Ric...

III

A Shakespeare Story

RETOLD BY ANDREW MATTHEWS
ILLUSTRATED BY TONY ROSS

ORCHARD

For Rob

A.M.

ORCHARD BOOKS

338 Euston Road, London NW1 3BH

Orchard Books Australia

Hachette Children's Books

Level 17/207 Kent St, Sydney, NSW 2000

First published in Great Britain in 2006

First paperback publication in 2007

This slipcase edition published in 2013

Not for individual resale

Text © Andrew Matthews 2006

Illustrations © Tony Ross 2006

ISBN 978 1 40780 981 6

A CIP catalogue record for this book is available from the British Library

Printed in China

Orchard Books is a division of Hachette Childrens Books,
an Hachette UK company.

www.hachette.co.uk

Contents

Cast List

Richard
Duke of Gloucester, later
King Richard III

Duke of Buckingham
Follower of Richard

Henry Tudor
Earl of Richmond,
later King Henry VII

King Edward IV

Prince Edward
King Edward's son

Richard, Duke of York
King Edward's son

The Scene
England in the fifteenth century.

And therefore, since I cannot prove a lover
To entertain these fair well-spoken days
I am determined to prove a villain

Richard; I.i.

Richard III

Visit the battleground at Bosworth Field
alone, and you will meet me without
knowing it. My restless spirit will seem to
be the sighing of the wind through the
branches of a tree, or the creeping shadow
of a passing cloud. Long ago, I was flesh
and blood like you. I was a king until
I came here. On this field I lost my crown,
my kingdom and my life.

Before I became King Richard, I was Richard, Duke of Gloucester, son of the house of York, though my deformed back and withered arm earned me other titles. 'Richard Crookback', my enemies called me, 'hedgehog' and 'spider'. I had many names and many enemies, chiefly in the house of Lancaster.

For almost thirty years the Yorkists
and Lancastrians made war to decide
who would rule in England. My brother
Edward was king, until he was overthrown
and exiled by King Henry; but he came
back, with me and our brother George,
Duke of Clarence, at his side. King
Henry was imprisoned in the Tower of

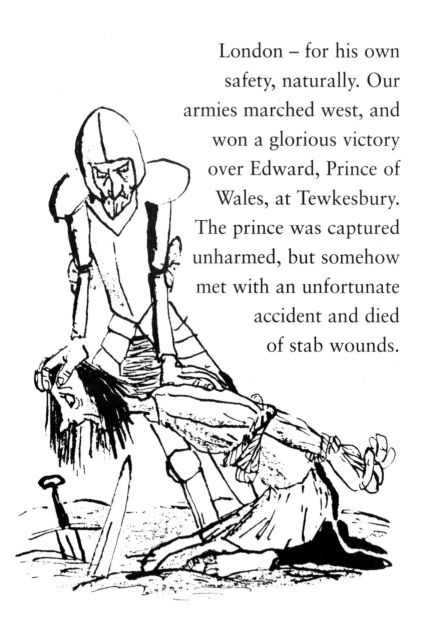

London – for his own safety, naturally. Our armies marched west, and won a glorious victory over Edward, Prince of Wales, at Tewkesbury. The prince was captured unharmed, but somehow met with an unfortunate accident and died of stab wounds.

While my brothers celebrated, I returned
to London, paid a secret visit to the king
in the Tower, and gave him the sad news
of his son's death. Poor Henry was too
gentle and too holy to live in this world,
so I sent him to the next with the point of
my dagger, and gave
it out that he had
died of grief.

The old king's
tragic death set
me thinking.

The Yorkists had triumphed over the Lancastrians, but the result was more like a truce than peace. Just below the uneasy surface lay mistrust, hatred and the desire for revenge. Given such a situation, it grieved me to consider what wickedness a mischievous person might do, simply by dropping hints and spreading rumours.

My way was clear. I could have supported my brother the king, and toiled to reconcile the houses of York and Lancaster, but peacemaking was not to my taste. The time was ripe for someone to play the villain, and I was determined to be that someone. I would deceive, and double-deal, and smile – even as I committed murder.

✳ ✳ ✳

When wars end, the victors often fall out, and so it was with us; I made certain of it.

During his exile, my brother Edward was struck with a wasting disease that gave him a hollow cough, and stretched his skin tightly over his bones. With the throne regained, he ruled England, but his sickness ruled him. He feared plots against him, and spoke daily with astrologers, fortune-tellers and the like.

The night I received news that the king had issued a warrant for the arrest of the Duke of Clarence, I hurried to Clarence's house and met him in the street outside, accompanied by armed guards.

"Why has our brother Edward done this, Clarence?" I cried.

Clarence laughed carelessly.

"Because my name is George," he said. "Some half-crazed wizard told him that his sons would be cheated of the throne by a man whose name begins with G."

"This is the queen's doing!" I growled. "She encourages the king's wild imaginings." The captain of the guard saluted me.

"I'm sorry, my lord Gloucester, but I was given orders that no one should be allowed to talk to the prisoner," he said.

"Please stand aside, and let me do my duty."

"Very well," I agreed.

"Don't worry, Clarence. I'll make sure that you're not imprisoned long."

As the guards marched their prisoner away to the Tower, I smiled to myself, for it was I who had taught the wizard what to say to the king, and paid him to say it.

"Ah, Clarence!" I sighed. "As your brother, I want only the best for you, and it would be best if your soul were safe in Heaven. I will arrange it soon, I promise you."

The first part of my plan had been successful. With a light heart, I made my way to Westminster to begin the second part – winning myself a bride.

* * *

The interior of the abbey was glowing
with candlelight. Great stone pillars
soared up into the darkness all around me
as I searched for the side chapel where the
coffin containing the body of the late
King Henry lay awaiting burial the
following morning. The coffin had been
placed on an altar, and draped with an

embroidered cloth. Before the altar,
dressed in mourning robes, Lady Anne,
the widow of Prince Edward. I had
heard her beauty praised, though she was
a little past her prime, but I had also
heard talk that she was weak-willed and
easily led. Now I was about to put the
rumour to the test.

Lady Anne turned as she heard me slip into the chapel. Her eyes widened in loathing.

"What black magician conjured you up, fiend?" she hissed.

I bowed. "I learned that you were keeping vigil here tonight, and I came to offer you my respects."

Lady Anne quivered.

"I don't want your respects, you filthy toad!" she raged. "I want the earth to open up and swallow you back down into Hell."

"I didn't know that angels could be so angry," I said, flinching. "Why do you speak so harshly to me?"

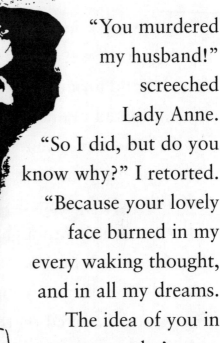

"You murdered my husband!" screeched Lady Anne. "So I did, but do you know why?" I retorted. "Because your lovely face burned in my every waking thought, and in all my dreams. The idea of you in someone else's arms was more than I could bear. Jealousy drove me out of my wits!"

Lady Anne's feelings showed in her look. She was both horrified and fascinated, as though she found me repellent, yet attractive.

Then came my master stroke.

I fell to my knees, drew my dagger, closed Lady Anne's hand around the hilt and bared my neck.

"If I can't have your love, give me your hate, and kill me!" I pleaded.

For a moment I thought that she would, but she faltered. The dagger dropped from her fingers and clattered on the flagstones.

I picked it up and pressed the edge of the blade to my throat.

"Tell me to kill myself!" I sobbed.

"No!" said Lady Anne. "No, I don't want you dead."

I gave her my most adoring gaze.

"But may I live in hope, my lady?" I murmured.

We were married five days later.

＊ ＊ ＊

Though the king's health was failing fast, he ignored the doctors who advised him to rest, and insisted on holding a banquet to honour my new bride. Invitations were sent out to the great and good, and also to those who were not so good.

On the morning of the banquet, I gave my faithful – and highly inventive – follower Tyrrel, a warrant permitting him and a companion to enter the Tower and question the Duke of Clarence. Tyrrel returned alone at dusk. I found his report most gratifying, almost amusing.

At the banquet, King Edward proposed a toast to the house of York, and added, "I have good news concerning my brother Clarence. I have signed his pardon, and he will be set free tomorrow."

I waited for the murmurs of approval to die down before I spoke.

"Your majesty," I said hesitantly. "Has no one informed you? Clarence is dead. He was found this afternoon in the cellars of the Tower, drowned in a barrel of wine. I often warned him of the dangers of drinking, but he paid me no attention."

The king fell back into his chair, and was wracked by a fit of coughing. Blood gushed from his mouth.

"Servants!" shouted
Queen Elizabeth.
"Carry the king to
his bed. Call the
royal physicians!"

As the guests
waited for news of
the stricken king,
they broke into
groups and chatted.

I found myself in company with the
Duke of Buckingham, a man with
a reputation for greed and treachery;
I admired him.

"I wonder what the queen's brother,
Lord Rivers, is discussing so earnestly
with Lord Grey, Lord Hastings and the
Earl of Richmond?" I said, as I poured
more wine into Buckingham's goblet.

"How to thwart your ambitions, my lord," he replied.

I pursed my lips. "Oh, and do I have ambitions?"

"You desire to wear the crown, my lord," said Buckingham.

"Suppose I did wear it, would you be for me or against me?" I enquired.

Buckingham took a sip of wine.

"I am loyal to whoever can afford me," he said.

"Would the earldom of Hereford buy your support?" I mused.

Buckingham inclined his head. "My lord, I am your man."

At that moment, the doors of the banqueting hall flew back and Queen Elizabeth appeared. Her hair was in disarray, and tears lined her pale cheeks.

"The king is dead!" she announced. "His dying wish was for his brother, Richard of Gloucester, to be appointed Lord Protector, and given guardianship of our young sons."

It was neither the time nor the place for grinning, so Buckingham and I smiled at each other with our eyes.

✳ ✳ ✳

And so I became guardian to my nephew
Edward, Prince of Wales, who was twelve,
and my namesake Richard, Duke of York,
who was ten. Edward would be crowned
king, and I would rule in his name until
he was twenty-one.

This arrangement caused me some
distress. To wield power for a few brief
years, and then surrender it to my nephew
seemed unsatisfactory to me. I thought
long and hard about what obstacles lay

between me and the throne, and how best to remove them. Buckingham and I burned out many candles in our secret night-time conferences, but our time was well spent.

The nation was rocked by a chain of sensational scandals. Papers came to light that proved Lord Rivers and Lord Grey were scheming to kidnap the young princes and hold them to ransom. The traitors were arrested, tried and beheaded.

To protect my nephews from other evildoers, I had them moved into the Tower, where I could keep a close eye on their welfare.

Meanwhile Henry Tudor, Earl of Richmond, suddenly left England for France.

Shortly after, my French spies reported that he was attempting to raise an army against me, but I was not alarmed by this. Henry Tudor had Welsh blood in his veins, and what Welshman had ever amounted to anything? More disturbing was a tale that Lord Hastings had boasted of how I would never be king while his head remained on his shoulders.

I had the strangest feeling that another shocking scandal was at hand.

It broke during a meeting that I called to decide on a date for my nephew's coronation. Hastings was present, along with Buckingham, Lord Stanley, and the Bishop of Ely.

Hastings made a long and flowery speech that ended with the suggestion that I should fix the day.

My response was a loud groan and a heavy sigh.

"Are you unwell, my lord?" asked Hastings.

"Sick at heart!" I replied. "Tell me, Lord Hastings, what sentence would you pass on those who used witchcraft to harm the royal family?"

"Why, death!" Hastings said without hesitation.

"Then you have passed sentence on yourself, my lord!" I exclaimed. "For you and the late King Henry's wife cursed me with your dark magic."

"No!" cried Hastings.

"No?" I echoed, raising my withered arm with its clawed hand for all to see. "If I was not cursed, how do you explain this?" Hastings's eyes were empty; I had him, and he knew it.

"I c–cannot explain it, my l–lord," he stammered.

The Bishop of Ely was dumbfounded.

"This man should stand trial at once!" he mumbled.

"No need for a trial," I said. "His guilt is written on his face. Guards, take Lord Hastings outside and put him to death!"

✳ ✳ ✳

The hardest blow of all was quick to follow. Buckingham chanced upon an old chronicle that made it plain that my brother Edward, while still an infant, had been betrothed to the daughter of a French nobleman. The betrothal had long been forgotten, and its rediscovery had far-reaching consequences. It meant that Edward's marriage to Queen Elizabeth had been unlawful. My nephews were illegitimate, and so barred from inheriting their father's crown. Imagine my feelings when I heard of this!

Bands of Londoners took to the streets, calling for me to be made king. These loyal outbursts were arranged by Buckingham, who also led the delegation of city worthies who implored me to take the throne.
I protested that I was weak and unworthy, but at last they persuaded me to put duty

before self, and I accepted the heavy
burden of kingship.

Events moved swiftly. Two days before
my coronation, I was told that Richmond
had set sail from France, in command of
an invasion fleet. I ordered my navy to
sink it.

At my coronation feast, my wife Anne
fell ill with stomach pains and sickness,
and had to take to her bed.

That evening, Buckingham brought grave news to my private chamber.

"Gales have kept your navy in port, sire," he told me. "Richmond has landed on the coast of Wales. Lord Stanley and the Bishop of Ely have joined forces with him."

"Ha!" I scoffed. "After I've crushed them, I'll have their heads spiked on London Bridge." I lowered my voice. "Buckingham, issue a proclamation that the queen is fast approaching her death."

Buckingham raised his eyebrows. "Is she, sire?"

"If she is not, I paid good money to an apothecary who lied about the poison he supplied me with," I said. "The queen is too old to give me the male heir I need.

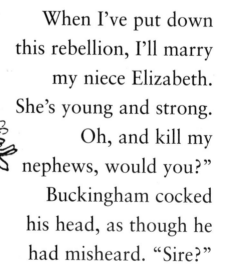

When I've put down this rebellion, I'll marry my niece Elizabeth. She's young and strong. Oh, and kill my nephews, would you?"

Buckingham cocked his head, as though he had misheard. "Sire?"

"My nephews are a threat to my royal line. I want them dead!" I snapped.

"Majesty!" blustered Buckingham. "Give me a little time to—"

"There is no time, Buckingham!" I interrupted.

Buckingham stiffened. "I'm afraid I must remind your majesty that you have not yet kept your promise to make me Earl of Hereford."

I smiled. "Promise, Buckingham?
I promised you nothing. Leave me. We
will speak again once your memory
has improved."

When Buckingham had gone, I softly
called out, "Tyrrel?"

Tyrrel flowed out of the shadows and
stood beside me.

"Sire?"

"I fear that Lord Buckingham will turn against me," I said. "He has no stomach for the business I discussed with him."

"Depend on me to deal with it for you, sire," said Tyrrel.

"Bear in mind that they are anointed princes," I warned. "Don't shed their precious blood."

"Not a drop, sire," Tyrrel vowed.

And he was true to his word, for later he described to me how he smothered my nephews.

* * *

War gathered like clouds in a stormy sky. More nobles deserted me for Richmond, including Buckingham, who was taken prisoner by one of my generals in the course of a minor skirmish. The general

sent me Buckingham's head, which
I regarded as a great kindness.

Richmond's forces marched east,
I marched my armies west to meet him,
until we faced each other at Bosworth Field.

The night before the battle, I dreamed
that I was visited by the ghosts of my
victims, who predicted my defeat.

I woke up in a cold sweat.

"My conscience gives me nightmares, but nothing else!" I muttered to the dark. "I won wealth and power without it, and made myself the man I am – the villain I set out to be!"

* * *

That sly viper Richmond outwitted me
and attacked before dawn, when my
forces were not fully prepared. His
artillery blew gaps in my front lines, and
his cavalry surged through. My soldiers
might have rallied, but my best

commander, the Duke of Norfolk,
was reported slain, and his troops
retreated in confusion. I tried to bring
up reinforcements, but the cowardly
Earl of Northumberland refused to obey
my orders.

The day was lost. The best that I could hope for was to make my escape. Then a volley of arrows cut my steed from under me. I staggered through the smoke of battle, shouting, "A horse! A horse! My kingdom for a horse!"

As if in reply, a horse appeared: a dapple-grey war horse galloped towards me, with Henry, Earl of Richmond, on its back.

I saw him lean sideways, saw light flash on the blade of his battleaxe as he swung it...

My memories end there.

I was wrong about Henry Tudor – he amounted to something after all. My crown was placed on his head, and he founded a line of monarchs that lasts to this day, for his distant descendants still live in royal palaces.

As for me, I have shrunk to a breath of wind, a trick of the light. When I am remembered, if I am remembered, I am Richard the Bloody, Richard the Tyrant who slaughtered the princes in the Tower.

Well, it is better than being completely forgotten. In the end, villainy has granted me a kind of immortality.

God and your arms be praised, victorious friends!
The day is ours. The bloody dog is dead.

Richmond; V.v.

Villainy in Richard III

Richard III was Shakespeare's first great popular success, and it remains one of his most frequently performed plays.

King Richard is a villain so ruthless and cruel that he comes close to being a pantomime character. What saves him from seeming ridiculous is his dark sense of humour. His witty asides to the audience win us over to his point of view. More than simply a mindless thug, he deliberately sets out to manipulate the weak characters who surround him, and we share his relish when he succeeds.

Shakespeare wrote the play between 1592 and 1593. Though he based the plot on the best historical sources of the day, Thomas More's *History of King Richard the Third*, and Holinshed's

Chronicles, the real-life Richard Plantagenet was nothing like as evil as his stage counterpart. There is no evidence to connect him with the disappearance of the princes in the Tower, nor is there any conclusive evidence that they were murdered.

Henry Tudor, Earl of Richmond, who appears as a character in the play, became King Henry VII, father of King Henry VIII and grandfather of Queen Elizabeth I. Tudor historians were anxious to portray Henry Tudor as a noble hero who ended the reign of a murderous tyrant, and established peace and stability after a period of bloody civil war.

In no way should this lack of accuracy spoil our enjoyment of the play. Shakespeare was not a historian, but a dramatist whose genius is still able to transport audiences out of their everyday lives, and plunge them into the exaggerated life of the stage.

Shakespeare and the Globe Theatre

Some of Shakespeare's most famous plays were first performed at the Globe Theatre, which was built on the South Bank of the River Thames in 1599.

Going to the Globe was a different experience from going to the theatre today. The building was roughly circular in shape, but with flat sides: a little like a doughnut crossed with a fifty-pence piece. Because the Globe was an open-air theatre, plays were only put on during daylight hours in spring and summer. People paid a penny to stand in the central space and watch a play, and this part of the audience became known as 'the groundlings' because they stood on the ground. A place in the tiers of seating beneath the thatched roof, where there was a slightly better view and less chance of being rained on, cost extra.

The Elizabethans did not bath very often and the audiences at the Globe were smelly. Fine ladies and gentlemen in the more expensive seats sniffed perfume and bags of sweetly-scented herbs to cover the stink rising from the groundlings.

There were no actresses on the stage; all the female characters in Shakespeare's plays would have been acted by boys, wearing wigs and make-up. Audiences were not well-behaved. People clapped and cheered when their favourite actors came on stage; bad actors were jeered at and sometimes pelted with whatever came to hand.

Most Londoners worked hard to make a living and in their precious free time they liked to be entertained. Shakespeare understood the magic of the theatre so well that today, almost four hundred years after his death, his plays still cast a spell over the thousands of people that go to see them.

Orchard Classics
Shakespeare Stories

RETOLD BY ANDREW MATTHEWS
ILLUSTRATED BY TONY ROSS

As You Like It	978 1 84616 187 2	£4.99
Hamlet	978 1 84121 340 8	£4.99
A Midsummer Night's Dream	978 1 84121 332 3	£4.99
Antony and Cleopatra	978 1 84121 338 5	£4.99
The Tempest	978 1 84121 346 0	£4.99
Richard III	978 1 84616 185 8	£4.99
Macbeth	978 1 84121 344 6	£4.99
Twelfth Night	978 1 84121 334 7	£4.99
Henry V	978 1 84121 342 2	£4.99
Romeo & Juliet	978 1 84121 336 1	£4.99
Much Ado About Nothing	978 1 84616 183 4	£4.99
Othello	978 1 84616 184 1	£4.99
Julius Caesar	978 1 40830 506 5	£4.99
King Lear	978 1 40830 503 4	£4.99
The Merchant of Venice	978 1 40830 504 1	£4.99
The Taming of the Shrew	978 1 40830 505 8	£4.99

Orchard Books are available from all good bookshops.

the official state religion through incorporation of the Lateran Pacts, giving special privileges to the clergy, as well as the outlawing of divorce.

The parties of the left, although renouncing a claim to a socialist Constitution (because the conditions, Togliatti said, were not right) aspired to what was described as a 'progressive democratic' republic. Their focus was less on the Fascist abuse of parliamentary democracy than on the weaknesses of the liberal order that had allowed fascism to come to power in the first place. Their proposals were to locate power in a single-chamber National Assembly, which would allow the 'will of the people' to prevail, and to incorporate in the Constitution a number of social and economic rights, or 'positive freedoms'. Their inclusion would provide a constitutional justification for – if not an obligation on – future governments to carry through policies of a socialist nature.

The overall result of this confrontation was a curious compromise, aptly captured in Piero Calamandrei's comment that, 'To compensate the left-wing parties for their failure to effect a revolution, the right-wing forces did not oppose the inclusion in the Constitution of the promise of a revolution'.[3] On the one hand, the left obtained the insertion of several articles relating to citizens' social and economic rights, which make the Italian Constitution stand out with respect to its counterparts in other Western countries, since they echo the content of constitutions found in the Communist world. Besides containing rights to work, to participate in the management of firms, to strike, and to receive a reasonable living wage, the Constitution also places an obligation on the state to address social and economic inequalities, and private enterprise can be limited with an aim to ensuring its 'social function'.[4] On the other hand, the Christian Democrats managed to obtain, besides their religious demands, a Constitution that was, among the post-war European democracies, one of the most strongly protected against abuse by the executive or a parliamentary majority. This was secured through several constitutional guarantees: a constitutional court, presidential counter-powers, genuine bicameralism, a self-governing independent judiciary, provisions for direct democracy (through abrogative referenda), a system of autonomous regional governments, and a National Council for the Economy and Labour.

The compromise was the outcome more of a series of hard fights (and votes) over incompatible proposals than of an effort to overcome differences in the name of anti-Fascist unity. True, there were moments when the latter appeared to prevail (e.g. the Communists' vote for the inclusion of the Lateran Pacts), but, for the most part, the compromises were the outcome of struggles that involved the constant amendment and re-amendment of various proposals. This had the effect of ensuring that several of the final articles were either self-contradictory or contradicted by other articles, or so watered down as to be largely meaningless.[5] The entire process, moreover, became more difficult as time went on, especially after the exclusion of the left from government, when the Constitution had to be completed in an intensely hostile atmosphere.

In short, the Constitution 'left all options and all solutions open: the ultimate decision was to be left to the political will of the groups which would prevail in Parliament and, to a lesser extent, to the interpretation the judiciary would give to the Constitution' (Vercellone 1972: 126). The judiciary, in fact, did not wait on the Christian Democratic victory in the April 1948 elections to snuff out the 'promise' of a revolution. In a ruling in February 1948, the (unpurged) Court of Cassation established a constitutional distinction between norms that were subject to immediate enforcement (*norme precettizie*) and those that were 'programmatic' and could therefore only be achieved at a later date. This not only nullified the intents of the proposers of the more progressive aspects of the Constitution, but at the same time justified the subsequent failure to repeal a large part of the Fascist penal code. This was subsequently used by Minister of the Interior, Mario Scelba, to create a large police force, suppress left-wing protests, and deny freedoms guaranteed by the new Constitution (Neppi Modona 1997). The judiciary as a whole became notorious for its uneven treatment of Fascist crimes (which often went unpunished) compared with partisan offences (which were vehemently prosecuted, even when the offences were trivial). The abundance of acquittals of Fascists and prosecutions of partisans 'seriously called into question the idea that the anti-Fascist "values of the Resistance" were in any way integral to the identity of the new Republic' (Duggan 1995: 4).

Perhaps more serious was the impact of the Christian Democratic election victory on the organizational aspects of the Constitution. Many of these had remained a 'promise' too, because it was up to Parliament to pass the necessary enabling legislation. However, having secured an electoral majority, the Christian Democrats and their allies lost their enthusiasm for 'checks and balances', and various institutions were established only after considerable delay: the Constitutional Court (1956), the National Council of the Economy and Labour (1957), the High Council of the Judiciary (1958), regional governments and referenda (1970). The failure to implement the regional system meant that the Prefect and the centralized state remained in full force. In the case of the National Council of the Economy and Labour, the enabling legislation effectively emasculated it as an organ with any influence. The left, on the other hand, despite having opposed various aspects of the Constitution, became the most ardent supporter of its full implementation.

To summarize, despite the prominence of anti-Fascist unity, the post-war settlement was characterized by a power struggle, one that took on an increasingly polarized character as the Cold War rapidly developed. In that struggle the left was unequivocally defeated. Its failure to secure an electoral majority in the first elections of the new Republic was only one aspect of this defeat. Already there were strong elements of continuity with the old state, the 1940s and 1950s being characterized by 'a curiously schizophrenic climate . . . in which calls for change and renunciation of the immediate past jostled uneasily with many indications that a large part of the country's former political baggage – both material and ideological – had simply passed unchanged into a new constitutional wrapper' (Duggan 1995: 3). This was made easier by the fact that the popular passions aroused by the Resistance and the Republic were increasingly overshadowed by an alternative view: that Fascism was best forgotten as a mere historical interlude during Italy's journey to democracy. From this perspective, Fascism had less to do with Italians than with 'a cast of outlandish buffoons' who had now been removed from the scene; the experience was not, therefore, to be taken seriously. Neo-fascism was quickly reborn as a party (the Italian Social Movement, MSI) and commanded a small but significant and growing vote, and the fear of a return to fascism constituted an important part of left-wing culture in the 1950s (Duggan 1995: 7–10).

All of this undermined both in feeling and substance the notion that a break with the past had occurred. While the most visible continuities were with what had just passed (fascism), perhaps of more significance were the continuities with the characteristics of the liberal order that had preceded Fascism, characteristics that Fascism had not changed in any way, since it had been unaccompanied by any socio-economic revolution. If one were to summarize (rather brutally) the main deficiencies of the liberal order (1860–1922), one would emphasize the low legitimacy of the regime as a consequence of several factors: a parochial political culture rather than a national integrative one, which was further undermined by the refusal of the Church to recognize the new State; the underdevelopment of the south (as a consequence of an alliance between northern capitalists and southern landowners, which kept the old southern clientelist system intact); oligarchic rule (only 2 per cent of the population having the vote); a failure to achieve genuine alternation in government (through governments' recourse to *trasformismo*, whereby the hostility of opposition deputies was constantly bought off); a highly centralized state; and the *de facto* delegation of state authority to other centres of power, especially in the south (the Mafia).[6]

If these deep-rooted features had produced a crisis of the State and little effort to save it from fascism, they were not destroyed *either* by Fascism *or* by the post-war settlement. Indeed, as the Christian Democratic 'party regime' developed in the post-war period, it became apparent that the features persisting since Unification had remained intact, albeit often in modified form. The parochial outlook of Italians continued to bedevil attempts to forge a national state and identity; up to a third of the population's votes were – in effect – wasted as a result of the *conventio ad excludendum* ('exclusion convention') operated by the parties to bar the Communists and (for a short period) Socialists from power; the south remained underdeveloped and became, through patronage, one of the pillars of Christian Democratic power; the nature of the party system ensured that there was no alternation in government, but only 'peripheral turnover'; the centralized system of government remained firmly in place; and the absence of state authority in the face of other power centres became commonplace.[7]

In short, in terms of continuity, the real menace was less the fascistic presence in the new State (alarming to many as it was), than what it represented in broader terms: the failure to enact a break with what had hampered the growth of democracy in the pre-1922 period, and what would distort the democratic development of the new Republic. However, of the various differences between the features of the liberal order and the post-war Republic, one stood out above all others: the presence in the latter of mass parties. *Trasformismo*, as a formula for perennial rule, had been predicated on the absence of disciplined mass parties. The post-war settlement witnessed a rapid change in this respect; but if this was a sign of political maturity, when overlaid with the other deficiencies, it also had some less welcome consequences.

THE ITALIAN POLITICAL SYSTEM UNTIL THE 1990s

There is little doubt that the new parties served a purpose that had gone unfulfilled under Fascism and the liberal order: the gradual integration of popular forces within the state and the (re)construction of collective identities. However, if before 1947–8, there could be said to have been a merging of party strategies and national interests, this was no longer the case once the Cold War descended on Europe (Battente 2001: 99–101). For different reasons, the impact of the Cold War on Germany and Italy was greater than it was on other Western nations. In Italy, this was because of the electoral strength of the left-wing parties, and especially the PCI, and the perceived threat it constituted through its links with the Soviet Union. This placed considerable focus on the largest political party, the DC, increasing its dependence on the United States and NATO. The domestic political situation therefore represented a microcosm of the international Cold War and the tensions prevailing therein. When combined with the Fascist experience from which the country was just emerging, it caused a grave legitimacy deficit, with Italian citizens feeling alienation, mistrust and detachment from the political system (e.g. Morlino 1991c). Apart from religion, civil society – in terms of civic, professional, cultural and interest groups – was weakly organized and certainly incapable of providing a foundation for the development of party politics, as had occurred in many other European democracies (Pasquino 2002b: 23) (see chapter 5). In a Cold War situation, the parties' subsequent integrative capacities heavily conditioned the manner in which consolidation of the regime occurred.

As different interpretations of the party system have indicated, the DC was, to some extent, compelled to govern indefinitely by the situation in which it found itself (see chapter 3). For the DC, the PCI threatened to overturn the political system *per se* if it ever came to power. Hence, the 'exclusion convention' which became the pivot on which the party system developed. It might be concluded from this – and from the destiny of the post-war settlement – that the DC's long period of rule was predicated on winning an 'ideological war' through a forceful and coherent strategy to establish and maintain hegemony, even at the cost of harsh repression of the left. Some evidence, furthermore, would tend to support this thesis: orienting the constitution in a majoritarian direction (through the DC's failure to implement key parts of it); the passing of the so-called 'swindle law' in 1953 (whereby the coalition of parties receiving 50 per cent plus one of the votes cast would have obtained two-thirds of the seats in the Chamber);[8] the severe repression of left-wing protests in the 1950s; and the failed attempt in 1960 to govern with the neo-fascists, the Tambroni government being brought down by popular protest.

Yet, if a DC plan to retain power existed, it was more complex and less coherent than this, if for no other reason than the fact that the outcome of the 'swindle law' and the Tambroni government demonstrated that a forceful hegemonic strategy was not viable. If it had been, then the result might have been an outlawing of the PCI; but De Gasperi resisted American pressures to do just this because of his fear that it would prompt a civil war (Leonardi 1991: 78). While the parties were engaged both publicly and secretly in an 'ideological war', the leaders of the parties were careful not to allow either the public image or the subterranean reality to translate into a confrontation in general political practice, because of their fear of the consequences (see chapter 6). It was, therefore, a war in which neither side was prepared ever to engage in battle (at least in public). In this way, 'ideology – paradoxically – did not divide, but unite; or, better, united at the same time as dividing' (Mastropaolo 1994: 72).

Italian polity and society were, therefore, structured around two competing 'churches', or solidarity systems, with the two main parties acting to mobilize and reinforce their respective worlds, since their legitimacy depended on them. This structured and stabilized voting behaviour and integrated the working classes into the political system (see chapter 4). The *modus vivendi* between party elites, meanwhile, allowed them to operate the rules of pluralistic democracy and achieve economic growth (Mastropaolo 1994), at the same time as the presence of extremist elements at the subterranean level reinforced hostility and destabilized any attempt to reduce ideological polarization.

This competitive structuring had a significant impact on the State, since it led to the development of a 'spoils system', originating in the weakness of the DC's organization and its fragmented and fragile social base, Catholicism and anti-communism (see chapters 2 and 4). In the 1950s, the Church was replaced by the State as 'the decisive pole of party activity'. Party reorganization in the 1950s, and the extension of the state sector into the economy (combined with an absence of formal state funding of parties until 1974) prompted a transformation of the DC from what were two distinct party types (a party of notables in the south and a mass party in the north) into a form of 'catch-all' party resembling a national 'syndicate of political machines' (Allum 1997: 23–9). The State became the vehicle by which the DC could provide the resources to make its electoral constituencies more secure. Yet, in keeping with the DC's aim of avoiding increased polarization and an actual confrontation, the 'spoils system' was not exclusive; rather, it included not only the ruling coalition partners but also, over time, the main opposition party (powerless to prevent it, but finding that the system suited its own institutional strategy). The DC's hegemony, in short, was 'soft', rather than monopolistic and rigorously imposed (Tarrow 1990). It was partly the product of the party's own strategic decisions, but also of the peculiarities of the Italian situation and the responses of other parties to that situation.[9]

In this way, Italy became a *partitocrazia* ('partyocracy') or 'partitocratic regime' (see chapter 3), which differed from the system of party government experienced in most other European democracies. This was due to the monopoly of party control exercised over government, on the one hand, and institutions, the economy and culture, on the other (e.g. Pasquino 1999: ch. 2; Pasquino 2002b: 17–18; Newell 2000b: 65; Hine 1990). The consolidation of democracy in Italy occurred, therefore, through the tutelage, or 'democratic pedagogy', of the parties, which provided channels through which citizens learnt the culture, values and procedures of democracy (Nevola 2003: 251–3). If this compensated for (but did not solve) the problem of the lack of legitimacy (Morlino 1991c), it also carried with it an inevitable degenerative impact on government, institutions, the economy and political culture.

'Partyocracy' produced weak and unstable governments, which fell almost always as a product of internal factional struggles in the main governing party, rather than any vote in Parliament (see chapter 7). The authority of the Prime Minister, Cabinet and Parliament were all undermined by the strength and dictates of the parties. This instability was overlaid with aspects of enduring stability in terms of the political parties making up the successive governing coalitions, the ministerial class and policy immobilism.[10] Indeed, if 'partyocracy' embodied a strong form of party control over state and society, it did not follow that it was a strong form of 'party government' *per se*. Vassallo (1994) uses two dimensions to measure the strength of party government – the power of nomination or resources of patronage, on the one hand, and the degree of policy direction exercised, on the other – and Italian party government was strong only in relation to the former. Italian policy making lacked any sense of broader national interest. It became geared towards producing *leggine* ('little laws') for clientelistic constituencies, and factionalism inside the main governing party grew as a consequence of the struggle for control over the vehicles of patronage (Pasquino 1999; Dente 1990; Cotta and Isernia 1996).

These effects had significant implications for institutions, the economy and political culture. Dahrendorf (1988) argues that the well-being of nations – the extent to which integration of society occurs – depends not just on citizens' access to the market (economic resources), but also on their access to politics and culture (entitlements). The development and guaranteeing of entitlements on a universal basis, moreover, depends on democratic institutions. Institutions become the basis for the diffuse sense of citizenship and identification with democracy (March and Olsen 1989). In Italy, as Cartocci (1994) argues, the economy successfully produced provisions, but institutions failed to produce universal entitlements. Due to the primordial role of political parties, institutions failed to function on the basis of efficiency and availability to all. When an institution becomes regulated by sectional or partisan (rather than universalistic) criteria, the capacity of the institution to promote integration in society declines. Entitlements (which place citizens on an equal basis) effectively become provisions: that is, the extension of favours. Institutions become a cause of social disaggregation because people 'cede entitlements to obtain provisions'. Consequently, in Italy, 'a culture of favours prevails progressively over that of rights', and institutions are held in low esteem (Cartocci 1994: 59–60). This explains the persistence of strong subcultures, as well as cultural traits such as 'amoral familism' – originally defined by Banfield (1958) as the inability to act together to achieve any common good beyond the material interest of the nuclear family – both of which have hindered the construction of a national identity and sense of community (see chapter 3).[11]

Furthermore, while the economy may have produced provisions, it did not escape the effects of the suffocating embrace of the parties. On the contrary, party penetration of what was the largest state sector of the economy in the Western world affected not only the nature of that sector but also the structure of, and competition within, the private sector (see chapter 10). Italian capitalism took on a distinctive character, dominated by a clannish power structure, which involved collusive practices and protection from competition through a network involving a few big banks, large private industry, state holding companies and political parties. Economic growth, moreover, was characterized by structural and territorial distortions, where the most spectacular successes occurred in areas and sectors where state regulation could be avoided and where political subcultures were strong (see chapter 11).

This 'model' of the Italian political system was not, of course, unchanging. However, the paradox was that the main features of change worked together to undermine the stabilities on which it rested, thereby making an 'earthquake', if not inevitable, at least increasingly likely by the 1980s.

THE DÉNOUEMENT OF THE SYSTEM

In the course of the post-war period, Italian society became increasingly secularized and modernized. This was combined with a decline of ideological hostility and the effective end of the 'Communist question' (see chapter 4). The sapping of two of the pillars of DC support (Catholicism and anti-communism) was compounded by the fact that the party's social base was strongest amongst two declining population groups – peasants and the independent middle class – and weakest amongst two growing groups: immigrant workers and the new middle class (Tarrow 1990: 319–23). If this was a factor contributing to a rising tide of societal dissent, it also had two other effects. The decline of Catholicism and anti-communism increased the party's dependence on its third pillar of support (patronage), and these changes in class structure made imperative a widening of the DC's political alliance. This widening occurred first through the PSI and later the PCI (in a more restricted and short-term manner that failed). The dissent that manifested itself in the late 1960s and the 1970s was, wherever possible, accommodated (or bought off). The widening of the alliance, in its turn, increased further the pressures on the party's patronage system as the newcomers expected a share of the spoils. This was not a problem while the economy was experiencing growth, but once this was called into question in the 1970s, the public deficit and debt began to spiral upwards under a combination of patronage and the accommodation of dissent (see chapter 2).

In this way, the logic of the system began to outlive its origins. By the 1980s Italy had become a modern society with ideology and traditional forms of militancy and social conflict in decline, and the international environment undergoing rapid change. These changes, while sapping the strength of the main parties, rendered obsolete the 'exclusion convention', thereby destroying the main rationale on which the system had rested (the need to avoid a full-scale confrontation). Yet, the parties, trapped within a clientelistic power logic, were unable (and unwilling) to draw the consequences of these changes in terms of either adapting their organizations in the way that other European parties were doing (Barnes 1994) or modifying existing political alliances to prompt alternation in government.

Instead, energies were channelled into vainly experimenting with neo-corporatist and institutional attempts at reforming the anomalies of the system (Mastropaolo 1994: 82–7). Neo-corporatism was never likely to succeed, in view of the peculiar nature of the way in which State–interest group relations had developed in the post-war period, constrained as they were within a 'partitocratic' logic (see chapter 5). Even in the presence of the supposed conditions facilitating it, neo-corporatism did not function, and was eventually killed off by the 1985 referendum on the *scala mobile* (Bull 1988; Lange 1986). Institutional reform was launched by Bettino Craxi (PSI leader) in 1983, and was combined with his attempt to make more powerful the Prime Minister's office. The issue dominated Italian political debate thereafter (see chapter 7). Yet, reform attempts were constantly sabotaged by the parties themselves, 'which feared that one way or another any institutional reform might curtail their power or their *political rents*, that is the advantages they were drawing from their political location in the party system and institutional system' (Pasquino 1998: 43). The impression was that the debate was designed to do little more than publicize an apparent commitment to reform.

The decline of the ideological premiss on which the system was based, but the failure of the parties to draw the consequences, increased the dependence on patronage and spoils, and the system began to degenerate. This degeneration was reinforced by the fact that those operating at the subterranean level had abandoned the strategy of anti-

Communist *coup* and terrorist threats in favour of securing influence over the system through more subtle methods involving finance and corruption (see chapter 6). Over time the relationship between clientelistic tendencies, maladministration and organized crime produced a level of corruption that became systemic. In other words, corrupt practices became so widespread and embedded that 'illicit governance' became the norm, punishing those who failed to acquiesce in it (Della Porta and Vannucci 1999a: 247). The *pentapartito* governing coalition that ruled Italy in the 1980s became increasingly obsessed with *lottizzazione* ('sharing out'), their programmes being based on a systematic and corrupt distribution of the country's resources to retain power and shore up legitimacy (Pasquino 1994). The economic boom of the 1980s encouraged this profligacy, despite the fact that the boom was achieved on the basis of an economic model whose distortions were still growing. In fact, the decade witnessed a growing public deficit and public debt that, in the long run, would be hard to sustain, but which were not tackled by the political class (see chapter 2).

All of this, moreover, ran counter to the demands of the broader international system, which were becoming increasingly difficult to meet (see chapters 10 and 12). Financial markets were demanding higher interest rates on Italian debt; the EU (through its regulations) was forcibly opening the Italian economy to foreign competition; and new corporate regulations were making it increasingly difficult to sustain the existing collusive and clannish practices. Economic internationalization and the EU were introducing 'a new style of politics into southern Europe, based more on northern "Protestant" or "technocratic" norms which fit ill alongside the personalised, clientelistic politics of the south' (Bull and Rhodes 1997a: 9). The structural adjustments needed to thrive, if not survive, in this changing economic system could not be carried through by the existing regime (Guzzini 1995).

If all this suggests that there was a certain inevitability about the dénouement of the system (Bull and Rhodes 1997a: 5–6), it nevertheless required a concatenation of factors to precipitate it. There were four key factors that became intertwined. The first two opened up two 'fault lines' in Italian politics that facilitated and enhanced the impact of the other two factors.

First, the collapse of communism in Central and Eastern Europe and the transformation of the PCI into a non-Communist party of the left effectively ended the 'Communist question'.[12] This had effects on voters (who no longer felt obliged to 'hold their noses and vote Christian Democrat' out of fear of communism) and on public prosecutors (who felt less constrained in investigating corruption in the governing parties for fear of assisting a Communist advance) (see chapters 3 and 8). It should also have had an effect on the ruling parties, but the reaction of the DC and the PSI to the PCI's operation was cynical and arrogant, if not disbelieving. It had always been assumed that the resolution of the 'Communist question' would place pressure on the governing parties to come to terms with the new party. However, the PCI's transformation was a protracted affair, lasting fifteen months, and threw the party into the deepest crisis of its history. For the DC and the PSI, therefore, locked into a stagnant power-sharing arrangement, symbolized by what was known as the CAF (Craxi–Andreotti–Forlani) axis, it became apparent that coming to terms with the former Communists might not be necessary at all. They seriously misread the seriousness of the situation and the wave of public indignation and protest that was about to engulf them.[13]

First, the party-political arena itself remains in some turmoil (see chapter 3). While the revolution in party politics ended the old party system and produced electoral reform, this did not automatically produce a new, stabilized party system. There has been a slow process of bipolarization, but the contours of the party system are still prone to considerable change.

Second, in this unstable situation, the party political sphere has none the less established its own dynamic, and political parties their own autonomy, with party strategies, as in the past, quickly focusing on party-political interests. Party competition has become embroiled in new issues that have caused deep divisions over questions of reform. This is not to suggest that parties are inherently against reform, but rather that the pressures to agree on reform produced by the sense of crisis and urgency of the early 1990s have long passed. As long as coalitions remain essential to achieve change, the parties can often act as veto players in relation to reforms that are not seen to be in their interests.

Third, this tendency is reinforced by the fact that the party-political sphere is not, of course, autonomous of broader economic and social interests, and in various quarters there is still stiff resistance to many of the changes often identified as necessary to open up Italian capitalism (see chapter 10). The lobby of politicians, bureaucrats, state holdings managers, financial institutions and trade unionists against the privatization and liberalization of the Italian capitalist model remains strong.

Fourth, the dramatic changes of the early 1990s produced a new dominant political party (Forza Italia) and politician (Silvio Berlusconi), yet whether their putative commitment to reforming the political system is genuine remains open to question. Berlusconi could be viewed as a quintessential product of the First Republic, and someone who launched his political career to try to protect his own personal interests. Despite his political rhetoric of reform, he has brought to the heart of Italian government a conflict of interests which has yet to be satisfactorily resolved. This is between his position as Prime Minister and his control of 90 per cent of private television networks, which currently secure 43 per cent of the total average of television viewers.[15] Furthermore, the Prime Minister's court cases (on various accusations relating to corruption) and his vitriolic accusations of a political witch hunt being conducted by a partisan judiciary provoked a grave institutional crisis, exacerbated by the involvement of the President of the Republic in his position as head of the High Council of the Judiciary.

The fact that Berlusconi has been the main political beneficiary of the collapse of the First Republic has had a direct bearing on the reform debate in two interrelated ways. The first is that policy reforms in several sectors have been subject to fierce opposition (at the parliamentary and societal levels) because they appear to have been formulated with the Prime Minister's judicial and commercial interests in mind. This has applied particularly to three areas: judicial policy, where several laws have been passed, all of which have had a direct bearing on trials involving Berlusconi and/or his former Minister of Defence (Cesare Previti); legislation designed to resolve Berlusconi's conflict of interests, which will not divest him of any of his holdings, the bill being widely regarded as inadequate to protect against possible abuses deriving from the Prime Minister's position (Hine 2002); and media policy, where the so-called Gasparri Law allows Berlusconi's media company, Mediaset, to expand even further and reinforce its dominant position in the Italian market.

Table 1.1   Italian satisfaction levels with functioning of Italian democracy, 1984–2004

	Italians 'very' or 'reasonably' satisfied with functioning of Italian democracy (%)				
		Those considering themselves			
Year	Whole electorate	Of the centre left	Of the centre	Of the right	Don't know
1984	52	45	55	59	48
1994	44	43	45	17	39
2004	34	23	37	47	33

Source: Eurobarometer data, as summarized in *Corriere della Sera*, 13 May 2004

The second way in which Berlusconi's position influences the reform debate is that many of those who once aspired to achieve a strengthening and stabilization of party government now have reservations as to the wisdom of such a development while he remains Prime Minister in a bipolarized system which privileges majority rule, and while the centre left remains so divided that it cannot present a credible governing alternative. This concern applies particularly to institutional or constitutional reform. There is a growing body of opinion in Italy (echoed in the respectable press abroad) that regards the Prime Minister's increasing concentration of media, economic and political power as alarming, and possibly tantamount to the construction of a new 'regime' (e.g. Sartori 2002; Santomassimo 2003; Ginsborg 2003). Under his second government elected in 2001, there has been a strengthening of policy direction, as a consequence of the presence of a clear (albeit often divided) governing majority, and a strengthening of control over resources of patronage. The dangers of the first are evidenced in the controversial nature of many of the policies, deriving from Berlusconi's peculiar position. The dangers of the second arise from the fact that *lottizzazione* inevitably works differently in a bipolarized system with a clear division between a majority and an opposition that expect to alternate in power. Patronage is more likely to become part of strengthening the government against an expected alternation. The government's passing of the Frattini Law (which allows the replacement of a large number of officials by an incoming government) and its actions in relation to appointments to RAI, ENI, ENEL, Finmeccanica and the postal services give an idea of the perceived importance of this power to the government (Donovan 2003: 240).

The above scenario has produced a complex situation, in which the pace and scope of reform vary across different sectors, but which overall is probably less than what was popularly expected by the revolution in party politics at the beginning of the 1990s. This is perhaps best reflected in the steep decline in the number of Italians (of all political persuasions) declaring themselves to be satisfied with the functioning of Italian democracy – from what were relatively low levels in the first place (see table 1.1).

The pressures being exerted on the Italian system are still present, and the Italian polity continues to undergo change, but the direction and outcome of that change are not clear. Change is mediated through a new party-political 'prism' that has the capacity to retard as much as to accelerate. This helps to explain why the Italian polity is currently characterized by areas of both dynamism and stagnation, with some sectors adjusting much more quickly to new challenges than others. The most ardent reformers view a constitutional revision as ultimately necessary to 'normalize' the political system; but, as noted, this is, in fact, one of the areas of most notable division and stagnation.

To conclude, in the broader political system (i.e. as opposed to the constitutional arena) there are a number of areas undergoing reform. These include the parties (organizations, alliances, party system); institutions (e.g. electoral reform, decentralization, administrative reform); governance (e.g. party government, prime ministerial authority); public policies (e.g. sound finance, macro-economic policy, welfare policy, education policy, policy for the south); the relationship between the State, employers and trade unions; the state sector of the economy; large private capitalist groups; the 'Third Italy'. The reforms are neither clear-cut nor complete. Several are subject to resistance, where they have not stalled altogether. Yet, whatever the caveats, it remains true that most of the reforms were largely unimaginable before the early 1990s. In this sense, irrespective of the constitutional order and the stagnation of reform in some sectors, we are witnessing the gradual passing of the former Italian political model and the emergence of a new one, whose key contours and characteristics remain to be shaped. It is to a more detailed treatment of the economic context of that model that we now turn.

THE POST-WAR ECONOMY AND MACRO-ECONOMIC POLICY MAKING

INTRODUCTION

In the post-war period Italy became integrated into a new international economic system dominated by the United States, later influenced by moves towards European integration. As a consequence, the Italian economy has experienced problems and patterns of development that are not dissimilar to those of many other West European economies across the decades. At the same time, there have been distinctive national traits to the Italian economy that have made it stand out from other economies in the West, and which have had a significant impact on its performance. These traits concern structural and territorial distortions, the nature of macro-economic policy, and regulation of the economy generally. This chapter (which adopts a historical approach to macro-economic policy making) and chapters 10 and 11 (which adopt a thematic approach to the economy's structural and territorial features) will emphasize the distinctiveness of the post-war economic model and its mode of state regulation, as well as analysing how this has begun to change in the period since the early 1990s.

FROM POST-WAR RECONSTRUCTION TO THE END OF THE ECONOMIC MIRACLE

At the end of the war, the Italian economy had low levels of industrialization, territorial and structural dualisms, high levels of unemployment and underemployment, inequalities in salaries and wealth, little advanced technology, and an absence of basic raw materials. The economy was also relatively closed and protected from the international economic environment. Its poor comparative wealth is perhaps best exemplified in per capita income which, in 1950, was only a quarter of that of the United States and little more than half that of most of the countries of northern Europe. Despite twenty-two years of fascism, Italy remained a largely agricultural society, with 43.9 per cent of employees in 1951 being employed in this sector, compared with 23 per cent in Germany and a mere 5 per cent in the United Kingdom (Valli 1982: 7–11).

This situation began to change in the 1950s, partly as a result of fundamental decisions made in the period of reconstruction. The late 1940s were characterized by a reassertion of the forces of economic liberalism, which involved two changes. First, at the domestic level, it meant reducing state intervention and giving freedom to market forces (in contrast with moves towards Keynesianism in Britain and France). Second, at the external level, it involved reducing protectionist controls and opening the economy to world competition. This was not just a reaction to the Fascist experience, but a product of Italy's insertion within the Western sphere of influence (GATT, OEEC-OECD, World Bank, IMF, NATO, initial moves toward European integration), as well as a reflection of the internal balance of power. The parties of the left, which might have chosen an alternative course, were gradually marginalized from political influence, and the line of De Gasperi (Prime Minister) and Einaudi (Governor of the Bank of Italy, then Minister of the Budget and, in 1948, President of the Republic) prevailed.

Nevertheless, the commitment to liberalization was not unequivocal. There were several influential economists (such as Sylos Labini, Bertolini, Fuà) and politicians (Fanfani and the *dossettiani*, who would become the most influential faction in the DC) who were less disposed towards a withdrawal of the State. The Fascist inheritance included a wide-ranging network of state holdings, not all of which was dismantled: the large state holdings, IRI (hydrocarbons) and AGIP (petrol), for example, were left intact. It was also apparent that some forms of state intervention would be necessary to carry out the tasks of reconstruction, specifically in public housing, public works (particularly major roads), agriculture and the south (Salvati 1984: 53–6). In short, while this period was marked by a rejection of pure Keynesianism (the Keynesian *Piano del lavoro* or 'Plan for work' proposed by the trade unions was hardly even considered by the government), this did not entail a complete abandonment of state intervention. The economic conditions, in fact, became conducive to the development of more extensive forms of state regulation, which would take on a peculiarly Italian character.

The 1950s and beyond were marked by stability and high levels of economic growth, and were quickly dubbed an 'economic miracle'. Figures for three successive periods (1951–8, 1958–63 and 1963–9) give some idea of the extent of the achievement. The most impressive period was 1958–63, when 'the Italian economy managed to realise three main achievements, seldom to be found simultaneously present in the same country: namely, a high rate of growth and capital accumulation, price stability, and balance of payments equilibrium' (Graziani 1991: 21). In fact, the figures confirm that strong economic growth continued through two decades (see table 2.1). In addition, inflation during the period was low (approximately 3.8 per cent for 1951–69), growth in productivity high (5.2 per cent on average per annum for the decade 1951–61, and 7.7 per cent specifically for industry), and there was a healthy surplus in balance of payments. Unemployment was the one exception to this achievement: it averaged 5.2 per cent for the period 1951–69 (which contrasted with an EEC average of 2.1 per cent).

Italy's 'economic miracle' has been cited as a classic example of export-led growth (Stern 1967; Graziani 1969, 1991). The contribution of government was not crucial, since little beyond fine-tuning was necessary. Rather, the 'miracle' is explained by several other factors. The opening up of the economy allowed it to exploit a general

Table 2.1   Economic performance in the 1950s and 1960s

	1951–1958	1958–1963	1963–1969
GDP*	5.3	6.6	5.3
Investments**	19.2	22.9	21.6
Industrial Production**	6.8	10.2	6.2
Exports**	9.2	11.3	14.0
Current Account Bal.**	−0.2	0.9	2.4
Population in Agric.***	42.2 ('51)	29.1 ('61)	17.2 ('71)

* Average annual growth rates.
** As per cent of GDP.
*** Per cent of active population.
Source: Reproduced from Balcet, *L'économie italienne* © Editions La Découverte, Paris 1995 (Balcet 1997: 51)

growth in world trade. Because of relatively low internal demand (albeit boosted by public expenditure in the south), Italian companies were forced to look abroad to sell their products, and they found them to be very competitive. Labour was available at low wage rates and was replenished by the exodus from agriculture and migration from the south, which also kept trade unions weak. The influx of new technology from the United States modernized what were particularly backward industrial structures, and this, combined with Einaudi's strict monetary policy, forced the industrial system to rationalize, boosting productivity along capital-intensive lines. Finally, there was a decline in the price of raw materials from abroad, notably oil.

Yet, if this was a success story, it was one that carried with it 'distortions' and imbalances, which to some extent were exacerbated by the rapidity of economic growth (Lutz 1975; Graziani 1969, 1972). First, the structural dualism persisted between a few capital-intensive giant corporations, on the one hand, and small, family-run firms, on the other. This was heightened by the opening up of the economy, since those sectors that were forced to seek overseas markets became more highly productive and dynamic, leaving other sectors to stagnate (Graziani 1969). Second, the economy's territorial dualism (between north and south) was exacerbated. The dynamism of the large corporations of the industrial north, coupled with the massive exodus of labour from the south, left the southern economy underdeveloped, despite the beginnings of state aid to the south in 1950. Third, the agricultural sector remained backward. Despite agricultural reform in the 1950s, agriculture had an average growth rate (2.5 per cent) which was lower than that achieved in Yugoslavia and Greece (Balcet 1997: 59). Fourth, the competitiveness of Italian industry was based largely on low labour costs rather than technological investment. Indeed, despite the injection of new technologies, levels of technological innovation remained lower than in most of Italy's main competitors, particularly in the large number of family-run firms. Fifth, there were high levels of unemployment, notably in the sectors of low productivity. Sixth, the exodus from the south towards the industrial triangle of the north placed rising demands on local governments there for services (in health, education, housing, public transport) of a quality which they proved unable to provide.

These economic distortions were compounded by the specific approach of the new political class to state intervention. State intervention was considerably expanded from the 1950s onwards, for three reasons: the underdevelopment of the south; a decision taken to develop heavy industry (e.g. steel, energy) by expanding the system of state holdings developed under Fascism, and the need for stronger social services and infrastructure to support industrialization. However, due to the hostile ideological climate of the 1950s and the fragility of the DC's social base, this expansion was exploited for more subtle purposes too. Swept to power on a wide inter-class base, but confronted with a strong delegitimized Communist party, the DC found itself confronted with something of a dilemma. If the party pursued reformist policies, it risked its support amongst the more traditional sectors (hence the plummet in its electoral support in the south in the 1952–3 local elections after the agrarian reform). Yet, if the party failed to introduce reforms, it would undermine its support amongst more progressive sectors, at the same time giving legitimacy to several of the PCI's demands. The DC's dilemma, then, was a reflection of the dualism existing in the economy.

In 1954, the DC's new party leader, Amintore Fanfani, saw it as imperative that the DC transform itself from what was largely a party of *notables* into a modern mass party with a strong organization, capable of mobilizing different sectors of the electorate. Whatever the policy's original objectives, modernization of the party became, over time, intimately linked to 'colonization' of the state sector of the economy. This allowed the DC to begin to use the new forms of state intervention to tie sectors of society to the party, particularly in the south. It enabled the party to preserve its inter-class base while, at the same time, making itself less dependent on the more traditional elements of southern politics. The policy also kept the south underdeveloped and depopulating, thereby hindering the development of class conflict.

Salvati (1972) described this situation as one of 'repressive development', or rapid economic growth 'underpinned by under-development'. Italian capitalism, he suggested, was therefore characterized by 'precocious maturity', a situation which was inherently unstable. Not surprisingly, therefore, once the factors facilitating growth began to disappear in the 1960s, the underlying problems of the economy surfaced, exposing the political class's failure to facilitate a stable political-economic equilibrium for long-term growth. In this way, the unfolding of several factors culminated in the explosion of social and worker militancy at the end of the decade, known as the 'hot autumn'.

First, despite reasonable rates of growth in the 1960s, the 'virtuous cycle' was arrested in the early part of the decade. Price and wage inflationary tendencies surfaced in 1962, which were largely a product of growing wage demands as employment reached peak levels in the north. Inflation rose from 2.8 per cent in 1961 to 5.7 per cent in 1963, and a series of strikes and wage increases in 1963–4 were followed by an increase in prices and a severe monetary squeeze in 1964–5. This deflationary policy affected business investment and profits, which could be maintained only through a rationalization of existing capacity, essentially through longer working hours. Consequently, the annual growth rate in this period (5.3 per cent for 1963–9) has been described as 'false', since, without increasing investment, it could only be temporary (and the recovery in economic activity in 1966–7 was not accompanied by any notable rise in investment).

Second, there was an increase in international competition, which made it difficult for companies to maintain profits by raising prices. Exports continued to expand until 1968, but this year represented a peak, and Italian companies experienced increasing difficulties in the 1960s in trying to expand their export markets. Export growth had occurred primarily in what were originally high-technology sectors (e.g. engineering, chemicals and vehicles). As these sectors became more standardized, they were prone to competition from less developed countries with cheaper labour. At the same time foreign companies had begun to compete more effectively in the Italian domestic market, resulting in an increase in imports.

Third, the trade unions and workforce increased their industrial and political muscle, partly due to the move towards full employment in the north, making it more difficult to sustain profits on low wages, and partly because of poor working conditions. There was a growing sense amongst the labour force that it had not enjoyed the fruits of the economic growth of the previous decade. Moreover, the tighter labour markets in the north highlighted the economy's territorial dualism, since there were large reserves of labour 'locked up' in low-productivity areas.

Early in the decade, there was hope that the government's management of the economy would be conducive to a resolution of these problems, since the centrist governing coalitions of the 1950s – DC, Liberals (PLI), Republicans (PRI) and Social Democrats (PSDI) – were replaced with the centre left formula. After the Socialists (PSI) had supported a DC-led government in 1962, a government was formed in December of 1963 consisting of the DC, PSI, PRI and PSDI (the PLI not entering the coalition). For the more progressive elements of the political class, the new political formula, combined with economic planning, was the means whereby the economy's structural distortions could be removed, at the same time as integrating an important part of the working class into the capitalist system. The main priorities of 'The National Economic Plan for the Five Years 1966–70' were to boost employment in specified areas, modernize and increase agricultural production, reduce the north–south divide, provide better social infrastructures and reform the State (Valli 1982: 120–2). Italian capitalism, it was argued, would be rationalized and stabilized, thus moving it closer to the European model.

However, the centre left was opposed at both ends of the political spectrum. On the one hand, it brought out fully the interests of the more backward-looking sectors of Italian capitalism (notably the right wing of the DC), which stood to lose from progressive reform. On the other hand, there were elements of the left in the PSI, PCI and trade union movement who interpreted the centre left experiment as a neo-capitalist plan designed to rationalize Italian capitalism's primary contradictions and split the working class in the process (which in fact occurred). The strength of opposition (particularly from the right) was sufficient to impede the approval of several reforms, and the plan of 1966–70 failed almost totally with regard to its major objectives. Unemployment increased in the south, the state of agriculture and the north–south divide worsened, social infrastructures in northern cities were hardly improved, and reform of the State was faltering and partial (Valli 1982: 122–6). The PSI, rather than becoming the agent of radical change by entering the *stanza dei bottoni* ('control room'), began to cultivate the practices of the existing governing parties, bent on securing its electoral future through the distribution of patronage. This had the effect of widening the constituencies in need of attention, thus distorting further the distribution of public resources in the system. This explains why the disastrous experience of economic planning, coupled with a struggling private sector, was not compensated by the performance of the state holdings system. The creation in 1956 of the Ministry for State

Participation confirmed the basic evolution of conglomerates such as IRI, ENI and EFIM into vehicles of patronage for the governing parties (see chapter 10). Paradoxically, this evolution was occurring at a time when the state holdings system was regarded as a model of good industrial performance, widely admired abroad.

The credibility of the centre left experiment effectively collapsed after the 1968 elections. Workers, lacking the benefits they might have expected from the 'economic miracle', became, by the late 1960s, an entrenched and unaccommodating group ready to use its industrial muscle.

FROM THE HOT AUTUMN TO THE CRISIS OF THE FIRST REPUBLIC

The hot autumn embodied a radical change in the power of industrial workers (see chapter 5). The trade unions used the spontaneous wave of strikes and militant action in 1969 to achieve several important changes: large wage increases (up to 15 per cent); the abolition of differences in wage scales; increased security of employment; a new pension law (providing two-thirds of a worker's final wage at the age of 60 with some indexing for inflation); a housing law (which provided for an increase in the stock of public housing); the right to 150 hours of paid education or training each year; and an increase in investment in the south.

The government's concession to these demands was coupled with a deflationary policy designed – as a decade previously – to weaken the labour market and undermine wage and other demands. Yet, while this had the effect of depressing economic activity, it failed to prevent the intense wage push of the first half of the 1970s, which was common across Western Europe, but particularly acute in Italy, for three reasons. First, a shift had occurred in the internal balance of power in the trade union movement towards both the plant level and specific industrial unions (such as the Metalworkers) that were less willing to compromise than most others. Second, Confindustria, representing business interests, was divided in its response. Small and medium-sized businesses wished to resist wage demands, while large-scale industry was open to bargaining with the trade unions. Meetings between the two sides held in 1971–2, however, proved to be failures. Third, the government lacked the cohesion and ability to carry through a deflationary strategy, largely because of the exhaustion of the centre left formula (Salvati 1979: 35). The PSI had, in 1966, reunited with the PSDI to form the United Socialist Party (PSU), only to split again after a poor showing in the 1968 elections. On the back of this failure, the PSI would only sanction the re-creation of the centre left if several trade union demands and parts of the centre left programme were acted upon. The DC was in too weak a position to resist these conditions, given that its coalition alternatives would have had to involve either the PCI or parties of the right (the monarchists and neo-fascists), and given the pressures being exerted by its own trade union, the CISL. The 1972 elections, moreover, which marked a shift to the right in the electorate and the formation of a centre right government, did little to change things, as both unions and business were opposed to a tighter monetary policy.

Consequently, government economic policy succeeded in depressing economic activity without resisting either higher wage demands or other increases in public expen-

Table 2.2   1970s: economic indicators

year	GDP growth*	Inflation	Unemployment	Public deficit**	Public debt**
1970	5.3	6.8	5.4	−3.3	41.2
1971	1.6	7.2	5.4	−4.8	46.6
1972	2.7	6.3	6.4	−7.0	53.4
1973	7.1	11.6	6.4	−6.5	55.0
1974	5.4	18.5	5.4	−6.4	54.5
1975	−2.7	17.5	5.9	−10.6	60.3
1976	6.6	18.0	6.7	−8.1	58.6
1977	3.4	19.1	7.2	−7.0	57.9
1978	3.7	13.9	7.2	−8.5	62.5
1979	6.0	15.7	7.7	−8.3	61.6
1980	4.2	20.8	7.6	−8.5	59.0

* In real terms; figures conform to ISTAT's 1987 revision of national calculations.
** As per cent of GDP.
Source: Reproduced from Balcet, *L'économie italienne* © Editions La Découverte, Paris 1995 (Balcet 1997: 78)

diture through social reform. In addition, since productivity gains in the 1960s had been achieved largely through a rationalization of existing capacity (e.g. longer working hours), improved working conditions resulted in a decline in productivity. Employers were also now less inclined to raise productivity through (capital-intensive) investment because of the increased security of employment – especially in a context of a general decline in world demand. The recovery of economic activity in the second half of 1972 enhanced the inflationary formula (more growth, more inflation) in the economy, and the rise in prices (to achieve profits) was matched by a rise in wages. Finally, the decision taken, in February 1973, to float the lira on the currency markets (until then it had been based on fixed exchange rates) led to its devaluation (by approximately 15 per cent in a year). This set in motion a devaluation–inflation–devaluation spiral that would endure throughout the decade.

The fourfold increase in oil prices in October 1973, therefore, had a severe impact on Italy, not just because of the country's high dependence on oil imports (it had little coal, oil, gas and nuclear power, so over 80 per cent of its energy needs were met by imported oil at substantial cost), but because the economy, in contrast with its European partners, was in a phase of 'inflationistic expansion'. The world recession and high oil prices shattered the assumption of continued economic growth in Western economies and gave rise to a new phenomenon: stagflation (the simultaneous rise of inflation and unemployment), combined with erratic growth. In Italy, stagflation was exacerbated by the emergence of an additional phenomenon that was to characterize the economy thereafter: a dramatic rise in the public sector deficit (see table 2.2). Even when drastic cuts became necessary after mid-1974, public expenditure continued to spiral upwards. This was caused by prior spending commitments (e.g. to the south and for social welfare policies), the failure to resist further wage demands (the trade unions' conditions for wage restraint – price stability, full employment and social reform – were not met), and the growing need to subsidize the state holdings sector.

Self-financing until then, this sector was now spiralling into debt. Industries such as steel and chemicals were, as elsewhere in Europe, suffering from world overproduction; but the problems were particularly acute in Italy as a result of poor management (party control) and a series of poor investment decisions in the late 1960s and early 1970s. IRI, for example, having broken even in 1973, was 500 billion lire in debt in 1975, 900 billion in 1977, 1,346 billion in 1979, and 2,200 billion by 1980, a figure representing 6 per cent of GDP (Balcet 1997: 70).

The government decision, in 1975, to increase the coverage of the wage (inflation)-indexation system (*scala mobile*) from the then 40 per cent to 100 per cent compounded the economy's problems. Proposed by Confindustria, the idea behind it was to reduce inflationary *expectations* in the economy, thus reducing shop-floor unrest, assisting a shift in power back to the trade union confederations with a subsequent moderation in wage demands (at the same time as giving the government room to control price increases). Yet, although shop-floor unrest was reduced, the agreement (which marked a peak in trade union power) had several other unforeseen consequences.

First, because inflation was running at more than 20 per cent per annum, in any given year the proportion of a worker's pay increase deriving from the *scala mobile* soon far outweighed the proportion secured from collective bargaining. This led to a 90 per cent rise in industrial labour costs between 1975 and 1978. By 1980 wage costs per unit of production were 39 per cent higher than in Germany or Britain. Profits fell, many firms going bankrupt. The rise in labour costs, moreover, undermined the effectiveness of the government's price-control policy. Second, wage indexation increased unemployment, because high labour costs deterred employers from taking on new workers. The expansion in scope of the state insurance fund (the *Cassa integrazione guadagni*), a trade union demand, by which workers would receive 80 per cent of their pay for a year if made redundant, made it easier for firms to release workers, the cost to be borne by the State. Third, it led more and more firms to retreat from the 'official economy' because of high production costs. There was a 'decentralization' of production, with thousands of firms adopting techniques that avoided wage regulations, unions, social security contributions and taxes. Production costs were said to be up to a third cheaper than in a standard factory. The performance of this sector of small and medium-sized firms helped to maintain the comparatively good performance of the Italian economy, but it did little for the state coffers.

With social and economic tensions high, the PCI, in the 1976 national elections, reached its post-war electoral peak (34.4 per cent of the vote). The two main parties (DC and PCI) agreed on a 'historic compromise' to overcome the crisis. This saw the formation of 'national solidarity' governments supported by the PCI during 1976–9. A 'Three Year Plan' was successfully negotiated with the trade unions. This involved pay restraint by the unions (real wages were due to remain constant for three years) in return for consultation on legislation affecting them, the creation of tripartite bodies (government, business, unions) as advisors on economic policy, and the carrying through of several social reforms. Economic conditions in the second half of the decade also improved. There was a rise in international demand which, coupled with the devaluation of the lira, gave a boost to exports. Inflation was brought down, some large debts repaid, and the exchange rate stabilized through Italy joining the European Monetary System (EMS) in March 1979.

Yet the 'national solidarity' pact was not destined to last. Despite trade union expectations that the PCI would achieve cabinet positions, conservative elements of the DC were never prepared to countenance this, and this unwritten premiss of the 'national solidarity' experiment effectively died with the kidnapping and murder by the Red Brigades of its chief architect, Aldo Moro, in 1978. The PCI, losing members and votes at local elections, pulled out of the experiment before the 1979 elections, in which the party suffered its first decline in votes in the post-war period. For the trade unions, the national solidarity governments failed to deliver. While several important reforms were achieved in this period (e.g. in relation to the tax system, the social security system and subsidies to small firms), others (e.g. those relating to industrial restructuring, youth employment, rent control, agriculture, universities) barely got beyond the drafting stage. This was due both to the protracted legislative process and to important elements of the DC who were not prepared to sacrifice the accommodation of their clientele: the more conservative elements of the small bourgeoisie, or *topi nel formaggio* ('mice in the cheese') (Sylos Labini 1974: 53).

Paradoxically, various reforms and government measures introduced in the 1970s not only raised public expenditure on a 'one-off' basis, but automatically committed the State to increased expenditure in the future – thus raising the structural deficit precisely at a time when adjustments were needed in the opposite direction (Balcet 1997: 68). The measures included the introduction of regional governments (1970), the Workers' Statute (1970), the 100 per cent coverage of the *scala mobile* (1975), the industrial restructuring law (1977), the new National Health Service (1978), reform of the fiscal system (1974–9), the creation of the *Cassa integrazione guadagni*, new legislation to salvage industries (on the part of the State), a widening of the coverage of the pensions system, increased state intervention in the south, and increasing subsidies to the state holdings system.

At the same time, state income failed to increase sufficiently. Total fiscal income rose from 26.9 per cent of GDP in 1970 to 31.1 per cent in 1980, while total expenditure rose from 33.1 per cent of GDP in 1970 to 42.2 per cent in 1980. Fiscal reform failed to prevent a rise in tax evasion (boosted by the rapid growth of the 'black economy'), since the DC was unwilling to withdraw what was seen as one of the privileges of its clientele. In this situation, the rapid deterioration of the public finances was not surprising. The size of the public debt and public sector deficit rose dramatically in the 1970s, and interest payments on the debt rose from a figure representing 1.7 per cent of GDP in 1970 to 5.3 per cent in 1980. In this situation, the second bout of oil price rises in 1980 had a considerable impact. There was a severe economic recession, the government responding with a tight credit squeeze and cuts in public expenditure (largely falling on health, welfare and education). Inflation rose to its highest ever annual rate of 21.1 per cent in 1981 and stayed at 15 per cent or above until 1984. Real growth plummeted for three years, and unemployment increased throughout the decade.

This recession, however, quickly gave way to a period of renewed growth that lasted almost until the end of the decade. Although unemployment and debt continued to rise, growth in GDP was consistently above 2.5 per cent, and inflation fell to more reasonable levels (see table 2.3). This turn-around was part of a recovery on a world scale, assisted by reflation of the American economy and falling oil prices, but it also

Table 2.3   1980s: economic indicators

year	GDP growth (%)	Public deficit*	Public debt*	Interest on debt*	Inflation	Unemployment
1980	4.2	8.5	56.9	5.3	21.1	7.6
1981	0.6	11.4	59.8	6.2	19.3	8.4
1982	0.2	11.3	64.9	7.1	16.3	9.1
1983	1.0	10.6	70.0	7.5	15.0	9.9
1984	2.7	11.6	75.2	8.0	10.6	10.0
1985	2.6	12.6	82.4	8.0	8.6	10.3
1986	2.9	11.6	86.5	8.5	6.1	11.1
1987	3.1	11.0	90.6	7.9	4.6	12.0
1988	4.1	10.7	92.7	8.1	5.0	12.0
1989	2.9	9.9	95.7	8.9	6.6	12.0
1990	2.1	11.0	97.8	9.6	6.1	11.0

* As percentages of GDP.
Source: Reproduced from Balcet, *L'économie italienne* © Editions La Découverte, Paris 1995 (Balcet 1997: 78)

had a distinctive Italian dimension to it. The decision to join the Exchange Rate Mechanism (ERM) in 1978, combined with the recession that followed, forced Italian industry to undertake radical restructuring, because devaluing the lira in order to safeguard growth was no longer an option. In fact, the recovery of profit margins in the late 1970s, a result of devaluation, had resulted in a sharp increase in investment, particularly in traditional industries, at a time of rapid technical progress in rationalizing production and improving quality. The repeated devaluations of the 1970s had, by chance, postponed rationalization until a particularly propitious moment. In the early 1980s, something like 80 per cent of industry's capital spending was allocated to plant rationalization and modernization, compared with only 30 per cent a decade earlier: 'Italian industry was able to renew its plant en bloc and incorporate the new technology' (Cipoletta 1995: 14). Large companies such as FIAT led the field in adopting new electronic and automated techniques, and there were a number of industrial mergers and takeovers.

The trade union movement could no longer resist this restructuring. Its power had been weakened by a rise in unemployment, a hardening of Confindustria's attitude towards rigidities in the labour market, and a decline in the vote for the PCI. A thirty-three-day strike in 1980 over FIAT's restructuring plans split the workforce, and was ended by a demonstration of 40,000 workers in favour of FIAT's terms. Other large companies followed FIAT's example, introducing new technology, even if redundancies were to result. The restructuring therefore increased unemployment, further weakening the bargaining power of organized labour. In 1983, the government, trade unions and industry reached an agreement that reduced labour market rigidities (specifically with regard to the hiring and transferring of workers), placed a limit on wage increases, and reduced the coverage of the *scala mobile*. The following year, the Socialist Prime Minister, Bettino Craxi, proposed a further reduction in the coverage of the *scala mobile*, on the grounds that the reduction would be more than compensated by the reduction in inflation that would occur. The trade unions were divided on how to respond, the CISL, UIL and Socialist component of the CGIL agreeing with the reduction, while the Communist component of the CGIL allied with the PCI to oppose it. Craxi passed the measure as a decree, and the subsequent attempt of the PCI to nullify it by referendum failed, 45.7 per cent voting for nullification and 54.3 per cent against. It marked the 'end of an era' of trade union power, which had begun in the Hot Autumn (Lange 1986).

The restructuring was accompanied by two other changes. First, there was a further decentralization of production. In the 1980s small and medium-sized firms became the backbone of employment in the industrial sector, and their economic performance made famous the 'made in Italy' mark, despite a strong lira that undermined exports (see chapter 11). Second, there was an improvement in the stability of the political situation, notably under the premiership of Craxi. Setting a record for government longevity (unsurpassed until the second Berlusconi government), Craxi attempted, with partial success, to develop a reputation for *decisionismo* ('decisiveness' – see chapter 7). This, coupled with an improved economic performance and a reduction in social tensions, seemed to bring Italy closer to her northern neighbours, increasing the confidence of foreign investors.

Yet, the economic boom did not lead to a resolution of problems of a more structural nature. On the contrary, it was achieved on the basis of a model whose distortions (and particularly the public deficit and debt) were growing, and which, in a changing international context, would lay the foundations for a renewed crisis in the early 1990s. Triglia (1996) has described what occurred in the 1980s as a form of 'perverse Keynesianism'. Where in other Western democracies, there existed the combination of a public deficit with a balance of payments deficit, there were pressures on central government to change public expenditure patterns, raise taxes and control inflation. But in Italy the sheer success of small firms in the 1980s helped to keep the balance of payments out of deficit and reinforced the traditionally high level of Italian family savings. This helped (through the issue of Treasury bonds) to finance the public deficit, so that the problem could be effectively postponed for several years. This allowed public expenditure to rise unchecked under the Craxi governments. It was fuelled by the new welfare policies launched in the 1970s and by the continued need to ensure electoral support through benefits policies in the south (an increasing stronghold of the governing parties). At the same time, it assisted the restructuring of large firms (since they could be supported by public policies on redundancy payments) and kept the domestic market buoyant, thus further helping small firms. These were losing competitiveness abroad, because the government could no longer choose to devalue the lira now that the currency was in the ERM.

By the end of the 1980s, therefore, Italy's economy was locked into a 'perverse enveloping growth model' (Baldassarri and Modigliani 1995). The national budget increased disposable income (via the explosion of spending and current account deficits), which was largely channelled into consumer goods, squeezing capital spending over the long term. The loss of competitiveness abroad in a context of sustained domestic demand led to a decline in exports and an increase in imports, and therefore a large balance of payments (current account) deficit, which, by 1991, had produced for the first time a foreign trade deficit (measured at constant prices for manufacturing). The combination of public deficit, public debt and current account deficit on the balance of payments left little choice but to keep interest rates high to ensure that Treasury bonds could be placed and the lira's exchange rate maintained. The high interest rates further squeezed investment in production, while generating transfers of income from the national budget to the private sector, helping to reinforce consumer demand. In this situation, the economy had a high inflation rate (despite coming down from the peaks of the early part of the decade, it was still 5–6 per cent by the end of the decade), a low (and declining) growth rate, and rising levels of public and external debt.

The real problem, however, was that there was no incentive to rectify these distortions. Apart from the manufacturing sector (roughly 4.3 million workers and 1.7 million entrepreneurs), which saw its profits squeezed, and future generations, which would have to pay interest on the public deficit and debt, the majority of Italians profited (Baldassarri and Modigliani 1995). In short, the perversity of the model allowed four-fifths of the population to improve their living standards while reducing real growth.

The growing amount of public and external debt suggested that this situation could not last; but two interrelated factors hastened change. The first was the economic downturn of the late 1980s and early 1990s that was common to most Western economies. The big industrial leaders, agricultural producers and the backbone of small firms all began to suffer, requiring new strategies, cut-backs and lay-offs. By 1991 the trade imbalance, low GDP growth (just over 1 per cent), high inflation (6.4 per cent), high unemployment (11 per cent) and huge budget deficit (over 10.5 per cent of GDP) revealed the costs of failure of successive governments' macro-economic policies.

These costs were brought into sharp relief by the second factor: moves towards Economic and Monetary Union (EMU). While joining the ERM in 1978 helped to effect a restructuring of industry and to bring down inflation, it did not enforce macro-economic discipline – where successive governments proved wanting. The perverse model of growth worked in such a way that the constraint did not in fact work, and the question of the public finances could be postponed. This was also because the ERM, in the first phase until the mid-1980s, operated with a degree of flexibility, with frequent realignments of the currencies inside the system. The ERM, therefore, could not break completely the basic approach to economic policy making that had characterized the 1970s – when a central role was played by public deficits, state subsidies to firms, and repeated devaluation of the lira to raise the competitiveness of exports, even though it exacerbated inflation and the size of the public debt (see Giavazzi and Spaventa 1988).

In the second half of the 1980s, however, the objective of integration was pursued with more determination. The realignments became less frequent, and in 1990 the lira entered the 'narrow band' of the ERM. This was accompanied by the complete liberalization of capital movements. The persistence of Italy's high inflation compared with that of other countries led to a depreciation in value of the lira. This increased the government's economic difficulties, making national budgets appear out of line with the new demands of EMU (Pizzuti 1994: xvii–xviii). Finally, the decision in 1990–2 to move towards EMU and the formulation of tough convergence criteria in the Maastricht Treaty raised a perilous spectre for Italian policy-makers: that of being left in the European 'slow lane', which would be immensely unpopular in one of the EC's most consistently pro-European nations. At the time of the Treaty's signing, Italy met only one of the five criteria. The two most demanding criteria were the stipulation that budget deficits should be no more than 3 per cent of GDP (Italy's was approximately 9 per cent) and that public debt should be no more than 60 per cent of GDP (Italy's was more than 100 per cent). In fact, by 1991, Italy had more outstanding debt than any country in the world except Japan and the United States. It was the biggest borrower in the EC, and its ratio of outstanding debt to GDP was roughly double the average of that of the other eleven countries. Italy therefore faced a very difficult struggle to meet the criteria. Significant cuts in public expenditure and increases in tax revenue would be required; the latter would be politically difficult to carry through, and the former threatened the clientelistic base of the ruling parties and their corrupt practices.

By the early 1990s, therefore, economic problems and the demands of EMU had taken on significant political implications, at the same time as intertwining with the unfolding of several political factors (see chapter 1). They produced a political and economic earthquake in 1992: the decimation of political parties began in the period after the April elections, and there was an alarming run on the currency. Despite the Bank of Italy using a substantial amount of its foreign reserves to defend it, the lira was withdrawn from the ERM on 13 September (Pizzuti 1994: part 1).

SOUND FINANCE AND ECONOMIC DECLINE SINCE THE EARLY 1990s

In the period since 1992 there has been a marked change in approaches to macro-economic policy making. This has been a consequence not just of the lira's exit from the ERM and the need to meet the Maastricht convergence criteria, but also of the dramatic political changes of the early 1990s. Since the exposure of widespread corruption, the demise of the DC and the PSI and their replacement by new political forces in the midst of an economic crisis, the 'perverse Keynesianism' of the past has been rejected, or at least has not constituted an option to follow. Operating within the European monetary constraint, the nine governments that have held office since 1992 (Amato I, Ciampi, Berlusconi I, Dini, Prodi, D'Alema I, D'Alema II, Amato II, Berlusconi II) have, to varying degrees, recognized the need to make fundamental changes in the economy and in economic management. In particular, when faced with the Maastricht deadline for joining the single currency, the self-styled 'transitional' governments of Amato I, Ciampi and Dini, together with the Prodi government, set about carrying out an overhaul of the public finances. Tight budgets were passed in order to reduce the public deficit and level of public debt, and significant inroads were made into the former. The overall level of public debt, however, has proved more difficult to reduce substantially, due largely to interest payments, which by 1993 had reached 12 per cent of GDP (accounting for the entire public sector borrowing requirement). However, the level of public debt in Italy has been reduced in the past decade, while the average level of that of the euro zone has risen (see tables 2.4 and 2.5).

The significant improvements in public finances resulted in Italy's entry into the single currency in 1999 with the first wave of countries. This was an outcome that had

Table 2.4   1990s and beyond: economic indicators

year	GDP growth (%)	Pub. sect. deficit*	Public debt*	Interest on debt*	Inflation	Unemployment**
1990	2.1	11.0	97.8	9.6	6.1	11.0
1991	1.2	10.0	100.6	10.2	6.4	10.9
1992	0.7	9.5	107.7	11.4	5.4	11.5
1993	−1.2	9.4	118.1	12.0	4.2	10.2
1994	2.1	9.3	124.3	10.8	3.9	11.3
1995	3.0	7.6	123.8	11.2	5.4	12.0
1996	0.7	7.1	122.7	10.3	3.9	12.1
1997	2.0	2.7	120.2	9.4	1.7	11.7
1998	1.8	2.8	116.4	8.3	2.1	11.8
1999	1.6	1.8	114.6	6.8	1.7	11.2
2000	2.9	0.5	110.5	6.5	2.6	10.4
2001	1.8	1.4	109.4	6.4	2.7	9.6
2002	0.4	2.3	108.0	5.8	2.3	9.1
2003	0.3	2.4	106.2	n.a.	2.4	8.7

* As percentages of GDP.
** In 1993, the criteria for defining unemployment became more restrictive, resulting in lower figures relative to those that obtain using the earlier definition.
Sources: Balcet 1997: 78; ISTAT (various years c); Bank of Italy annual reports; OECD Economic Survey 2003

Table 2.5   Italy's public debt over ten years compared with principal competitors

	1993	1994	1995	1996	1997	1998	1999	2000	2001	2002
Italy	**118.2**	**124.3**	**123.8**	**122.7**	**120.2**	**116.4**	**114.9**	**110.6**	**109.5**	**106.7**
France	45.3	48.4	54.6	57.0	59.3	59.5	58.5	57.3	57.3	59.5
Germany	46.9	49.3	57.0	59.8	61.0	60.9	61.2	60.2	59.5	60.8
UK	45.4	48.5	51.8	52.3	50.8	47.7	45.1	42.1	38.9	38.4
Av. Euro area	66.7	69.0	72.9	74.5	74.3	73.5	72.0	69.5	69.1	69.1
Av. EU	65.3	67.3	71.2	73.1	71.4	69.3	67.8	63.9	63.0	62.5

Source: Adapted from Table 8. International comparisons of gross public debt in the EU, *OECD Economic Surveys: Italy – Volume 2003 Issue 13*, © OECD, 2003 (OECD 2003: 60)

been considered by many observers as almost impossible at the time of the signing of the Treaty, and, in the case of some observers, as late as two years before the dead-line.[1] Salvati (2000: 83) describes the turn-around of the 1990s as 'a small miracle, a miracle of fiscal and financial adjustment'.

The 'small miracle' of the past decade has been characterized by four features. First, there has been a mixture of public expenditure cuts, tax increases and new taxes (including a new 'European tax' levied specifically in order to meet Maastricht). The cuts have mainly concerned welfare, health, pensions, public works and local govern-ment. Second, there have been moves towards reform of the welfare state and the pen-sions system. Third, new agreements have been reached with the trade unions that have allowed relaxation or elimination of certain labour market rigidities. In July 1992 the *scala mobile* was abolished through an accord on labour costs with the trade unions. In July 1993, a new agreement was reached on labour costs and conditions, making wage increases dependent on the projected inflation rate, allowing perform-ance-related pay by individual companies and introducing greater flexibility for start-ing salaries. Barriers regarding hiring regulations by firms have been removed, and an insurance system for the purpose of mass redundancy has been created. Fourth, a sig-nificant programme of privatization was begun in 1992, and although the programme has since slowed down (if it has not faltered), several important privatization meas-ures have been implemented (see chapter 11). The significant capital raised by these measures was used to wipe out the debts of companies in the state holdings system.

Cumulatively, therefore, the governments of the 1990s achieved significant successes and raised Italy's credibility abroad.[2] A culture of stability and sound finance appears to have taken hold as a consequence of the 'European constraint' (see chapter 12), and in the period until qualification for the single currency, there was a mood of optimism regarding the prospects for the Italian economy. Yet, by the latter half of the decade it was becoming apparent that the 1990s was as much about economic 'chickens coming home to roost' as it was a 'turning point' in sound finance. The long overdue improvement in public finances was not accompanied by an economic turn-around, despite the lira depreciating by approximately 30 per cent between September 1992 and January 1995 (thus assisting exports). Indeed, economic performance in the 1990s was worse than in any other decade since the war. Growth between 1990 and 2001 averaged only 1.7 per cent – almost half that of the preceding decade, and below the European average. Industrial productivity increased by an average of only 1.4 per cent over the same period (compared with 2.6 per cent over the previous decade), and figures for the key sectors (and notably manufacturing) show Italy lagging behind its main competitors (see table 2.6).

The competitiveness of Italian goods has fallen sharply since 1995, as reflected in the country's share of world trade, which has declined more steeply than that of its chief European competitors (see table 2.7). In terms of the world's largest exporters, Italy fell two places (from sixth to eighth), dropping behind China and Canada (see tables 2.7 and 2.8) (Trento 2003: 1093).

Finally, Italy has ongoing long-term structural and territorial problems regarding unemployment, leading to much higher rates than the EU average, especially in rela-tion to youth unemployment, which is almost double (see table 2.9).

There are four interrelated factors that explain this economic decline. First, it can be viewed as a necessary part of the structural financial adjustment that has occurred as a consequence of Italy joining the single currency. The lira crashing out of the ERM could be seen, with hindsight, as the last of a long series of currency devaluations that have assisted Italian competitiveness abroad, and that are now ruled out by the single currency. The euro, after an initial period of depreciation against the dollar, began to appreciate considerably. Moreover, the depressive effect of the restrictive monetary policies and tight budgets that were necessary to join the single currency has not been fully lifted, because the European Growth and Stability Pact transformed two of the Maastricht criteria into permanent requirements. The European Central Bank's approach has been governed by the need for low inflation and monetary stability. For

Table 2.6 Italy's output, employment and productivity, 1990–2001, against principal competitors

	Italy	Germany	France	UK	Av. EU	Av. OECD
Av. GDP growth	1.7	1.5	1.9	2.2	2.1	2.6
of which:						
Productivity	1.4	1.4	1.2	1.9	1.5	1.6
Employment	0.2	0.1	0.7	0.3	0.6	1.0
of which:						
Unemployment*	0.1	−0.2	0.1	0.1	0.0	0.0
Labour force	0.2	0.3	0.7	0.2	0.6	1.5
Demographics**	0.1	0.2	0.8	0.2	0.4	1.6
Participation						
rates***	0.0	0.2	−0.1	0.0	0.2	−0.1
Labour productivity growth in selected industries:+						
Total manufacturing	1.9	2.7	3.5	2.7	n.a	n.a
Electricity, gas and water supply	3.1	5.1	3.7	10.5	n.a.	n.a
Construction	0.1	0.1	−0.5	2.4	n.a.	n.a
Wholesale, retail trade, restaurants, hotels	1.1	−0.6	0.7	1.8	n.a.	n.a
Transport, storage, communication	3.2	7.6	2.9	4.3	n.a	n.a

Figures for Germany, EU and OECD start with 1992.

* A positive sign indicates that unemployment has declined and contributed to increasing output growth.

** The contribution comprises changes in the size and age composition of the working-age population.

*** Measures the effect from changes in age-specific participation rates.

+ 1990–2000, except France (1990–99) and Germany (1992–2000).

Source: Adapted from Table 9. Output employment and productivity 1990 to 2001 *OECD Economic Surveys: Italy – Volume 2003 Issue 13* © OECD, 2003 (OECD 2003: 65)

Table 2.7 Reduction (%) in share of world trade (exports), 1995–2002: Italy compared with principal European competitors

Italy	**−20.0**
France	−16.7
Germany	−18.7
UK	−18.5

Source: Adapted from Visco 2004: 35

Italy, therefore, the macro-economic regulatory framework governing the economy since the war has changed. By choosing to enter the single currency, Italy has replaced regulation of collective behaviour through the constraint of the market (i.e. the risk of a monetary crisis) with regulation through an institutional constraint (the European Growth and Stability Pact and the financial rules accompanying it). In view of its economic history, the adaptation required is considerable (Signorini 2001: 161).

Table 2.8   The world's top ten exporters, 2002

		Value of exports (billions of dollars)	Share (%) 2001	Share (%) 2002
1.	United States	694	11.8	10.8
2.	Germany	610	6.7	9.3
3.	China*	418	5.8	6.5
4.	Japan	416	6.5	6.5
5.	France	331	5.2	5.2
6.	UK	278	4.4	4.3
7.	Canada	252	4.2	3.9
8.	**Italy**	**251**	**4.0**	**3.8**
9.	Netherlands	243	3.7	3.8
10.	Belgium	209	3.1	3.3

* Includes Hong Kong's re-exported goods of Chinese origin. The value of these was $92 billion, constituting a share of 1.4% in 2002 (against 1.5% in 2001).
Source: Adapted from Onida 2004: 84

Table 2.9   Italian unemployment compared with the EU average (2001)

	Italy	EU avge
Unemployment rate*	**9.0**	7.6
Long-term unemployment⁺	**63.4**	43.7
Youth unemployment rate	**27.0**	13.9

* Data refer to 2002.
⁺ As per cent of total unemployment.
Source: Adapted from Figure 31. Unemployment rates in selected areas, 1996–2002, *OECD Economic Surveys: Italy – Volume 2003 Issue 13* © OECD, 2003 (OECD 2003: 111)

Second, the economic decline reflects the difficulties Italy has experienced in exploiting the so-called 'new economy', which has developed since the collapse of Communism in Central and Eastern Europe and the end of the Cold War (Trento 2003: 1088–91; Signorini 2001: 161–5). The early 1990s saw the rapid diffusion of information and communication technologies that had, until then, been reserved for military and defence operations. Other European countries have benefited more than Italy from these new opportunities, through existing firms adopting new technologies to improve their productivity and new businesses being developed around those technologies. Two factors explain the low levels of diffusion of these new technologies in Italian firms. The first is that the largest and most productive part of Italy's industrial structure is comprised of small and medium enterprises. These are, generally speaking, based on more traditional methods of production and are less inclined than large firms to invest in new technology. The second factor is that the national framework – or facilitating conditions – which determines how quickly and efficiently firms can exploit the new opportunities, remains largely unreformed. Italy is saddled with an archaic and collusive (rather than competitive) industrial financing system, change in which

Table 2.10   Foreign direct investments exiting investing countries, as percentage of world totals: Italy compared with France, Germany and the UK

	Flows 1990–1995 (av.)	Flows 1995–2001 (av.)	Stock 1990	Stock 2001
Italy	2.5	1.6	3.3	3.0
France	9.4	10.7	7.0	7.1
Germany	9.3	8.4	8.6	7.7
UK	10.1	15.5	13.3	14.8

Source: Adapted from Onida 2004: 90

Table 2.11   Foreign direct investments entering beneficiary countries, as percentage of world totals: Italy compared with France, Germany and the UK

	Flows 1990–1995 (av.)	Flows 1995–2001 (av.)	Stock 1990	Stock 2001
Italy	1.7	0.9	3.1	1.8
France	7.2	4.5	5.3	4.1
Germany	1.9	6.7	6.4	7.2
UK	7.8	8.0	10.9	7.0

Source: Adapted from Onida 2004: 91

has been slow since the early 1990s (see chapter 10). When new technologies are introduced, they usually provide a short-term advantage to more advanced nations because of the speed of adoption, the less advanced sectors and nations eventually catching up. Italy's competitors, starting from a more advanced base, were therefore quick to improve further the efficiency and quality of their financial markets, leaving Italy still to catch up. Yet, the poverty of facilitating conditions goes beyond financial markets. Firms are subject to excessive regulation and red tape. With regard to the setting up of new businesses, for example, Italy has the highest costs in the OECD, and is second slowest in terms of the length of time it takes (twenty-one weeks). There are considerable barriers to product innovation; labour market rigidities remain relatively high; investment in research and development and infrastructures is low, and the educational system is in need of reform. Despite privatization, state control remains an important feature of the industrial structure, and firms are subject to heavy fiscal pressure compared with that existing in other advanced economies.

Third, the diffusion of information technologies has been part of a broader process of globalization of the world economy in terms of capital, technology and services. The degree of competitiveness of national economies is increasingly shaped by their levels of integration into the international economy, as evidenced not only in exports versus imports, but incoming and outgoing foreign direct investment (FDI). This is a sign both of the capacity of national firms to establish a direct presence in international markets and of the attractiveness of a country's political economy to a multinational presence. In Italy, FDI is very low on both counts, and is both a cause and a symptom of the problems (see tables 2.10 and 2.11). Italy does not attract foreign investment because of the high costs of setting up and doing business there and because of the low innovative capacity of existing firms. Since FDI is, in its turn, an important means of diffusion of technological and managerial innovation, the lack of such investment exacerbates the deficiencies in innovation of Italian exports, and reduces the likelihood of Italian firms increasing FDI abroad. The low figures for FDI abroad stem from a long tradition of firms prioritizing domestic investment (particularly in the south) over investment overseas (especially firms in the public sector), combined with the economic crisis that many large firms have experienced in the past decade (see chapter 10) (Onida 2004: 78–81; OECD 2003: 40–1).

Fourth, the economic decline is attributable to the severe challenge by China to the exporting capacity of Italy's small and medium-sized firms. The so-called Chinese threat is affecting Italy more than other nations because it is focused on precisely those goods (the 'made in Italy' brand) where Italian small and medium enterprises have become market leaders in the past three decades (see chapter 11). This challenge, moreover, has highlighted the structural (and territorial) imbalances that characterize the Italian economy, where 95 per cent of firms are very small in size, and 10 per cent account for 90 per cent of exports. The impact of Chinese competition is, therefore, more far-reaching than it might otherwise have been, for it is striking at the heart of a formula that has kept the Italian economy abreast of its competitors.

In this new climate the national debate has shifted from a concern, in the early 1990s, with an economic crisis, to a focus, from the late 1990s onwards, on Italy's economic decline (e.g. Toniolo and Visco 2004). Furthermore, the element of optimism that accompanied the debate in the early 1990s (due to the transformation of the political landscape) has largely vanished, as the limitations of politics have become apparent (see chapter 1). Yet the roots of this decline lie not just in macro-economic policy making, but also in the peculiar structural and territorial distortions of the post-war politico-economic model, which will be the subject of chapters 10 and 11.

POLITICAL PARTIES AND THE PARTY SYSTEM

INTRODUCTION

Between the end of the Second World War and the end of the Cold War, the Italian party system reflected the division of the post-war world into Communist and anti-Communist camps. For one thing, the development of the Cold War served to sustain the electoral strength of the two largest parties, the Christian Democrats (DC) and the Communists (PCI), which between them averaged 64.3 per cent of the vote in the period from 1946 to 1992. For another thing, the fundamental determinant of coalition formation was the *conventio ad excludendum*, permanently excluding the PCI from office. This allowed the DC, as party of relative majority, to sustain itself permanently in office by constructing constantly shifting coalitions with the smaller parties of the centre – the Liberals (PLI), Republicans (PRI) and Social Democrats (PSDI) – and (from 1963) with the Socialist Party (PSI) (see ch. 3 appendix). Sartori (1966, 1976) famously interpreted this party system in terms of 'polarized pluralism' – where a fragmented party system spread over a large ideological distance, together with 'bilateral oppositions', led to an absence of alternation in government.

Italian polarized pluralism had consequences for government stability, policy making and the role of the parties in public life that both political analysts and the general public tended to view in highly negative terms. Consequently, when in the period between 1992 and 1994 the traditional parties of government disintegrated, there was a sense in which it could be said that the party system characterizing the first half-century of republican Italy's existence had sown the seeds of its own destruction. Therefore, in what follows we shall first describe the basic contours of the old party system and its perceived dysfunctions. Second, we shall explore how these dysfunctions contributed to the profound transformation of the party system that took place in the 1990s. And finally, we shall describe the most salient characteristics of both the system and the parties that have emerged since then.

COMPONENTS OF THE TRADITIONAL PARTY SYSTEM, AND ITS DYSFUNCTIONS

If, for fifty years, the DC was the largest party, and thus the mainstay of every feasible governing coalition, then it owed its initial conquest of this position to the internal and external resources it could draw upon to establish an electoral following in the period between the announcement of the armistice on 8 September 1943 and the elections held in 1948. The resources were four in number. First, the party had a particularly elastic ideology that could appeal to a wide spectrum of voters. On the one hand, its record of anti-fascism allowed it to appeal successfully to a northern working class and peasantry that had been mobilized by the Communist-dominated resistance movement and by the dramatic events of 1943–5. On the other hand, landed proprietors and leading members of the capitalist class, who had supported the Fascists but now deemed it advisable to abandon the sinking ship, were not slow to see the advantages of the party's disguised appeals to class collaboration; so they too were willing to throw in their lot with the new party (Ginsborg 1990: 48–9).

Second, the party was able to count on the backing of two enormously powerful actors: the Catholic Church and the United States government. Once the Vatican had decided to swing the Church behind the DC, it brought with it the more than two million members of Catholic Action,[1] the 25,000 members of the clergy, and in 1948 the 300,000-strong army of the 'civic committees' organized by Luigi Gedda, a leading figure in Catholic Action. The power of the United States government was ideological, economic and military. Its ideological power was revealed by the famous 'letter-writing campaign' of 1948, when more than a million letters from the large Italo-American community sought to warn voters of the dangers of a Communist victory in that year's election. In case this message didn't get through, the US administration warned the Italians that all assistance under the Marshall Aid plan would cease immediately in the event of the DC being defeated by the Communist–Socialist Popular Front. If this too failed, there was always military intervention, and in the weeks preceding the election, US warships anchored in the waters off the main Italian ports (Ginsborg 1990: 11–16).

Third, the party was blessed in this period by an extremely astute leader in the person of Alcide De Gasperi. Although the party, in De Gasperi's conception, was to draw its inspiration from Church teachings, he was very well aware of the electoral dangers were it to become a straightforward 'confessional' party. Therefore, though the party might draw its leaders, activists and voters from the ranks of Catholics, De Gasperi was insistent from the beginning that the DC be quite independent of the Church in the fields of policy making and party activity. In addition, De Gasperi was able to ensure that the nature and timing of the first post-war elections – those of 1946 and of 1948 – were such as to maximize the chances of DC success. On the one hand, the longer the 'molten lava of 1945' had time to cool, the better the chance he had (Ginsborg 1990: 90). On the other hand, the Communists and Socialists, fearful of Allied intervention and convinced that the Christian Democrats represented a potentially progressive force in Italian society, were prepared to make substantial concessions for the sake of maintaining intact the alliance they then enjoyed with the DC as partners in government (prior to their expulsion in May 1947). Consequently, De Gasperi was able to ensure that the Constituent Assembly elected in June 1946 would not have legislative powers but that its functions would be limited simply to drawing up a new constitution and that, only at a later date, once the Assembly had completed its work, would proper legislative elections take place.

Finally, therefore, responsibility for the DC's initial conquest of power must also be laid at the feet of its Socialist and Communist opponents themselves. Though the presence of the Allied armies meant that socialist revolution was not a possibility, reform was a different matter; for its domination of the Resistance movement and the Committees for National Liberation gave the left a position of considerable strength. Yet in the fluid situation of the 1943–5 period, it failed to use this resource to achieve any kind of reform that might have shifted the balance of political forces permanently in its favour, accepting, rather, that all the critical questions concerning the nature of post-war Italy, the nature of the new State and so on, were to be postponed until the deliberations of the new Parliament. Relieved of this pressure, the conservative forces in Italian society 'acted, decided, manoeuvred and, not surprisingly, triumphed' (Ginsborg 1990: 47).

Meanwhile, however, the growth of political participation which arose from the Resistance allowed both main parties to consolidate their positions as mass-based organizations. This enabled them to exercise 'a profound influence over the reconstruction of social organizations and interest groups' (Hine 1990: 68), capturing many of them and, through the development of 'flanking organizations', establishing social networks that would serve to inculcate among members of such organizations appropriate feelings of partisan solidarity. These strategies were particularly successful in the parties' subcultural strongholds of the north-eastern and central regions respectively (see chapter 4).

The PCI's successes with these strategies, and the electoral consolidation that they brought with them, created a fundamental strategic dilemma for the third largest party, the PSI, which found that it could only escape subordination to the PCI at the cost of subordination to the DC, and vice versa. Having signed a 'Unity of Action' pact with the PCI in 1934, the Socialists found that they were caught in a vicious circle. For the disunity to which the alliance gave rise meant, in its turn, that the party had less strength to resist the slide towards becoming in fact, and being seen to become, a mere electoral adjunct of the PCI. Partly in order to break out of this vicious circle, the Socialists in the years following 1956 moved towards a governing accommodation with the Christian Democrats, a process culminating in formal entry into government in December 1963. However, the party did not benefit electorally, and for the next thirty years it remained firmly confined, through a variety of ups and downs, to the 9–15 per cent range, constantly in danger that its distinctive identity would be merged with that of its larger ally (Hine 1979: 140).

The vote of the smaller centre parties that were also periodic coalition partners for the DC never exceeded the combined total of 14.5 per cent which they won at the 1963 election. The PRI and the PLI both remained small as a result of the DC's success in monopolizing the broad centre right. Like the PSI after it, the PSDI, having been sucked into the DC's orbit, quickly degenerated into 'a party of office holders and electoral opportunists' (De Grand 1989: 138), with few clearly discernible ideals to pursue, and it never exceeded the 7.1 per cent it won in 1948.

Finally, the neo-Fascist and violently anti-Communist Italian Social Movement (MSI), formed in 1946 by a group of young Fascists who had been junior officers in Mussolini's *Repubblica di Salò*, averaged 5.5 per cent of the vote between 1946 and 1992. Its unacceptability as a governing coalition partner was dramatically put to the test between March and July of 1960, when the Tambroni government held office with the external backing of the MSI. The disturbances to which this gave rise merely served to confirm the centrality of anti-fascism to the dominant ideology, and thus the rule of Italian politics that the road to DC reliance on the MSI to help sustain it in office was permanently closed (Ginsborg 1990: 257–8).

At the other end of the political spectrum, the unavailability of the PCI as a potential coalition partner stemmed from its self-perception, and the perception of those around it, that, though reformist in its practice, it aimed not simply at providing the State with its leading personnel, but at its replacement (albeit by peaceful means) with a qualitatively new kind of state. It was of little avail that the party had made a considerable contribution to the drawing up of the republican Constitution or that it consistently defended it as the heritage of the entire nation. Nor did it matter that the party was thoroughly 'social democratic' in terms of its day-to-day actions in local government and the trade unions. Since it continued to hold on to the idea that the sort of change it would introduce if and when it won office would be both *structural* and *permanent*, it continued to be perceived, by both supporters and opponents alike, as millenarian, anti-system and revolutionary.

The unavailability of both left and right extremes and the consequent permanence in office of the DC in alliance with the smaller parties in its orbit had several significant consequences. First, since the DC and its allies knew that they were virtually guaranteed a place in government regardless of election outcomes, the collapse of a government was always more or less quickly followed by the installation of a new government composed of some more or less altered combination of the same parties. This meant that they were under little or no pressure to enact coherent legislative programmes, and therefore that they were under little pressure to construct governments with any real power *vis-à-vis* the legislature. Consequently, senior party leaders with the power to impose discipline on their followers tended not themselves to be cabinet ministers but rather to delegate these positions to secondary figures. And the fact that it was not they, but the powerful party secretaries, who chose their cabinet colleagues meant that prime ministers had little authority.

Second, the weakness of prime ministers and executives meant that governments, and the parties staffing them, had little power to carry through coherent legislative programmes. Consequently, whilst the main basis of support for the governing parties in their competition with the main party of opposition was ideological (that is, anticommunist), small-scale distributive measures, allowing them to establish clientele relationships with their followers, became the parties' preferred means of mobilizing and retaining electoral support in competition amongst themselves. Thus the substance of negotiations leading to the formation of governments essentially concerned how the various ministries and under-secretarial positions were to be distributed (a process pejoratively referred to as *lottizzazione*) among parties anxious to control them for patronage purposes.

This had two consequences of crucial significance for the party system transformation of the early 1990s. First, it allowed the parties to penetrate vast areas of the State and society – a state of affairs that came to be dubbed *partitocrazia* or 'partyocracy'. Second, by virtue of this, it reinforced still further the inability of the system to respond to popular demands through coherent policy making. For, '[g]iven its obvious character as a distributive exercise, direct party control of nominations became fertile ground for the activities and the development of sub-party actors (factions etc.) thus helping to reduce the parties as such to mere agents of mediation between such actors' (Cotta

1996: 23). Close to being complex constellations of interests (each with a power of veto whenever policy change was considered), rather than unitary actors endowed with their own programmatic profiles, the parties, as a consequence, found it difficult to take decisive initiatives in the most significant areas of public policy. Hence their role in policy making tended to be a predominantly reactive one. Typically, some external event linked to the action of interest groups, the state of the economy or the international scene would make necessary a policy initiative on the part of the government. In such situations, the role of party actors would be to try to direct and channel the policy response, seeking to limit, as much as possible, any consequent damage to the interests they represented.

By the late 1980s, therefore, *partitocrazia* and policy-making difficulties had created for the governing parties significant organizational and electoral weaknesses. In organizational terms, since it was membership numbers that within the DC determined the power of each faction at provincial and national congresses, the function of membership enrolment had inevitably come to serve not so much 'interparty competition as the intraparty struggle for positions and power' (Caciagli 1982: 279). The Socialists too found that being so thoroughly pervaded by the practices of political power brokering had disastrous consequences for the quality of the grass-roots membership. Since the motives for joining in the first place tended to be highly self-regarding, the party lacked a membership with a sufficient degree of the ideological commitment necessary for maintaining the effectiveness of the party on the ground. This in turn meant that its very existence as a free-standing organization was inherently fragile. In electoral terms, by having their names associated, in the public mind, with control of a wide range of public institutions and administrative bodies, the parties were inevitably held responsible for all the inefficiencies of such bodies – whose performances the parties' policy-making weakness prevented them from improving, however. By choosing to remain outside government, while taking a predominantly reactive stance in the process of policy making, the behaviour of the party leaders frequently came to acquire, in the public perception, the connotations of illegitimate interference in public affairs (Cotta 1996: 22).

In short, the governing parties were giants with feet of clay, the *range* of whose control over political processes was matched by severe limits on the *strength* of that control (Cotta 1996). It is this dual feature that explains both the rapidity of the parties' disintegration in the period between 1992 and 1994 and the popular emergence at this time of the terms First and Second Republic. These gave expression to the view that, by contributing to a process of party system transformation, the old parties' extinction marked the onset of a period of regime transition whose outcome, it was hoped, would be a better form of democracy than had been experienced hitherto (Bull and Newell 1993: 203).

THE PARTY SYSTEM TRANSFORMATION OF THE 1990s

Although the rule of Italy's traditional governing parties had already shown signs of crisis with the electoral changes discussed in the next chapter, there can be little doubt that the crisis entered a radically new, and altogether more severe, phase with the collapse of the Berlin Wall and the concomitant decision of PCI leader, Achille Occhetto, to announce the beginning of the transformation of his party into a non-Communist party with a new name – the Partito Democratico della Sinistra (Democratic Party of the Left, PDS) (Newell and Bull 1997). The move was motivated by the realization that the attempt to balance the party's need to adapt its programme to 'the logic of majority politics' (Esping-Andersen 1985: 8) with its need to maintain its identity as the means to preserve unity was no longer sustainable, and that the implications of the East European revolutions were such that the conflict between the internal and external pressures operating on the party would have to be confronted head on (Bull 1991a).

The most immediate result of Occhetto's proposal was to unleash an unprecedented degree of internal conflict and to promote a major party split, leading to the formation of Rifondazione Comunista (Communist Refoundation, RC), which would not accept the change. Hence, the first party system consequence of the PCI's transformation was to leave Italy with two significantly sized left-of-centre parties in place of the previous one. A second consequence was to create significant difficulties for the DC (and, to a lesser extent, all the governing parties). Since by far the largest of the PCI's two heirs was in effect declaring that it was no longer a Communist party, the governing parties' capacity to prevent significant proportions of their voters now choosing 'exit' as their response to a long-standing dissatisfaction with their performance was definitively destroyed. If this directly benefited the Northern League (see chapter 4) as the principal spearhead of anti-governing party protest, at least in the north, then the governing parties' plight was compounded by their mistaken belief that, since resolution of the Communist question was accompanied by a major crisis of the Communist Party itself, far from losing, they might actually gain. The PSI leader, Bettino Craxi, in particular appears to have been convinced that the final outcome of the PCI's crisis would be a reorganization of the left under his own leadership – a belief in which he was encouraged by the results of the regional elections of 1990, which saw the PSI's vote advance to 15.2 per cent while the PCI lost 6 per cent. In the meantime, the electoral decline of the DC had allowed the PSI to acquire a position of indispensability in the formation of any coalition led by the DC. Hence the Craxian Socialists felt free to concentrate on an extortion of spoils in the present, comfortable in the belief that their position was secure in the future: this would be marked by bipolar competition between the DC on the one side and themselves on the other as the leaders of a reconstructed left. The DC for its part – or at least for the most powerful factions within it – was content to conclude, with the PSI, a long-term power-sharing arrangement which, while acknowledging the DC's dependence on the Socialists, would at least bring predictability to, and contain conflict between, the two parties (see below). Thus, instead of reacting to the end of the Communist issue by engaging in political renewal, the two principal parties of government preferred to try to maintain their stranglehold on change at a time when economic recession together with moves towards European integration (especially the terms of the Maastricht Treaty) were exacerbating economic and social tensions (Newell 2000b: 22; and see chapter 12).

A third feature of the transformation of the PCI was its connection to the onset of the Mani Pulite ('Clean Hands') anti-corruption investigations and the associated Tangentopoli ('Bribe City') scandal at the start of 1992. For while, prior to 1992, there had only been a few celebrated instances of judges using their authority to pursue the powerful in corruption cases, the resolution of the Communist question subverted whatever ideological justifications there had once been for being lenient towards the more dubious clientele practices of the governing class. The judges, therefore, supported by public opinion, became keener to use their powers as the champions of a campaign to moralize public life. Likewise, it has been argued that the end of Communism made entrepreneurs more willing to co-operate in judicial investigations than they might otherwise have been, in that big business, faced with the increasing costs of corruption (Della Porta 1993) concluded, for the first time in forty-five years, that it 'could foster a major crisis of the political system without risking its own survival' (Calise 1993: 556).

Tangentopoli undermined the governing parties not only *indirectly*, through the electoral effects discussed in the next chapter, but also *directly* through its impact on the parties' finances and membership bases. During the 1970s and 1980s, the parties had become increasingly dependent on corrupt forms of funding, while also facing mounting accumulated debts. Though state funding of parties had been introduced in 1974, the amounts available could be changed only by legislation, and meanwhile the parties were facing growing costs as a result of the media and office revolutions and changes in the balance of power between them. In particular, the Socialists' indispensability as a coalition partner from the mid-1970s had allowed them to extract an increasing share of the public positions available through the process of *lottizzazione*, thus increasing the attractiveness of the party for 'business politicians' – persons with little or no civic morality and an almost entirely instrumental attitude to politics (Della Porta 1996). As, consequently, money increasingly became the key to success and to positions of power within the parties, competition between individuals and groups (encouraged by factionalism and the system of preference voting) soon gave rise to an inflationary dynamic whereby the pressure to obtain higher and higher amounts of illicit funding became unremitting. Therefore, by reducing the amounts available from illegal sources of financing to just a trickle, the investigations pushed all the traditional parties fairly quickly towards bankruptcy (Rhodes 1997). Meanwhile, by cutting off the flow of resources that in large numbers of cases had provided the *raison d'être* for party membership in the first place, the investigations led to the parties' organizational disintegration as predominantly venal memberships just melted away.[2]

Finally, if the decomposition of the traditional parties and party system was the outcome of a series of events set in motion by the transformation of the PCI, then the emergence of new parties, and *re*composition of the party system was – via the electoral law referenda of 1991 and 1993 – the outcome of a series of events ultimately set in motion by pressures originating from within the DC. In 1983 the DC had achieved its worst electoral result since the war, confirming for the third time in succession its inability to make up a governing majority without the PSI (see table 3.1 and fig. 3.1) and allowing the latter to capture the premiership. Proceeding to build on his reputation for decisiveness and attempting to construct, for his party, the image of one capable of delivering efficient and stable government, PSI leader and Prime Minister Bettino Craxi was a considerable thorn in the DC's side. Though his record in office was not especially noteworthy, his first government (August 1983–June 1986) was, at 1,058 days, by far the longest-lasting in the history of the Republic to that

Table 3.1 Party representation in the Chamber of Deputies: percentage of seats won per party, 1948–1992

Party	Election 1948	1953	1958	1963	1968	1972	1976	1979	1983	1987		1992
DC	53.1	44.6	45.8	41.3	42.2	42.2	41.8	41.6	35.7	37.1		32.7
PCI	31.9[a]	24.2	23.5	26.3	28.1	28.4	36.0	32.0	31.4	28.1	PDS	17.0
											RC	5.6
PSI		12.7	14.1	13.8	14.4[b]	9.7	9.0	9.8	11.6	14.9		14.6
PSDI	5.7	3.2	3.7	5.2		4.6	2.4	3.2	3.7	2.7		2.5
PRI	1.6	0.8	1.0	1.0	1.4	2.4	2.2	2.5	4.6	3.3		4.3
PLI	3.3	2.2	2.9	6.2	4.9	3.2	0.8	1.4	2.5	1.7		2.7
MSI	1.0	4.9	4.0	4.3	3.8	8.9	5.6	4.8	6.7	5.6		5.4
Monarchists	2.4	6.8	4.2	1.3	1.0							
Radicals								0.6	2.8	1.7	2.1	1.1
DP								1.0	1.0[c]	1.1	1.3	
Greens										2.1		2.5
LN										0.2		8.9
Rete												1.9
Others	1.0	0.6	0.8	0.6	4.2	0.6	0.6	0.9	1.0	0.9		0.8
Total	100.0	100.0	100.0	100.0	100.0	100.0	100.0	100.0	100.0	100.0		100.0

[a] In 1948 the PCI and PSI fielded joint lists of candidates as the 'Democratic Popular Front'.
[b] In 1968 the PSI and the PSDI fielded joint lists of candidates as the 'United Socialist Party'.
[c] Democratic Party of Proletarian Unity (PdUP) in 1979.
Source: Calculated from figures given in Hine 1993a: 71–6, table 3.1

point; the improving health of the economy during his premiership was widely hailed as a 'second economic miracle', and he made assertive use of decree powers and parliamentary procedures to obtain the legislature's consent to government measures. At the following general election, in 1987, the PSI achieved its greatest electoral success since the war (14.3 per cent), so that, though its own vote recovered slightly, the DC was even more dependent on the PSI than ever. Moreover, it had begun to encounter increasing difficulties in maintaining its distinctiveness as compared to the Socialists. No longer was it the only large party seeking to defend the free market, because the Socialists had also become its convinced supporters. No longer was it the only significant channel of access to the resources of patronage and clientelism, as the Socialists increasingly provided such access as well. No longer was it the only bulwark against communism, as the Socialists, seeking to defend their political space against a centre-moving PCI, engaged in frequent, fierce attacks on Leninism, Togliatti and other elements of the PCI's heritage (which the PCI was then forced to defend).

The origins of the electoral law referenda thus ultimately lay in the conflict, within the DC, over the best means of managing its growing dependence on the Socialists. On the one hand, leaders such as Ciriaco de Mita saw the solution in terms of party reform that would allow the DC to compete more effectively with the Socialists. This in turn would involve the attempt to overcome the DC's factionalism by means of strong leadership – which would allow the party to overhaul its image as a party of clientelism and bad government and present itself, instead, as a 'modern conservative

1948

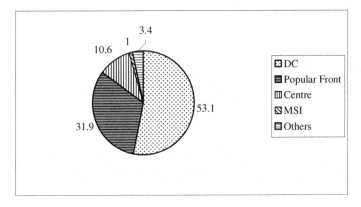

1953

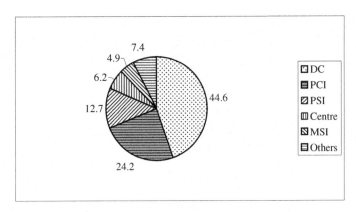

1958

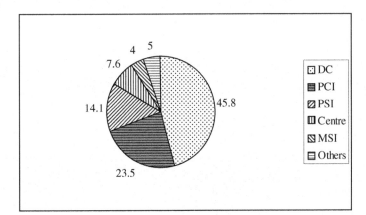

Figure 3.1 Party representation in the Chamber of Deputies: percentages of seats won by parties and party groupings, 1948–1992. 'Centre' refers to the combined percentage of seats won by the PSDI, PRI and PLI, except in 1968, when it refers to the combined percentage for the PRI and PLI only (since in that year the PSI and the PSDI fielded a joint list of candidates under the label PSU). *Source*: Calculated from figures given in Hine 1993a: 71–6, table 3.1

1963

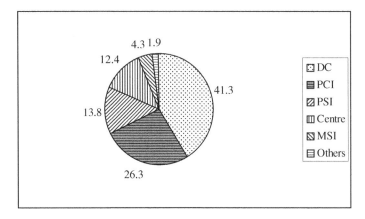

1968

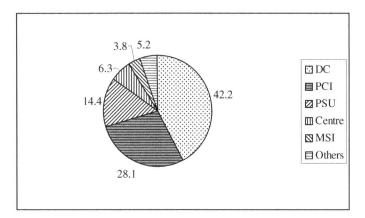

1972

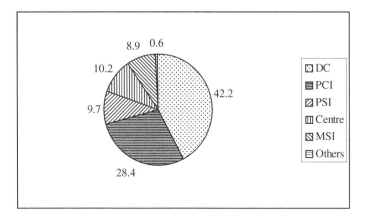

Figure 3.1   *(continued)*

1976

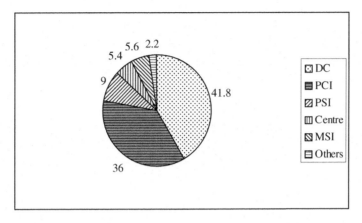

1979

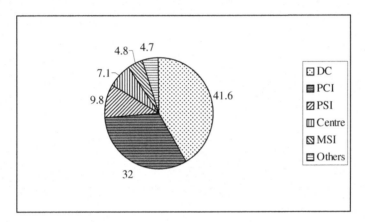

1983

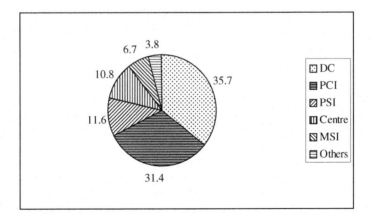

Figure 3.1 *(continued)*

1987

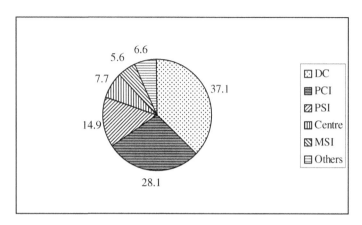

1992

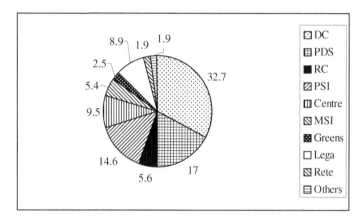

Figure 3.1 (*continued*)

party capable of sound economic management and attractive to the growing numbers of managers and technocrats' (Daniels 1988: 269). On the other hand, internal rivals of de Mita, faction leaders Giulio Andreotti and Arnaldo Forlani, wished not to pose as competitors of, but rather to reach an accommodation with, the PSI – convinced that, by negotiating with the Socialists on terms of equality, ceding control of this or that part of the State as necessary, they could draw the Socialists even further into the networks of *partitocrazia*, ensuring that they became so dependent on clientelism and illegal sources of party funding that it would be impossible for them credibly to pose as the leaders of a genuinely reformist alternative (Colarizi 1998: 639; Daniels 1988: 269). Ultimately, it was the second of these strategies that gained the upper hand – in the form of the so-called CAF axis: a long-term power-sharing arrangement between Craxi and the DC factions headed by Andreotti and Forlani, which would govern Italy until the next election. Premissed on the defeat of de Mita and his project of Christ-ian Democratic renewal, in essence, the CAF agreement represented the renunciation of attempts to regain hegemony for the DC, and an acceptance of its dependence on the Socialists. In return for this, Craxi, for his part, was to agree not to attack the DC, thus depriving himself of that freedom of movement which had brought him electoral success in the past – circumstances that would allow division of the spoils of *parti-tocrazia* to proceed peacefully between the PSI and the relevant factions of the DC. As a naked power-sharing arrangement, uninformed by any strategic vision or reformist intent, whose sole purpose was preservation of the *status quo*, the CAF agreement was driven by the recognition that an impasse had been reached and that the governing parties had lost all capacity or desire for programmatic renewal.

If the DC was incapable of finding within itself either the will or the power to reform itself, then, for dissident Christian Democrat, Mario Segni, reform of the electoral laws would force it to do so (Colarizi 1998: 703). He began to gather the signatures nec-essary to request the holding of referenda on a variety of electoral law reforms – of which the one concerning preference voting survived the obligatory examination of constitutional admissibility carried out by the Constitutional Court. Largely because he was supported in his efforts by individuals from across the political spectrum, and by a variety of civil society organizations – while being opposed by all of the govern-ing parties – Segni's 'referendum movement' quickly acquired the connotations of a popular movement of protest against the entire governing class, the referendum itself being perceived as a challenge to the entire system of *partitocrazia*. Thus called upon, in effect, to cast a vote of no confidence in this system, on a turn-out of 62.5 per cent, 95.6 per cent of voters duly did so. Encouraged by this result, Segni's movement then set about gathering the signatures necessary for the holding of a referendum on a ques-tion which, framed in such a way as to meet the Constitutional Court's earlier objec-tions, would change the method of election to the Senate (and thus force Parliament, since the Senate and the Chamber have co-equal legislative powers, to change the method of election to the latter body too). On a turn-out of 77.1 per cent, this pro-posal was supported by 82.7 per cent of voters when put to them in the referendum held on 18 April 1993.

With this result, all the elements were in place that would lead to the restructuring of the party system that took place between then and the general election of March 1994. The sheer number of high-level politicians caught up in the Mani Pulite inves-tigations – by 17 June the previous year, 422 requests for the lifting of parliamentary immunity had been issued against 212 members of the Chamber of Deputies (Bellu 1993) – meant that by the summer of 1993, the legislature elected the previous year had been thoroughly delegitimized. If this pointed in the direction of fresh elections to restore Parliament's authority, the outcome of the April referendum implied that these could be called only once the necessary legislation had been passed in order to give effect to what had seemed to amount to a popular vote in favour of a predominantly majoritarian electoral system for both chambers of Parliament. As in the ensuing months the legislation was put in place, and as the membership and votes of the tra-ditional governing parties continued to collapse, the results of mayoral elections held in the autumn had a decisive impact on the shape of the electoral coalitions which the new voting system would oblige each party to form with other parties in its political vicinity in order to minimize the risk of more distantly located parties taking seats at their collective expense. Held on the basis of the double ballot system, with a run-off between the top two candidates if none managed to reach 50 per cent, the autumn mayoral contests revealed that the PDS and other parties of the left had a much better capacity to construct alliances around common candidates – and thus to win – than did parties of the right. They revealed, too, that if the DC was now decisively compromised as a force able to withstand the left on its own, then none of the other significant forces on the right – neither the MSI, nor the Northern League – had the strength to undertake this task single-handedly either. Thus it was that on 26 January 1994, the media magnate, Silvio Berlusconi, announced his intention to join the political fray with a new party, Forza Italia (FI), in order to forge an alliance capable of 'saving Italy from communism'. Though neither the Northern League nor the MSI was willing to contemplate an alliance with the DC, given its record, and though neither would spontaneously ally itself with the other (the one standing for centralized government and the welfare state, the other for decentralization and free markets), each was prepared to ally itself with Berlusconi. Consequently, in the run-up to the 1994 election, Berlusconi was able to form, in the north of the country, an alliance with the Northern League known as the 'Freedom Alliance' and, in the south of the country, an alliance with the MSI, known as the 'Alliance for Good Government'. On the left, the Progressive Alliance brought together eight formations stretching from Communist Refoundation on the left to left-leaning ex-Christian Democrats in the centre. The bulk of the DC, having changed its name to the Italian People's Party (PPI), refused to ally itself with the left or the right.

THE PARTY SYSTEM AND THE PARTIES SINCE 1994

The above developments changed the party system in three fundamental respects. First, the parties that once occupied the positions furthest to the left and the right on the political spectrum – the PCI and the MSI – are no longer regarded as ineligible for government. Second, as a consequence of this, the non-governing parties no longer lie on both sides of the political spectrum, but on one side only (that is, opposition is no longer bilateral but unilateral). Third, therefore, there no longer exists a centre party able to maintain itself permanently in office by excluding left and right extremes. In short, Italy's party system now has a bipolar, rather than a tripolar, format.

The PCI's success in overcoming the preclusion against it was, of course, intimately bound up with its transformation into the PDS. For, in declaring that it was no longer a Communist party, it was saying, in effect, that it was giving up the search for structural changes of an irreversible kind, and that its policies would henceforth be decided almost exclusively by their expedience in terms of the *existing* political game. The MSI's escape from the political ghetto also involved a transformation of identity, one that was a direct consequence of the legitimacy conferred on it by Berlusconi's offer of an alliance in the run-up to the 1994 election, and the prospect of unprecedented electoral gains that this offered. In taking 13.5 per cent of the vote in 1994, the MSI saw its support rise to almost three times its post-war average. As a consequence, in the aftermath of the election, MSI leader Gianfranco Fini decided to seek approval to dissolve the MSI into the less ideologically distinctive Alleanza Nazionale (National Alliance, AN). This committed itself to the principles of liberal democracy and to the declaration that anti-fascism constituted an important part of the democratic renewal of the post-war order (Ruzza and Schmidtke 1996: 157).

The second fundamental change in the party system – the disappearance of bilateral oppositions – is inseparable from the third change: the disappearance of a centre party able to maintain itself permanently in office. In turn, the latter change must be seen as both cause and consequence of the transformation of the two parties at the ends of the political spectrum. On the one hand, the collapse of the DC and its role as a dam against the opposing extremes removed the most fundamental, and hitherto insurmountable, obstacle in the way of the MSI's overriding ambition of finding a partner or partners in the construction of a conservative, anti-left pole. On the other hand, it had been the PCI's transformation that had removed the last of the three pillars (Catholicism, clientelism and anti-communism) on which electoral support for the DC had traditionally rested, thus hastening that party's demise in the first place. The bipolar party system that has gradually consolidated itself over the two elections since 1994 – those of 1996 and 2001 – is, then, built upon two party coalitions: one of the centre left, the other of the centre right, each competing for overall majorities of seats.

The coalition of the centre left, known as the Ulivo (or Olive-tree Alliance), came into existence in the spring of 1995 as a means of extending towards the centre the earlier Progressive Alliance and providing a vehicle for the prime-ministerial ambitions of economics professor and ex-president of IRI, Romano Prodi. The requirement that the coalition opposing Berlusconi in 1994 extend its embrace towards the centre, seemed to be apparent from the figures for that year's election, which, for 46.4 per cent of the vote, had given the centre right 63.6 per cent of the seats distributed according to the plurality formula. The centre and left, with a combined vote of 50.0 per cent, had taken only 35.3 per cent of these seats. The Progressive Alliance had also suffered from its lack of a clearly designated leader – and thus from its inability, unlike the centre right, to specify whom it envisaged becoming Prime Minister in the event that it was victorious. The opportunity to give effect to the Ulivo project, launching Romano Prodi as the coalition's prime-ministerial candidate, came in February 1995 when the PPI, aware that non-alignment had been unproductive in 1994, split – one half joining Berlusconi as the Cristiani Democratici Uniti (Christian Democratic Union, CDU), the other half retaining the name of the Italian People's Party and joining the centre left.

The historic *rapprochement* between former Communists and ex-Christian Democrats that the Ulivo represented was, then, in the first instance an electoral coalition born of necessity. However, it was also something more than this, since, for senior figures such as ex-Communist Walter Veltroni, as well as for Prodi himself, the hope and the desire was that the coalition's victory in the 1996 election, together with the experience of government thereafter, would produce a qualitative change, transforming the Ulivo 'into a real political actor capable of imposing its political sovereignty on its component parts and thus eventually of absorbing them' (Massari and Parker 2000: 49).

That this vision has not been realized in the intervening period must be attributed to the effect of six interrelated factors undermining the coalition's capacity to act as an effective political force. The first of these is its extreme fragmentation. At the 1996 election, it presented five separate lists,[3] formed by no fewer than fourteen parties and 'quasi-parties'[4] (new formations and formations that had emerged as 'successors' to the 'traditional' parties during and after the upheavals of the 1992–4 period).[5] A complex sequence of amalgamations, splits and acquisitions from the centre right in the subsequent period then saw to it that at the 2001 election, the number of lists (four)[6] and the number of individual formations (eight)[7] it housed would be only somewhat lower (see figure 3.2).

Such fragmentation has always made difficult the search for a unity of intents sufficiently powerful to overcome divergences in the long-term strategic visions of each of the parties making up the coalition. On the one hand, there are those parties, such as the Democrats, and most of the DS,[8] which see themselves as secular, centre left, reformist parties firmly committed to the consolidation of majoritarian democracy and a bipolar future. On the other hand, parties such as the PPI and RI[9] stand in the tradition of Christian Democracy, which made its fortune by exploiting its location in the centre of the political spectrum in a tripolar party system involving exclusion of the extremes. Some politicians within this tradition (notably UDEUR leader Clemente Mastella) see their long-term political fortunes as being tied to the resurrection of a centre party capable of engineering a return to such a party system and retaining power on the same basis. Consequently, their commitment to coalition unity remains highly conditional.

Partly reflecting its fragmentation has been, third, the absence of a single party within the Ulivo able to act as a 'coalition maker'. Consequently, there has never been a party powerful enough to be able to impose upon the remaining parties in the coalition the unitary vision that Veltroni and Prodi wished to realize. From the start, the PDS, as the coalition's largest party, aspired to the status of 'coalition maker' – but it was never able to achieve it owing to its own difficulties. In particular, the transformation from the PCI considerably weakened the party's extra-parliamentary organization by undermining the Communist ideology, while creating a high level of internal conflict over

Figure 3.2 Evolution of main party organizations and alliances, 1991–2001. AD: Democratic Alliance; AN: National Alliance; Bianco: Biancofiore (White Flower); Bonino: Bonino List; Casa: House of Freedoms; CCD: Centre Christian Democrats; CDU: Christian Democratic Union; CS: Social Christians; CU: United Communists; DC: Christian Democrats; Dem.: Democrats; Dem. Eur.: European Democrats; DP: Proletarian Democracy; DS: Democrats of the Left; FDS: Democratic Socialist Federation; Fed. Lib.: Liberal Federation; FI: Forza Italia; Fiamma: Tricoloured Flame; Gira.: Girasole (Sunflower); Lega: Northern League; Lista Pannella: Panella List; Marg.: Margherita (Daisy); MID: Italian Democratic Movement; MSI: Italian Social Movement; Pact: Pact for National Renewal; PCI: Italian Communist Party; PdCI: Party of Italian Communists; PDS: Democratic Party of the Left; PLI: Italian Liberal Party; Polo: Freedom Alliance; PPI: Italian Popular Party; PR: Radical Party; PRI: Italian Republican Party; PS: Socialist Party; PSDI: Italian Social Democratic Party; PSI: Italian Socialist Party; PSI-n: New Italian Socialist Party; RC: Communist Refoundation; Rete: Network; RI: Italian Renewal; Riformatori: Reformists; SD: Social Democrats; SDI: Italian Democratic Socialists; SI: Italian Socialists; SVP: South Tyrolese People's Party; UD: Democratic Union; UdC: Union of the Centre; UDEUR: Union of Democrats for Europe; UDR: Union for a Democratic Republic; Ulivo: Olive Tree Alliance; Unità rif.: Reformist unity; Valori: Italy of Values; Verdi: Greens.

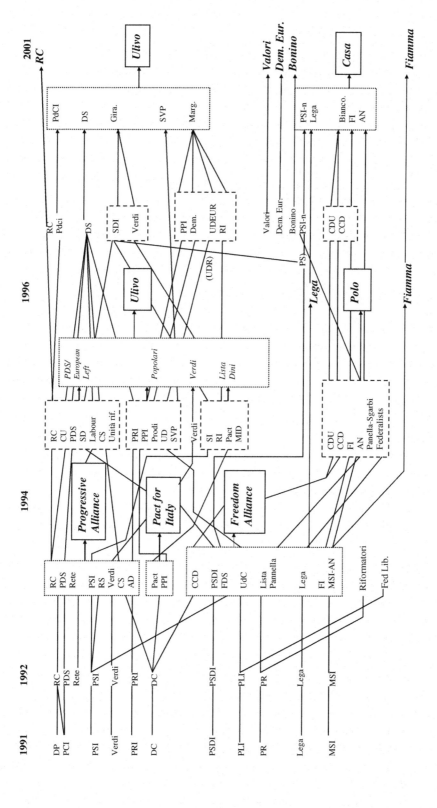

the alternative to be put in its place. All of this has taken its toll on its electoral performance (which has remained essentially flat).

At 16.6 per cent in 2001, the party's vote share was only 2.1 per cent above that of the second largest formation in the coalition, the Margherita, which had provided the coalition's prime-ministerial candidate. The election returns suggested not only that the Margherita fished in the same pool of voters as the DS, but also that it had benefited quite considerably from providing the coalition's leader. Together, these factors have rendered the relationship between the coalition's two largest parties inherently competitive, while ensuring that the Margherita's Francesco Rutelli has been unable to count on the unconditional support of the DS, since the party believes that there are electoral gains to be had by itself providing the leadership.

The leadership would be stronger were there agreed-upon mechanisms in place for selecting the leader via democratic processes from the bottom up. As it is, however, the absence of such mechanisms ensured that Rutelli and, before him, Prodi remained hostages to the party leaderships that selected them. Moreover, by denying opportunities for rank-and-file participation in the life of the coalition, it also ensured that the latter would experience difficulties in maintaining the links with its natural supporters that are necessary to ensure its effectiveness outside Parliament, on the ground.

Finally, all of the above factors have contributed to depriving the coalition of a clear agreement on which forces should belong to the coalition and which should not, such an agreement being essential to a clear identity and a minimum of organizational cohesion. In 1994 the Ulivo's predecessor had included RC within its boundaries while excluding the PPI in the centre. In 1996 the Ulivo's boundaries had included within them the centre – while only partially including RC.[10] In 2001 they had excluded RC altogether, as well as important centre-based forces (di Pietro's *Italia dei Valori*, or 'Italy of Values', IV) – while including, however, a number of migrants (Mastella's UDEUR) from the centre right.[11] If lack of clarity over the coalition's boundaries is, perhaps, an inevitable consequence of the many divergences in the policy and programmatic outlooks of its constituent parties, then it constitutes a significant electoral handicap for the coalition.

In each of the above six respects, the coalition of the centre right – known as the House (or the 'Home') of Freedoms – is much better placed. In contrast with the centre left, it has in essence almost always had a stable membership of four essential components: FI, AN, former Christian Democrats (in the Christian Democratic Centre and the Christian Democratic Union (CCD–CDU)) and the Northern League. True, it has at various times offered a home to other minor formations. But, in contrast with small formations within the Ulivo, such parties have never been able to exercise any significant influence within the coalition. Not only has this been due to their very small size compared to the 'big four', but above all because of the power of FI to act as a coalition maker.

Unlike the PDS within the Ulivo, FI is *so* much more powerful than its partners that its leadership of the coalition (with all that this implies in terms of its right to provide the coalition's leader and prime-ministerial candidate) is undisputed – a position it owes to three factors above all. First, it has provided a home for that large pool of voters in the centre and on the centre right who were orphaned by the collapse of the First Republic's traditional governing parties and, owing to the charisma of Berlusconi and an electoral appeal which is closely tied to the age-old communism/anti-communism division running through Italian politics, it is a particularly appetizing proposition for these voters.

Second, in part cause, in part consequence, of its electoral popularity, FI enjoys a thriving membership and organization, having moved beyond the 'plastic' or 'business-firm' model (Hopkin and Paolucci 1999) held to characterize it in the period immediately after it was founded. Since then, though real power in the party continues to remain highly concentrated in the hands of its leader, FI has acquired a more firmly rooted territorial organization. This, while featuring the network of locally based elective bodies that is typical of the traditional 'mass' party, is, however, one whose centre of gravity lies among the party's elected representatives. If this model has given FI a degree of autonomy from its environment, allowing it to achieve effective institutionalization, then its novelty has allowed it to continue to deploy a propaganda weapon of inestimable importance: namely, the claim to be a very different political animal from the parties that governed the First Republic.

Third, the party naturally benefits from the strategic difficulties faced by its allies. Of these, AN suffers from the abiding fear that, despite the 'customs clearance' (*sdoganamento*) that was accorded it in 1993–4, it has still not yet been completely accepted as 'a party like all the rest' (Tarchi and Poli 2000: 70) and that, therefore, the risk persists that it might once again be pushed back to the fringes and relegated to a position of isolation. Such anxieties severely limit the party's room for manoeuvre. On the one hand, they drive it to support its larger coalition partner even on issues on which it is vulnerable and which threaten, in the long run, to undermine its own distinctive appeal (for example, Berlusconi's struggle with the judiciary – see chapter 8). On the other hand, they prevent the party from complaining when its partner takes actions that are directly damaging to it (for example, Berlusconi's 1998 decision to abandon the Parliamentary Commission for Constitutional Reform).

Meanwhile, the Northern League, having been the principal spearhead for the popular protest involved in the collapse of the First Republic, has, ever since the emergence of FI, found itself driven hither and thither in the constant struggle to maintain visibility and a distinctive identity in the shadow of its larger ally.[12] Thus, having been relegated to a position of parliamentary isolation despite its best-ever electoral performance in 1996, it responded by embarking on a long, colourful campaign for northern 'independence'. If this brought it media attention in the short term, in the long run it produced only electoral set-backs among a constituency whose embrace of 'autonomy' had everything to do with the inefficiencies and the tax demands of the central state, and almost nothing to do with quixotic notions of a northern 'Padanian' nation. If the stance on independence set up a vicious circle, raising the League's political isolation, thus undermining its electoral base still further, a point was reached when it became clear to Bossi that a new alliance with Berlusconi was the only way of avoiding permanent marginalization. Like AN, the League too has been forced to accept a position of fundamental subordination with respect to FI (moderating its demands for northern autonomy while continuing the search for distinctiveness through an emphasis on alternative issues, notably, anti-immigrant and xenophobic themes, thus seeking to occupy political ground left vacant by AN in its continuing search for respectability).

Finally, former Christian Democrats in the CCD–CDU (now the *Unione dei Demo-cratici Cristiani*, Union of Christian Democrats, UDC) show periodic signs of the desire to disrupt the two coalitions and engineer a return to tripolarity by the creation of a centre grouping able to play a pivotal role. The clearest example of this came with the formation of the *Unione Democratica per la Repubblica* (Democratic Union for the Republic, UDR) in February 1998 from most of the CDU, part of the CCD and a number of more or less independent politicians, which managed to bring about the creation of a centre left government without RC, seeing this as the first step on the road to ensuring RC's permanent isolation from the rest of the centre left (Donovan 2002: 109).[13] However, the UDR never managed to build a centrist formation strong enough to disrupt the coalition of the centre right in a similar way and, as has become apparent, the electoral conditions necessary for the creation of such a formation simply do not exist. A large proportion of voters place themselves in the middle of the politi-cal spectrum, and, in aggregate, they occupy a median position between left and right in terms of their political attitudes. Importantly, though, this is not because they occupy median positions individually, but because they are a heterogeneous group in which left-wing attitudes cancel out right-wing attitudes, and vice versa, and they prefer to vote for parties located distinctly on the left or the right (Mannheimer and Sani 2000). Given this, and given the effects of the electoral system, it is not surprising that none of the centre-based political forces fielded independently of the two main coalitions at elections since the end of the First Republic has ever managed to attract sufficient votes, and therefore seats, to allow it to play the pivotal role to which they aspire. Despite the 'centrist temptations' of the House of Freedoms' ex-Christian Democrats, there-fore, they too are forced to accept that their position *vis-à-vis* the coalition's largest partner can ultimately only be one of subordination.

Given the coalition's relative lack of fragmentation, then, and its relatively clear-cut boundaries – *but above all because of FI's ability to play the role of coalition maker within the centre right* – the three remaining factors which cause such problems on the centre left (namely, divergences in the long-term strategic visions of each of the parties making up the coalition, the absence of a democratic method of leadership selection, and the inability of the coalition to acquire any kind of sovereignty over its compo-nent parts), though they exist for the House of Freedoms too, are not nearly as prob-lematic. Where the House of Freedoms does have a major weakness, of course, is in its extreme dependence on Berlusconi. If the coalition is held together largely because of the strength of Forza Italia and if, to a large degree, Forza Italia owes its strength to the role within it, and the electoral appeal, of its leader, the question naturally arises as to what would happen to the coalition in the event of a sudden enforced removal of Berlusconi.

The uncertainty of the answer to this question highlights the extent to which, though the party system has clearly undergone significant change, its structure remains fluid and unconsolidated – which in turn raises the question of the extent to which it can, in fact, be captured by the term frequently used to describe it: namely, 'bipolarity'. As Pappalardo (2002) points out, the defining characteristic of bipolar party systems is centripetal competition. This implies a relatively small ideological distance between the relevant parties or coalitions, and thus a willingness of voters to switch between left and right. At first glance, the evidence of bipolarity, thus defined, seems rather thin.

What struck observers of the 2001 election, for example, was relative stability in the distribution of the vote between the two main coalitions, the apparently small numbers of voters prepared to switch between the two, and the way in which changes in the parties' alliance strategies appeared to have played a larger role in the alternation that took place than did altered vote distributions.[14] This seemed significant; for, if it left open the question of whether sufficient voters were available and willing to move in order for alternation to be a realistic possibility in most ordinary circumstances, then it raised the possibility that parties might find centripetal competition within a bipolar format unrewarding (Newell and Bull 2002). On the other hand, as Pappalardo (2002: 212) points out, the claim that changing alliance patterns count for more than shifting votes in explaining election outcomes implies that the vote is structured from above, by the parties, rather than from below, by the exogenous preferences of individuals. Yet this is not an issue that can be decided by observing how the vote changes when, for example, the PPI joins the centre left, the League leaves the centre right, and so forth. For the number of observers who maintain that votes simply fall into line, there is at least an equal number who maintain that 'the People's Party voter who in 1994 had confirmed his centrist inclinations . . . modified the political significance of his vote by voting, in 1996, for the Ulivo or the Freedom Alliance' (Corbetta and Parisi 1997: 18, quoted by Pappalardo 2002: 212). In the absence of information about the significance that the vote has for the voter him- or herself, a given change lends itself as much to an interpretation which locates its source in the behaviour of voters, as it does to an interpretation locating its source in the behaviour of parties – and which of the two is correct is something destined to remain undetermined.

Meanwhile, whatever the proportions of voters willing to switch between the two main coalitions, those most likely to shift are located in the centre of the political spectrum, thus rendering profitable convergence of the two coalitions on the median voter. This has underpinned, since 1992, the repeated failure and declining fortunes of third poles lying between left and right. None of this is to deny that centre-based forces may seek a determining role for themselves, passing from one pole to the other (Pappalardo 2002: tables 7.6, 7.9 and 7.10). But this phenomenon is rather usual in a number of bipolar systems, where, since the basic choice before voters remains one between two alternative governing coalitions, competition retains its centripetal character. For all of these reasons, the term 'bipolar' would, then, seem to capture the Italian case accurately.

CONCLUSION

In this chapter we have sought to describe the most salient features of the tripolar party system that took root in Italy in the war's immediate aftermath, attributing its persistence until the early 1990s to the occupation of left and right poles by parties that, for almost fifty years, were perceived as 'anti-system' and ineligible as governing partners. We then sought to relate these features to a number of concomitants in terms of the parties' role in policy making and in public life generally – concomitants which, together, served to render the parties fragile both organizationally and electorally. Consequently, when the collapse of the Berlin Wall brought an end to the anti-system connotations of the party occupying the left pole, a series of events was set in motion leading to the party system's 'destructuration'. The centre parties' unwillingness or inability to reform themselves, meanwhile, set in motion that series of events which, via the electoral law referenda of 1991 and 1993, put in place the conditions necessary for the system's 'restructuration' and its acquisition of a new, bipolar format. Articulated around two coalitions, one of which is much more robust than the other, the new system's structure, though fluid, has not prevented the emergence of centripetal competition, which constitutes the defining characteristic of bipolar systems.

One of the most salient features of *partitocrazia* as it existed prior to the party system's transformation was the very close relationship between political parties and specific organized interests. These acted, in effect, as 'transmission belts' for the distribution of resources from the top down, and for the corresponding mobilization of electoral support – discussed in chapter 4 – from the bottom up. One of the most significant consequences of the party system upheavals, then, has been major change in the ways in which organized groups seek and obtain representation of their interests. We discuss this issue in detail in chapter 5.

Government	Dates	Composition	Duration (in days)
Provisional governments			
Badoglio I	25 July 1943–17 April 1944	Military government	268
Badoglio II	22 April 1944–8 June 1944	Government of national unity	48
Bonomi I	18 June 1944–10 Dec. 1944	DC, PCI, PSI, PLI, PRI, PdL, Pd'A, PSIUP	176
Bonomi II	12 Dec. 1944–19 June 1945	DC, PCI, PLI, PdL, Pd'A, PSIUP	190
Parri	21 June 1945–8 Dec. 1945	DC, PCI, PSIUP, PLI, Pd'A, DL	171
De Gasperi I	10 Dec. 1945–1 July 1946	DC, PCI, PSI, PLI, DL, Pd'A	203
Constituent Assembly (election: 2 June 1946)			
De Gasperi II	13 July 1946–20 Jan. 1947	DC, PCI, PSI, PRI	191
De Gasperi III	2 Feb. 1947–13 May 1947	DC, PCI, PSI	100
De Gasperi IV	31 May 1947–12 May 1948	DC, PSLI, PRI	347
1st legislature, 8 May 1948–4 April 1953 (general election: 18 April 1948)			
De Gasperi V	23 May 1948–12 Jan. 1950	DC, PLI, PSLI, PRI	599
De Gasperi VI	27 Jan. 1950–16 July 1951	DC, PSLI, PRI	535
De Gasperi VII	26 July 1951–29 June 1953	DC, PRI	704
2nd legislature, 25 June 1953–14 March 1958 (general election: 7 June 1953)			
De Gasperi VIII	16 July 1953–28 July 1953	DC	12
Pella	17 Aug. 1953–5 Jan. 1954	DC	141
Fanfani I	18 Jan. 1954–30 Jan. 1954	DC	12
Scelba	10 Feb. 1954–22 June 1955	DC, PSDI, PLI	497
Segni I	6 July 1955–6 May 1957	DC, PSDI, PLI	670
Zoli	19 May 1957–19 June 1958	DC	396
3rd legislature, 12 June 1958–18 February 1963 (general election: 25 May 1958)			
Fanfani II	1 July 1958–26 Jan. 1959	DC, PSDI	209
Segni II	15 Feb. 1959–24 Feb. 1960	DC	374
Tambroni	25 March 1960–19 July 1960	DC	116
Fanfani III	26 July 1960–2 Feb. 1962	DC	556
Fanfani IV	21 Feb. 1962–16 May 1963	DC, PSDI, PRI	449
4th legislature, 16 May 1963–11 March 1968 (general election: 28 April 1963)			
Leone I	21 June 1963–5 Nov. 1963	DC	137
Moro I	4 Dec. 1963–26 June 1964	DC, PSI, PSDI, PRI	205
Moro II	22 July 1964–21 Jan. 1966	DC, PSI, PSDI, PRI	548
Moro III	23 Feb. 1966–5 June 1968	DC, PSI, PSDI, PRI	833
5th legislature, 5 June 1968–28 February 1972 (general election: 19 May 1968)			
Leone II	24 June 1968–19 Nov. 1968	DC	148
Rumor I	12 Dec. 1968–5 July 1969	DC, PSU, PRI	205
Rumor II	5 Aug. 1969–7 Feb. 1970	DC	186
Rumor III	27 March 1970–6 July 1970	DC, PSI, PSDI, PRI	101
Colombo	6 Aug. 1970–15 Jan. 1972	DC, PSI, PSDI, PRI	527
Andreotti I	17 Feb. 1972–26 Feb. 1972	DC	9
6th legislature, 25 May 1972–1 May 1976 (general election: 7–8 May 1972)			
Andreotti II	26 June 1972–12 June 1973	DC, PSDI, PLI	351
Rumor IV	7 July 1973–2 March 1974	DC, PSI, PSDI, PRI	230

Government	Dates	Composition	Duration (in days)
Rumor V	14 March 1974–3 Oct. 1974	DC, PSI, PSDI	203
Moro IV	23 Nov. 1974–7 Jan. 1976	DC	410
Moro V	12 Feb. 1976–30 April 1976	DC	78
7th legislature, 5 July 1976–2 April 1979 (general election: 20–1 June 1976)			
Andreotti III	29 July 1976–16 Jan. 1978	DC	536
Andreotti IV	11 March 1978–31 Jan. 1979	DC	326
Andreotti V	20 March 1979–31 March 1979	DC, PRI, PSDI	11
8th legislature, 20 June 1979–4 May 1983 (general election: 3 June 1979)			
Cossiga I	4 Aug. 1979–19 March 1980	DC, PLI, PSDI	228
Cossiga II	4 April 1980–27 Sept. 1980	DC, PSI, PRI	176
Forlani	18 Oct. 1980–26 May 1981	DC, PSI, PSDI, PRI	220
Spadolini I	28 June 1981–7 Aug. 1982	DC, PSI, PSDI, PRI, PLI	405
Spadolini II	23 Aug. 1982–13 Nov. 1982	DC, PSI, PSDI, PRI, PLI	82
Fanfani V	1 Dec. 1982–29 April 1983	DC, PSI, PSDI, PLI	149
9th legislature, 12 July 1983–28 April 1987 (general election: 26 June 1983)			
Craxi I	4 Aug. 1983–27 June 1986	DC, PSI, PSDI, PRI, PLI	1,058
Craxi II	1 Aug. 1986–3 March 1987	DC, PSI, PSDI, PRI, PLI	214
Fanfani VI	17 April 1987–28 April 1987	DC, independents	11
10th legislature, 2 July 1987–2 February 1992 (general election: 14 June 1987)			
Goria	28 July 1987–11 March 1988	DC, PSI, PSDI, PRI, PLI	227
De Mita	13 April 1988–19 May 1989	DC, PSI, PSDI, PRI, PLI	401
Andreotti VI	22 July 1989–29 March 1991	DC, PSI, PSDI, PRI, PLI	615
Andreotti VII	12 April 1991–24 April 1992	DC, PSI, PSDI, PLI	378
11th legislature, 23 April 1992–16 January 1994 (general election: 4 April 1992)			
Amato I	28 June 1992–22 April 1993	DC, PSI, PSDI, PLI	298
Ciampi	28 April 1993–16 April 1994	DC, PSI, PSDI, PLI	353
12th legislature, 15 April 1994–16 February 1996 (general election: 27 March 1994)			
Berlusconi I	10 May 1994–22 Dec. 1994	FI, LN, AN, CCD, UdC	226
Dini	17 Jan. 1995–17 May 1996	Independents	486
13th legislature, 9 May 1996–9 March 2001 (general election: 21 April 1996)			
Prodi	18 May 1996–9 Oct. 1998	PDS, PPI, Dini List, UD, Greens	876
D'Alema I	27 Oct. 1998–18 Dec. 1999	Ulivo, PdCI, UDEUR	423
D'Alema II	22 Dec. 1999–19 April 2000	DS, PPI, Democrats, UDEUR, PdCI, Greens, RI	119
Amato II	25 April 2000–11 June 2001	DS, PPI, Democrats, UDEUR, SDI, PdCI, Greens, RI, independents	398
14th legislature, 29 May 2001– (general election: 13 May 2001)			
Berlusconi II	12 June 2001	FI, AN, LN, CCD–CDU, independents	

Sources: <http://www.governo.it/Governo/Governi/governi.html>; <http://www.cronologia.it/governi2.htm>

Political Culture, Elections and Voting Behaviour

Introduction

Elections are important. Since they provide an institutionalized means of choosing political leaders, elections give citizens a channel for the legitimate expression of grievances and thereby help to confer legitimacy on the actions of those duly elected. In this way they bestow power. And because they simultaneously disempower those out of office (by depriving them of the authority to make legally binding decisions), elections create a powerful incentive on parties to gear their activities primarily to the winning of them. This usually entails parties moderating policies as they seek to extend their bases, beyond the ranks of their die-hard supporters, to take in voters who would otherwise be captured by rival parties. Elections thus make a huge contribution to the maintenance of political stability, and nowhere in post-1945 Europe has this contribution been of greater significance, arguably, than in Italy, affected as it was by the existence of two such all-embracing and implacably opposed subcultures as the Catholic and the Marxist. Understandably, therefore, attempts to explain Italian voting behaviour and election outcomes have attracted some attention.

Social and political cleavages

With varying impact over time, four social divisions more than any others have conditioned Italian voting behaviour in the post-war period. These are religion, ideology, territory and class.

Religion

The influence of religion in electoral politics has historical roots stretching back to the foundation of the State itself. As a result of Italian unification in 1861, the Church was deprived of all of its territories in the peninsula with the exception of Veneto and

Rome. The former was then annexed in 1866, the latter in 1870. The Church therefore refused to recognize the new State and forbade Catholics to participate in political life. Later, with the rise of socialism and the threat to its moral and spiritual authority that this posed, the Church tempered its ban on involvement, and the Catholic People's Party was formed in order to compete with the left for the allegiance of the newly enfranchised masses. Having been complicit in the rise of Fascism, the Vatican was then able to secure its long-term influence on Italian affairs by negotiating, with the Mussolini regime, the Lateran Treaty. This made religious instruction in schools compulsory, established Church jurisdiction over marriage, provided for state financing of the priesthood, and stipulated that, as long as they abstained from political involvement, Catholic Action and the Church's other lay organizations could continue their educational, cultural and recreational activities unhindered. In this way, the Church was not only able to survive the totalitarian pretensions of Fascism, but was enabled to emerge as one of the most powerful social institutions at the war's end. For, in a largely rural society where well over 40 per cent of the active population was engaged in agriculture, low levels of geographical mobility and relatively undeveloped state provision in areas such as sickness and old age meant that the Church, with its myriad collateral associations was bound to be the most significant organizational presence in the everyday lives of citizens. And in the immediate post-war years the Vatican frequently and assiduously exploited its influence for explicitly political objectives – most notoriously when the Cold War was at its height and fear of communism led Cardinal Siri, archbishop of Genoa and head of the Italian Episcopal Conference, along with other members of the episcopate to warn that it was a mortal sin to vote 'for lists and candidates who do not give sufficient assurances of respecting the rights of God, the Church and mankind' (Ginsborg 1990: 117).

Not surprisingly, given such pervasive influence, the overwhelming majority of Italians were and are Catholic in terms of religious affiliation. What has made Catholicism a politically significant social division has been its tendency to create a distinction between those for whom Catholicism is a matter of *active adherence* to their faith and those for whom their religious self-identity is a *purely nominal affair* or who, in spite of their nominal self-identity, are outright opponents of the Church on many issues. And, as measured in terms of Church attendance, there has been continuous change in the proportions on either side of the divide, with 69 per cent of the adult population claiming, in 1956, to have attended mass the previous week, 37 per cent in 1976, and only 30 per cent by 1990. There was also, as the post-war years went by, a steady decline in the intensity of the divide, clearly discernible in the declining political homogeneity of the faithful. In 1968, 77 per cent of practising Catholics voted for the Christian Democrats (DC), whereas in 1985 only 63 per cent did so (Mannheimer and Sani 1987: 96). These developments were essentially due to record levels of economic growth from the 1950s (levels exceeded only by Japan, and that became known as the 'economic miracle' – see chapter 2) bringing with them urbanization, greater privacy and new leisure opportunities; new mobility and a weakening of local attachments; the spread of education and less unreflecting attitudes towards politics. As a consequence, the DC was faced with the dual problem of a decline in the size of its principal support group in conjunction with a decline in the propensity of the *remaining* members of the group to vote for the party.

Ideology

As immortalized in many popular stories, such as those based on the comical fiction character Don Camillo,[1] the religious cleavage in Italian society was to a considerable degree, even if not entirely, coterminous with the ideological cleavage, which, in conjunction with the former, gave rise to the existence of two territorially based subcultures, the Catholic and the Marxist. One side of the divide was marked by strong feelings of identity with the working class and a conviction that the latter was destined to play a central role in the process of social transformation; solidarity with the Soviet Union and the countries of Eastern Europe; a strong adherence to the values of antifascism and the Resistance. On the other side, the division meant a strong attachment to the Church and to the ecclesiastical hierarchy, and an acceptance of the Church's guidance in matters personal, social and political. Within this framework, communism, both national and international, was considered to be a mortal danger, being perceived not only as a threat to religion and religious institutions, but as the sworn enemy of the family, morality, private property and individual freedom (Mannheimer and Sani 1987: 87).

That such a cleavage should have become firmly rooted in the consciousness of ordinary Italians in the period following the announcement of the armistice on 8 September 1943 is hardly surprising. The collapse of the Fascist state, and German occupation of most of the country, created a void in which the Church and the Resistance movement became the only points of reference and of contact for Italians who had no other authority to whom to turn except the Nazis and Fascists (Galli and Prandi 1970: 14). On the one hand, the Church, having deep roots in civil society through its parishes and collateral associations, became a rallying point for working out ideas and attitudes. On the other hand, popular backing for the Resistance, dominated as it was by the Communist Party (PCI), gave to the latter authority and legitimacy.

Just as the capacity of religious observance to structure the vote declined as the postwar years went by, so too did the capacity of the ideological divide. In 1987 – by which time Gorbachev had come to power in the Soviet Union, and the Cold War had clearly lost much of its previous intensity – Mannheimer and Sani noted that 'the figures for the mid-eighties would seem to indicate a diminution in the level of preclusion [against the PCI]', while other indicators suggested a growing legitimation of this formation (1987: 110). Anti-communism had always been one of the principal pillars on which support for the DC had rested, but whereas 'in 1968, 74 per cent of the most anti-Communist and in 1972 73 per cent said they supported the DC', in 1985 only 48 per cent of the most anti-Communist (that is, those rating the PCI between 0 and 20 on a 100-point 'feelings thermometer') did so (Leonardi and Wertman 1989: 181).

After the collapse of the Berlin Wall in 1989 had led Occhetto, the PCI leader, to propose transforming the party into a non-Communist party with a new name, many DC supporters no longer felt compelled to vote for the party as the main bulwark against communism, yet the PCI was unable to benefit. Having made efforts, through the 'historic compromise' and other initiatives, to increase its appeal by lowering the temperature of ideological conflict, the decline in its vote share after 1976 (see table 4.1) suggested that increasing moderation and liberalization were, just possibly, leading

Table 4.1   Percentage share of the valid vote received by parties at general elections between 1948 and 1992

Party	Election year										
	1948	1953	1958	1963	1968	1972	1976	1979	1983	1987	1992
DC	48.5	40.1	42.4	38.3	39.1	38.7	38.7	38.3	32.9	34.3	29.7
PCI	31.0[a]	22.6	22.7	25.3	26.9	27.2	34.4	30.4	29.9	26.6	16.1[b]
RC											5.6
PSI		12.7	14.2	13.8	14.5[c]	9.6	9.7	9.8	11.5	14.3	13.6
PSDI	7.1[d]	4.5	4.6	6.1		5.1	3.4	3.8	4.1	3.0	2.7
PRI	2.5	1.6	1.4	1.4	2.0	2.9	3.1	3.0	5.1	3.7	4.4
PLI	3.8[e]	3.0	3.5	7.0	5.8	3.9	1.3	1.9	2.9	2.1	2.9
PNM	2.8	6.9	4.9[f]	1.8[g]	1.3[g]	8.7[h]	6.1[h]	0.6[i]			
MSI	2.0	5.8	4.8	5.1	4.5			5.3	6.8	5.9	5.4
PSIUP					4.5	1.9					
DP							1.5	2.2	1.5	1.7	1.2
PR							1.1	3.4	2.2	2.5	0.8
Greens										2.5	2.8
LN										1.8[i]	8.6
Rete											1.9
Others	2.3	2.8	1.5	1.2	1.4	2.0	0.7	1.3	3.1	1.6	4.3
Total	100.0	100.0	100.0	100.0	100.0	100.0	100.0	100.0	100.0	100.0	100.0

[a] In 1948 the party presented a combined list with the Socialists, called the Democratic Popular Front.
[b] By 1992 the party had changed its name to 'Democratic Party of the Left'.
[c] The figure refers to the percentage obtained by the PSI and PSDI combined during their brief period of unity as the United Socialist Party.
[d] Candidates ran under the label 'Socialist Union'.
[e] Candidates ran under the label '*Blocco Nazionale*'.
[f] The figure refers to the proportion of the vote received by the combined list fielded by the PNM and the *Partito Monarchico Popolare*.
[g] In these years, candidates took the label '*Partito Italiano di Unità Monarchica*'.
[h] In these years the monarchists fielded joint lists with the MSI called '*Movimento Sociale Italiano – Destra Nazionale*' (National Right).
[i] At this election, candidates took the label '*Destra Nazionale*'.
[j] Lega Lombarda.
Source: Petrarca (2004)

to disillusionment and apathy. By making its programme increasingly similar to those of other parties, the PCI was, perhaps, bound to disappoint its *own* supporters while creating little incentive for the supporters of *other* parties to change loyalties.[2]

Territory

The declining power of ideological conflict and of religion to anchor support to the two main parties helped to alter the way in which territorial divisions structured the vote. Prior to the 1990s, it was traditional to divide Italy into four zones according to

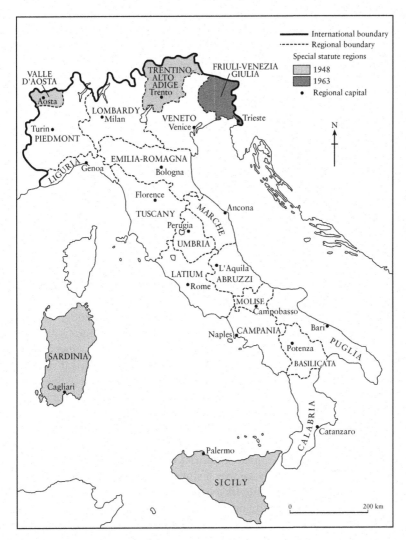

Figure 4.1   Map of Italy showing regional boundaries. The 'white belt' is traditionally thought of as corresponding to the regions of Veneto, Trentino-Alto Adige and Friuli-Venezia Giulia, the 'red belt' to the four central regions of Emilia-Romagna, Tuscany, Marche and Umbria. There are of course various ways in which the country may be divided according to the purposes of the investigator, but the majority of such divisions define the 'north-west' as corresponding to the regions of Liguria, Piedmont, Valle d'Aosta and Lombardy. Finally, the 'south' is almost always defined as consisting of the regions of Abruzzi, Molise, Puglia, Basilicata, Campania, Calabria, Sicily and Sardinia.

their rather distinct patterns of political behaviour: the 'white' and 'red' belts (corresponding to the north-eastern and central regions respectively), the north-west and the south (including Sicily and Sardinia) (see figure 4.1). The 'white belt' was the heart of the Catholic subculture, the area where the world of Catholic associationism had traditionally been at its most vibrant, and therefore the influence of the Church and the

DC at their strongest. In the 'red belt', the heart of the Marxist subculture, the Social-ist tradition of the area stemmed largely from the fact that it had formed part of the Papal States before 1860, the papal abuse of temporal power giving rise to a fierce anticlericalism and the growth of a popular radical tradition. The north-west was an area where, in a relatively industrialized and urbanized environment, the forces of the left and the right tended to be more or less evenly matched. Finally, the south was an area which, until the 'economic miracle' of the 1950s and 1960s got under way, was largely populated by a peasantry that was desperately poor, brutally exploited and in constant competition within itself for what meagre resources were available (Ginsborg 1990). In such an environment, fatalism, mistrust and what Edward Banfield (1958) famously described as 'amoral familism' were the most characteristic socio-political attitudes. Hardly surprisingly, the world of Catholic associationism was able to gain only a limited foothold, and the DC (whose best performances outside the 'white belt' were traditionally registered in the south) managed to consolidate its position by gaining control over the distribution of public resources, which thus allowed its politi-cians to establish clientelistic relations with their voters.

The period from the 1960s saw the emergence of the so-called Third Italy in the central and north-eastern regions (see figure 4.2), where the desire of large-scale indus-try to cut labour costs by subcontracting led to the spread of small-scale enterprises which were able to compete successfully in world markets through 'flexible special-ization' and short production runs (see chapter 11). In these regions the political sub-cultures facilitated the emergence of small-scale enterprise, as Cento Bull and Gilbert (2001: 79) explain, for they 'performed more than just a political role, creating an environment of mutual trust and social co-operation . . . As well as being the product of weakly polarised societies, both subcultures encouraged the formation of local political institutions bent on mediating between sectoral interests so as to promote class collaboration.' However, Christian Democracy in the white belt gradually lost its ability to represent the interests of small businesses effectively. As we have seen, a very significant way in which it sustained support for itself was by means of clientele pol-itics. At first, the Third Italy's dynamism helped to shore up clientelism and its atten-dant public mismanagement and inefficiency by sustaining, through traditionally high levels of savings, the public sector deficits on which the former rested (Trigilia 1994: 433). However, because clientele politics mainly tended to benefit the south and the large-scale industries of the north, during the 1980s, as small firms came under increas-ing competitive pressure from abroad, they began to feel the effects of public mis-management in terms of the inadequacy of policies for professional training, research and innovation, and collective services in general (Trigilia 1994: 433). At the same time, the poor quality of public services helped to heighten the salience of the taxa-tion by which they were partly funded.

Therefore, as the DC revealed itself decreasingly capable of defending the small busi-ness interests that were now in conflict with its clientelistic support in the south, and given that the ideological and religious bases of the DC's voting support were also declining, from the late 1980s the way was opened for a new political actor, the auto-nomist Northern League, to step in as a new spokesperson for the interests of north-ern small business. By claiming that the larger proportion of the total tax take needed to finance public expenditure necessarily came from the richer north, and by blaming

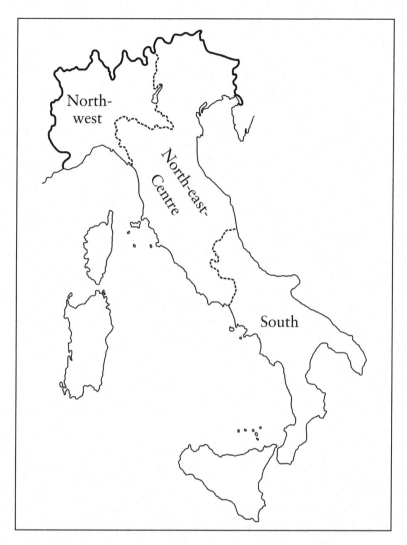

Figure 4.2   Map showing the 'three Italies'. Arnaldo Bagnasco's (1977) 'three Italies' correspond to: (1) the 'north-west', as defined in figure 4.1; (2) the 'red' and 'white belts' (with the additional of Latium), where dynamic small enterprises have given rise to the so-called Third Italy; (3) the south and the islands, characterized by slower economic development.

the inefficiency of public services on the efforts of a corrupt, party-dominated bureaucracy in far-away Rome to maintain its clientele-based power in an underdeveloped south, the League was able to tie small-business discontents firmly to its own autonomist concerns. It did this by arguing that a set of federalist arrangements were needed, as these – by limiting the functions of the State to external defence, internal security, the administration of justice, and the provision of only the most indispensable of additional public goods – would remove from the central authorities all those functions which allowed it to tax the north while giving little or nothing in return.

Class

Given that what appeared to underlie support for the Northern League was a desire to defend specific, small-business, economic interests, it was possible to interpret the emergence and growth of the League as one manifestation of the influence of the class structure upon party politics.

As Hine (1993a: 79) points out, class had a major impact on shaping the structure of the Italian party system. Conflict between employer and worker and between land-lord and peasant was often intense during the first half of the twentieth century, and from the 1890s onwards, Italy generated a class-based party of the left, the Socialists, formed from an alliance of industrial and agricultural trade unions, peasants' co-operatives and Marxist intellectuals. After 1921, the Socialists' place as the largest party claiming to represent the working class was taken by the PCI, born of a split within the Socialist Party itself, which, in the post-war period went on to become the largest Communist party in the West. In view of the discrediting of the forces of the right through their complicity in the rise of Fascism, the bourgeoisie of the immediate post-war period gave its almost unanimous support to the DC, whose cross-class appeal offered, in the circumstances, the best prospects of defending bourgeois inter-ests through keeping the Communists at bay. Class therefore played a considerable role in the genesis and evolution of the Italian *party* system.

However, the impact of class on *voting* patterns, in the post-war period, was always relatively modest as compared with the other social divisions we have discussed. Partly this had to do with the relative strength of the religious cleavage, which, by cross-cutting that of class, meant that voters with the same economic interests often found that they failed to share the same socio-cultural characteristics. Workers who attended mass regularly, for example, might feel that to give support to the traditionally anti-clerical forces of the left would be to do violence to their religious outlooks, and hence levels of 'working-class solidarity' in voting would be correspondingly reduced. A second reason for the relatively modest impact of class had to do with the subcultural bases of voting, where voters' identification with either the Catholic or the Marxist subculture allowed the DC and the PCI, as the parties representing each, to act as 'catch-all' parties, winning votes across the social class spectrum within the 'white' and 'red' belts in the north-east and centre respectively. Finally, the impact of class was further weakened, in the course of the post-war period, by those same socio-economic changes that brought a decline in the power of religious observance to structure voting patterns: namely, high levels of economic growth with their concomitant homogeniz-ing tendencies in terms of life-styles and their tendencies to promote less unreflecting, less structurally determined attitudes to politics.

To sum up this section: with the passage of time, the behaviour of Italian voters became decreasingly constrained by the main social divisions that had emerged as the principal influences on voting patterns in the years following the war's immediate aftermath. Secularization and the waning of the Cold War both gradually undermined the power of religion and ideology to anchor the support of voters to the two main parties. The decreasing ability of the DC to deal with the contradictions inherent in its choice of clientelism as a means of maintaining support for itself changed the electoral implications of territorial divisions and was an added factor in its decline. The class structure, already weak in terms of its capacity to deliver 'occupationally homogeneous' blocks of voters to the parties became increasingly so.

ELECTORAL DISCONTENT

The combined consequence of the above was evidence of growing electoral instability from the mid-1970s onwards, as, through the process of intergenerational turnover, the electorate came increasingly to consist of cohorts whose formative years, and therefore political outlooks, had been most heavily affected by the profound social changes associated with the 'economic miracle'.

Prior to the election of 1976, observers had been wont to comment on the very high, stable levels of support shown for the established parties. Thus, between 1948 and 1976, turn-out at elections never fell below 92 per cent, while support for the Christian Democrats showed rock-like stability: if one excludes the 1948 election, when it reached 48.5 per cent, support for the party varied between a high of 42.4 per cent (in 1958) and a low of 38.3 per cent (in 1963). Meanwhile, support for the PCI was almost equally stable: it managed to increase its vote by only 4.6 per cent over the two decades between 1953 and 1972.

For some observers this was puzzling, given the nature of Italian political culture. This has traditionally been characterized by a lack of interpersonal trust, something that has been reflected in a mistrust of authority, a lack of confidence in the State, the absence of a sense of citizenship, and hence a lack of pride in the country's institutions of government. Moreover, these feelings tended to be sustained in the period after the war by parties' actual performances in government, where their inability to enact coherent programmes of policies, together with their practice of clientele politics and the corruption to which this was often linked, meant that surveys carried out by the Eurobarometer consistently found Italians to be far less satisfied with 'the way democracy works' in their country than the citizens of other countries in the European Union (Morlino and Tarchi 1996). Why, then, the high, stable levels of voter turn-out and party support?

In fact, the seeming paradox is easily explained by the impact of the social and political divisions discussed above. The Cold War-induced 'Christ or communism' ideological conflict, for example, concerned the fundamental characteristics of the polity, and therefore tended to present the voter with a choice not of alternative *programmes* but of alternative *systems*. It was thus likely to make the voter feel that he or she did not really have a 'choice' at all, so radically different were the alternatives on offer. Any political choice is a choice made in opposition to the alternative not chosen, and if this alternative is seen as being sufficiently negative, the characteristics of the alternative that *is* chosen may be of little relevance. Under these circumstances, voters were often found supporting parties with whose performances they were dissatisfied and in whom they had little confidence, simply because this was the only way of blocking parties on the other side of the ideological divide. It was a situation aptly captured in 1976 by Indro Montanelli, editor of the conservative newspaper *Il Giornale*, when, in the face of the PCI's predicted advance, he famously exhorted his readers to hold their noses and vote Christian Democrat.

Similarly, the territorially based 'red' and 'white' subcultures also tended to deprive the voters of a sense that they were exercising a choice. In the process of mediating sectoral interests, as described above, the subcultures gave rise to 'a dense network of institutions co-ordinated by the dominant party' (Trigilia 1986: 47–8). Given such dominance, individual members of the subculture would be the carriers of a distinct world-view sustained by participation in a variety of political and recreational organizations and by exposure to flows of communication specific to the subculture itself. Under such circumstances, voting tended to be the expression of an automatic, unreflecting, subjective identification with the political party, seen as an entity linked organically to the social group to which the voter belonged. The vote was thus a *voto di appartenenza* ('vote of belonging') rather than a *voto d'opinione*: that is, the result of a weighing-up of the alternative policy proposals presented by the parties (Parisi and Pasquino 1977).

Finally, even clientelism could sustain high, stable levels of party support. For, though bound to sustain discontent with the way in which parties and institutions functioned *collectively* (because, by creating a whole series of vested interests, each with a power of veto, it tended to create policy paralysis), it could sustain support for parties *individually* as long as those parties were able to ensure that resources continued to be forthcoming. Under these circumstances, it was rational for the individual citizen to continue supporting his or her chosen party *regardless* of what he or she thought of the performances of the parties collectively.

As we have seen, at a certain point, the practice of clientelism began to undermine support for the DC in its heartland areas, because it was inimical to the continued economic prosperity of those areas. Meanwhile, rapid economic growth and its attendant social changes undermined the capacity of the subcultures to form political allegiances. The gradual attenuation of the Cold War undermined the significance of ideology in electoral choice. As a consequence, the impact of voters' lack of confidence in the State and their dissatisfaction with parties' performances was less effectively held in check, and the high, stable levels of support for the established parties gave way to declining turn-out, growing fragmentation and increasing aggregate volatility.

Between 1976 and 1979, voter *turn-out* fell from 93.4 per cent to 90.6 per cent, and it declined at every subsequent election, to reach 82.7 per cent in 1996. Adding to these figures those who cast either blank or spoiled ballot papers, it reveals a rising trend in support for the so-called non-vote party (NVP), which, by 1996, had reached 23.2 per cent of the electorate – a larger percentage than that given to any other party. Of course, the level of NVP support does not necessarily measure dissatisfaction: some abstentions will be involuntary, as will some spoiled ballot papers, and intentional abstentions and spoiled ballot papers may be the expression of any one of a number of different possible motivations. Only from blank ballot papers does it seem reasonable to infer a desire to protest. However, because support for the NVP rose at almost every election over the 1980s and 1990s, and we have no reason to believe that the most common causes of involuntary abstention or spoiled ballot papers (failure to consign electoral certificates, sickness and intellectual incapacity) rose concomitantly, and because the spread of this voting behaviour took place concomitantly with the growth of new formations – Radicals, Proletarian Democracy and, from the late 1980s, the Greens and the Northern League (see table 4.1) – whose aims clearly *did* have a protest character, a desire to express dissatisfaction seems to be the most reasonable inference to draw. With respect to *fragmentation*, between 1968 and 1987 the number of separate party lists presented at elections rose from 229 to 442, and at the same time the number of parties in the Chamber of Deputies rose from nine to fourteen. In 1992 the number grew to sixteen, and in 1994 to twenty. The proportion of the electorate voting for the three largest parties (DC, PCI, Socialists) declined from three-quarters in 1976 to under half in 1992. *Aggregate volatility*, as measured by Pedersen's index,[3] rose from an average of 5.8 between the election pairs of 1953–8 and 1972–6 to an average of 9.1 between 1976–9 and 1987–92.

In short, the period after 1976 gradually began to reveal an electorate that was, in aggregate, more volatile, more fragmented and more inclined to protest by abstaining or casting blank or spoiled ballot papers than the electorate of the previous two decades. In so far as a willingness of voters to abandon established parties is a necessary condition for the emergence and growth of new ones, such electoral instability made a significant contribution to the demise of the traditional parties of government in 1992–3 in the wake of the Tangentopoli ('Bribe City') corruption scandal, and to the consolidation of a new party system format following the passage of a new electoral law in 1993 and the election of 1994. It is to the analysis of electoral behaviour in this new context that we now turn.

Changes since the early 1990s

The immediate electoral consequences of Tangentopoli (which rumbled on through 1993) can be seen from table 4.2, which shows the results of the regional, provincial and communal elections which took place between the general elections of 1992 and 1994. The figures are not comparable, of course, because of the differing electorates in each case, but they do serve to document the sheer scale of the electoral disaster provoked for the governing parties by Tangentopoli. By the time of the series of elections that took place on 6 June 1993, all the traditional governing parties had begun to experience breakaways on the part of local federations, which felt that the only way to save themselves was to field, in defiance of the national leadership, their own lists of candidates under different names or joint lists with other parties. Hence the very low, and non-existent, figures for governing party candidates in columns 4, 5 and 6 reflect not only voter disenchantment, but also the fact that the disintegration of these parties as organizations had already become irreversible.

Meanwhile, popular dissatisfaction with the performance of the parties that had governed Italy since 1945 provoked a range of cross-party organizations into exploiting the constitutional provision allowing the holding of referenda on laws and parts of laws in order to engineer, in 1993, a change in the electoral law for the two chambers of Parliament. By forcing a change from a proportional to a largely single-member, simple plurality system, thus obliging parties to form electoral coalitions whose leaders would be natural candidates for the premiership, reformers hoped that the new system would result in voters being presented with a straightforward choice between a coalition of the left and one of the right. This would allow them to determine directly both the composition of the government and the identity of the Prime Minister, who, in virtue of the receipt of a popular mandate and competition from the Opposition, would enjoy sufficient authority to be able to impose discipline on the governing coalition.

Table 4.2   National, regional, provincial and communal elections, April 1992–November 1993 (votes %)

	(1)	(2)	(3)	(4)	(5)	(6)	(7)	(8)
DC	29.7	14.0	24.3	22.3	18.7	12.1	14.3	10.7
PSI	13.6	7.2	9.9	4.7	2.5	0.6	0.6	1.2
PRI	4.4	1.5	3.6	1.7	0.7	0.2	0.5	0.2
PSDI	2.7	0.8	4.9	1.6	0.8	0.4	0.9	0.9
PLI	2.8	1.2	2.9	1.3	0.2	–	–	0.1
MSI	5.4	3.2	7.2	8.3	4.0	5.3	7.4	12.0
PDS	16.1	17.8	11.4	9.9	7.7	19.8	4.6	12.1
RC	5.6	6.7	6.3	5.5	5.1	8.0	1.3	5.3
Greens	2.8	2.4	1.6	5.4	1.0	3.4	3.4	3.5
Pannella	1.2	–	0.8	–	–	–	–	0.9
Rete	1.9	2.7	4.0	1.8	2.0	1.8	5.2	3.1
League	8.7	33.9	13.7	26.7	11.7	30.5	9.6	6.2
Others	5.1	8.6	9.4	10.8	45.6	17.9	52.2	43.8
Total	100	100	100	100	100	100	100	100

(1) General election, 5 and 6 April 1992.
(2) Provincial elections, Mantova, 28 September 1992.
(3) Communal elections, 55 communes, 14 December 1992.
(4) Regional elections, Friuli-Venezia-Giulia, 6 June 1993.
(5) Partial communal elections (1,192 communes), 6 June 1993.
(6) Provincial elections (Gorizia, Ravenna, Viterbo, Mantova, Pavia, Trieste, Varese, Genova, La Spezia), 6 June 1993.
(7) Regional elections, Trentino Alto Adige, 21 November 1993.
(8) Partial communal elections (424 communes), 21 November 1993.
Source: Newell 2000b: 27, table 2.2

Consequently, it was hoped that in place of the old system of governance, based, as it had been, on unstable coalitions whose composition owed more to behind-the-scenes negotiations after the votes had been counted than to the voting choices of citizens, the changed electoral law might bring with it a new, bipolar, system providing greater stability, responsiveness and popular accountability.

The 1993 law, then, provides for three-quarters of the seats in both chambers of Parliament to be distributed according to the single-member, simple plurality system, one-quarter proportionally. In the case of the Senate, the country is divided into 237 single-seat colleges, within which the voter chooses his or her preferred candidate. The candidate winning the most votes is elected. The remaining seventy-eight seats are distributed among the country's twenty regions according to size, and are allocated proportionally according to the d'Hondt highest average formula. Within each region, the parties' vote totals are calculated and then discounted by the votes received by candidates that have been elected outright in the single-member colleges. This is the so-called *scorporo* (or 'deduction of votes'). Seats are then given to the (not already elected) candidates of parties entitled to receive seats in accordance with the size of such candidates' vote shares.

In the case of the Chamber, twenty-seven constituencies are subdivided into 475 single-member colleges, within which the voter makes a choice of candidate, and the candidate winning the most votes is elected. Candidates in the single-member colleges must be supported by at least one of the party (or party coalition) lists presented at constituency level for the distribution of the remaining 155 seats. The voter has a second ballot with which to make his or her choice among these lists. The proportionally distributed seats are allocated only to those lists that receive at least 4 per cent of the national total of valid list votes cast. Seats are then allocated to lists in three steps. First, in each constituency, each qualifying list's 'electoral total' is calculated. This is its vote total minus, for each of the party's candidates elected in single-member colleges in the constituency, a sum of votes equal to the total obtained by the second-placed candidate. Again, this is known as the *scorporo*. Second, the sum of all qualifying lists' electoral totals is divided by the number of proportional seats allocated to the constituency, to obtain the constituency electoral quotient. Third, each party's electoral total is then divided by the quotient to determine the number of seats to which it is entitled.[4]

One of the most significant implications of this new system is that election outcomes since its passage have, in a sense, been less heavily dependent on the choices of voters than elections in the past were. That is to say, prior to 1993, when the electoral system was highly proportional, essentially the only factor influencing the distribution of parliamentary seats among competing parties was voters' decisions about how to distribute their votes among the alternatives on offer. But in an electoral system of the kind that Italy now has, election outcomes also depend upon parties' decisions about electoral alliances and upon the way in which the electoral system converts a given distribution of votes between the given alternatives into a given distribution of parliamentary seats. Moreover, the three variables are not independent of one another. Parties' decisions about alliances and candidatures will be affected by their knowledge of the likely impact of such decisions on voters' behaviour and by their knowledge of the effects of the electoral system. Voters' decisions will be affected by their willingness or otherwise to support a party regardless of its alliance decisions and by their knowledge of the implications of the electoral system for the impact of a vote cast one way or the other. In the 2001 election, for example, the centre right coalition is widely thought to have won, not because of any significant shift in the distribution of votes in its favour (see table 4.3), but because it had a more efficient system of electoral alliances than the centre left. In particular, many observers were wont to suggest that had the centre left Olive-tree Alliance and the left-wing Communist Refoundation (RC) managed to agree on joint candidatures for the Senate race, the centre right might even have been deprived of its majority in that chamber. However, it could not be considered *inevitable* that this state of affairs would work to the centre right's advantage. For it was also possible to think that the *absence* of an agreement between RC and the Olive-tree might attract to the ranks of the centre left sufficiently large numbers of more centrally located voters who, if the centre-left *had* been allied with RC, would under those circumstances have refused to support it. In short, a great deal depended on the *summability* of votes.

It is possible to assess this by virtue of one of the characteristis of the new electoral system: namely, the fact that for Chamber of Deputies elections, voters have two

Table 4.3 The Chamber of Deputies elections of 1996 and 2001

1996 Plurality vote Coalition	Vote (%)	Seats (no.)	Proportional vote Parties and alliances	Vote (%)	Seats (no.)	2001 Plurality vote Coalition	Vote (%)	Seats (no.)	Proportional vote Parties and alliances	Vote (%)	Seats (no.)
			PDS-Sin. Eur	21.1	26				DS	16.6	31
			P. Sardo d'Az	0.1	0				Margherita	14.5	27
			Verdi	2.5	0				Girasole	2.2	0
			PPI-SVP-PRI	6.8	4	l'Ulivo-SVP	1.6	8	PdCI	1.7	0
			RI	4.3	8	l'Ulivo	43.7	184			
l'Ulivo	42.3	247	Total	34.8	38	Total	45.3	192	Total	35.0	58
Progressisti	2.6	15	Rif. Com.	8.6	20				Rif. Com.	5.0	11
l'Ulivo + RC	44.9	262		43.4	58	l'Ulivo + RC	45.3	192		40.0	69
			CCD-CDU	5.8	12				CCD-CDU	3.2	0
			Forza Italia	20.6	37				Forza Italia	29.5	62
			Alleanza Nazionale	15.7	28				Alleanza Nazionale	12.0	24
Polo libertà	40.3	169	Total	42.1	77				Nuovo PSI	1.0	0
Lega	10.8	39	Lega	10.1	20				Lega	3.9	0
Polo + Lega Lista	51.1	208		52.2	97	CdI	45.4	282	Total	49.6	86
Pannella	0.2	0	Pannella	1.9	0	Bonino	1.3	0	Bonino	2.2	0
MSFT	1.7	0	MSFT	0.9	0	MSFT	0.3	0	MSFT	0.4	0
Others	2.0	5	Others	1.6	0	Italia Valori	4.1	0	Italia Valori	3.9	0
						Dem. Eur.	3.6	0	Dem. Eur.	2.4	0
						Others	0.0	1	Others	1.5	0
Total	99.9	475		100	155	Total	100	475		100	155

Source: Newell and Bull (2001)

separate ballot papers for the seats distributed according to the simple plurality formula and for those distributed proportionally. So, though the procedure involves making possibly unwarranted inferences about the behaviour of individuals from aggregate data, we can compare voting behaviour under different conditions of political supply, as D'Alimonte and Bartolini (1997) point out. It is not necessarily the case, for example, that a voter who chooses one of the centre left's parties with the proportional vote will choose the centre left's candidate for the seat in his or her single-member college. At the 1994 and 1996 elections, for example, it appears to have been the case that in those colleges where its candidate was drawn from RC, the centre left's plurality vote was substantially lower than the sum of the proportional votes cast for its constituent parties in those same colleges (D'Alimonte and Bartolini 1997: 126–7). So, although by allying itself with RC at these two elections, the centre left avoided the risk of separate RC candidatures resulting in seat losses by depriving it of left-wing votes, the strategy was not cost-free in so far as it seems, to a degree at least, to have been counterbalanced by vote losses among (presumably) more centrally located supporters unwilling to support the coalition when its candidate was from a party as far to the left as RC. In the 2001 election, the absence of an alliance with RC failed to win over voters able to give the centre left a Senate majority by being sufficiently numerous to compensate for the votes lost by separate RC candidatures.

The possibility and the fact of 'split-ticket' voting has been taken by electoral analysts as one piece of evidence of a heightened importance of leader characteristics in electoral choice as compared to the period prior to the 1990s (reflecting what is clearly a more 'presidential' style of electoral campaigning in the new bipolar world of Italian party politics).[5] For example, in 1994, when the centre right won significantly more votes in the plurality than in the proportional arena (see table 4.4), its victory was attributed, at least partly, to an apparent capacity of Berlusconi's leadership of the coalition to attract voters beyond those who were for the centre right in terms of their choice of individual party. By contrast, in 1996, when the centre left chose Romano Prodi as its coalition leader (thus making up for its failure in 1994 to identify a prime-ministerial candidate prior to polling day), not only did it win the election, but it managed to attract some half a million more votes in the plurality than in the proportional arena (while the centre right now won fewer plurality than proportional votes; see table 4.4). Again, therefore, there was evidence that an effective coalition leader had the capacity to attract voters from other camps.

That said, voters do not switch camps easily. In 2001, for example, fewer than three in a hundred voters split their votes between the two main coalitions. Similarly low proportions switch allegiance between the two main coalitions at successive elections. Thus, between 1994 and 1996, only 5.5 per cent of those voting at both elections did so; between 1996 and 2001, only 7.6 per cent. Moreover, as one who is without strongly held political beliefs, and who decides his vote at the last moment, the voter who switches in this way seems to be rather different from the broadly well-educated and informed voter responsible for the earlier electoral volatility described in the previous section (see ITANES 2001: ch. 6). Overall, then, it would seem to be the case that, following the instability of the late 1970s and the 1980s, and in the aftermath of the party system earthquake of the early 1990s (when the allegiances of unusually large proportions of voters *necessarily* changed, simply because the profile of the choices

Table 4.4 The Chamber of Deputies elections of 1994

Parties and alliances	List votes N (millions)	%	Proportional seats N	%	Plurality seats N	%	Total seats N	%
PDS	7.86	20.4	37	23.9	72	25.2	109	17.3
RC	2.33	6.0	12	7.7	27	5.7	39	6.2
Greens	1.04	2.7	0	0.0	11	2.3	11	1.7
PSI	0.84	2.2	0	0.0	14	2.9	14	2.2
Rete	0.72	1.9	0	0.0	6	1.3	6	1.0
AD	0.45	1.2	0	0.0	18	3.8	18	2.9
C-S				0.0	5	1.1	5	0.8
RS					1	0.2	1	0.2
Ind. left					10	2.1	10	1.6
Total Progressive Alliance	13.24	34.3	49	31.6	164	34.5	213	33.8
PPI	4.27	11.1	29	18.7	4	0.8	33	5.2
Patto Segni	1.79	4.7	13	8.4	0	0.0	13	2.1
Total Pact for Italy	6.06	15.7	42	27.1	4	0.8	46	7.3
FI	8.12	21.0						
FI			25	16.1	74	15.6	99	15.7
CCD			7	4.5	22	4.6	29	4.6
UdC					4	0.8	4	0.6
PLD					2	0.4	2	0.3
Riformatori					6	1.3	6	1.0
AN	5.20	13.5	22	14.2	87	18.3	109	17.3
Northern League	3.24	8.4	10	6.5	107	22.5	117	18.6
LP	1.36	3.5	0	0.0	0	0.0	0	0.0
Total Freedom Alliance	17.92	46.4	64	43.1	302	63.6	366	58.1
SVP	0.23	0.6	0	0.0	3	0.6	3	0.5
Lista Valle d'Aosta					1	0.2	1	0.2
Lega d'Azione Meridionale	0.06	0.2	0	0.0	1	0.2	1	0.2
Social-democrazia	0.18	0.5	0	0.0	0	0.0	0	0.0
Lega Alpina Lumbarda	0.14	0.4	0	0.0	0	0.0	0	0.0

Table 4.4   *(continued)*

Parties and alliances	List votes		Proportional seats		Plurality seats		Total seats	
	N (millions)	%	N	%	N	%	N	%
Verdi-Verdi	0.03	0.1	0	0.0	0	0.0	0	0.0
Other leagues	0.13	0.3	0	0.0	0	0.0	0	0.0
Autonomist lists	0.03	0.1	0	0.0	0	0.0	0	0.0
Other lists	0.57	1.5	0	0.0	0	0.0	0	0.0
Total others	1.37	3.6	0	0.0	5	1.1	5	0.8
Total	38.59	100.0	155	100.0	475	100.0	630	100.0

1. The list votes won by CCD (which presented a separate list only in Molise) have been included under 'Other lists'; the seven proportional seats obtained have been attributed to CCD candidates on the lists presented by FI.

2. Of the total 302 plurality seats attributed to the Freedom Alliance, 164 were won by the Freedom Alliance (of which Northern League 107, FI 38, CCD 8, *Riformatori* 6, UdC 3, PLD 2); 129 by the Alliance for Good Government (of which AN 79, FI 36, CCD 13, UdC 1); 1 by FI-CCD; and 8 by AN running alone.

Source: Bartolini and D'Alimonte (1994): table 2

they were presented with changed so radically), both the scale and the significance of instability have shrunk.

Two further important changes as compared with the past are worth mentioning. First, religion is no longer a factor of any significance in structuring electoral choices. As we have seen, already well before the 1990s, the DC had changed from being *the* party of Catholics to *a* party of this group. Then, as part of the party system upheavals that took place in the wake of the Tangentopoli investigations, the disintegration of the DC led to the formation of several 'successor' parties, each of which found itself aligned with other parties on one or other side of the left–right divide in the country's emerging bipolar system. Not very surprisingly, then, what we now find is that, even among the most religiously observant, the distribution of the vote differs very little from the corresponding distribution among the electorate as a whole. In 2001, for example, among the electorate as a whole, the distribution of the Chamber plurality vote between centre right, centre left and others was 46.2 per cent, 44.3 per cent and 9.6 per cent respectively, whereas the corresponding proportions among those who go to church every Sunday were 50.8 per cent, 39.1 per cent and 10.0 per cent (ITANES 2001: 84). Second, and perhaps partly because of the virtual disappearance of the religious cleavage in Italian politics, social stratification now appears to be more significant in structuring the vote. From the data gathered through the 2001 Italian National Election Study survey, two fairly sharp distinctions are apparent: between the votes of the employed and the self-employed, on the one hand, and the votes of public- and private-sector employees, on the other. Among the self-employed, support for the centre right in the Chamber plurality vote was higher than support for the centre left by 22.5 per cent, while among the electorate as a whole the corresponding difference was only 1.7 per cent. Among public-sector employees 30.6 per cent and 58.8 per cent voted for the centre right and centre left respectively, whereas among private-sector employees the corresponding proportions were 44.1 per cent and 43.7 per cent (ITANES 2001: 60–3).

CONCLUSION

By the beginning of the twenty-first century the electoral landscape had been completely transformed as compared to the early years of republican Italy's existence. The old divisions of religion and ideology had essentially ceased to exist. The Catholic and Marxist subcultures, which these divisions helped to sustain, had been gradually eroded by higher levels of geographical and social mobility, an expansion of the mass media of communications, and rising standards of living – all consequent upon rapid rates of economic growth. Fewer and fewer voters cast what Parisi and Pasquino (1977) had come to call a *voto di appartenenza*, and more and more cast a *voto d'opinione*. The negative quality of most such opinions was for long nurtured by the inability of the governing parties to respond effectively to popular expectations and desires, so that, when the traditional anchors – religious, ideological, subcultural and clientelist – holding voters to the established parties began to lose their grip, an essential pre-condition was created for the profound party system upheavals of the early 1990s.

In the few years that have passed since those upheavals, Italian electoral behaviour appears to have settled down into a new pattern within the framework of the country's new, largely bipolar, party system. When voters collectively have the power to determine the composition of governments directly, and when the disappearance of traditional ties and divisions of the kinds we have discussed render electoral markets relatively open, then we expect electoral choice to become, above all, about assessing government competence. If voters *are* moved by such assessments, then we expect to see a degree of electoral movement between competing coalitions – although, as mentioned, this is something we have not seen so far. Until it happens, it is difficult to see how one can reasonably expect competing coalitions to alternate in government for any reasons other than the effects of their alliance decisions coupled with the arbitrary effects of the electoral system. What significance, then, should we attach to the party system upheavals of recent years? This, in a sense, is the question to which the book as a whole is addressed. In the following chapter, we discuss the significance of the party system upheavals for the representation of interests, before examining, in the chapter following, the upheavals' significance for the role of informal institutions in the Italian polity.

THE REPRESENTATION OF INTERESTS

INTRODUCTION

In chapter 3, we saw that after the fall of Fascism, the newly emergent political parties were able to penetrate vast areas of the state and society, and thereby to consolidate a type of rule that was widely referred to as *partitocrazia*. This was a type of rule in which political power was exercised through the party leaders more than through an executive accountable to Parliament (Partridge 1998: 69); in which recruitment to positions therefore took place primarily according to the criterion of political party affiliation and only secondarily, if at all, according to technical competence to perform the job in question; and in which, therefore, there was a considerable degree of overlap between the personnel of the parties, on the one hand, and interest groups and administrative positions, on the other, making it difficult to draw clear boundaries between these entities.

While, from one point of view, the parties' capacity to gain control of interest groups spoke to their strength, from another point of view, that of the groups themselves, it helped to make them weak. For it tended to undermine the capacity of parties to filter and aggregate demands, leading them instead to function as instruments of the groups, transmitting to governmental structures demands that were narrow and indicative of an unwillingness to compromise (LaPalombara 1964: 8). This in turn tended to perpetuate a view of the State as something to be conquered by one's own group to the disadvantage of others, rather than as an entity that could reasonably be relied upon to further the general interest. In this way it added a further mechanism by which the authority and standing of the State among ordinary citizens was weakened and undermined.

If this implies that an analysis of the Italian political system's difficulties since 1945 would not be complete without an analysis of the part played by pressure groups, then it is also the case that 'only a small, if not very small number of pressure groups, is truly significant for the purposes of explaining the operations of a political system' (Sartori 1959: 39; quoted by Morlino 1991: 35).[1] Alongside the groups that meet this criterion in most democratic capitalist systems – namely, the trade unions and employers' organizations – in the Italian case one also finds the Church and its lay organizations, and, for much of the post-war period, the small farmers' organization, the Coltivatori Diretti (or Coldiretti, Direct Cultivators). These organizations played a significant part in shaping and sustaining the principal characteristics of Italian democracy as it emerged after the war – while, in their turn, the characteristics of Italian democracy had a significant impact on the specific ways in which pressure groups articulated interests and sought to influence public policy. Beginning with the trade unions, the focus of this chapter is, in the following two sections, therefore, the specific mechanisms through which these reciprocal influences were exerted in the case of the four organizations we have mentioned. In the final section, we explore the implications of the 1990s party system transformation for these organizations' activities.

PRESSURE GROUPS AND THE TRANSITION TO DEMOCRACY

The unions were reconstituted by the main political parties towards the end of the war, when the struggle for liberation was still proceeding, and indeed, they were reconstituted 'as part and parcel of that struggle' (Bedani 1995: 1). If this meant that they came to be seen as an indispensable element of the fabric necessary to ensure the country's development as a stable democracy, then, because they were brought into being by an anti-Fascist coalition whose representatives were otherwise separated by deep ideological divisions, union activity inevitably reflected, and was driven by, these divisions.

Initially, it suited both Catholic and Communist trade unionists to work together, within the framework of a single confederation, the Confederazione Generale Italiana del Lavoro (General Confederation of Italian Labour, CGIL), founded in June 1944. The concept of a single confederation chimed with the Communists' commitment to the principle of working-class unity; the Catholics were worried that their own separate confederation might leave them weak and at risk of being ignored in industrial negotiations. This then encouraged the Socialists to favour unity, because, by including the Catholics, the united confederation reduced the risk that either of them would end up being hegemonized by the Communists. However, precisely because of the strong ideological and organizational ties between these various tendencies, and the corresponding political parties, the confederation was inherently exposed to the risk that it would fail to survive the break-up of the government of which all three parties then formed part. Even more was this the case bearing in mind the highly centralized structure of the movement. For if decisions within it were the preserve of its leaders, 'these leaders were the most vulnerable to party pressures' (Bedani 1995: 33). The precipitating factor in the secession of the Catholics – who in May 1950 formed the Confederazione Italiana Sindacati Lavoratori (Italian Confederation of Workers' Unions, CISL) – was the reaction of the CGIL executive, in calling a general strike allegedly in violation of the confederation's statutes, to the July 1948 assassination attempt against Communist Party (PCI) leader Palmiro Togliatti. With the Catholics gone, and wishing to avoid the risk of domination by either Communists or Catholics, republicans and social democrats in March 1950 set up a third, smaller confederation, Unione Italiana dei Lavoratori (Italian Workers' Union, UIL).

Division between the confederations helped to sustain the anti-communism that was so important to DC power and influence, in three ways. First, freed of the obligation – as the price of unity – to keep the parties at a certain distance, Catholic and Communist components of the trade union movement could now become unequivocally identified – in perception and broadly in reality – as collateral organizations of the DC and the PCI respectively. This made it easier, given the intensity of the Cold War atmosphere, for government and employers to delegitimize the CGIL and thus to exclude it from collective bargaining agreements. Second, as an organization in competition with the CGIL, the CISL developed its industrial relations strategy (with its emphasis on workplace bargaining) in opposition to that of the former organization (with its preference for national bargaining as more conducive to workers' solidarity). Given the perceived party affiliations of the two organizations, the CISL's strategy inevitably fostered the by no means mistaken impression that there was a strong anti-Communist critique implicit in it. Third, the hostility of the CISL helped to push the CGIL even more firmly into the embrace of the PCI, which came to be perceived, in accordance with Leninist principles, as the PCI's 'transmission belt': the party's 'industrial arm' whose policies it had an obligation to put into practice. In this way the CISL's stance played its part in heightening perceptions that communism was a dangerous ideology capable of penetrating the workplace and thus undermining the post-war economic recovery.

Such perceptions were also fostered by the Coltivatori Diretti that was formed in October 1944 as a result of the contrasting attitudes towards agricultural labour of the Communist and Catholic parties to the negotiations leading to the formation of the CGIL. While Catholic negotiators sought a place for small farmers within the organization, as a means of extending Catholic influence within it, Communists objected that the small farmers needed a separate organization which, by championing their specific aspirations, could provide the basis for joint action with the trade union confederation. By being based on real points of convergence, it was argued, such action 'would stand a better chance of success than policies worked out on the basis of a confused and generic unity which ignored important differences' (Bedani 1995: 22). In the light of uncertainty about which of these views would win the day, the DC stole a march on the Communists, establishing the small-farmers' organization under the leadership of a 34-year-old Catholic political activist from Piedmont, Paolo Bonomi, an individual capable of using a variety of clientelistic means to tie his organization's members firmly to the DC and thus entrench them, ideologically, in the political camp dominated by anti-communism and the Catholic Church.

The Church, meanwhile, was prepared, at Fascism's fall, to 'extend its hand' to any organization able to counter the appeals of 'atheistic Marxism' and ensure that the Lateran Treaties would remain in force into the post-war period. Naturally, this meant using its enormous influence among the population to ensure that individuals voted as Catholics, and that they voted as a single bloc. Prudently, until it became clear that the DC rather than some other party would emerge as the vehicle through which this would happen, the Vatican's instructions were that 'Catholics may vote only for those candidates, or lists of candidates that give assurances that they will respect and defend the observance of divine law and the rights of religion and the Church in public and private life' (quoted by Magister 1979: 54). By eschewing mention of specific parties, the Vatican was careful to avoid, in its initial pronouncements, anything that could be interpreted as the 'formal investiture' of a single party above others. For it was aware that there were deep divisions among Catholics (for example, on the future of the monarchy), and it wished above all to avoid doing anything that would spawn competing Catholic parties and thus strengthen the position of the left. Later, the sheer power of the Church over the fate of the fledgling DC was illustrated by the contents of the March 1947 letter from Vittorino Veronese, leader of the Church's laypersons' organization, Catholic Action, to Alcide De Gasperi: unless DC representatives in the Constituent Assembly voted compactly for incorporation of the Lateran Treaties in the new Constitution, it was difficult to predict how Catholics would vote in future general elections (Magister 1979: 87–8). That this was no empty threat had already been revealed at the local elections the previous November, when numerous priests had openly supported the right-wing Fronte dell'Uomo Qualunque ('Common Man's Front'), causing considerable set-backs for the DC, especially in Rome. At the 1948 elections, the party was heavily reliant on Catholic Action's Civic Committees under the leadership of Luigi Gedda, who, along with others close to the Vatican, frequently sought to exploit such reliance to condition the political line of the party in the years thereafter. It was the awareness of De Gasperi that, by too closely resembling a purely confessional party, the DC would unnecessarily limit its electoral appeal, that in the 1950s under Fanfani the party undertook to become organizationally and financially independent of the Church by 'colonizing' a wide range of public bodies which it could exploit for patronage purposes.

Finally, Confindustria played a more passive role in the transition from Fascism to post-war democracy, for it had a legitimacy problem. In terms of personnel and bureaucratic resources, it inherited more from its Fascist predecessor than it cared to admit, while the close collaboration between industry and government that had taken place through its Fascist predecessor was likewise an embarrassment for it. If this led it to adopt robustly *laisser-faire* political and economic positions – something that would help it to distance itself, in the popular imagination, from the Fascist experience – then it also led it to avoid party-political ties which, by recalling too forcefully its earlier involvements, carried risks for its public image. Therefore, while its leaders worked closely with those of the Liberal Party – whose *laisser-faire* outlooks were in particular accord with those of Confindustria – the collaboration remained strictly informal, and was never underpinned by any organizational links or any overlap in the leadership of the two organizations. Towards the remaining parties of the centre right the Confindustria assumed a position that was essentially one of neutrality, and it was not until the exclusion from government of the parties of the left, in May 1947, that Confindustria finally abandoned its reservations towards the governments that were overseeing the process of transition from Fascism to the institutions of the post-war regime.

That is not to say that Confindustria was of little consequence for the characteristic features of post-war Italian democracy or the consolidation of its party system. On the contrary: after all, with the marginalization of the left, and with the DC firmly in the saddle after April 1948, it was reasonable to hope that privileged relationships with the governing parties might lead to policies of benefit to industrial interests without the risk of their being abolished or overturned in the short term. During the first post-war legislature, Confindustria was able to obtain a 'duopolistic' approach to industrial and economic policy, involving the reduction to a minimum of public economic intervention, together with the marginalization in economic and industrial policy making of all groups other than Confindustria itself. In exchange for the advantages thus obtained, Confindustria offered the DC financial and electoral support, recognized its role as guardian of the points of access to government decision making, and fully accepted that, as the best guarantor of political stability, its place in government was permanent. The Liberals, meanwhile, came to be seen as a means of constraining the DC from the right, in the event that the bigger party deviated from the aforementioned approach to economic and industrial policy making (Mattina 1991: 273–4).

After the end of the first legislature, Confindustria's relations with the principal party of government became less harmonious and more complex. In order to explicate these, it is necessary now to reverse perspectives, examining how the characteristic features of Italy's post-war democracy affected the ways in which pressure groups sought to advance their members' interests.

CHRISTIAN DEMOCRATIC HEGEMONY AND THE ARTICULATION OF INTERESTS

In a celebrated volume, LaPalombara argued that access of organized groups to the points of decision and policy within the public bureaucracy depended in large measure on their ties of *parentela*, involving 'a relatively close and integral relationship between certain associational interest groups on the one hand, and the politically dominant Christian Democratic Party on the other' (1964: 306). Such relationships, in turn, derived from the DC's overwhelming electoral superiority as compared to other parties; its permanence in office; its willingness to intervene in the administrative process on behalf of groups affiliated with the party; the groups' capacity, based on their 'vote-delivering prowess' (LaPalombara 1964: 337), to condition the party's actions; and structural characteristics of the Italian bureaucracy such as the extreme centralization of authority within it. For the most significant interest groups, such as the Coltivatori Diretti, CISL and Catholic Action, ties of *parentela* also meant having their representatives sit on the DC's directive bodies and getting them elected, as DC candidates, to Parliament. In this way *parentela* meant being able to condition policy in both the rule-making and rule-applying spheres of the political system, by means of links *internal to* the dominant party. Significant interest groups, such as Confindustria, unable to establish ties of *parentela* with the DC, were forced, instead, to develop with the bureaucracy ties of *clientela* as the main means of seeking to influence administrative actions. Such ties existed when the interest group succeeded in becoming 'in the eyes of a given administrative agency, the natural expression and representative of a given social sector which, in turn, constitute[d] the natural target or reference point for the activity of the administrative agency' (LaPalombara 1964: 262). In this way, Confindustria was able to establish privileged relations with the Ministry of Industry and Commerce, whereby the latter came to act as the peak association's unofficial but acknowledged representative within the sphere of government, in exchange for the efforts of Confindustria, when necessary, to apply pressure on other branches of government on the Ministry's behalf. In this way, *clientela* acted as a means whereby the interest group could influence policy in the rule-making and rule-applying spheres of government through ties that were *external to* the dominant party.

This analysis helps to make sense of the growing estrangement between the DC and Confindustria in the years after 1953, hinted at above. As an organization external to the DC, Confindustria was not in a position to influence directly the composition of the party's leadership or its parliamentary contingent. Neither (as would be revealed by the 1958 general election) was the proportion of enterprises – especially small enterprises – affiliated to it sufficiently large, or its influence among them sufficiently great, to allow it to control large numbers of votes. In essence, therefore, it relied on its members' money as the means by which to condition the party. For the DC, from 1954 under the control of Fanfani and the left-leaning faction, Iniziativa Democratica, this situation was problematic. It created a relationship of dependence on Confindustria. In addition, as a party whose Catholic values were, to a degree, at odds with those of unbridled free enterprise, and as 'a brokerage party consisting of a number of groups that [were] in conflict with one another' (LaPalombara 1964: 224), the DC was under pressure to respond to the demands of those, such as the CISL, that were internal to it. The party was therefore under pressure to reduce the scope of the policy concessions accorded to large-scale industry, and the privileged access accorded to its organized representative, and to do so in a way that would allow it to escape from its financial dependence on the latter. It is in this light that the DC's 'colonization' of vast areas of the State with resources to dispense must at least in part be understood.

Part of this operation involved the creation or overhaul, under party control, of such state holding companies as IRI and ENI, whose subsidiary firms broke away from Confindustria in 1956 to form a rival organization, Intersind. Not only did this undermine Confindustria's ambitions to establish a monopoly on representation of the interests of industry, but it reversed the approach to economic and industrial policy making of the first legislature, which, as mentioned, had involved the marginalization of industry representatives other than Confindustria itself. Faced with this attempted invasion, by the DC, of its own sphere of action, Confindustria fought back by establishing Confintesa, a committee bringing together the General Confederation of Italian Agriculture, the Italian Confederation of Commerce, and itself, in an attempt to encourage DC voters, in 1958, to cast their preference votes for its preferred candidates, and other voters to vote for the Liberal Party. In other words, it sought to acquire for itself that same vote-mobilizing capacity on which rested a large part of the power of groups enjoying *parentela* ties with the DC. The substantial failure of this effort essentially confirmed Confindustria's status as a group which – when faced with the DC's decision to sacrifice its interests to the demands of groups more directly able to influence the composition of its leadership and its electoral support – would be able to condition the party only from the outside.

The full significance of this can best be appreciated by considering the radically contrasting situation of the Coltivatori Diretti. The organization was large, both in absolute terms and in terms of its coverage of the social category whose interests it sought to advance (Lanza 1991: 58–9).[2] Partly because of this, it managed to gain control of large numbers of the agricultural consortia, which were relevant for a range of activities of direct economic importance to farmers, so that not being a member of the Coltivatori Diretti was likely to involve a heavy material price for the individual farmer concerned. This was even more the case after 1954, when the organization managed to secure legislation extending to small farmers the provisions of Italy's compulsory health insurance legislation and establishing, for each of the relevant localities, sickness benefit funds (*Casse Mutue*) – the vast majority of which the Coltivatori Diretti won control of through the elections to their boards of directors. As a member, the farmer could be relied upon to vote in the way Bonomi's henchmen told him to, thanks to the Italian electoral law's provision for preference voting.[3] In return for the support thus engineered, the individual farmer could expect the provision of clientelistic favours of both an immediate and individualistic kind (such as help in obtaining the award of old age and invalidity pensions), as well as favours of a more general kind. In other words, in return for his support he could expect the parliamentarians so elected to use their influence within the ranks of the DC's legislators to secure passage of a range of laws of direct interest to him.

There is no doubt that in the early post-war years the Coltivatori Diretti wielded considerable power within the corridors of Parliament. The fact that the DC was a brokerage party allowed Coltivatori Diretti parliamentarians to operate as a kind of 'peasants' party' within the larger party itself (Lanza 1991: 84). And given that Coltivatori Diretti deputies accounted for 7.5 per cent, 12.6 per cent and 12.8 per cent of DC deputies respectively in the first three legislatures (Lanza 1991: 89–90), their group was not one that could be easily ignored.

That said, it is important not to overlook the very real limits on the Coltivatori Diretti's power. First, precisely because the nature of the DC *did* allow the small farmers to act as 'a party within a party', the DC itself was forced to act as a 'ring keeper', arbitrating between the claims of its competing groups, and it was by no means a foregone conclusion, when it came to the taking of crucial decisions of relevance to the entire political system, that such decisions would go in the small farmers' favour. Second, while the Coltivatori Diretti had considerable vote-mobilizing power and was very influential in the selection of DC candidates, in terms of its presence in the controlling bodies of the party apparatus, it appears to have been somewhat less influential. Third, the highly particularistic nature of its concerns prevented its leaders from developing the kind of theoretical perspectives that might have given them both prestige and the capacity to mobilize support around political visions of a general nature. Consequently, with the growth, from the 1950s, of factional rivalry within the DC, the organization's influence was rendered less than it might otherwise have been by its capacity to do little more than attach itself to whichever faction seemed to be in the ascendant at the moment in question (Lanza 1991: 86).

Over time, additional limits were placed on the Coltivatori Diretti's power – limits deriving essentially from the 'economic miracle', which had two effects. First, by stimulating massive internal migration, mainly from rural to urban settings, it considerably reduced the size of the organization's catchment area (see table 5.1). Thus, while in 1951 small farming accounted for 30 per cent of the employed population, by the mid-1990s, it had declined to around 5 per cent (Bruzzone 1994: 230). Not surprisingly, already by the mid-1980s the number of families associated with the Coltivatori Diretti had declined to 1,070,460 (Capo 1985: 1077) from the figure of 1,683,141 in 1958. By the mid-1980s, the number of local sections, which in 1958 had amounted to 13,556, had declined to 10,345 (Capo 1985: 1077). By 2004, they had declined by

Table 5.1   Economically active population by sector of employment, 1951–2001 (%)

Sector	Year	1951	1961	1971	1981	1991	2001
Agriculture		42.2	29.1	17.2	11.1	8.5	5.0
Industry		31.3	39.5	42.0	39.5	32.0	31.7
Tertiary							
sector		26.5	31.4	40.8	49.4	59.5	63.3
Total		100.0	100.0	100.0	100.0	100.0	100.0

Source: Adapted from Perulli (1994): 444 and Lelli (2004): 301, table A9

a further 533, to 9,812.[4] Second, by bringing about a dramatic growth in per capita income, the 'economic miracle' reduced considerably the organization's vote-mobilizing capacities. Thus, even for those who remained small farmers, rising incomes generally brought exposure to new influences on political attitudes – such as television and the increasing possibilities of combining small farming with part-time, non-agricultural employment – competing with the influence of the hundreds of ecclesiastical counsellors retained by the Coltivatori Diretti. Moreover, the establishment, in 1978, of a fully-fledged national health service, itself a product of economic growth, resulted in the Casse Mutue being absorbed into new Local Health Units (Unità Sanitarie Locali) – and thus in the loss of control of the small-farmers' organization over the distribution of health resources. For the individual farmer, therefore, it became somewhat less essential to pay heed to the organization's political instructions.

The Church saw its political influence decline as a result of very similar factors. One of the most significant effects of the economic miracle was the decline in church attendance, as rising incomes expanded the range of accessible leisure pursuits. Furthermore, the exposure to an increasing range of alternative sources of political information reduced the inclination of those who continued to attend church to draw given political conclusions from their religious commitment (see chapter 4). These processes inevitably also brought declining membership in the laypersons' organizations – Catholic Action and the Associazione Cattolica dei Lavoratori Italiani (Italian Workers' Catholic Association, ACLI) – through which, in the early post-war years, the Church had sought to further its interests at the mass level. Widely considered as the most powerful of the DC's internal pressure groups in the 1950s, Catholic Action saw its membership figures decline from about 3 million in the 1950s to 1.6 million in the late 1960s and about 600,000 in the early 1980s (Spotts and Wieser 1986: 255–7). The ACLI – formed in 1944 as a parallel organization, alongside the unions, with the object of shielding Catholic workers from the influence of class struggle ideologies and teaching them the principles of 'responsible' trade unionism – saw its membership decline from about 1 million in the early 1960s to about half that twenty years later.

If its sponsorship of mass-membership organizations was one way in which, in the early post-war years, the Church had sought to further its interests, another had been by means of direct political intervention at the elite level. This too underwent a gradual decline in significance, due to a series of political events and changes that took place in tandem with the sweeping economic and social changes. Four stand out as having been of particular importance.

First, the failure of Italian bishops to obstruct the 'opening to the left' (marked by the eventual entry of the Socialists into government in December 1963) considerably strengthened the DC in its relations with the Church. Opposed to the development on principle, the Italian Episcopal Conference (CEI) was eventually forced to give way by parliamentary and electoral arithmetic and by practical demonstrations (such as the experience of the 1960 Tambroni government) of the consequences for political stability of refusing to entertain the possibility of collaboration with the Socialists. In one of those coded messages, so typical of the Church's elite-level interactions with the DC, Pope John XXIII made it clear, during the course of a state visit by Fanfani to the Vatican on 11 April 1961, that he would not stand by the CEI – a move which, by virtue of the overriding Church imperative of the political unity of Catholics, disarmed the Italian bishops. Given the position of the Pope, the imperative made it impossible to condemn the DC or to respond to its 'disobedience' by encouraging the project that had long been nurtured in some clerical circles: namely, the setting up of a rival Catholic party open to political alliances with the far right.

Second, of possibly equal significance in tempering ecclesiastical passions for political involvements, was the gradual decline – to which Pope John XXIII was himself a significant contributor – in the intensity of the Cold War conflict. Of particular significance in this connection was the papal encyclical *Pacem in Terris*. Warning of the need to make a clear distinction between 'a false philosophy' and 'economic, social, cultural, and political undertakings', even when such undertakings draw their origin and inspiration from that philosophy, the document went on to ask: 'Besides, who can deny the possible existence of good and commendable elements in these undertakings, elements which do indeed conform to the dictates of right reason, and are an expression of man's lawful aspirations?'[5] Given such sentiments, it was not surprising, perhaps, that publication of the document should coincide with a change in the tone of the customary instructions issued by the CEI to its bishops prior to elections – instructions whose strident anti-communism now tended to give way to blander reminders of the need for the political unity of Catholics around the DC, while also inviting the bishops to abstain 'from involvement in any struggle between the factions of the party itself' (Magister 1979: 285).

Third, the Second Vatican Council helped to dilute the ecclesiastical passion for elite-level intervention in Italian politics. Convened with the purpose of considering the spiritual renewal of the Church and of reconsidering its position in the modern world, not only its substantive decisions (such as those permitting vernacularization of the liturgy), but the way in which it was conducted (according to principles of democracy) and the circumstances in which it was conceived (by an 'unconventional' Pope just three months after his election), all pointed in the direction of a growing awareness that the Church would have to pay a price in terms of a greater acceptance of heterodoxy if it was to retain influence in a rapidly changing world. Indicative of this changed outlook, then, were signs of a growing willingness on the part of some Church intellectuals to explore what common ground there might be between Catholic social teaching and political ideas inspired by communism and the left; an increasing number of clergymen willing to question publicly the principle of the political unity of Catholics around the DC, and a tendency of the Vatican to make its views on Italian political matters felt through formal diplomatic channels rather than by means of direct pressure on the DC.

Finally, on 1 December 1970, the so-called Fortuna–Baslini law (after its sponsors, the Socialist Loris Fortuna and the Liberal Antonio Baslini) made divorce legal in Italy. Not only did this touch on an issue that went to the heart of Church teaching, but the law's passage appeared to conflict with the Lateran Treaties outlawing divorce and providing that any revision of the treaties was to be undertaken only with the consent of *both* parties. If, among members of the Church, there had been any lingering faith in the capacity of the DC to act as a vehicle for the furtherance of their interests, then the divorce referendum of May 1974 forced them to recognize that by then it had become 'vain to rely on the DC to promote Church policy' (Donovan 2003: 103). For not only had the DC been unable to prevent passage of Fortuna–Baslini in the first place, but in the referendum itself, despite a vigorous campaign by most of the DC against divorce, 59.2 per cent of those casting a vote nevertheless voted against the law's abrogation. Part of the explanation of this outcome had to do with the fact that the DC was not, in fact, wholly united in its opposition to the law. This in its turn reflected a highly telling change of approach to political propaganda, one that had been forced on both the party and the Church by the growing sophistication of the voters of the economic miracle. It was a change that could be seen in the CEI's February 1974 declaration, which argued that nobody should be surprised if the clergy sought to enlighten the consciences of the faithful or if the latter sought to defend the indissolubility of marriage by making use of the referendum instrument. What was significant about this appeal was that it sought to justify its claims, not, as in the past, in terms of dogma or the authority of the Church, but in terms of the individual's conscience, and in terms of *reason*. And, if the debate was to take place on the terrain of *reason*, then this made it possible for *other* Catholics and DC members to argue, in equally rational terms, that while the indissolubility of marriage should indeed be protected and reinforced as an ideal, it was quite another matter to suggest that indissolubility should be imposed on the population by law. Significantly, then, the divorce referendum both contributed to and reflected a much less authoritative role for the Church in a world where rapid economic and social change was helping to produce voters whose outlooks were much more *critical* than those of their parents.

This willingness on the part of ordinary citizens to question and contest established values and practices was readily apparent in the trade union and industrial relations sphere at this time – indicating that the unions had overcome many of the weaknesses that had been typical of them in the 1950s. Of these, the most significant had been the ideological divisions, undermining as they did the impact of the unions as vehicles for collective bargaining, thereby contributing to low levels of union membership (see figure 5.1), and hence perpetuating the unions' organizational dependence on the parties – whose demands however, especially in the case of the CISL, often conflicted with the demands of workers' solidarity and the defence of workers' interests.

The at least partial supersession of ideological divisions was both crucial to the success of those union initiatives that contributed to the so-called hot autumn – the worker discontent that was reflected in a wave of unofficial protests beginning in 1968 that underpinned the striking successes of the CGIL-CISL-UIL in official contract nego-

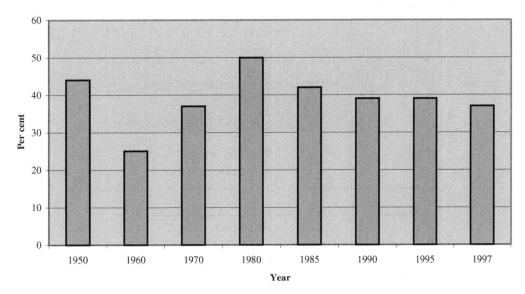

Figure 5.1   Union density, 1950–1997.
Source: Adapted from Jensen 2004: 13, table 4

tiations in the autumn of 1969, and that continued to make itself felt into the early 1970s (see figure 5.2). While bound up with the broader processes of economic and social change affecting most Western democracies at this time, the discontent was also fuelled in the Italian case by successive governments' economic growth strategies, based on openness to international competition and the assumption that international demand was to be the primary stimulus to growth. If this required low labour costs and the freedom for employers to hire and fire at will, then it also guaranteed that governments would not embark either on policies to stimulate domestic demand (which risked strengthening the labour movement and undermining the discipline of international competitive pressures) or on policies to mitigate the intense exploitation of labour that took place through the furious pace of machine operations in the factories (Lange, Ross and Vannicelli 1982: 112; Bedani 1995: 146).

The unofficial protests to which the discontent gave rise took a variety of forms, and were based on a variety of demands. What they had in common was that the demands went beyond those that the official unions had made until then; that they saw the official unions 'either pushed to the margins or forced to present to management demands decided directly at workers' assemblies over which they had little control' (Bedani 1995: 149); that they saw a breakdown, in the popular assemblies and committees, of traditional distinctions between Catholic and Communist workers – thus putting pressure on the unions to strive for unity. Practical unity came when, in advance of national contractual negotiations, 'the three metalworkers' federations, the FIM, FIOM and UILM, after the most extensive rank-and-file consultations ever witnessed, took the unprecedented step of organizing a conference at which they jointly

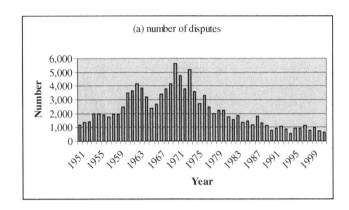

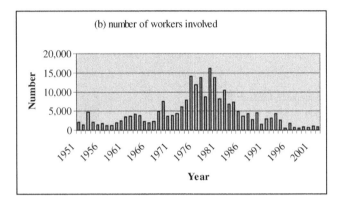

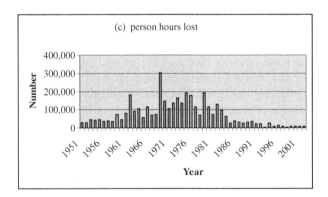

Figure 5.2 Labour disputes 1951–2001.

Source: Calculated from the figures given in ISTAT 1955a: 311, table 356; 1960a: 322, table 357; 1965a: 357, table 361; 1970a: 322, table 345; 1975a: 395, table 345; 1980a: 305, table 294; 1983a: 302, table 303; 1988a: 231, table 7.9; 1993a: 214, table 7.10; 1998a: 244–5, tables 9.12 and 9.13; 2003a: 226–7, tables 9.16 and 9.17

prepared the platform of demands they would present to the Confindustria for the whole industry' (Bedani 1995: 153). Later, a national general strike, called by the three confederations on 19 November 1969, set a number of social policy objectives for the movement in the areas of housing, health and taxes. The success of these initiatives was crucial in ensuring that the trade union confederations would emerge from the 'hot autumn' with unprecedented strength: between 1969 and 1971, membership of the CGIL and the CISL rose by 20 per cent, with union membership density peaking in 1978 at 49 per cent of the active labour force (Regalia and Regini 1998: 471); the direct forms of worker involvement and participation that had been characteristic of the 'hot autumn' enabled the unions for the first time to obtain a significant organizational presence *within* firms and on the shop floor, and although formal unification of the three confederations did not succeed, 'there was a qualitative increase in the cooperation among the unions at all levels' (Lange, Ross and Vannicelli 1982: 126).

The principal long-term consequence of the confederations' new strength was that it led to the development of a novel strategic perspective shared by the confederations – one that in its essentials remained intact throughout the 1970s and 1980s. This represented a synthesis of the traditional strategic perspective of the CGIL (with its emphasis on the union as an agent of the working class, on long-term gains applicable to all workers, and on the importance of macro-economic policy in achieving them) and that of the CISL (with its emphasis on the union as an association of its members, on immediate gains for such members, and on the factory as the arena in which to achieve them). It was based on the idea that the unions were to be active in *both* the market *and* the political arenas, exploiting their new power in the former arena to pursue objectives in the latter.

If the confederations' joint strategy thus envisaged the unions becoming a much more significant, and pro-active, player in the field of economic and industrial policy making, then this objective was achieved in part. On the one hand, the convergence of their traditional strategic outlooks initially allowed the confederations to make significant advances towards unification (1972 saw the creation of a federation of the confederations), and as both cause and consequence of this, they were able to acquire a greater degree of independence from the political parties – thus increasing their capacity to recruit and to act as an autonomous political actor in pursuit of reforms. On the other hand, they found it difficult to translate their market power 'into political power capable of changing the basic lines of government policy' (Lange, Ross and Vannicelli 1982: 139). For one thing, while they could negotiate with governments over reforms to be pursued in this or that area, such reforms then had to be passed by Parliament. And since clientelism was so much a part of the policy-making process – creating, as it did, a constellation of vested interests each with a power of veto over any proposed shifts from the *status quo* – governments' abilities to 'steer' Parliament were weak at best (see chapter 7). Second, it was impossible to translate market power into a vote-delivering capacity with which to punish enemies and reward friends: the leftward shift signalled by the 'hot autumn' did not prevent DC supporters from voting for their party as before, and certainly the confederations were in no position, on pain of sacrificing their unity, to urge their supporters to vote for this party rather than that one. Finally, the pursuit of politico-economic objectives and social change tended to create tensions and the potential for divisions within the union movement. For it soon became apparent that aggressive strategies in the market might undermine the prospects for growth needed in order to make the politico-economic objectives viable. But if this suggested the desirability of some kind of 'social contract', or a policy of 'trade-offs', with reforms to be given in exchange for austerity and sacrifice, the danger was that such an agreement inevitably had the potential to enhance the political fortunes of the party achieving it – and thus the potential to arouse the opposition of those within the union movement who retained partisan attachments to rival parties.

Just such a scenario came to pass in the mid-1980s when Craxi's PSI, wanting to enhance co-operation with labour as a means of enhancing its political fortunes, was instrumental in achieving a tripartite agreement to promote economic stability and in promoting a plan to reduce levels of wage indexation. With the CISL and the UIL, along with the CGIL Socialists, supporting the plan, and the remainder of the CGIL opposed, the result was to produce the most serious split in the trade union movement since the 1950s. By the end of the 1980s, therefore, it was apparent that if the trade unions' behaviour since the war had been subject to the drastic changes brought about by the 'hot autumn' watershed, then it was also characterized by strong continuities arising from the specific features of the political and party systems. The final section of this chapter therefore considers the implications of the party system changes of the 1990s for the processes of interest articulation carried on by the unions, as well as by the other important groups considered earlier.

THE 1990S AND THE IMPLICATIONS OF PARTY SYSTEM TRANSFORMATION

One important consequence of the changes of the 1990s was to create an apparently less hospitable environment for pressure group activity – at least as far as the trade unions were concerned. The unrest associated with the 'hot autumn' watershed resulted in four significant public policy concessions, each with major implications for levels of public expenditure: the protection of incomes, a generous pension scheme for wage earners, health services and university access (Della Sala 1997: 22). Partly (but not only) as a consequence of this (see chapter 2), the level of public debt grew at a significant rate in the years following. Consequently, when in 1991 the Italian government signed the Maastricht Treaty, it was clear that there would be considerable difficulties in meeting the convergence criteria for admission to the single currency with the first wave of countries. Awareness of these difficulties had two effects. First, since the possibility of 'missing the European train' was viewed with alarm by policy-makers and most voters, it placed governments under pressure to tackle overall spending levels with uncustomary vigour, and this allowed the State to acquire a 'harder shell' (Della Sala 1997) than it had had in the past – stronger and less permeable to the demands of societal interests and pressure groups. Second, by the same token, Maastricht and its provisions played a significant part in hastening, if not precipitating, the process of party system transformation that began and took on increasing momentum following the collapse of the Berlin Wall in October 1989. The bipolar system that has emerged from this process has arguably made its own contribution to the hardening of the State: because all parties are accepted as legitimate political actors, not only has alternation in government become possible, but in 2001 it actually took place. That voters on that occasion compared what the incumbent government had done with the proposals of its centre right challengers is one of the major findings of the Italian National Election Study (ITANES 2001: 163–4). This made it clear that 'the politics of buckpassing and outbidding [had] been superseded by the politics of accountability' (Pasquino 2004: 6). Governments that are effectively accountable to mass electorates in this way (unable to escape the full rigours of accountablity in the way that the parties of the First Republic had been able to do) are usually better placed, because of what is at stake for them, to resist the pressures of particularistic demands. One is therefore led to expect pressure groups to have had a more difficult time in influencing public policy to their liking in the period since 1990 than they did in the earlier period.

In the case of the trade unions there are three pieces of evidence that point in this direction. First, either because they were legitimized by the national economic emergency[6] or because they were directly legitimized by electoral outcomes, or both,[7] governments of the 1990s managed to secure a series of tripartite agreements that differed fundamentally from those attempted in the 1980s.[8] Unlike those of the earlier period, the agreements of the 1990s were based to a much lesser extent on social policy concessions as the price of making them stick than they were on perceptions of the existence of shared problems (Regini and Regalia 1997). As a consequence, the trade unions were under pressure to play a restraining role in relation to their members, with the result that the period saw the assertion on the part of governments of a degree of economic policy authority that they had rarely enjoyed in the past. Second, in the period after 1996, the imposition of restraining functions on the unions was considerably assisted by the fact that governments were for the first time the expression of *all* of the parties with which the three main confederations had traditionally been associated. As a result, the earlier vulnerability of the confederations to divisions arising from the divergent policies of the parties with which they were associated was effectively overcome. Third, once membership of the single currency had been secured and had thus, in effect, put an end to the 'national economic emergency', the 2001 Berlusconi government was able to take office committed to putting an end to 'concertation' and to the trade union 'veto' over economic policy making that concertation supposedly entailed. As a result, strengthened by his decisive election victory, the new Prime Minister was able to pursue labour market reforms which, by the summer of 2002, had succeeded in engineering significant new divisions between the CGIL and the two remaining confederations.[9]

For Confindustria, on the other hand, the period since 1990 has arguably brought about a climate rather *more* hospitable to the pursuit of its members' interests. There are a number of theoretical and empirical arguments that support this view. First, if business had frequently complained that there was no real industrial culture in Italy (Sassoon 1997: 143), then the 1990s saw the demise of the governing party, the DC, whose Catholic values had arguably been largely responsible for this absence.[10] Second, if one accepts the argument that states in capitalist societies are structurally dependent on capital (so that business is not required to lobby explicitly in order to influence the content of public policy but can do so merely by virtue of its routine investment decisions), then, from the end of a 'politics of buckpassing and outbidding' and the eventual emergence of a 'politics of accountability' (Pasquino 2004: 6), it follows that governments will have become more sensitive than ever to the needs of private enterprise. Third, if the years leading up to the adoption of the euro were ones in which governments were under special pressure to improve national competitiveness, then this suggests the likelihood that such governments were sensitive to the needs of private enterprise to a greater degree than is suggested by the 'structural dependency' thesis alone. Fourth, in the course of the 1990s, Italian capitalism began to move away from a model whereby enterprise finance was secured mainly through the banks and inter-locking ownership networks towards one involving a greater reliance on stock markets (see chapter 10). At the same time, interest-rate reductions were reducing the attrac-tiveness of state bonds, while pension funds were beginning to expand. The conse-quence was a notable increase in the proportion of household savings – up from 22.5 per cent in 1990 to 49.3 per cent in 1999 – that were invested in unit trusts and shares. If this in turn meant a growth in the exposure of household savings to relatively high levels of risk, then it also meant the likely emergence of significant numbers of voters with a desire to see low interest rates and high levels of enterprise profits (Della Sala 2001: 207). Fifth, the new Prime Minister, in April 2001, sought to emphasize the overlap between his own programme and that of Confindustria (Accornero and Como 2003: 239), while the industrialists' peak organization acquired a new president, Antonio D'Amato, famous for his no-nonsense, combative approach to the pursuit of business interests.

If the period since 1990 has thus seen the emergence of a Confindustria that has apparently become more aggressive in seeking to further its aims, then the Church arguably represents the mirror image of this, in that, in one respect at least, it has given up seeking to further its aims at all. As Donovan (2003b: 95) points out, the collapse of the DC and party system transformation 'obliged and enabled the Vatican finally to break its nearly 50-year-long support for Catholic party politics in Italy'. For, with the failure of the DC's principal successor party, the Italian Popular Party, to remain united, and with its remnants eventually surfacing on *both* sides of the coalitional divide in the new bipolar world of Italian party politics, it was not in the Vatican's interests to be publicly associated with one coalition to the exclusion of the other. The 1990s, therefore, saw the Vatican assume a new position *super partes*, one of non-alignment in relation to party politics.

This has meant that the Church has had to place greater reliance on alternative means of seeking to influence public policy, one of these being straightforward appeals, through its allied publications and other media, to members of the general public. In this way it has sought to champion positions in relation to bio-ethical issues, state funding of private education, immigration and opposition to war. While large pro-portions of Italians disregard, if they do not feel openly hostile towards, Church teach-ing in matters of faith and personal morals, the Vatican continues, as the millennium events demonstrated (Donovan 2003b: 96), to speak with authority, and could prob-ably influence the votes of about 15 per cent of the electorate, which is far from neg-ligible (McCarthy 2000: 148). Therefore, another way in which the Church seeks to lobby for change is by urging Catholics to support candidates who will guarantee to defend its fundamental values in matters of human dignity, economic justice and freedom, international peace and solidarity. In this way, the Church's political position eschews neutrality while continuing to be one of non-alignment. A third way in which the Church has sought to promote its policy agenda is by taking on an active role in the health, welfare and voluntary sectors. This has the potential to allow the Church to push its agenda not simply by bringing its volunteer workers into direct contact with those being treated, but more profoundly by allowing it to demonstrate 'that capitalist and public-sector economies are not the only kind and that the non-profit sector might offer new approaches to such problems as health care' (McCarthy 2000: 151).

Finally, if in the 1990s the Church gave up seeking to lobby through privileged ties with a political party, then so too did the Coltivatori Diretti. 'Feeling that it received shabby treatment from the DC because of the failure to defend it in the face of the [Tangentopoli] corruption scandal and its decreased interest in the agricultural sector, [in November 1993] the Coldiretti adamantly declared its autonomy from all political parties' (Koff and Koff 2000: 91). The DC's attitude was, perhaps, not surprising: as suggested by the continuing slide in agricultural employment – to 6.8 per cent in 1997 (ISTAT 1998: 187) – of the four major interests and associated pressure groups we have examined, the one to have declined furthest and fastest in political significance was arguably agriculture and the Coltivatori Diretti. Of far greater, and some continuing, significance in the 1990s was a rather different legacy of Italy's rural past: the Mafia. It is therefore to this and to related phenomena that we turn in the following chapter.

INFORMAL INSTITUTIONS

INTRODUCTION

Political science is paying increasing attention to the impact of so-called informal institutions on the functioning of liberal democracies. 'Informal institutions' constitute vehicles through which influence is exercised on the democratic functioning of a polity, beyond the channels of participation provided by the formal institutions of government. Examples include clientelism, corruption, the Mafia, civil disobedience, *coup* threats and other destabilizing activities. All countries have varying degrees of influence exercised by these institutions, as well as a mix of different types, and they should not be overlooked, since 'without the inclusion of informal institutions, the analysis of a democracy remains incomplete' (Lauth 2000: 45).

The Italian case is very pertinent in this regard, for two reasons. First, there is a long-standing historical debate focused on the disputed existence of a 'parallel' or 'dual' state. Several authors argue that Italian democracy was effectively subverted in the period until the early 1990s by the occult, illegal and undemocratic activities of the secret services and other groups, aimed at preventing the PCI from ever coming to power (e.g. Cucchiarelli and Giannuli 1997; Tranfaglia 1997; Silj 1994; Dossi 2001). This thesis is rejected by others for being politically motivated and based largely on conspiracy theories, or *dietrologia* (e.g. Bedeschi 2002; Battista 2002; Sabbatucci 1999). Second there is a wide consensus on the significance of the Mafia, clientelism and corruption in the development of the post-war Republic.

This chapter therefore assesses the role played by informal institutions in Italian post-war politics by analysing two broad and overlapping groupings in the period between the 1940s and the end of the 1980s: first, the secret services, terrorism and international penetration; and second, clientelism, corruption and the Mafia. In a final section, the chapter then assesses the extent to which the role of informal institutions may have changed and declined in the watershed period since the early 1990s.

THE SECRET SERVICES, TERRORISM, AND INTERNATIONAL PENETRATION, 1940s–1980s

The Cold War and 'dual loyalty'

The Cold War had a significant impact on Italy because of the country's geo-political strategic importance and the presence of the largest Communist party in the West. The Americans felt that Italy represented Moscow's best hope of dividing NATO. With the exclusion of the PCI and the PSI from the government of 'national solidarity' in 1947, the anti-fascist pact was effectively shattered, and Italian politics became ideologically polarized around the Communist threat (see chapter 1). For the governing political class (around the Christian Democrats), it created what De Felice (1989) has defined as a situation of 'dual loyalty' (*doppia lealtà*): to the 1948 Constitution, on the one hand, and the Atlantic Alliance, on the other. As long as there was a possibility of the PCI legally coming to power, the two loyalties remained fundamentally incompatible, and provided the rationale for unconstitutional actions on the part of elements of the political class and state bureaucracy. The polarization penetrated deep into Italian society. Former President of the Republic Francesco Cossiga described it as 'an invisible iron curtain, cutting across people, classes and consciences', and creating 'two political realities, civil and moral, two political communities, almost two nations' (quoted in Fasanella et al. 2000: 10–11). The two political communities, moreover, were internally divided. There were members of the DC who wished to have the PCI outlawed, while the PCI contained an orthodox Marxist faction (around Pietro Secchia) still committed to overthrow of the State.

In this situation, important and secret developments began to take place. The PCI, assisted by Soviet support, built up a defensive structure for use in the event of a *coup d'état* or being outlawed. The party housed a clandestine structure (the so-called Gladio rossa), which had developed out of the 'red' partisan movement and the arms it still possessed, and whose members received assistance and training in Czechoslovakia and the Soviet Union. The party was assisted by the provision of millions of dollars by the Soviet Union between the late 1940s and the 1980s, when it was redirected towards Armando Cossutta's pro-Soviet faction. The funding was supplemented by a tax levied on companies doing business with Moscow. The PCI, in fact, received more funding than any other Western communist party (Fasanella et al. 2000: 35–6).

On the other side, the Italian secret services, in conjunction with some former 'white' partisans, set up a secret organization called Gladio, as part of NATO's post-war strategy of creating 'stay-behind' forces in European countries (to become operable in the event of a Soviet invasion). The members were trained (many by the British intelligence services) in information gathering, sabotage, communications and the hiding of arms caches. However, whatever its original *raison d'être*, Gladio and the United States became concerned more with the electoral threat of the PCI than the possibility of a Soviet invasion, thus prompting the establishment of other clandestine organizations as the perceived threat became greater. Italy became the target for the largest covert political action programme in the CIA's history. Covert operations were planned in the event of the PCI coming to power (De Lutiis 1996: ch. 1), and these were given massive financial support. Between 1945 and 1966 the CIA provided more than $65 million in financial assistance to non-communist parties in Italy, mainly the DC. The programme of funding was renewed in 1971, to the tune of $11.5 million, and (to the consternation of the CIA) placed under the direction of the then American ambassador to Rome, Graham Martin, where much of it went directly to the Italian secret services. A further $2 million was sanctioned in the mid-1980s (Silj 1994: 171–2; Willan 1991: 114–15).

There is sufficient evidence to suggest that the two underworlds were aware of each other's activities, but there was a mutual reluctance to expose their clandestine operations because of the likely consequences: an outlawing of the PCI and a damaging civil war. Both worlds were also aware that, with Italy's location in NATO, a communist *coup* was not really feasible. A delicate balance was therefore maintained, based on a mutual fear of the consequences that might follow from bringing the conflict of the two subterranean worlds into the open (Fasanella et al. 2000: 38 and 53–4).[1] Knowledge of these activities beyond the two worlds, however, was not widespread, and the subterranean worlds themselves were small. The PCI's democratic centralism ensured that the relevant information was restricted to the most senior personnel only, while the Italian parliament was kept in the dark about Gladio for forty years. It was only in 1990 – in response to a parliamentary motion from the left demanding that the government report on an 'an occult, parallel structure that allegedly operated within our military secret service with the aim of influencing the political life of the country' – that Prime Minister Andreotti admitted its existence. Until then, those in power had constantly denied knowledge of it, despite evidence that had emerged in judicial and parliamentary investigations and other studies.[2] The secret services decided which politicians should be informed and how much they should be told, something which was done on quite an arbitrary basis, depending on the dependability and likely curiosity of those holding the relevant offices of state.[3] In fact, few politicians who were informed considered it necessary to ask for further explanations, and Gladio was, therefore, largely uncontrolled throughout the post-war period.

This murky anti-Communist underworld (Gladio, other clandestine organizations, elements of the state security apparatus) established links with organizations of the extreme right, which would be responsible for the strategy of tension and terrorist atrocities in the late 1960s and early 1970s. They were to be assisted by covert American funding provided through Ambassador George Martin, who delegated most of the funding to top individuals in the Italian secret services with close links to right-wing extremist organizations. This relationship of the security services with the far right was, in some ways, not surprising. It reflected the emergence by the mid-1960s of a general 'cultural *milieu*' comprising a mix of leaders of the armed forces, the political class, the judiciary and some industrial sectors, all of whom were subject to a conflict of loyalties.

In short, when the Constitution's anti-fascist basis was undermined by the Cold War, there emerged a 'white' (moderate) form of anti-communism alongside the traditional 'black' (fascist). The launch of the Italian Social Movement, a barely disguised party for former Fascists, combined with the halt in the purging of state personnel, provided a pool of reliable recruits to indulge in activities to combat communism. Black and white anti-communism would be brought together by developments in the 1960s, rendering unstable the delicate balance between the two underworlds.

The strategy of tension

The origins of the strategy of tension lay, paradoxically, in the international trend toward *détente* in the late 1950s. This had its expression in Italy in the 'opening to the left' (the entry of the PSI into government). Military circles began to fear the new climate, and forged closer links with the extreme right. The strategy was predicated on the basis of spreading a climate of fear (through indiscriminate terrorist attacks), to provide a perceived necessity for a restoration of public order, either through a *coup* or through the political consequences following from an awareness by politicians of preparations for a *coup*.

The *Piano Solo coup* plot of 1964 was the first of several planned undemocratic attempts to manipulate the Italian political system. Based on the paramilitary police and the head of the *Carabinieri*, General De Lorenzo, the plot included plans to round up left-wing politicians and place them in concentration camps in Sardinia, one of which (Capo Marrargiu) was the official training centre for Gladio. The *coup* was not carried out, but this should not necessarily be interpreted as a failure, since there were disagreements over the desired outcome of the *coup* preparations. While hardliners saw the logical outcome as a *coup* itself, others were more interested in subtly using the threat of a *coup* (an *intentona*) to produce a change in government composition, and this in fact occurred (Fasanella et al. 2000: 48–52; Willan 1991: 35–6).[4]

In the period 1968–70 there was recourse to violence through several indiscriminate bombings, including the Piazza Fontana bombing in Milan, which caused twelve deaths. These were prompted by the high levels of government instability (the centre left formula was effectively viewed as exhausted in 1968), the electoral defeat of the United Socialist Party (PSU, an attempt to forge a strong but moderate social democratic party[5]), and the rise of student and worker militancy. This phase came to an end with a *coup* plot organized by the right-wing Fronte Nazionale (led by Valerio Borghese) in December 1970, the *coup* being called off at the last moment, possibly by national or international figures above Borghese. The event marked a turning point in the perceptions of the secret services and those elements bent on undemocratically conditioning the direction of Italian democracy. In Pellegrino's words (Fasanella et al. 2000: 72):

from that moment onwards, a very clear message reached all of the diverse and, at times, conflict-ridden underworld: that Italy was not like Greece, but a country which could count on a substantial political left that was deeply-rooted in society. In short, it was not military force, but more refined plans of institutional modification, to which one should turn to achieve a change in the political 'balance'.

What followed, therefore, was an operation by the secret services and state security apparatus to break its links with right-wing terrorist groups, with a view to shifting the strategy of tension on to a new, less violent, level. This proved more difficult than expected, since several of the groups were not inclined to renounce their tactics. The violent bombing campaign and *coup* plots (e.g. by Rosa dei Venti, Sogno, Fumagalli) that followed in the early 1970s were, therefore, in large part a form of refusal by right-wing terrorists to renounce the original strategy of tension (some of their targets, in fact, being the *Carabinieri*). Judicial investigations of these crimes were subsequently hindered, sabotaged or blocked (by use of 'state secret' arguments) by members of the security services, anxious to protect the secrecy of their clandestine anti-Communist networks and the links that had formerly been established with the right-wing terrorist groups.

The mid-1970s witnessed a final turning point in the abandonment of the idea of a *coup* or *coup* threat, in the context of a changing international situation. With the fall of the Portuguese and Greek authoritarian regimes and the weakening of the Nixon–Kissinger axis (as a consequence of the Watergate scandal), the CIA and US administration began to rethink the wisdom of supporting far right authoritarian regimes. In Italy, the head of the secret services, General Maletti, was replaced, and (by his own later admission) Andreotti explicitly reminded the secret services of their duty of loyalty to the Constitution, and indicated that a change in their activities had to occur.

The new climate provided a context for the growth in influence of the secret Masonic lodge, P2, under its head, Licio Gelli. Gelli had long-term close links with the secret services, and various investigations have revealed evidence linking the P2 to right-wing terrorist organizations. The membership of the P2 included politicians from all the main political parties (except the PCI and the Radicals); cabinet ministers and former ministers; senior members of the police, air force, navy, army and judiciary; the heads of the secret services; several managers of banks and public companies; and senior civil servants. There were in total over 400 employees of the public administration, most of them at a senior level, amounting to a significant and widespread presence of the Masonic lodge in the state apparatus.[6] The lodge, in Pellegrino's words (Fasanella et al. 2000: 115–16), became a 'refuge for "Atlantic extremism"'. Its members were made up of a mix of former *golpisti* (those who had earlier been in favour of a *coup* or *intentona*), and more generally those who were passionately committed to the anti-Communist imperative of the Atlantic Alliance.

Under Gelli, the P2 became the main protagonist of the new phase of the strategy of tension (which ended in 1981 with the exposure of the P2 and its membership list). Gelli's strategy was based on a 'Plan for Democratic Renewal'. This was predicated on the notion that Italy was undergoing a crisis that could provoke a *coup*, and that the best alternative to this scenario was an institutional modification of the Republic, essentially along Gaullist – but also technocratic – lines. While many of the proposals in the plan were not necessarily undemocratic, if undoubtedly right-wing in nature, the means to implement the plan revealed the fundamentally undemocratic intentions of its drafters. Instead of military force, financial means and corruption were to be used to begin a process of infiltrating and gaining control of the mass media, the political parties and the state apparatus more generally, and of marginalizing the influence of left-wing parties and the trade unions. Effectively, therefore, it aimed, in former Prime Minister Giovanni Spadolini's words, at 'the overthrow of our system, through its undermining and control from within' (quoted in Silj 1994: 225).

The process was to be assisted by measures that helped to keep the Italian political system in a situation of instability and tension. It was for this reason that, as black terrorism became more sporadic, red terrorism (which developed from the early 1970s) was seen as potentially useful through its effect of spreading fear. There is evidence to suggest that the Red Brigades (BR) may have been infiltrated by the secret services with the aim of manipulating their activities (Willan 1991; Tranfaglia 1997). Certainly, it is undeniable that the response of the authorities to several atrocities was grossly – and suspiciously – inadequate. After the capture of BR leaders Renato Curcio and Alberto Franceschini in the mid-1970s, the organization was on the verge of destruction; yet, instead of the security services striking a final blow, the group was allowed to reorganize itself.[7] This suggests that, even if the red terrorists were not being manipulated, their continued activities were useful to those seeking to shift the political axis in a rightwards direction. The response of the authorities to the kidnapping of the DC leader Aldo Moro in 1978 fitted this pattern.[8] Moro stood for everything the right fiercely opposed: reaching an agreement with the PCI that would see the party's entry into government. Moro had originally (from outside government in the late 1960s) dubbed this the 'strategy of caution' (*strategia dell'attenzione*). Later he described it as the Republic's 'third phase' (after the first two phases: the DC and its centrist allies; the centre left), while the PCI (under Enrico Berlinguer) used the term 'Historic Compromise' for its own analogous strategy. However coined, it can be viewed as a response to the strategy of tension (Fasanella et al. 2000: 107–8). Moro was kidnapped by the BR on his way to Parliament on the morning that a new government, with Communist support, was to be announced. He was found fifty-five days later murdered in the back of a car left in a street equidistant between the PCI and DC headquarters. His policy towards the PCI effectively died with him. Moro's kidnap witnessed a catalogue of errors and a level of incompetence on the part of the State, the dimensions of which suggested that there were influential elements within the state apparatus with an interest in Moro not returning. The failure to secure Moro's release was made all the more glaring when the secret services subsequently made Mafia-style bargains to negotiate the release of more minor political figures.[9]

There is sufficient evidence to indicate a foreign (and especially US) presence behind much of the 'secret politics' of the Republic, but its exact nature and extent remain obscure (Bull 1992: 477). Recent research has suggested that, while the Americans were concerned about the size and influence of the PCI, and were prepared to take measures to reduce that influence, they did not think that the Yalta settlement was in danger, even in the event of the PCI coming to power.[10] The Americans also did not consider a Communist *coup* in Italy as ever being realistic. Yet, there were other American interests at stake concerning the Mediterranean, which cut across the Communist question, and which engaged other countries too, including Britain, France, Germany and Israel. Italian foreign policy, although generally low key, tended to sway between being pro-European and pro-Mediterranean (in the sense of pro-Arab), and moves towards making foreign policy more dynamic took the form of a more activist Mediterranean component. The Italian government in the late 1960s and early 1970s had ambitions to become a much more central player in this arena, and other countries feared that an overly activist Italian Mediterranean policy might threaten their interests. For example, there is little doubt that both American and British interests suffered directly from the Ghedaffi *coup* in Libya in 1969, which Italy supported in order to expand its influence in that zone. Consequently, for these countries it was useful to keep Italy in a state of instability and tension: a faithful ally, but not one that would become too strong, independent and active in the Mediterranean area. The North–South (Mediterranean) issue therefore overlaid the East–West (Communist) question.

Whether or not they were aware of it, the diverse national elements that engaged in the strategy of tension for reasons of anti-communism were, at the same time, also serving certain international geo-political interests.[11]

Clientelism, corruption and the Mafia, 1940s–1980s

Clientelism and corruption

Clientelism was a long-established feature of Italian political culture, which was particularly prevalent in the south, where patron–client relations became established after Unification. This was an important explanation behind the failure of the south to undergo socio-economic modernization (Graziano 1980) (see chapter 11). Clientelism in the post-war period, however, developed in a different form. The 1950s witnessed a rapid decline in the importance of agriculture, and therefore in the clientelistic power of the southern landowners. Traditional clientelism was transformed into bureaucratic and political clientelism, under the aegis of the Christian Democratic Party (DC), which, confronted with an ideologically hostile but large Communist party, wished to expand its social base and consolidate its position of power (see chapter 2).

The new clientelism had two interrelated facets. The first was the replacement of the southern notables with the political parties (and especially the DC) as the 'mediators' between citizens and the State (Gribaudi 1991). Their role was made possible by the introduction of universal suffrage in the specific economic circumstances of the south in the immediate post-war period, where many of the inhabitants were extremely poor and dependent on the State for industrialization and development (Allum 1973b: 166). The second was the expansion of the state sector of the economy and the politicization of the new state agencies on the basis of a 'sharing out' (*lottizzazione*) between different parties and factions according to their relative bargaining power.

Clientelism allowed the governing class to use state economic resources in order to win consent and hold on to power. McCarthy (1995: 62) defines it as 'the attainment and retention of power through the private expropriation of public resources, and through the use of the state to expropriate private resources'. Clientelism conditioned the political practices of the Italian Republic; indeed, it became effectively a system of rule operated by the governing parties. Its significance lies in the fact that it represents a denial of the value of universalism. It constitutes a form of protective relationship based on a 'personalized use of power' and an individualistic exchange for mutual benefit between patron and client. It therefore undermines the principles of modern democracy by transforming 'rights' into 'favours' (consideration of the individual), so undermining confidence in institutionalized authority and reinforcing the use of arbitrary power (Graziano 1980: 53; De Bernardi 1994: 86) (see chapter 1). Some of the consequences of this system have been explored in other chapters. It helped to ensure the persistence in government of the DC with its allies over a fifty-year period (chapters 1 and 7); it produced grave distortions in economic policy, especially in the south (chapters 2 and 11); it helped cause bureaucratic and state inefficiency and maladministration (chapters 8 and 10); and it also laid the basis for the development and spread of corruption.

Della Porta and Vannucci (1999a: 255–65) outline three 'vicious circles' involving corruption and, respectively, maladministration, clientelism and the Mafia. Maladministration increases the demand for corruption; clientelism increases its supply; and organized crime reinforces the stability of corrupt exchanges, since the threat of violence can be used to underwrite illegal deals. Corruption itself facilitates the emergence of different forms of behaviour and new norms that help to reinforce existing pathologies of the political system. It also embodies its own self-generating dynamic, since there is an inverse relationship between the extent of corruption and the risks associated with it. On the one hand, attempting to bribe in a society where corruption is already widespread carries fewer risks than in a society in which it is rare, of provoking moral outrage and being reported to the authorities. On the other hand, 'where there is corruption the non-corrupt are led to collude with it, or at least accept it, in order to obtain political advantage' (Della Porta and Vannucci 1999a: 10). The moral threshold thus drops, since corruption is seen as increasingly acceptable if everyone else appears to be indulging in it. It was this dynamic which allowed corruption in Italy to feed on itself.

The dynamic was reinforced by several other factors, which acted as catalysts to the growth of corruption (Newell and Bull 2003: 38–43): a reduction in income flows to the parties (through a decline in provision from the US and the Soviet Union, combined with the outlawing of donations from public sector companies in 1974); the rising costs of campaigning and politics generally; a decline in the level of ideological conflict between the DC and PCI, and the development of *consociativismo* (see chapter 7), which allowed inclusion of the Opposition in illegal financing; the direct running of state agencies by politicians to increase their control over public funds; private entrepreneurs' growing lack of trust in the efficiency and impartiality of public action in a context of legislative uncertainty and administrative inefficiency; and changes to the parties themselves (notably to the PSI), with the rise of the so-called business politician (see chapter 3).

The combination of these factors caused corruption to spread in the 1970s and 1980s with a rapidity such that it came eventually to infect 'every sector of the state, local, and central administrations, public agencies and enterprises, the military apparatus, and the bureaucracy, including the judicial power' (Della Porta and Vannucci 1999a: 15). Corruption, and especially the payment of *tangenti* (bribes) by entrepreneurs to political parties in order to secure public works contracts, came to be the accepted mode of operation for most participants. It thus came to operate in a systematic and routine manner, despite the breathtaking sums of money that were involved and the complex channels that were often used in order to transfer them (Barbacetto et al. 2002).

Corruption's self-generating dynamic means that 'corruption *in* a democracy is always the corruption *of* a democracy, something not true of other political systems' (Della Porta and Vannucci 1999a: 10). In Italy, by the late 1980s, it had undermined the formal mechanisms of Italian democracy by introducing a competing 'parallel' set of illicit rules and practices – ones more powerful than those of the State, that became the 'real' norms: 'Those occupying the principal public roles moved around easily within this pervasive system of hidden exchange, legislating and directing the affairs of the state and of public entities ... At the same time, they acted as guarantors for the functioning of the illegal market, which directed every public action of any economic importance' (Della Porta and Vannucci 1999a: 15).

Mafia

The Mafia originated in the far south of Italy because it was a society characterized by strong notions of 'self-help' (i.e. with little reliance on formal organizations), peripheral from the national culture and characterized by a relative absence of state power (either through inability or unwillingness). Relationships tended to be clientelistic in nature, and the State effectively delegated authority to private organizations. It originally developed as a form of private power, offering protection of persons and property and the general maintenance of public order within a given territorial location.[12]

In order to maintain this power, it developed certain distinctive attributes. These included a 'code of honour' (the central aspect of which forbade giving information to the public authorities), to which the *mafioso* owed absolute allegiance, a private monopoly of violence and instrumental friendship (i.e. based on an exchange of resources). The traditional Mafia, therefore, was an overt form of private authority that obtained honour and respect through its maintenance of public order (Hobsbawm 1971; Catanzaro 1985, 1988).

After its suppression by Fascism, the Mafia resurfaced during the war for liberation, assisted by the Americans, who used it to prepare the invasion of Sicily and help run many municipalities once the occupation was completed (Lewis 1984: ch. 1; Silj 1994: 3–13). It set its sights on quickly regaining control of the land. Yet circumstances had changed dramatically, with the rise of peasant and leftist movements demanding land ownership. The agrarian reform of 1950 marked a defeat for the Mafia in this respect, since the land lost its key economic and social function. This defeat was combined with the rapid eclipse by the DC of the parties which the Mafia had earlier decided to support (separatists, liberals, monarchists), and, during the 1950s, the commencement of the party's clientelistic strategy in the south, based on new economic and welfare policies (see chapter 2).

The Mafia therefore quickly shifted its allegiance to the DC, and set about exploiting the new social and economic programmes through collusion with politicians and administrative officials.[13] The emergence of political and bureaucratic clientelism caused a transformation in the Mafia. Clientelism served the DC primarily to secure votes, and this meant bartering with whomever could deliver them. In Sicily this meant the Mafia, and so the party's alliance with it was 'not an aberration but rather a logical, if extreme, extension of clientelism' (McCarthy 1995: 63). With this relationship in place, the Mafia, in the late 1950s, gradually abandoned the countryside for the cities, where the economic boom and demographic revolution were creating new opportunities for collusion and exploitation: the construction industry; transport; provision of water; control of tobacco, petrol, drugs and so on.

When, in the early 1970s, the construction boom came to an end, the Mafia moved into two lucrative markets which transformed the organization's wealth and power (Arlacchi 1988; 1996: 88–9). The first was international drug trafficking, in which, by 1980, Sicily was producing 30 per cent of the heroin sold on the American market.

The second was public works contracts. This required collusion with public officials and entrepreneurs, and often involved a contract being awarded to a 'clean' business, but on the understanding that subcontracts were subsequently awarded to Mafia-controlled companies. Exploiting public works contracts became more important as the Sicilian share in the American heroin market declined, and by the mid-1980s the main Sicilian family (the Corleonesi) was making more profits from this than from the drugs trade. The 1970s also witnessed a form of territorial expansion, through the rapid growth of two existing Mafia groups on the mainland: the 'ndrangheta based in Calabria and the Camorra in Naples. These groups used a similar mix of activities to secure their wealth and power: protection rackets, bribery and extortion, exploitation of public works contracts, and the smuggling of arms and drugs.

The extraordinary increase in illicit activity in the 1970s and 1980s turned Mafia families into major international enterprises. Their power was so complete that all business contracts relating to their areas added 15 per cent for the 'Mafia risk'. Their wealth, if estimates were accurate, made the Mafia bigger than Exxon, at the time the largest American corporation listed in *Fortune 500*. This success caused a transformation of the Mafia as an organization.[14] Its function of mediation was effectively replaced by one of capital accumulation; its former rigid territorial divisions became less relevant; it became an *occult* power, in stark contrast with the former 'man of honour'; it became a more formally structured organization;[15] and it was run increasingly by a new breed of *mafiosi* who were willing to use violence against each other to regulate competition amongst groups for the new economic opportunities.

Yet, perhaps more important than these factors was the transformation that occurred in the Mafia's relationship to political power. Traditionally the Mafia's success had been predicated on an *absence* of the State in the Italian southern periphery. The State had effectively delegated to the Mafia the task of maintaining social and political order (Arlacchi 1996: 89). Mafia leaders exerted considerable political influence, and in exchange for ensuring the election of the majority of the Sicilian members of Parliament, they received favours and protection.[16] Indeed, some politicians were 'Men of Honour' themselves, and subject therefore to a form of dual loyalty, 'to the Mafia and to democratic institutions' (Arlacchi, 1995: 160).

This was a largely stable relationship whose main focus was local (Sicilian) politics. However, with the change in the Mafia's activities, a more covert and tense relationship developed with politicians. As the traditional delegation of 'community' functions by the State became redundant, the Mafia sought influence with political power to maintain its illicit activities. Local Sicilian politics and the Mafia became completely interpenetrated, personified in the career of Vito Ciancimino, who became mayor of Palermo in 1970 (Chubb 1982: 149). This also led to greater involvement of the national political level, anxious to protect its interests, and therefore 'the emergence of an evenly matched confrontation between leaders of Cosa Nostra and national political figures' (Arlacchi 1996: 91). Giulio Andreotti was the foremost politician in this regard, his faction being represented in Sicily by the son of a *mafioso*, Salvo Lima. Like Ciancimino, Lima built up a powerful clientelistic machine through which the Mafia was obliged to work in order to advance its interests.

The effective withdrawal of the State's 'delegated' power meant that Mafia power was no longer 'legitimated' by the State, and this destabilized the relationship, making it potentially more confrontational. The Mafia's economic clout and political autonomy grew, but it was now exposed to the possibility of the State taking a more aggressive stance towards it if the climate of opinion began to place pressure on governments and the judicial authorities to act. The Mafia's response was to develop much closer relations with secret Masonic lodges, which provided new avenues for covert activities, money and the exercise of professional violence (Silj 1994: 400–2; Arlacchi 1996: 92–3), and it also began to focus its violence on public figures responsible for judicial or political anti-Mafia operations (*delitti eccellenti*). The Mafia, in short, was prepared to use violence or the threat of violence to maintain its privileged relationship with political power.

Until the 1980s, the State's response to the Mafia problem was, perhaps unsurprisingly, minimal. It amounted to the convening of parliamentary commissions, which spent years analysing an abundance of information, but which concluded with little prescription and conveniently overlooked the collusion of politicians in fostering the Mafia's growth.[17] This changed after the death in 1982 of General dalla Chiesa, who, after having been given the task of defeating the Mafia, was not provided with the special resources and powers he repeatedly requested, and was then murdered after only four months in post (Stille 1996: 64–71). This provoked a massive civil protest that prompted the government into action. Assisted by the first break in the Mafia code of *omertà* (when Mafia leader, Tomasso Buscetta, arrested in 1984, decided to turn state's witness), the government initiated a major anti-Mafia operation, under the general leadership of the public prosecutors Giovanni Falcone and Paolo Borsellino. This resulted in the so-called maxi-trial, at which 474 Sicilians were tried, including almost the entire Mafia leadership.

Yet, by the late 1980s it was evident that the operation had not achieved the expected impact. Despite securing more than 300 guilty verdicts, many of the convicted were released on appeal, the trials had became discredited through delaying tactics, and there were accusations of surreptitious attempts to derail police and judicial investigations. Finally, the anti-Mafia team of prosecutors was wound up (Sabetti 1990). The Mafia presence in Italy was, by the end of the 1980s, as strong as ever, and its ties with political power still intact.

REGAINING SOVEREIGNTY FROM INFORMAL INSTITUTIONS SINCE THE EARLY 1990s

To summarize the period between the 1940s and the late 1980s, the development of informal institutions in Italy exemplified the dangers which theoretical analyses of these institutions have highlighted. In situations where a number of informal institutions emerge together there develops a self-reinforcing logic, with far-reaching consequences for democracy. The sovereignty of the State, the rule of law and democratic processes generally are all undermined. Citizens' trust in formal norms and institutions is affected, thus hindering the development of a civic culture. In this way, young democracies can develop into defective or poorly functioning democracies (Lauth 2000: 45).

Italian politics generated a set of informal institutions that became more expansive and mutually reinforcing over time. The 'domain of covert power' was extensive, the different actors (the secret services, the political and administrative class, conspirators, terrorists, bankers, entrepreneurs, *mafiosi*, overseas actors) constituting a distinctive milieu, which was partially, loosely and unsystematically co-ordinated through the influence of Lico Gelli and the P2. The practices of these different actors (manipulation, clientelism, corruption) reinforced a trend towards 'cryptogovernment' (Bobbio 1980: 200), where important public decisions were taken outside the arena of formal democratic institutions (Della Porta and Vannicelli 1999a: 165–75). These informal institutions engaged the participation of a substantial part of the political class responsible for the management of formal institutions, a consequence of the existence of a situation of 'dual loyalty'. There is sufficient evidence that these informal institutions influenced and conditioned the development of Italian democracy, suggesting that the formal political system had 'limited sovereignty' in the period between the 1940s and the late 1980s. How much sovereignty has been regained since the early 1990s?

The period since the early 1990s has witnessed a decline in the influence of informal institutions, even though the importance of their continuing presence should not be underestimated. The Communist threat, which had been used to justify the collusion of the political class with anti-democratic elements, ended in the early 1990s. In fact, anti-communism had been losing its credibility during the 1980s, as the international situation changed (see chapter 1). The more explicit secret service activities of the 1970s had gradually given way to those characterized more by corruption and irregular financing. Anti-communism remained their justification, but they increasingly took on a life of their own, fuelled by the need for power and influence. The CAF axis (see chapter 3) was symptomatic of this state of affairs. Both the DC and PSI had become dependent upon corruption to survive in power, and both continued to use the anti-Communist card. However, the collapse of the Berlin Wall and the transformation of the PCI into a non-communist party of the left definitively ended the question, perhaps best symbolized in 1996 when the former Communist Party entered government. The end of the Cold War also led to the public exposure of the Gladio network and the creation of various parliamentary commissions (or continuation of those begun in the 1980s) investigating various informal institutions: *coup* plots, the Mafia, the P2, the Moro affair and the manipulation of terrorism. In short, in the course of the 1990s the conditioning effect of anti-communism on the Italian polity evaporated. While the secret services remained active on various fronts, the necessity to engage in secret plots and collude with external interlocutors in order to fight the Communist menace became largely a thing of the past.

The end of the Communist question was one of a concatenation of several factors that lay behind the dramatic collapse of the DC's 'party regime' in the early 1990s. Another of those factors was the exposure of corruption and the Mani Pulite ('Clean Hands') campaign by Italian magistrates. Indeed, it is difficult to separate the exposure of corruption in that period from broader changes to the political system, since what occurred was the collapse of a *system* of corruption. The 'vicious circles' of corruption outlined earlier are inherently fragile and prone to violent crises, because they cannot produce legitimacy and stability for the political system over the long term. Under these circumstances, a combination of external factors and internal actors can, if the timing is right, play a role in setting in motion a 'virtuous circle' which can cause the collapse of the system of corruption (Della Porta and Vannucci 1999a: 265–72).

This is what occurred in Italy, where external factors (the ending of the Communist question, economic recession, the signing of the Maastricht Treaty, the rise of new protest movements, the 1992 electoral defeat of the governing parties) changed the climate and encouraged the judicial investigators to deepen their investigations. The investigations proved immensely popular, something which prevented the politicians from using tactics they had until then employed to curb judicial investigative power and maintain a wall of silence, and there was a chain reaction of entrepreneurs arriving at the public prosecutors' doors to reveal all. The result was a spectacular collapse in legitimacy of the political class, the arrest of thousands of politicians and entrepreneurs, the ending of the political careers of most of the influential members of the political class, and the electoral and organizational disintegration of the main parties of government. The most significant impact on the political system occurred in the two years 1992–3, which are popularly associated with Mani Pulite. However, the arrests, court cases and convictions continued for a decade, with some still ongoing. By March 2002, ten years after the first arrest, 4,520 persons had been subject to investigation; 3,200 of them had been issued with *avvisi di garanzia* (an official warning that they were under formal investigation); and 1,121 had received definitive sentences (Barbacetto et al. 2002: 704–5).

The collapse of the system of corruption put the Mafia's position in jeopardy. There was exposure of Mafia involvement with politicians in corruption in the south, the loss of political protection (with the DC and the PSI under immense pressure), and a consequent resurgence in anti-Mafia action on the part of the State (Jamieson 2000). The murders, between March and July 1992, of Salvo Lima, Giovanni Falcone and Paolo Borsellino marked a watershed in the relationship between the Mafia and politics. Lima's murder was interpreted as punishment for the DC having failed to secure the nullification of the maxi-trial on procedural grounds, and marked the ending of high-level collusion with the DC.[18] The murders of Falcone and Borsellino, the architects of the maxi-trial, marked the beginning of a new aggressive strategy of all-out war against the State now that the Mafia's political protection was unravelling. The State inaugurated a vigorous anti-Mafia campaign, quickly passing many of the tough anti-Mafia measures that Falcone and Borsellino had been demanding for several years. Some astounding results were achieved, including the break-up of various criminal organizations, the arrest of leading *mafiosi* who had been on the run for years (including Totò Riina, head of the Mafia in Sicily, and Carmine Alfieri, head of the Neapolitan Camorra), and the sequestering of illegal assets. This campaign was assisted by a strengthening of the laws assisting *pentiti* (those turning state's witness), with a consequent increase in *mafiosi* prepared to expose their relationships with politicians, entrepreneurs, magistrates and police officials. These revelations confirmed the existence of a system of corruption in the south similar to that exposed in the north, except that the former had included the Mafia as a participant.[19]

The Mafia, therefore, although not defeated, is experiencing considerable difficulties (Paoli 2001). Most of the family heads have been arrested, and some of those in prison have indicated the possibility of dissociating themselves from the cause. The long-standing links between the Mafia and politics have been exposed, making relationships between politicians and 'men of honour' much more risky than in the past. Many of the Mafia's financial assets have been sequestered, and its income has been affected by a reduction in the extent of its control of the international drugs market, as drug refineries have increasingly been established in the areas of drug origin (as opposed to the drugs being refined in Sicily). This has increased the importance of territorial areas of control and the exploitation of public resources. Yet, public expenditure going to the south has been drastically curtailed as a consequence of the ending of special intervention there in the early 1990s (see chapter 11). Finally, the internal codes of the organization have been severely shaken by the significant breach in *omertà* that has occurred. In the period until the 1990s, there were very few (albeit significant) *pentiti* (e.g. Tommaso Buscetta, Salvatore Contorno, Francesco Marino Mannoia, Antonio Calderone). Since 1992, however, over a thousand *mafiosi* have agreed to collaborate with justice.

Nevertheless, if the influence of clientelism, corruption and the Mafia has undoubtedly declined in the past decade (largely as a consequence of more resolute state action), the long-term significance of these changes remains to be seen. After the intensity of the 'Clean Hands' campaign in its first few years, there has been a gradual shift in the debate and the balance of power between the judiciary and the politicians, to the clear advantage of the latter. In the early 1990s, the members of the judiciary had been hailed as heroes rooting out a corrupt political class. However, their anti-corruption campaign was so extensive and ended so many political careers that the new (and partly recycled) political class (perhaps fearing for its own future survival) began to question the value of the continued corruption investigations, as well as the motives of the judiciary. More generally, politicians raised the question of the dangers for Italian democracy of such an active judiciary, and wished to reassert the autonomy of the political sphere. In this, they were assisted by a waning of popular enthusiasm and interest in revelations about corruption, and by the fact that the most prominent new member of the political class, Silvio Berlusconi, was under investigation for corruption himself. The charges against him included money laundering, links with the Mafia, tax evasion and bribery (Lane 2004). His becoming Prime Minister in 1994 and 2001 has reinforced the clash between the judiciary and the political class, and raised it to a major institutional level. Berlusconi and his party view the allegations against him and his former Minister of Defence (Cesare Previti) as a political witch hunt designed to overturn the will of the people and oust him from office.

These factors help explain the paucity of measures passed by successive Italian governments specifically regarding the containment of corruption. While it is true that privatization has closed off many channels of clientelism, and public administration reforms have reduced the conditions favouring corruption (see chapters 8 and 10), the anti-corruption records of both the centre-left governments of 1996–2001 and the Berlusconi government elected in 2001 have been found wanting. Indeed, various measures passed by the latter have been explicitly concerned with assisting Berlusconi's and his colleagues' judicial defence by making it more difficult procedurally for the magistrates to prosecute them, thus making all anti-corruption cases more difficult in the future. The Italian political class – wittingly or unwittingly – seems to have missed the opportunity presented by the 'Clean Hands' campaign to try to free Italian democracy from the influence of corruption (Della Porta and Vannucci 1999b).

The danger is less that old practices will re-emerge than that they have never, in fact, been fully stamped out. In terms of the vicious circles of corruption, Della Porta and

Table 6.1   Italian public perceptions of corruption in public life in 2004 compared with 1992

Do you think that corruption in Italian public life with respect to 1992 has . . .	%
Gone up a lot	13.7
Gone up a little	11.0
Remained unchanged	46.5
Gone down a little	3.3
Gone down a lot	20.7
Don't know/no response	4.8
Total	100.0

Source: Eurispes 2004: 691

Table 6.2   Italy's ranking in Transparency International's Corruption Perceptions Index, 1995–2004

Year	Position*	CPI score**	Position in relation to other EU countries
1995	33	2.99	Lowest
1996	34	3.42	Lowest
1997	30	5.03	Lowest
1998	39	4.6	Lowest
1999	38	4.7	Lowest
2000	39	4.6	Lowest
2001	29	5.5	Greece lower (42)
2002	31	5.2	Greece lower (44)
2003	35	5.3	Greece lower (50)
2004	42	4.8	Greece lower (49)[+]

* The higher the number, the more corrupt relative to other countries.
** Between 0 and 10, where 10 = least corrupt.
[^] As before the expansion of 1 May 2004.
[+] Other countries level with or above Italy include Hungary (level 42), Costa Rica, Tunisia, Malaysia, Qatar, Jordan, Cyprus, Taiwan, Bahrain, Slovenia, Estonia, Botswana, United Arab Emirates, Oman, Uruguay, Israel, Malta, Japan, Barbados, Chile, USA, Hong Kong, Canada, Australia, Singapore.
Source: <www.transparency.org/cpi>

Vannucci (1999a: 269) suggest that 'the action of the magistrates has broken only one of the rings in the chain of reciprocal causality'. This is by having increased substantially perceptions of the *risks* involved in indulging in corrupt practices. The other conditions facilitating corruption (clientelism, organized crime, inefficient public administration) remain in place, albeit somewhat weakened. While, therefore, it is doubtful that corruption continues on the same scale (or at the highest levels), the continuing revelations, perceptions of the Italian public (see table 6.1) and Italy's poor results in the annual Transparency International Corruption Index (see table 6.2) suggest that the phenomenon persists.

Table 6.3 Italian public perceptions of the 'Clean Hands' anti-corruption campaign, twelve years on (2004, in %)

Judgements	Extent of agreement					
	Very much in agreement	**Generally in agreement**	**Not much in agreement**	**Definitely not in agreement**	**Don't know/no response**	**Total**
Tangentopoli was never stopped, and the system of corruption continues to operate as it used to do.	32.5	37.9	17.0	6.6	6.0	100.0
Corruption has always existed and always will exist, and there is nothing that can be done about it.	31.8	25.1	21.5	16.9	4.7	100.0
Di Pietro and the Mani Pulite judges did not have the chance of completing their work because the politicians blocked them.	29.3	31.9	16.1	12.5	10.2	100.0
The Mani Pulite judges were discriminatory, investigating only certain parties while overlooking others.	21.3	26.1	20.5	17.9	14.2	100.0

Source: Eurispes 2004: 702

The assessment of the Mani Pulite campaign by its leading judicial protagonists is that its overall contribution to containing corruption and 'purifying' public life has been modest.[20] The Italian public's judgement is even harsher, and also reflects a belief not only that politicians were able to hinder the investigation, but also that corruption is to a large extent inevitable and impossible to eradicate (see table 6.3). The corruption investigations, while bringing down an entire political class, failed, beyond intellectual circles, to induce any widespread reflection on those cultural traits of clientelism, nepotism and tax evasion which lie at the root of the development of many corrupt practices (Ginsborg 1996a). The failure of Parliament and government to tackle corruption more energetically, therefore, can be seen as tied, to a degree, to popular attitudes concerning law and its supposedly 'negotiable' nature, and to the lack of trust between citizens and the State. These attitudes are further reinforced at the elite level by Berlusconi's arguments that the Milanese prosecutors are politically motivated. Not only is Italy a long way from ridding itself of corrupt practices, therefore, but the very attempt to root out corruption of judicial investigators has degenerated into a major institutional conflict between the political class and the judiciary.

The continuation of corruption also provides the Mafia with significant opportunities to reconsolidate its presence and expand its operations, especially in view of the gradual waning of the state offensive. Anti-Mafia prosecutors describe the period from July 1992 (Paolo Borsellino's death) to Spring 1994 (election of the first Berlusconi government) as a 'magic moment' (Stille 1996: 406). Yet, from there onwards much of the resolve and momentum of the anti-Mafia campaign was dissipated. The Mafia, to be successful, has need of political patrons and (especially with its decline as an international economic entrepreneur) public money. The fact that Forza Italia, in the 2001 elections, won all twenty-seven seats in Sicily has generated various allegations about possible Mafia infiltration of the party, at least at local levels.

It can be concluded that the degree to which Italian politics is currently conditioned by informal, unseen influences has declined. The Italian political system has wrested back some of its sovereignty, especially in relation to the activities of the secret services and related groups. However, Italian democracy is far from being free from the influence of informal institutions, and old features such as clientelism, corruption and the Mafia persist, albeit in weakened form.

THE GOVERNMENT, PARLIAMENT AND THE PRESIDENT

INTRODUCTION

The focus of this and the following chapter is on the institutions of national government: Parliament, the executive, the bureaucracy and the judiciary. These institutions lie at the core of the policy-making process, which is itself 'the pivotal stage of the political process' (Almond and Bingham Powell, Jr. et al. 1992: 91), in the sense that it connects the input of demands from political parties, pressure groups and so forth to political outputs in the form of policies designed to respond to and shape such demands. Governmental institutions 'lie at the core of' policy making in so far as they are the basic structures through which policy is made. In describing how these structures work and are related to each other, we begin by spelling out the basic features of the Italian Constitution. For if constitutions can be defined as sets of rules specifying how the political process is to be carried on, then by that token they define what governmental structures exist in the first place.

THE CONSTITUTION

In setting out the institutional geography of the Republic, the Constitution reveals the anti-Fascist concerns of its drafters through the limitations it places on the possibilities of a centralized concentration of power. Thus, it deliberately refrains from establishing any mechanisms which would allow the executive to protect itself against the erosion of its parliamentary majority (such as, for example, the German 'constructive vote of no-confidence', which makes it possible for the Bundestag to express its lack of confidence in the Federal Chancellor only by electing a successor); and it establishes a number of institutions – a Constitutional Court, sub-national units of government, referenda – designed to restrain the power of a cohesive parliamentary majority. It was intended that restraint on parliamentary majorities would be achieved by each of the three institutions as follows: by the Constitutional Court in virtue of the fact that it is invested with the power to determine the constitutionality of ordinary legislation; by sub-national units of government (regions) in virtue of the fact that their existence is constitutionally guaranteed (hence they cannot be abolished except by means of a change in the Constitution itself); by the referendum device in virtue of the fact that, if invoked by the signatures of 500,000 electors or the request of five regional councils, it gives the electorate the opportunity to repeal unwanted legislation (see chapter 7 appendix).

Besides reflecting the political breaks that are also, usually, responsible for them, constitutions typically have several further features in common. One is some provision for their amendment, and here a distinction is commonly made between 'flexible' constitutions, on the one hand, and 'rigid' constitutions on the other – where 'flexible' constitutions are those whose texts can be changed by means of the same procedures that are used for ordinary legislation (such would be the British case), while 'rigid' constitutions are those requiring some special procedure designed to make amendment relatively difficult. Italy has a rigid constitution in this sense. Proposed amendments must be passed by both chambers of Parliament at an interval of three months; on the second occasion, the majorities concerned must be of the chambers' members; less than two-thirds majorities on the second occasion will trigger a referendum if requested by a fifth of the members of either chamber, 500,000 electors or five regional councils.

A third feature which the Italian Constitution shares with the constitutions of most other liberal democracies is its tripartite division of political authority between executive, legislative and judicial agencies. As in other parliamentary regimes, so in Italy, the executive consists of a cabinet, or 'Council of Ministers' (*Consiglio dei Ministri*), which is responsible to the legislature and remains in office only as long as it enjoys the confidence of the latter. Unusually for a parliamentary regime, the cabinet in Italy must retain the confidence of both branches of the legislature (the Chamber of Deputies and the Senate). Nor is there the usual constitutional requirement that ministers be members of Parliament – a fact that, as we shall see, was of considerable importance in maintaining political stability in Italy in the period following the 1992 elections. Otherwise, however, the Italian executive shares most of the characteristic features of parliamentary executives elsewhere: ministers are individually and collectively responsible to Parliament, and the executive is 'bicephalic' – in other words, there is a head of state (the President) in addition to a head of government (the Prime Minister). Presidents (see table 7.1) are elected for seven-year terms by both branches of the legislature and three delegates from nineteen of the twenty regions plus one from the Valle d'Aosta region; and, as in other parliamentary regimes, the incumbent is endowed, along with the usual ceremonial functions, with the power to appoint the Prime Minister and other members of the cabinet, to dissolve and convoke Parliament, and to promulgate laws. Unlike the situation in most parliamentary systems, however, these powers are not circumscribed by constitutional provisions that make the cabinet in fact responsible for official acts of the President. The latter's role is therefore by no means purely symbolic, as we shall see.

The Italian legislature is bicameral, but it is also 'perfectly bicameral', meaning that each branch has identical legislative power. Identical authority and tasks mean that the 630 members of the Chamber and the 315 members of the Senate have to be elected in accordance with very similar electoral laws for each house. Electoral laws that diverged too radically might result in houses with very different political complexions, with serious consequences for the possibility of stable and effective governance. Theoretically, the two houses could have different political complexions even if their electoral systems were identical; for article 58 of the Constitution restricts elections to the Senate to those aged 25 and over (the voting age for the Chamber is 18), while article 59 stipulates that, besides being themselves entitled to a Senatorial seat for life, outgoing presidents have the right to nominate five life Senators from among individuals who have distinguished themselves in the 'social, scientific, artistic and literary fields'. However, such constitutional niceties have not created problems so far.

The judicial agency, like its counterpart in other liberal democracies, is intended by the Constitution to be independent of the other two agencies, meaning that it is not subject to the authority of the other two, and neither are its members responsible to any or all of the members of the other two. Thus it is intended, in time-honoured fashion, that the individual be afforded a measure of protection against arbitrary action on the part of state officials and on the part of the State as a whole. Further protection against arbitrary action by the State is sought by means of the power vested in the Constitutional Court to pronounce definitively on the constitutionality of legislation. The independence of the judiciary is sought by means of a free-standing *Consiglio Superiore della Magistratura* (High Council of the Judiciary) having (almost) sole discretion in the appointment and dismissal of judicial personnel. Since March 2002, when its number was reduced from thirty, it has consisted of twenty-four members, two-thirds of whom are elected from among the various branches of the judiciary itself, one-third of whom are chosen by Parliament, which must make its selection from among members of the academic law community and practising lawyers. It is presided over by the President of the Republic. Finally, the citizen is afforded a measure of protection against arbitrary action by the judiciary itself in the form of article 111 of the Constitution, which enshrines the right of the citizen to appeal sentences to the Court of Cassation (the highest appeal court for the ordinary judicial system) 'on grounds of violation of the law'.

A fourth, and final, dimension in terms of which the Italian Constitution may be compared with constitutions elsewhere is in terms of how it distributes authority geographically. Here a distinction is commonly drawn between 'federal states' and 'unitary states', where the former are those in which there are two orders of government, a general government and regional governments existing in their own right under the Constitution, each with their own spheres of competence (Watts 1991: 229), the latter those in which the authority and existence of regional governments can be changed by a unilateral decision of the general government. From this point of view, Italy has a hybrid Constitution. On the one hand, the sub-national units of government (regions, provinces and communes) are specified in the Constitution; they therefore exist in their own right and cannot be abolished without constitutional amendment, and, as a result of constitutional changes introduced in 2001, the regions have in certain areas acquired legislative powers of the exclusive variety. On the other hand, the Constitution can be unilaterally amended by the central government without the regions' consent, for there is no second chamber, representative of the regions, that would give them joint control, with central government, of the procedures of constitutional change (see chapter 9). The territorial division of authority in Italy also reflects the historical conjuncture in

Table 7.1 Presidents of the Republic

Name	Born	Died	Biographical note	Term of office
Enrico de Nicola	9 Nov. 1877	1 Oct. 1959	Law graduate; elected to Parliament for the first time in 1909; withdrew from public life during Fascism; elected Provisional Head of State by the Constituent Assembly on 28 June 1946.	1 July 1946– 11 May 1948
Luigi Einaudi	24 Mar. 1874	30 Oct. 1961	Law graduate; worked as journalist until 1926; economist; Governor of the Bank of Italy 5 Jan. 1945–11 May 1948; cabinet minister in the fourth De Gasperi government.	11 May 1948– 11 May 1955
Giovanni Gronchi	10 Sept. 1887	17 Oct. 1978	One of the founders of the Italian People's Party in 1919; withdrew from public life during Fascism; member of the Constituent Assembly; elected President of the Chamber of Deputies, 8 May 1948.	11 May 1955– 11 May 1962
Antonio Segni	2 Feb. 1891	1 Dec. 1972	Law graduate and founder member of the Italian People's Party. During Fascism, withdrew from public life and taught law at various universities. Member of Constituent Assembly and Prime Minister 1955–7. Resigned as President in Dec. 1964 due to ill health.	11 May 1962– 6 Dec. 1964
Giuseppe Saragat	19 Sept. 1898	11 June 1988	Graduate in economics and commerce. Member of Socialist Party, later founder member of PSDI. Member of Constituent Assembly. Foreign Minister in the first and second Moro governments.	29 Dec. 1964– 29 Dec. 1971
Giovanni Leone	3 Nov. 1908	9 Nov. 2001	Graduate in law (1929) and political and social science (1930). Taught law at various universities. Joined DC 1944; member of the Constituent Assembly; Prime Minister in 1963 and 1968. Resigned as President six months before expiry of mandate, following accusations of nepotism.	29 Dec. 1971– 5 June 1978

Name	Born	Died		Term
Sandro Pertini	25 Sept. 1896	24 Feb. 1990	Graduate in law and political and social science. Imprisoned for political activity under fascism; sentenced to death by SS during Nazi occupation; secretary of Socialist Party; member of Constituent Assembly; elected President of Chamber of Deputies in 1968 and 1972.	9 July 1978– 23 June 1985
Francesco Cossiga	26 July 1928		Law graduate. Joined DC at 17. Cousin of PCI leader, Enrico Berlinguer. Elected to Parliament in 1958; Prime Minister in 1979 and 1980. At age 57 is youngest person to have held the Presidency of the Republic. Resigned as President in Apr. 1992, ten weeks before expiry of mandate.	24 June 1985– 28 Apr. 1992
Oscar Luigi Scalfaro	9 Sept. 1918		Law graduate; member of Constituent Assembly; Member of Parliament continuously from 1948; Minister of the Interior in 1983, 1986 and 1987. Elected President of the Chamber of Deputies, 24 Apr. 1992.	28 May 1992– 15 May 1999
Carlo Azeglio Ciampi	9 Dec. 1920		Joined Bank of Italy in 1946 and was its Governor 1979–93. Prime Minister, 1993–4. Treasury Minister in centre left governments 1996–9 in which capacity bore most of the responsibility for Italy's success in qualifying for first-wave membership of the Euro.	18 May 1999–

Source: <http://www.quirinale.it/ex_presidenti/expresidenti.htm#> and <http://www.cronologia.it/storia/tabello/tabe1548.htm>

which the Constitution was born; for it was essentially fear on the part of the Christian Democrats and their allies of the parties of the left (with their perceived dedication to a nationalized economy under central control) that gave rise to the provision for a constitutionally guaranteed regional tier of government.

Before turning to analyse the role of the principal institutions in the policy-making process – Parliament, Cabinet and Prime Minister, President – and how they have changed in the post-war period, it is important to emphasize the general dissatisfaction with the operation of the Republic's institutional framework in the post-war period. In contrast with many European democracies, where the institutional framework is generally unquestioned, in Italy the perception has been widespread that institutions lie at the root of the country's problems, and that what is needed is their root-and-branch overhaul. In 1983 the Socialist leader, Bettino Craxi, launched the *grande riforma* ('great reform') which constituted the first significant attempt at institutional reform, and the quest for institutional reform has remained central to Italian political debate since that date (Fusaro 1998; Pasquino 1998). Successive attempts at reform (one in the 1980s and two in the 1990s) all failed because the political parties, all of which sought to ensure that their individual interests would be protected if not furthered in any changed system (Pasquino 1998: 43) found it impossible to reach agreement. The most significant attempt at reform was that of the Bicameral Commission in 1997–8. This generated considerable expectations, because it followed the dramatic collapse of the old party regime. It therefore seemed destined to produce a constitutional revision and the formal birth of the so-called Second Republic, thus ending the so-called political transition. However, after eighteen months, the Bicameral Commission's work was sunk in Parliament when Berlusconi announced his party's withdrawal of support for the project. While Berlusconi's motives were said to be linked largely to the Commission's failure to circumscribe the role of the judiciary, it is also true that the Commission's proposals overall were widely regarded as poorly conceived and unlikely to produce the desired effects (Pasquino 2000a). Yet the quest for comprehensive institutional reform remains firmly on the agenda, with the second Berlusconi government elected in 2001 making a further such attempt (Ignazi 2003). In spite of the failure to achieve an overall reform of the institutional framework, each of the major institutions individually has undergone change and piecemeal reform, especially in the period since the early 1990s.

Parliament

With one or two significant exceptions such as the United States Congress, legislatures even in liberal democracies are usually thought of by political scientists as having rather little influence over policy. For it is argued that where parties are disciplined, and especially where one party commands an absolute majority of seats, the cabinet and prime minister are able effectively to take control of the legislature, and so assure themselves of the adoption of nearly all the legislation they propose. In such circumstances the role of the legislature is not so much to make policy as to ratify it. Italy's parliament was, until the 1990s, usually ranked alongside the US Congress as another significant exception to this rule. For, thanks to the nature of the party system, governments were

unable, as we saw in chapter 3, to wield the kind of power over their parties' followers that would have allowed them to subordinate Parliament to their will.

Partly reflecting this state of affairs, a number of features of its internal procedures
gave the legislature additional means of resisting executive dominance. First, until 1988
when the practice was all but completely abolished, the individual articles of legislative proposals could be made subject to a secret vote at the request of a minimum
number of representatives.[1] The effect of this was not only to give ordinary Deputies
and Senators considerable power to determine the precise shape of government legislation (by giving them power to bury certain parts of a bill while retaining others) but
also to give governments' own supporters a means of resisting attempts to control
them. In the light of this it was hoped that the success of the De Mita government in
1988 in severely curtailing the circumstances under which secret voting could be used
would make it easier for governments to manage their parliamentary majorities.

Second, article 77 of the Constitution allows governments 'to issue emergency executive decrees having the force of law. They must be converted into ordinary law by
Parliament within sixty days or they lapse' (Hine 1993a: 149). While this facility in
theory allowed governments to circumvent the parliamentary obstacles lying between
their legislative proposals and the statute book at least temporarily, the Constitution's
authors, of course, had envisaged that resort to decrees would be an exceptional matter
– and the fact that their use eventually became anything *but* exceptional (their number
rising dramatically in the period after 1970 to reach 477 during the eighth legislature)
was frequently taken as proof, not of government power, but of the inability of governments to get Parliament to take their legislative proposals seriously. Indeed, article
77 gave Parliament considerable leverage over the government inasmuch as it could
decline to convert decrees into ordinary legislation – and the image of governments as
beleaguered entities was added to by the habit they eventually adopted of responding
to stalling tactics on the part of Parliament by resorting to reissuing the same decrees
several times over.

Third, article 72 of the Constitution – unusually from a comparative point of view
– enables the Chamber and Senate, with few exceptions,[2] to give law-making authority to their committees such that legislation can be passed by these bodies without
having to be referred back to the whole house for final approval. However, this
committee-only route can be overridden at the request of one-tenth of the whole house,
in which case the bill in question must be referred back to the plenary session. 'This
gave the opposition considerable concealed power over the government since it could,
if it so desired, choke the work of the whole chamber by demanding that all legislation be subject to the full legislative procedure' (Hine 1993a: 178). Moreover, it was
through the committees acting in *sede legislativa* (in a law-making capacity), away
from the public gaze, that the governing parties were able to get on with the business
of mobilizing electoral support through the passage of large numbers of patronage-
based measures. Therefore, its capacity to block the passage of such legislation, and
its willingness to forgo doing so, gave the PCI a valuable means of providing evidence
of its 'responsible' intentions, bearing in mind that the depth of the ideological divide
separating it from other parties meant that it was engaged in a perpetual search for its
own legitimacy as the only means of extending its electoral support beyond its heart-
lands. By the same token, such *consociativismo*, as it was called, perpetuated the

legislature's ability to resist executive control.[3] It was by no means coincidental, there-fore, that academic and popular conceptions of Parliament emphasizing its 'centrality' – that is, the notion that it, not the executive, was, and should be, the central, supreme institution in the management of the State – were at their most influential in the 1970s: precisely the period in which the PCI's power and influence were at their height (Cotta 1994: 66).

During the 1970s and 1980s, other changes in the distribution of power within and between parties brought with them signs that governments were finding the process of bargaining to push forward their legislation an increasingly uphill struggle. The DC's 'colonization' of parts of the State allowed it to escape the dilemmas confronting it as a party trying to hold together a cross-class base of support in the stormy ideological climate of the 1950s (see chapter 2). However, struggle for control of the patronage resources used to achieve this also meant that the DC became an increasingly fac-tionalized party as time went by, and thus a party that was increasingly difficult to manage from the point of view of compelling cohesive behaviour on the part of its parliamentary representatives. Not entirely unrelated to this difficulty was the fact that the relative political weight and influence of the party as a whole, outside and within the legislature, began slowly to decline (see table 3.1, figure 3.1 and table 4.1). In 1971 the DC was forced to accept a change to the internal procedures of Parliament whereby power to determine the parliamentary timetable was shifted from the presidents of the two houses (offices that had almost always been staffed by DC politicians) to the leaders of the parliamentary groups (including the groups representing opposition parties), whose decisions had to be based on unanimity. This meant that the legisla-ture could, in effect, prevent attempts by governments to dominate by giving their own legislation privileged treatment. Not surprisingly, then, while the success rate for gov-ernment bills averaged 83 per cent in the period 1948–1972, over the next twenty years it averaged only 56 per cent. Emblematic of the difficulties faced by governments at this time was the experience of the relatively long-lived Craxi government, of 1983–6, which notoriously 'went under' 163 times, or almost once a week, as a con-sequence of the actions of the so-called *franchi tiratori* ('snipers') who used the secret vote to rebel against their parties' leadership. In order to overcome their difficulties, governments attempted increasingly to bypass Parliament by issuing decrees – the point even being reached, as mentioned, where governments would 'keep alive' decrees that had not been converted within the constitutionally required sixty days simply by re-issuing them as many times as was necessary until they had been converted.

With the party system transformation of the 1990s, it was reasonable to think that governments would acquire a new vigour *vis-à-vis* the legislature. For, with a sufficient degree of approximation in 1996, and unambiguously in 2001, the governments that took office following these elections in these years were staffed by single coalitions formed *prior* to the ballot and seeking to win overall majorities – rather than being formed, as governments had been previously, by coalitions whose make-up was decided by negotiations only *after* the election results were known. Each government, too, was faced with a unilateral (if not especially united) opposition. Unilateral oppositions tend to make alternation a more realistic possibility than it was prior to the 1990s, while governing parties' fortunes would seem to depend more than previously on the enact-ment of coherent programmes. For both these reasons, it was reasonable to anticipate greater cohesion on the part of governing parties than had been true of the past, and thus that the position of governments relative to the legislature would be rather more robust.

The available evidence presents a mixed picture. Party cohesion, in the sense of the willingness of Members of Parliament to act in concert does, on the whole, seem to have increased (Newell 2000c). Meanwhile, the proportion of legislative output accounted for by private member bills (Verzichelli and Cotta 2002) declined from 30 per cent between 1987 and 1992 to 10 per cent between 1996 and 2001. On the other hand, the rate of success of government-sponsored bills, though higher between 1996 and 2001 than during the two previous legislatures was, at 50 per cent, no higher than it was during the 1987–92 legislature (Verzichelli and Cotta 2002). In short, while there is some evidence in favour of the inferences to be drawn from the party system changes, further evidence – and therefore time – will be required before we can be certain of the degree of discontinuity with the past.

Paradoxically, precisely that feature of Parliament which gave it such power 'to block, amend, hassle and so forth' (Cotta 1994: 60) – namely, the ability of the national party elites to act as powerful institutional gatekeepers controlling both Parliament and the executive – also made it rather ineffective in exercising the functions of scrutiny and oversight for most of the post-war period. True, the rules of procedure adopted by the two houses in 1948 made provision for a number of *ex ante* checks on government action, and to these were subsequently added a range of *ex post* tools of inquiry (Verzichelli and Cotta 2002: 10). As one would expect, such checks and tools include motions and resolutions; orders of the day (containing instructions on how legislation, motions and so forth are to be interpreted or implemented); the power to establish commissions of inquiry (with the power to compel the presence of witnesses, sequester documents and search premises); questions and interpellations, as well as the power, through the passage of ordinary legislation, to set up supervisory committees (such as the *Commissione di vigilanza, RAI*, the commission for supervision of the state television network), to compel the presentation of periodic reports on the activities of given public actors (such as the police), and so forth. However, the structure of incentives operating on individual legislators was not such as to induce them to give oversight activities a particularly high priority. Such priority might have been expected had the activities in question related to the legislator's chances for re-election or promotion. But 'vigorous participation in formal Parliament business [was] likely to preclude the kind of network-building . . . required for junior members if they wish[ed] to ensure their re-election and to place themselves well in a strong faction' (Furlong 1990: 62). Moreover, the need to create and maintain a loyal network of local government and party supporters combined with the effects of the preference vote meant that constituency pressures tended to dominate role perceptions for large numbers of Italian MPs (Hine 1993: 173) and this arguably made it difficult for them to develop the kind of policy expertise that would have been necessary for oversight activities to be effective. The situation was not helped either by the fragmentation of party groups within Parliament and the blurring of the distinction between governing and opposition roles that was implicit in *consociativismo*, for both meant that it was, in a meaningful sense, difficult to identify the political actor that was to be the *object* of scrutiny and oversight in the first place (Verzichelli and Cotta 2002: 9).

This is not to suggest that ministers and governments were, in effect, unaccountable. The fact that ministers and their junior ministerial colleagues would often be drawn from different parties provided 'a watch-dog system' (Verzichelli and Cotta 2002: 91), whose effectiveness was not necessarily undermined on those occasions when governments were staffed entirely from the ranks of the DC (the so-called *monocolore* governments). On such occasions, the deep diversity of the social and political beliefs of ministers and junior ministers coming from the different party factions 'created a very similar game of mutual control'. Moreover, *consociativismo* and 'the centrality of Parliament', to a degree at least, served to enhance accountability by virtue of the emphasis they placed on the rights of the opposition parties and the rights of the 'popular representative' (Verzichelli and Cotta 2002: 10 and 20). Nevertheless, the 'blockage' of Italy's democracy and the consequent absence of cohesive governing coalitions able to impose discipline on the majorities that sustained them, did seem to have as a counterpart a relative weakness of the degree to which Parliament could exercise its accountability function (at least as compared to systems of the 'Westminster' variety with their bipolar party systems and the regular alternation of cohesive governing and opposition parties or coalitions).

With the 1990s shift in the nature of Italian party politics towards something more closely resembling this model, the situation in terms of scrutiny and oversight appears to have improved somewhat. New instruments of control have been introduced – notably, Prime Minister's question time and urgent interpellations – while, as measured in terms of the frequency of use of its associated instruments, the exercise of oversight went up dramatically in the 1992 and subsequent legislatures. Thus the use of such instruments as motions, resolutions, questions, interpellations and so forth rose from approximately thirty instances per day during the 1987–92 legislature to over fifty during the subsequent three legislatures to 2001. What is also striking is that whereas prior to the 1990s the instruments were exercised predominantly by opposition parliamentarians, over the past decade government backbenchers have become increasingly involved in their use (see table 7.2). Capano and Giuliani (2003) interpret this phenomenon in terms of a decline in the legislative function of Parliament since the end of the First Republic. First, the ability of governments to bend Parliament to their will in the pursuit of a legislative agenda has not increased, for, despite the majoritarian and adversarial trends set in motion by the 1993 electoral law, governments remain coalitions,

characterised by a series of internal cleavages. As a result, they cannot continually constrain their parliamentary majority to behave passively and simply follow the executive's guidelines. To compel Parliament is a really dangerous thing, since it constitutes an incentive to MPs and parliamentary groups to use all the powerful tools their institution disposes of [in the absence of incisive reform of Parliament's internal procedures] to fight Government. (Capano and Giuliani 2003: 29)

Second, as a consequence, governments, acting under the pressure of such processes as European integration, and with the added legitimacy that their 'direct investiture' brings,[4] have attempted to gain autonomy from Parliament by increasingly governing outside it altogether. They have managed to achieve this through an increasing resort to legislation which delegates to them powers to adopt legislative decrees in defined

Table 7.2 Measures of selected oversight activity, 7th–14th legislatures

Legislature	Interpellations				Motions and Assembly resolutions			
7th (1976–1979)	803	(22.3)	Majority	31.5% (7.0)	156	(4.3)	Majority	29.5% (1.3)
			Opposition	67.5% (15.1)			Opposition	68.6% (3.0)
8th (1979–1983)	3169	(64.1)	Majority	25.6% (16.4)	452	(9.1)	Majority	26.5% (2.4)
			Opposition	70.1% (44.9)			Opposition	73.0% (6.7)
9th (1983–1987)	1706	(35.3)	Majority	26.7% (9.4)	456	(9.4)	Majority	35.3% (3.3)
			Opposition	73.3% (25.9)			Opposition	64.7% (6.1)
10th (1987–1992)	2557	(43.7)	Majority	22.7% (9.9)	991	(16.9)	Majority	26.4% (4.5)
			Opposition	72.3% (31.6)			Opposition	71.3% (12.1)
11th (1992–1994)	1654	(68.8)	Majority	19.2% (13.2)	459	(19.1)	Majority	22.0% (4.2)
			Opposition	79.5% (54.7)			Opposition	77.8% (14.9)
12th (1994–1996)	1274	(50.7)	Majority	40.8% (20.7)	473	(18.8)	Majority	35.1% (6.6)
			Opposition	52.5% (26.6)			Opposition	59.0% (11.1)
13th (1996–2001)	4168	(67.7)	Majority	28.6% (19.4)	1369	(22.2)	Majority	38.3% (8.5)
			Opposition	50.5% (34.2)			Opposition	50.5% (11.2)
14th (2001–)	305	(39.8)	Majority	45.6% (18.1)	121	(15.8)	Majority	45.5% (7.2)
			Opposition	38.0% (15.1)			Opposition	44.6% (7.0)

Absolute figures, monthly figures in brackets. Percentages show distribution between majority and opposition parties of each type of activity. Percentages sum to less than 100 owing to the activity of Deputies belonging to the mixed group (not shown). Activity in 14th legislature updated to 13 Feb. 2002.
Source: Capano and Giuliani 2003: 26, table 2, <http://www.essex.ac.uk/ECPR/standinggroups/parliaments/papers/italianparliament_capano_giuliani.pdf>

policy areas, pursuant to the principles set out in the legislation, without the need to refer further to Parliament. Therefore – third – confronted with their decreasingly significant role in the legislative process (reduced even further by the impact of decentralizing institutional reform, and the fact that the government is the only player in the EU arena),

[t]hrough ex-ante (motions and resolutions) and ex-post oversight (interpellations), opposition groups and majority backbenchers are trying to restore their role in the parliamentary political process, thus somehow limiting or fixing the independence of the executive. The more the latter pushes for self-determination and decisiveness, the more the former need to exploit all the political and statutory resources they possess. (Capano and Giuliani 2003: 22)

In summary, then, the party system upheavals of the 1990s have given rise to significant changes, both in Parliament's role in the legislative process and in its relationship to the government. The upheavals have also given rise to significant changes in the way in which Prime Minister and Cabinet relate to each other.

PRIME MINISTER AND CABINET

As we have seen, prior to the 1990s, the never-questioned assumption of the governing parties that collectively they would permanently exclude the Communist opposition from government meant that they were left with no incentive 'to maintain government stability for its own sake' (Furlong 1990: 57). Governments might have been somewhat longer-lived and less fragile, had prime ministers had the kind of authority and discretion in managing their cabinets that was clearly envisaged by the framers of the Constitution and that are often found elsewhere. Article 95 of the Constitution states that the Prime Minister 'conducts and is responsible for the general policy of the government. He assures the unity and consistency of the political and administrative programme by promoting and co-ordinating the activity of the Ministers.' However, until 1988, there was no substantive legislation spelling out how this was to be done, and in any case, as the heads of coalition governments, prime ministers were deprived of the source of leverage over the conduct of their ministers that goes with the power to hire and fire. Since the composition of cabinets was in essence a matter of negotiation between the party leaders, prime ministers were forced to act as mediators rather than genuinely authoritative government leaders. This meant that there were significant restrictions on the degree to which they could exert influence on, and effectively co-ordinate, the policies of their governments. Themselves owing their positions to inter-party agreement, prime ministers were constrained – given their interest in maximizing their time in office – to *avoid* taking audacious policy initiatives that might alienate one or more of their governing partners, and to spend most of their time negotiating agreement between such partners.

During the 1980s strenuous attempts were made by at least two prime-ministerial incumbents to shift the influence that prime ministers could bring to bear on policy somewhat closer to the one implied by the constitutional ideal. Attempts were both informal and formal, the first kind being exemplified by the Craxi incumbency between 1983 and 1987. Because the role of Prime Minister is so broadly defined, its powers are heavily dependent – within the general constraints outlined – on the prevailing political circumstances and on the personality of the incumbent at the time. The abrasive Craxi, who was keen to make as much electoral capital as possible out of the potential of the office, deliberately set about using his incumbency to attempt, as far as he could, to build a reputation for vigorous and effective leadership. In this he was considerably helped by the problems faced by the Christian Democrats, whose electoral difficulties had forced them to concede the premiership in the first place, and which now gave Craxi some scope to lead from the front and to take independent policy initiatives. 'If his coalition partners dared to remove him' – so Craxi gambled – 'they would have to account to the electorate for doing so' (Hine and Finocchi 1991: 88). Although the political circumstances underpinning Craxi's position proved to be only temporary – the DC recovered its strength at the general election of 1987 – his attempts at power acquisition were significant because, as always with imprecisely defined offices, prime-ministerial powers are heavily dependent on what people expect them to be; incumbents who successfully make claims to influence thereby increase the range of acceptable influence thereafter.

Attempts to increase the formal powers of the Prime Minister centred on efforts to strengthen the organization of the weakly organized Prime Minister's office (known as the *Presidenza del Consiglio dei Ministri*, PCM). The problem was that performance of the constitutionally ascribed task of policy co-ordination was effectively undermined by the lack of legislative definition of the prime-ministerial role and by the lack of a separate budget for the PCM, something which meant that large numbers of senior officials in the office would have to be seconded from other parts of the government machinery, and hence would be subject to the same rate of turnover as prime-ministerial incumbents themselves. This obviously militated against continuity and the development of institutional memory. The response to this problem was an attempt on the part of the Republican party and managerially oriented Prime Minister Giovanni Spadolini (July 1981–December 1982), to pass legislation which would give to key features of the PCM a definite legal status, permanent staffing and a proper budget. After several changes of government and the slow process of negotiating the details through Parliament, the legislation finally reached the statute book in August 1988 as law 400 (Discipline in Government and Regulation of the Presidency of the Council of Ministers). It allows prime ministers, in cases of conflicts of competence between ministers, to suspend the administrative or political actions of the latter pending a ruling by Cabinet; and it insists that prime ministers should be able 'to agree with ministers concerned on the public statements that they plan to give whenever they wish to involve the general politics of the government, beyond their normal ministerial responsibility' (quoted by Barrera 1990: 10–11). It gives the PCM 'its own permanent staffing, and the capacity to hire either full- or part-time outside advisors paid directly out of its own budget' (Hine 1993: 214). The intention behind the law was clearly to strengthen the role of the Prime Minister, therefore. However, to the extent that it was necessarily confined to the administrative and organizational aspects of that role, the law could achieve little in the short term: unable to address the underlying political causes of prime-ministerial weakness, it remained a statement of aspirations rather than the actual conferment of enhanced powers that its authors wanted it to be.[5]

Since the party system upheavals of the 1990s – and very much as a consequence of these upheavals – the role of Prime Minister has been considerably strengthened.

Already in 1992 – when, in the wake of the Tangentopoli scandal, the traditional parties were in full retreat from their positions of power in the interstices of the State – Amato had been able to engineer the introduction of a series of economic recovery measures that would have been unthinkable just a few years previously.

In 1996 Prodi came to office as the designated prime-ministerial candidate of a pre-constituted coalition that then went on to win a majority of seats in that year's election. Since he owed his position as Prime Minister directly to the election outcome itself, rather than to inter-party negotiation after the election, he too found himself in a more authoritative position *vis-à-vis* his cabinet than was typical of post-war Italian prime ministers. Unfortunately for the authority that he and his immediate successors were able to command, Prodi was not the leader of any one of the parties belonging to the coalition at whose head he stood, and he had been chosen as the centre left's candidate not by means of any democratic, bottom-up process of selection among the coalition's *followers*, but merely by means of an agreement among its *leaders*. This meant that though he was recognized as the coalition's prime-ministerial candidate and subsequently as the leader of the Ulivo *government*, he never completely acquired the undisputed status of leader of the *coalition*. The notion that 'the premiership is not the leadership' (Pasquino 2001a: 29) became even more firmly established after the fall of Prodi, with the advent of the D'Alema and the Amato governments, when the power of the parties appeared to reassert itself.

In 2001 the advent of Berlusconi seemed to mark the apotheosis of the growth of prime-ministerial power. Like Prodi, Berlusconi came to office with his position reinforced by his having been the pre-designated prime-ministerial candidate of a coalition that then won a majority. But, unlike Prodi, he was also the undisputed leader of his coalition's largest component – while the election result reinforced his position still further by revealing that only one of his coalition partners would be numerically essential to the survival of his government. Finally, in the process of assuming office, Berlusconi made a significant move that seemed likely to reinforce his position. This was to include each of the main party leaders within government or in positions very close to the government. This is unusual for post-war Italy, which, as we mentioned in chapter 3, had been characterized by a tendency for the most senior party leaders to remain outside government and to delegate ministerial tasks to less powerful party figures. Not only had this allowed the party leaders to keep Cabinet and Prime Minister in a state of relative weakness – often agreeing policy away from the arena of Cabinet altogether, within the framework of periodic 'majority summits' (Criscitiello 1993) – but it also made it easier for parties to decline responsibility for, and avoid the electoral consequences of, unpopular policies. So, by including the party leaders in his cabinet, Berlusconi binds the prospects of any one of the parties individually much more closely than is normal to the success or otherwise of the government as a whole, in the process strengthening his own position *vis-à-vis* his cabinet (and that of the Cabinet *vis-à-vis* Parliament).

To be sure, Berlusconi will, in the long run, in no sense be exempt from the obligation to manage the centrifugal tendencies that are present in even the most compact of coalitions – the members of his own coalition retaining a certain veto power simply by virtue of the threat to the government's image, if not its numerical survival, that is posed by insubordination or, in the extreme case, abandonment of the coalition.

Berlusconi's position is thus fully characteristic of the tension between the old model of prime ministers as mediators and the new model of prime ministers as authoritative leaders that has been typical of governments since the early 1990s (Campus 2002: 290) – and since taking office, Berlusconi's actions have exemplified both. The transition to more authoritative prime ministers, more closely resembling their British counterparts, cannot, therefore, yet be said to be an accomplished fact. What does seem clear, however, is that Berlusconi's premiership has pushed the office closer to the 'authoritative leader' end of the spectrum than it has yet come so far.

If the foregoing discussion demonstrates that the role of the Prime Minister has changed quite considerably despite an absence of change in the constitutionally prescribed aspects of the office, then so too have the effective powers of the presidency been very much a function of the ebb and flow of political circumstances.

THE PRESIDENT

The fact of coalition government and cabinet instability has had a considerable impact on the exercise of at least two of the three most important of the President's constitutionally ascribed powers: namely, the power to dissolve and convoke Parliament, and the power to appoint the Prime Minister and other members of the Cabinet.

In the exercise of his power to dissolve Parliament, the President has been a crucial source of political stability in the post-war period. Coalition instability has prevented the development of a clear, unambiguous constitutional convention limiting the head of state's discretion; on the contrary, coalition instability means that dissolution cannot be granted automatically, and that presidents have to give requests for dissolution very careful consideration. Therefore, it has become a convention of the Constitution that when governments collapse, presidents will do all in their power to assist in the construction of a new government and will have recourse to dissolution only as a last resort. Moreover, they are enjoined to dissolve Parliament only if it is no longer representative of the actual political forces in the country, or if it is impossible to form a stable parliamentary majority, or if there is an irremediable political conflict between the two houses (Certoma 1985). The attempt by a President to dissolve a Parliament against its will would almost certainly provoke a constitutional crisis.

Paradoxically, the requirement that the power of dissolution must always be exercised with the clear intent of ensuring political stability and continuity makes it difficult sometimes for the President to avoid political controversy. For example, when Silvio Berlusconi's government collapsed at the end of 1994, President Oscar Luigi Scalfaro refused a dissolution – despite the fact that no obvious alternative could be found to the now clearly untenable coalition formula – on the grounds that an election held so soon after the previous one would clearly be destabilizing. This decision led to loud protests on the part of Berlusconi and his Forza Italia parliamentarians that the FI–AN–Lega electoral coalition that had come to power the previous March had, by virtue of the new electoral system, in effect received a Westminster-style mandate and that, since one of the coalition partners (the Lega) was no longer willing to respect that mandate, the latter ought to be passed back to the electorate for fresh conferral in new elections. The fact that Scalfaro was successful in resisting this line of reasoning was a measure of the failure of Berlusconi to implant a new convention in the Italian Constitution.[6]

In appointing the Prime Minister and other members of the Cabinet, the degree of latitude available to presidents depends on the prevailing political circumstances, which, again, can be traced to the lack of precision in the text of the Constitution. The latter states simply, without any further specification, that 'The President of the Republic appoints the President of the Council of Ministers and the Ministers who are proposed by him' (article 92) – thus leaving unanswered the fundamental question of how much discretion the President is authorized to exercise in making his nominations, and therefore what the constitutional position would be were the preferences of a President to conflict with those of other significant political actors. When there is a high level of agreement among a group of parties clearly able to command a parliamentary majority, the President is said to play a 'notarial' role (Calandra 1986: 56): his choices are *de facto* limited to those individuals whose names emerge during the intense rounds of consultations which presidents hold with the party leaders following the collapse of a government. And things could hardly be otherwise given the stipulation, contained in article 94 of the Constitution, that governments must have the confidence of the two houses of Parliament. Nevertheless, it was clear, from the birth of the Republic on, that imprecision in the constitutional text would prevent the parties from turning the President into a mere puppet. For example, in 1987 the second Craxi government came to the end of its life as a result of the DC's attempt to wrest the premiership from the PSI (see above) in accordance with an agreement between the two parties that had supposedly included an undertaking by Craxi to hand over the premiership in March 1987. This so-called *staffetta*, or 'relay', agreement was widely criticized (particularly on the left), on the grounds that it deprived the President of his constitutional right to appoint the Prime Minister.

By the 1980s, a constitutional principle seemed to have been established to the effect that in the appointment of governments, the President has a role that is essentially confined to the one once attributed to the British monarchy by Walter Bagehot: the right to be consulted, to encourage and to warn. This seemed to be made clear by the so-called 'moral question', an expression used to refer to the requirement that public officials perform their tasks in such a way as to leave no doubt about the propriety of their acts while avoiding contact with any organizations of dubious legality. During the formation of the first Cossiga government (August 1979–March 1980) and then again during the formation of Forlani's government (October 1980–May 1981), the 'moral question' led President Pertini to raise objections to the appointment of certain ministers. The fact that he confined himself to the despatch of letters to the prime ministers-designate reminding them of the professional and ethical standards required of ministers was widely interpreted as proof that there was no constitutional right of presidents to veto appointments or to refuse to appoint persons undesired by the President.

Later, in a very different political context, the room for presidential discretion appeared to be much wider. Following the referenda of April 1993 and the consequent resignation of the Amato government, the by then imminent collapse of the old party system, together with the bitter unpopularity of the governing parties, in effect gave the President sufficient latitude for a more or less literal interpretation of article 92 of the Constitution. This, to the benefit of political stability, allowed for the appointment of a government composed largely of technocrats untainted by the scandals that were by then decimating the ranks of the traditional parties. In effect, the outcome of the April 1993 referendum on the electoral law could be interpreted as a demand for a greater influence of ordinary voters on the formation of executives (Pasquino and Vassallo 1994). Therefore, if the party leaders no longer had the necessary authority to dictate the composition of governments, and if ordinary voters were not yet able to do it, then the person to assume this responsibility had to be the President, given the constitutional requirement that he 'represent the unity of the nation'.

But if the constitutional parameters of the President's powers of dissolution and of appointment of governments defy precise specification (something which has provided that constitutional flexibility necessary to allow presidents to carry out effectively their role of 'constitutional guarantor'), it is also clear that in exercising these powers presidents have frequently been able to exert considerable extra-constitutional, behind-the-scenes influence on the course of political events. By such means they have been able to influence government programmes, coalition formulae and the composition of governments. A recent example of this informal type of influence concerns President Carlo Azeglio Ciampi and Berlusconi's decision to propose the non-party technocrat Renato Ruggiero for the position of Foreign Minister in the immediate aftermath of the 2001 election. Ciampi was particularly committed to the idea of Italy playing a positive role in the process of European integration and wished to secure Ruggiero's appointment in order thereby to have some sort of guarantee that the government would not deviate from a pro-European foreign policy. On the other hand, Berlusconi was concerned, at the outset of his premiership, by the less-than-total credibility he and his government enjoyed in the other chancelleries of Europe, owing to his conflict of interests, his legal difficulties and the presence in government of parties with a dubious ideological heritage, such as AN. He was therefore especially keen, where possible, to avoid rifts with an internationally highly respected President whose public displays of support would help to give him and his government the international credibility they lacked. By this means, the President (along with the president of FIAT, Gianni Agnelli, who also pressed for Ruggiero's appointment) was able to influence both the composition of the new government and (prior to Ruggiero's resignation in January 2002) some aspects of its policy.

The third important presidential power is that of promulgating laws. At first sight, this power appears to be a limited one. Though it gives the incumbent the power to veto legislation temporarily, constitutionally the President is obliged to promulgate laws which, having been returned to Parliament for reconsideration, have then been passed by that body for a second time. However, as with the powers to dissolve Parliament and to appoint members of the government, so too the power of promulgation is not always limited – as the December 2003 decision by President Ciampi to refuse to promulgate the Gasparri law shows.[7] It was the Prime Minister, not the President, who was forced to back down, in that the presidential veto obliged Berlusconi, politically, to reconsider important parts of the proposed legislation. On the other hand, some would argue that the 'manifestly unconstitutional' character of the proposed law in effect obliged President Ciampi to withhold his signature. For this reason it could be argued that the episode confirmed the President's inclination to avoid institutional conflict with Berlusconi wherever possible, seeking instead to counter the Prime Minister's predilection for pursuing legislation of doubtful legitimacy by 'moral suasion' behind the scenes. The most spectacular example of this was on 10 October 2002, a few weeks before final passage of the Cirami law. President Ciampi took the unprecedented step, during a meeting with Berlusconi at the presidential palace, of personally re-drafting parts of the proposal as the *quid pro quo* for forgoing the exercise of his right to use the suspensive veto.[8]

CONCLUSION

This chapter has attempted to map out the various sources and channels of influence on policy and on the process of government that can be discerned from an analysis of the day-to-day interaction between the institutions of Parliament, Cabinet and Prime Minister, and President of the Republic. Such are the checks and balances built into the Italian political system that it has not been possible, for most of the post-war period, to attribute clear pre-eminence to any one institution over the others. What is clear, however, is that if any pre-eminent source of power *could* be identified, then, for most of the period, it lay less in the formally defined institutions of government than in the periodic *vertici* (summit meetings) between the party leaders which, prior to the 1990s, superintended the work of governing coalitions.

Since 1992, the post-war political system has been undergoing a still incomplete process of transition: the Amato government saw a gradual reduction in the power of the traditional governing parties as the results of the Mani Pulite investigations forced them, against a background of growing unpopularity, to cede control over ministries and other parts of the state apparatus; the formation of the 1993–4 Ciampi government saw the long-awaited demise of the *conventio ad excludendum*; new political parties have replaced old ones; a new electoral system was introduced in 1993 in the hope that it would lead to a bipolarization of the party system and more cohesive governing coalitions – hence more authority for the Prime Minister over his cabinet colleagues, a strengthening of the executive in relation to the legislature, and thus more efficient and effective policy making.

Some of these hoped-for effects do indeed seem to have been realized, with the authority of the Prime Minister, for example, having been considerably increased. The days when government programmes would be negotiated at party summits often without the participation of the Prime Minister at all are over (Calise 1994). That other hoped-for change – a shift in the balance of power from legislature to cabinet – has been somewhat slower to emerge, as a result of the absence, until 2001, of its fundamental political prerequisite: a united governing coalition sustained by a disciplined majority. Meanwhile, the presidency has seen its effective powers expand and contract like the accordion with which ex-Prime Minister Giuliano Amato once famously compared the office (Pasquino 2003).[9]

In essence what we have seen is significant change in the way in which the principal institutions of government function and relate to each other that is almost entirely a consequence of change in factors *external to* them – while, constitutionally, the institutions themselves have changed hardly at all. In the absence of constitutional reform, moreover, the permanence of many of the changes we have discussed must remain an open question.

The fact that failure to achieve such reform has always been due to the interlocking vetoes of the parties in a fragmented Parliament may explain why the attempt of the second Berlusconi government to achieve constitutional reform since 2001 has differed from previous efforts. Until the late 1990s, there was an unwritten agreement that institutional reform should be carried through with the consent of all significant political forces (the Bicameral Commission was symptomatic of this approach). But, in 1999, the centre left government set a precedent by unilaterally carrying through a reform of Title V of the Constitution using the strength of its parliamentary majority (see chapter 9). Berlusconi, once elected, decided to adopt an analogous approach, at the same time expanding the scope of constitutional reform. A small committee of 'wise men' was appointed to draft a reform project. In January 2004, their proposals were considered, and approved, by the Senate's Constitutional Affairs Commission, which represents the first step in the reform's long passage. However, the opposition parties abandoned the Commission in protest, and the reform will be subject to intense resistance, including a possible referendum. There are also considerable reservations about the reform within the majority coalition, so it remains unclear as to whether or not a reform can be achieved.

The substance of the proposals is controversial (especially in relation to the powers of the Prime Minister and regional devolution), as are their putative origins (to keep the Northern League happy and to reinforce the personal position of Berlusconi). But perhaps of greater significance at this stage is the *manner* in which they are being driven through. Constitutional revision in Italy appears to have lost the 'extraordinary' character that is so important to reinforcing the sanctity of the document itself (Ferrajoli 1996). The constitutional rules of the game are perceived by the parties as potentially subject to continual tinkering, through the exercise of majority rule, until the 'right formula' is reached. This despite the fact that it is very difficult to predict with any certainty the likely impact of major change, especially in circumstances where the party system – the oil in the constitutional motor – remains in transition. Whether or not comprehensive constitutional change is achieved, piecemeal change and the reform of individual institutions is certain to continue, as is exemplified in the case of the bureaucracy, judiciary and sub-national government, to which we turn in the next two chapters.

Appendix: Results of referenda 1946–2003

	Electorate	Voters	Turnout (%)	Non voters	Valid vote As % of electorate		%		%	Total	Invalid votes Spoilt ballots	As % of voters	Blank ballots	As % of voters
2 June 1946 Republic or monarchy	28,005,449	24,947,187	89.1	3,058,262	10.9	Republic 12,718,641	54.3	Monarchy 10,718,502	45.7	23,437,143	1,509,735	6.1	1,146,729	4.7
12 May 1974 Divorce	37,646,322	33,023,179	87.7	4,623,143	12.3	Yes 13,157,558	40.7	No 19,138,300	59.3	3,295,8582	727,321	2.2	425,694	1.3
11 June 1978 Public order	41,248,657	33,489,688	81.2	7,758,969	18.8	7,400,619	23.5	24,038,806	76.5	31,439,425	2,050,263	6.1	1,091,213	3.3
Financing political parties	41,248,657	33,488,690	81.2	7,759,967	18.8	13,691,900	43.6	17,718,478	56.4	31,410,378	2,078,312	6.2	1,091,213	3.3
17 May 1981 Public order	43,154,682	34,257,197	79.4	8,897,485	20.6	4,636,809	14.9	26,524,667	85.1	31,161,476	3,095,721	9.0	2,222,040	6.5
Life sentences	43,154,682	34,277,194	79.4	8,877,488	20.6	7,114,719	22.6	24,330,954	77.4	31,445,673	2,831,521	8.3	1,978,371	5.8
Firearms licences	43,154,682	34,275,376	79.4	8,879,306	20.6	4,423,426	14.1	26,995,173	85.9	31,418,599	2,856,777	8.3	2,014,303	5.9
Abortion	43,154,682	34,270,200	79.4	8,884,482	20.6	3,588,995	11.6	27,395,909	88.4	30,984,904	3,285,296	9.6	2,353,545	6.9
Abortion	43,154,682	34,277,119	79.4	8,877,563	20.6	10,119,797	32.0	21,505,323	68.0	31,625,120	2,651,999	7.7	1,733,769	5.1
9 June 1985 Scala mobile	44,904,290	34,959,404	77.9	9,944,886	22.1	15,460,855	45.7	18,384,788	54.3	33,845,643	1,113,761	3.2	476,829	1.4
8 November 1987 Civil liability of judges	45,870,931	29,866,249	65.1	16,004,682	34.9	20,770,334	80.2	5,126,021	19.8	25,896,355	3,969,894	13.3	2,616,217	8.8
Commission of enquiry	45,870,409	29,862,670	65.1	16,007,739	34.9	22,117,634	85.0	389,011	15.0	26,007,745	3,854,925	12.9	2,549,984	8.5
Nuclear power	45,869,897	29,871,570	65.1	16,007,521	34.9	20,984,110	80.6	5,059,819	19.4	26,043,929	3,818,447	12.8	2,536,648	8.5

Contributions, local bodies	45,870,230	29,871,570	65.1	15,998,660	34.9	20,618,624	79.7	5,247,887	20.3	25,866,511	4,005,059	13.4	2,654,572	8.9
ENEL	45,849,287	29,855,604	65.1	15,993,683	34.5	18,795,852	71.9	7,361,666	28.1	26,157,518	3,698,086	2.4	2,388,117	8.0
18 June 1989														
Hunting	47,235,285	20,482,359	43.3	26,752,926	56.6	17,790,070	92.2	1,505,161	7.8	19,295,231	1,187,128	5.8	647,630	3.2
Access of hunters to private funds	47,235,471	20,274,101	42.9	26,961,370	57.1	17,899,910	92.3	1,497,976	7.7	19,397,886	876,215	4.3	574,812	2.8
Pesticides	47,232,383	20,364,370	43.1	26,868,013	56.9	18,287,687	93.5	1,270,111	6.5	19,557,798	806,572	4.0	499,572	2.5
9 June 1991														
Preference voting	47,377,843	29,609,635	62.5	17,768,208	37.5	26,896,979	9.6	1,247,908	4.4	28,144,887	1,464,748	4.9	574,744	1.9
18 April 1993														
Local health units	47,946,896	36,845,706	76.8	11,101,190	23.2	28,415,407	82.6	5,997,236	17.4	34,412,643	2,433,063	6.6	1,400,309	3.8
Drugs	47,946,896	36,911,398	77.0	11,035,498	23.0	19,255,915	55.4	15,529,815	44.6	34,785,730	2,125,668	5.8	1,315,445	3.6
Party finance	47,946,896	36,896,256	77.0	11,050,640	23.0	31,225,867	90.3	3,373,039	9.7	34,598,906	2,297,350	6.2	1,291,367	3.5
Banks	47,946,896	36,856,051	76.9	11,090,845	23.1	31,046,262	89.8	3,524,781	10.2	34,571,043	2,285,008	6.2	1,515,546	4.1
Ministry of state holdings	47,946,896	36,851,158	76.9	11,095,738	23.1	31,234,897	90.1	3,428,899	9.9	34,663,796	2,187,362	5.9	1,443,777	3.9
Electoral law	47,946,896	36,922,390	77.0	11,024,506	23.0	28,936,747	82.7	6,034,640	17.3	34,971,387	1,951,003	5.3	1,207,710	3.3
Ministry of agriculture	47,946,896	36,868,634	76.9	11,078,262	23.1	24,325,394	70.2	10,313,117	29.8	34,638,511	2,230,123	6.0	1,411,824	3.8
Ministry of Tourism	47,946,896	36,863,866	76.9	11,083,030	23.1	28,528,528	82.3	6,143,898	17.7	34,672,426	2,191,440	5.9	1,412,783	3.8
11 June 1995														
Trade union representation	48,458,754	27,730,224	57.2	20,728,530	42.8	12,291,330	50.0	12,305,693	50.0	24,597,023	3,133,201	11.3	2,433,279	8.8
Trade union representation	48,458,754	27,702,339	57.2	20,756,415	42.8	15,097,799	62.1	9,197,089	37.9	24,294,888	3,407,451	12.3	2,675,273	9.7
Public employment	48,458,754	27,795,464	57.4	20,663,290	42.6	15,676,385	64.7	8,562,040	35.3	24,238,425	3,557,039	12.8	2,788,290	10.0
Cautionary exile	48,458,754	27,740,783	57.2	20,717,971	42.8	15,373,288	63.7	8,768,941	36.3	24,142,229	3,598,554	13.0	2,864,624	10.3

Appendix: (continued)

					Valid vote						Invalid votes			
	Electorate	Voters	Turnout (%)	Non voters	As % of electorate		%		%	Total	Spoilt ballots	As % of voters	Blank ballots	As % of voters
Privatization RAI	48,458,754	27,807,196	57.4	20,651,558	42.6	13,736,435	54.9	11,286,527	45.1	25,022,962	2,784,234	10.0	2,203,648	7.9
Commercial licences	48,458,754	27,739,462	57.2	20,719,292	42.8	8,741,584	35.6	15,792,453	64.4	24,534,037	3,205,425	11.6	2,587,737	9.3
Trade union dues	48,458,754	27,753,466	57.3	20,705,288	42.7	13,945,919	56.2	10,850,793	43.8	24,796,712	2,956,754	10.7	2,403,721	8.7
Local electoral laws	48,458,754	27,814,402	57.4	20,644,352	42.6	12,154,969	49.4	12,452,250	50.6	24,607,219	3,207,183	11.5	2,595,495	9.3
Shop opening hours	48,458,754	27,788,647	57.3	20,670,107	42.7	9,348,000	37.4	15,646,779	62.6	24,994,779	2,793,868	10.1	2,188,321	7.9
TV franchising	48,458,754	28,133,946	58.1	20,324,808	41.9	11,620,613	43.1	15,357,997	56.9	26,978,610	1,155,336	4.1	834,900	3.0
TV advertising	48,458,754	28,164,078	58.1	20,294,676	41.9	11,985,670	44.3	15,044,535	55.7	27,030,205	1,133,873	4.0	803,308	2.9
TV advertising	48,458,754	28,139,312	58.1	20,319,442	41.9	11,713,935	43.6	15,161,934	56.4	26,875,869	1,263,443	4.5	872,585	3.1
15 June 1997														
Privatization	49,054,410	14,790,505	30.2	34,263,905	69.8	9,539,459	74.1	3,340,893	25.9	12,880,352	1,910,153	12.9	1,330,347	9.0
Conscientious objection	49,054,410	14,860,894	30.3	34,193,516	69.7	9,561,009	71.7	3,775,660	28.3	13,336,669	1,524,225	10.3	1,045,553	7.0
Hunting	49,054,410	14,817,553	30.2	34,236,857	69.8	10,936,576	80.9	2,581,753	19.1	13,518,329	1,299,224	8.8	850,293	5.7
Judicial careers	49,054,410	14,791,735	30.2	34,262,675	69.8	10,786,069	83.6	2,123,452	16.4	12,909,521	1,882,214	12.7	1,321,648	8.9
Journalists	49,054,410	14,735,975	30.0	34,318,435	70.0	8,322,166	65.5	4,380,284	34.5	12,702,450	2,033,525	13.8	1,454,225	9.9
Extra-judicial obligations of magistrates	49,054,410	14,812,238	30.2	34,242,172	69.8	11,160,923	85.6	1,879,923	14.4	13,040,846	1,771,392	12.0	1,206,304	8.1
Ministry for Agricultural Policies	49,054,410	14,742,261	30.1	34,312,149	69.9	8,589,746	66.9	4,258,863	33.1	12,848,609	1,893,652	12.8	1,331,923	9.0

18 April 1999														
Electoral law	49,309,060	24,447,521	49.6	24,861,539	50.4	21,161,866	91.5	1,960,022	8.5	23,121,888	1,325,633	5.4	566,065	2.3
20 May 2000														
Reimbursement electoral and referendum expenses	49,067,694	15,796,834	32.2	33,270,860	67.8	10,004,581	71.1	4,073,688	28.9	14,078,269	1,718,565	10.9	1,248,244	7.9
Electoral law	49,067,694	15,918,748	32.4	33,148,946	67.6	11,637,524	82.0	2,551,963	18.0	14,189,487	1,729,261	10.9	1,231,529	7.7
High Council of the Judiciary	49,067,694	15,634,781	31.9	33,432,913	68.1	9,125,465	70.6	3,805,250	29.4	12,930,715	2,704,066	17.3	2,102,915	13.5
Judiciary	49,067,694	15,681,225	32.0	33,386,469	68.0	9,237,713	69.0	4,150,241	31.0	13,387,954	2,293,271	14.6	1,757,217	11.2
Extra-judicial obligations of judges	49,067,694	15,696,528	32.0	33,371,166	68.0	10,200,692	75.2	3,360,487	24.8	13,561,179	2,135,349	13.6	1,637,121	10.4
Dismissals	49,067,694	15,953,385	32.5	33,114,309	67.5	4,923,381	33.4	9,834,046	66.6	14,757,427	1,195,958	7.5	829,774	5.2
Union dues	49,067,694	15,800,947	32.2	33,266,747	67.8	8,632,445	61.8	5,331,053	38.2	13,963,498	1,837,449	11.6	1,373,612	8.7
7 October 2001														
Amendments to title V, part II of the Constitution	49,462,222	16,843,420	34.1	32,618,802	65.9	10,433,574	64.2	5,816,527	35.8	16,250,101	593,319	3.5	236,561	1.4
15 and 16 June 2003														
Employment rights	47,246,810	12,141,547	25.7	35,105,263	74.3	10,251,471	87.4	1,477,901	12.6	11,729,372	254,972	2.1	121,415	1.3
Electricity pylons	47,246,810	12,165,896	25.7	35,880,914	74.3	10,125,868	86.3	1,607,567	13.7	11,733,335	279,815	2.3	158,157	1.3

There are two sets of data for abortion on 17 May 1981 and for trade union representation and TV advertising on 11 June 1995 because there were two referenda held simultaneously on these issues (because sponsored by different groups).

Sources: Ministry of the Interior, <http://cedweb.mininterno.it:8880/referendum/ind_ref.htm>, for referenda from 1946 to 2001. Data for 2003 referenda calculated from Lelli, (2004): 324–5, tables B12, 13

THE BUREAUCRACY AND THE JUDICIARY

INTRODUCTION

If there is a single theme underlying the analyses undertaken in the previous chapters, it is the weakness of the State and citizens' relative lack of confidence in its ability to provide services delivered efficiently, according to norms of due process. Much of this has to do with aspects of the political culture handed down from the past (see chapter 4). In essence, economic and social diversity, together with a restricted suffrage and the hostility of the Church, combined to ensure that, after Unification, the new State found it difficult to win the allegiance of its citizens – which in turn meant that it had difficulty in asserting its authority against alternative, unofficial power centres organized around local elites. If this allowed local notables to manipulate state institutions in their own interest, then it also reduced the State's capacity to offer protection and public order, and to ensure the fulfilment of contractual obligations. By sustaining feelings of diffidence and low levels of interpersonal trust in general, this situation also sustained mistrust of public officials and the institutions they represented – thus ensuring that the State's weakness and inefficiency were, in effect, self-perpetuating.

This state of affairs was given a further twist in the first four post-war decades by the nature of the party system and the behaviour of the parties (see chapter 3). By stimulating the governing parties to 'colonize' vast areas of the State for patronage purposes, the Cold War-induced shape of the party system undermined the State's capacity for coherent policy making and ensured the persistence of strong elements of particularism in the distribution of resources. If this provided confirmation of popular perceptions of the State's inadequacies, then such perceptions were further reinforced by the authorities' manifest unwillingness or incapacity to exercise proper control over the activities of their institutional underworld, something that was also a product of the Cold War (see chapter 6). While this highlighted the importance of informal, and thus to some degree autonomous, centres of power in the workings of the Italian state, the dispersal of power was also a product of the country's constitutional architecture and the design of its formal institutions (see chapter 7). By fragmenting power, the design of Italy's national-level political institutions arguably placed a further limitation on effective government.

In this chapter we retain the focus on the State's difficulties in meeting the aspirations of its citizens since 1945 by exploring the organization and functioning of the bureaucracy (that is, those institutions associated with central government and the ministries which, in concerning themselves with administration, are linked by hierarchical structures of authority to the Cabinet) and the judiciary.

THE BUREAUCRACY UNTIL THE EARLY 1990S

It is probably because of their adherence to the notion that the public administration was a neutral entity, whose activities could be clearly demarcated from those of the political sphere, that the drafters of the Constitution were not concerned to include any articles establishing the boundaries of the public administration or its internal organization, thus leaving unchanged the structures they had inherited from the pre-war period.

The organizational model to which the post-war period thus became heir was one which, in its essentials, dated back to the so-called Cavour reform, a Piedmontese law of 1853. This sought to give effect to the liberal principle of ministerial responsibility by bringing together, within single government ministries, the functions of policy formulation and its implementation, and by establishing within each ministry a hierarchical form of organization, having the shape of a pyramid and established by law. The ministries were thus conceived of as machines, each of which would ensure the mechanical (that is, the rapid and precise) execution of the political instructions coming in from above (Melis 1996: 27).

However, since administrative procedures were to be governed by rules having the force of law, and since personnel were to be subject to rules of conduct, rights and duties, also having the force of law, public administration in Italy tended to be pervaded by a legalistic ethos. This rendered the efficiency and effectiveness of administrative action less than it might otherwise have been, for it engendered a heavy focus on the formal correctness of actions rather than on the contribution they might make to achieving desired outcomes. From the beginning of the twentieth century, this set in motion a process known as the 'flight from state supervision', referring to the emergence of so-called parallel administrations – structures existing within the orbit of the ministries but endowed with varying degrees of managerial and financial autonomy. Set up from time to time, their purpose was to deliver, on an *ad hoc* basis, the new services required by industrialism and the corresponding growth of the welfare state – and to do so with the necessary degree of managerial flexibility, unencumbered by the controls limiting freedom of action of the traditional bureaucracy. In this way, organizational pluralism emerged as a significant feature of the public administration.

The expansion in the size and range of functions of the public administration was accompanied by a growing tendency for it to draw in officials from the southern regions, where alternative employment opportunities were much more limited than in the north. And since the public administration had a position of near monopoly in the labour market for southern school-leavers and graduates, a strong incentive grew among public employees to demand conditions of employment that would give them security of tenure, as well as guarantees concerning career progression and earnings. Moreover, the public administration was sometimes used as an instrument for ensuring employment levels and reducing disequilibria in the labour market. From time to time, therefore, the rules governing career progression would be relaxed so that, instead of possibilities for advancement being limited by the frequency with which places further up the hierarchy became available, new places would be created. If this led to tasks being divided ever more minutely, making it increasingly difficult for the employee to retain sight of the overall purpose of his work, then it also allowed the popular perception to take hold that inefficiency in the public administration could be attributed to the cultural shortcomings of its (southern) personnel. Administrative delays and complications could be laid at the feet of employees supposedly attached to 'a cultural model typical of the peasant world . . . oriented to the conservation of one's property' (Cassese 1994a: 18) and therefore inclined to view their positions in terms of ownership rather than of service (Ginsborg 1998: 411). By providing a ready-made explanation for bureaucratic shortcomings, such beliefs ensured that popular frustration with the public administration would help perpetuate among northerners latent attitudes of hostility towards southerners – as would be demonstrated, much later, by the emergence and growth of the Northern League.

The final noteworthy feature of the public administration bequeathed to post-war generations was put in place by Fascism, and it concerned a proliferation of the numbers and types of parallel administrations as the instruments through which state involvement in the economy and welfare provision would be effected. On the one hand, the structural weaknesses associated with Italian economic development, combined with economic recession in the 1930s, gave rise to a tradition of active industrial policy symbolized by IRI (*Istituto per la Ricostruzione Industriale*), the state holding company established in 1933. On the other hand, in response to the unemployment of the Depression years, a number of previously voluntary social insurance schemes were made compulsory and run by several large sectoral agencies. Finally, a large number of agencies were established for specific industrial and agricultural sectors in order to enable producer and consumer groups to regulate production in their markets, to exercise quality controls, to manage professional registers and so forth.

Throughout the First Republic, any thoughts of rationalizing the structure bequeathed by the pre-war period were effectively vanquished by the consideration that to do so would be to upset the delicate balance of power subsisting between the governing parties. The problem was twofold. On the one hand, the process of distributing ministries and under-secretarial positions among parties and factions tended to be an extremely delicate and complex one, so much so that it was for long a matter of folklore that there existed a manual – the *Manuale Cencelli*, named after its supposed originator, a director of the personal office of the DC leader Mariano Rumor – designed to guide the participants in the negotiations (Furlong 1994: 116). On the other hand, any reform proposal would not only have had to find a majority in a highly fragmented Parliament, but it would also have had to be successful in dealing with the interlocking vetoes arising therefrom, and from the complexities just described, in order to obtain that majority in the first place.

The nature of the First Republic's party system also made its own distinctive contribution to bureaucratic inefficiency. In any industrialized democracy, ministers need senior officials to assist them in the making of policy by providing information, advice and operational solutions to the problems posed by policy objectives. On the other hand, such a need leaves ministers vulnerable to 'bureaucratic capture' – to the danger that they are unable to resist accepting *officials'* views about what policy should be in the area in question. This danger was particularly great in post-war Italy, given the weakness of governments and high turnover of ministers. But if this potentially made senior officials especially powerful *vis-à-vis* ministers, then in another respect it made them especially weak. For a high turnover of ministers combined with the fact that all senior-level appointments had to be approved by the minister, had potentially disastrous consequences for job security (leaving the administrative elite particularly vulnerable to attempts by politicians to use an American-style spoils system as the means to avoid bureaucratic capture, for example). So in order to avoid such a scenario, officials came to an unwritten agreement with politicians whereby, in exchange for their acceptance of an essentially marginal role in most major policy decisions, politicians agreed not to use their discretionary power to interfere with established patterns of promotion based on seniority (Cassese 1983). In such a situation, the outlook of officials tended not to be pro-active: since neither they nor the politicians conceived of their role as involving the exercise of much discretion, they tended not to be especially willing to take autonomous decisions – with obvious ill effects on management and the process of administration in general. Moreover, in order to overcome such effects, politicians tended to legislate in a very detailed way, setting out the fine particulars of administrative procedures – which only limited the discretion of officials even further, encouraging them to refuse to take initiatives that risked them exceeding their powers and hence exposing them to sanctions.

In a situation in which, precisely because of the legalism pervading them, administrative procedures were lengthy and complex, officials acquired a discretion arising from their power to help citizens overcome and circumvent bureaucratic obstacles in response to particularistic inducements. This is a very different kind of discretion to that which is deployed when the official undertakes autonomous action in a general cultural context of impartiality (Ginsborg 1998: 407). And the fact that citizens were highly unequal in terms of the influence they could bring to bear – and thus in terms of the service they could reasonably expect to receive – merely served to reinforce popular attitudes of cynicism and hostility towards the public administration.

Reforms designed to tackle this and other shortcomings tended to be piecemeal rather than systematic and co-ordinated (Della Cananea 1997: 203). Thus, in 1983, a new public employment law sought to bring greater uniformity to pay structures and terms of employment across the various sectors of the public administration; in 1988 there was the reform of the Prime Minister's office (see chapter 7), and in 1990 law no. 241 sought to streamline administrative procedures – but none of these was connected by any overall vision.

THE JUDICIARY UNTIL THE EARLY 1990s

Like the public administration, the judiciary has also been heavily influenced by party-political developments. Debate in the Constituent Assembly was heavily influenced by two contrasting positions concerning how the judiciary should be organized in the post-war period. On the one hand, the 'liberal' position argued for an apolitical judiciary subject only to the law, one enjoying strong forms of independence from other branches of the State. On the other hand, the Socialists and the Communists were conscious of the role which judges had played in repressing protest and the movement of opposition to Fascism, and were dubious about the commitment to democracy of an institution that had been almost completely untouched by the post-war *epurazione* (purge). Consequently, they wanted mechanisms that would prevent judicial independence allowing the institution's members to escape all forms of popular accountability.

The constitutional arrangements that were made for the judiciary in the end, in many ways represent a compromise between these two positions. On the one hand, the Constitution contains a number of articles which, in conformity with the liberal perspective, guarantee the judiciary a high level of independence from other branches of the State. For example, at the beginning of the section dedicated to the organization and functioning of the judiciary, article 101 stipulates that its members are 'subject only to the law' – the clear corollary being that they must be allowed to carry out their functions in complete autonomy, free of orders, directives or pressures of any kind and from whatever source. Practical assurance of this is then sought by means of articles 104 and 105, which, in establishing the free-standing *Consiglio Superiore della Magistratura* (High Council of the Judiciary, CSM), stipulate that two-thirds of its members are to be elected by members of the judiciary themselves, and that it is to have control over judicial appointments, assignments, transfers, promotions and disciplinary measures. Finally, article 112 stipulates that public prosecutors have a duty to initiate criminal proceedings – meaning that they are obliged to initiate an investigation whenever they become aware of evidence that a crime has or may have been committed. In this way the Constitution seeks to remove from other branches of the State the power to interfere in the administration of justice in such a way that the law is applied in a discriminatory manner. Thereby, the article seeks to ensure the equality of all citizens before the law.

On the other hand, the Constitution also contains a number of articles which, in conformity with the perspective of the Socialists and the Communists, are designed to prevent independence from allowing members of the judiciary to carry out their functions entirely free of any external or popular constraints. First, while two-thirds of the CSM are elected by members of the judiciary themselves, one-third is elected by Parliament from among full professors of law faculties and lawyers of at least fifteen years' standing. Second, the pre-war Ministry of Justice was retained; and while the final decision in disciplinary proceedings lies with the CSM, the Minister may initiate such proceedings. Third, article 102 gives effect to the aspiration to achieve forms of popular participation in the administration of justice by stipulating that special sections, with the participation of suitably qualified laypersons, may be established within judicial bodies for dealing with specific matters. In this way, the Constitution has made possible the involvement of outside experts in judicial decisions concerning, for example, minors, drug addicts and prisoners on parole.

The two contrasting perspectives – 'liberal' and Socialist/Communist – gave expression to the fundamental dilemma that lies at the heart of the judicial role. This is the dilemma that arises from the fact that, in applying the law, judges inevitably interpret and therefore create the law. If this implies the need for mechanisms of accountability in order to prevent judges from acting in conflict with popular aspirations, the insistence on accountability carries the risk of compromising judicial independence and, thus, impartiality. In the period since the Constituent Assembly completed its work, the dilemma, concomitantly with the growing assertiveness of the judiciary as an autonomous actor within the political system, has been increasingly keenly felt.

In the initial post-war years this autonomous role was very little in evidence. In fact, notwithstanding the strong guarantees of judicial independence provided by the Constitution on paper, in practice, the traditional pre-war capacity of the executive to condition judicial activity remained very strong. Essentially, this was due to the fact that the enabling legislation giving life to the CSM had to wait until 1958. In the meantime, though legislation passed in 1946 gave the judiciary a share in some of the executive's pre-war powers in matters of judicial appointments and promotions, internally the institution remained strictly hierarchical. The interests of the higher ranks of the judiciary in ensuring the continuation of hierarchy thus came to coincide with the interests of justice ministers in ensuring judicial compliance with their circulars and requests. The two sides had other reasons for wishing to collaborate at this time, one being their relationship of mutual dependency. If, on the one hand, judicial officers compromised by Fascism were potentially vulnerable to *epurazione,* on the other hand, ministers had no alternative but to work with a judicial corps the overwhelming majority of whose members had to one degree or another made their careers under Fascism. Finally, if the 1950s were conservative years, ones in which 'centrist governments . . . continued to use Fascist legislation to control, socially and politically, the left opposition and to obstruct implementation of the guarantees of freedom enshrined in the Constitution' (Neppi Modona 1997: 123), then this too facilitated the development of an essential convergence of outlooks between governments and the higher ranks of the judiciary. Thus it was that, notwithstanding the constitutional assurance (in article 107) that members of the judiciary differed only in terms of their functions, the achievement of the institution's so-called internal independence – the faculty of each judicial official to make decisions free of the influence of relations of hierarchy or dependence of one position on another – was delayed for several years after the war.

The first signs of a breakdown in hierarchy within the judiciary came when the Constitutional Court, provided for by article 134 of the Constitution, came into being in 1956. Before it was established, its role in settling disputes concerning the constitutionality of legislation and the relative powers of the different branches of government was performed by the Court of Cassation, the highest court of appeal for the system of ordinary law. Unsurprisingly, the new Court's establishment was viewed unfavourably by the highest-ranking judicial officers associated with the Court of Cassation, as it threatened their monopoly on interpretations of constitutional legitimacy, and in so doing gave a new freedom to junior members of the profession. For it was now open to them, during the course of proceedings, to request rulings on the constitutionality of laws of a court not composed of officials having direct authority over them.[1]

By giving rise to the widespread practice of seeking constitutional verification of laws, this new facility gave power within the judiciary to the efforts of those seeking reform of its internal structures. For, by helping to ensure the gradual implementation of the democratic principles that the Court of Cassation had previously obstructed, the habit of making use of the Constitutional Court helped to feed demands for greater democracy within the judicial profession as well. This process was also assisted by the natural process of generational turnover. That is, with the passage of time, the judiciary came to be increasingly composed of persons who had entered the profession after the Liberation. However, as the judiciary was a hierarchical organization, the change affected the lower ranks far earlier and to a far greater degree than the higher ranks, so that the passage of time saw the opening up of an increasingly wide rift between the innovative outlooks of the junior ranks and the more conservative outlooks of the senior ranks.

The substantial modification, if not elimination, of the significance of hierarchy within the judiciary was achieved with the passage of three items of legislation in 1963, 1966 and 1973. Essentially the legislation uncoupled 'career' and 'function', in the sense that advancement was detached from the availability of posts further up the hierarchy. Thus it became possible to move to higher grades and to achieve the corresponding salary increases while continuing in the same role.

A significant part in the achievement of this reform was played by the judiciary's professional body, the *Associazione Nazionale Magistrati* (National Association of Magistrates), which came into being after the fall of Fascism.[2] As an organization that sought to speak to the professional concerns of members of the judiciary, while bringing together all ranks on terms of equality, its very existence had inevitable egalitarian implications. If this led majorities within the Association to campaign for the abolition of judicial hierarchies, and by extension for democratization of the CSM (see below), then it played a significant role in bringing about the breakaway from the Association of the higher ranks that was marked by the formation of the *Unione dei Magistrati Italiani* (Union of Italian Magistrates, UMI) in 1961. Meanwhile, the dramatic social and economic changes of the 1960s, with their internal migrations and record levels of growth, acted as a stimulus for reflection within the Association on the role of the judiciary in contemporary society (Pizzorusso 1990: 51; Bruti Liberati 1997: 157). One of the most significant indicators of this reflection was the growing significance of factions within the Association – something that was marked by the emergence, in 1964, of *Magistratura Democratica*, a left-leaning faction, alongside the existing, more 'moderate' factions, *Terzo Potere* and *Magistratura Indipendente*. Left by the UMI split under the control of younger magistrates – ones who tended to reject the notion that legal interpretation could be reduced 'to a purely formalistic activity, indifferent to the substance and the actual impact of the law on the life of the country' (quoted by Pizzorusso 1990: 51–2) – the Association would play a significant role in the change in the method of election of the CSM in 1975.

When the law giving life to it was passed in 1958, the CSM was endowed with an electoral system that reserved a position of pre-eminence within the organization for members of the Court of Cassation. Of the fourteen members elected by the judiciary, six had to be members of the Court of Cassation, four had to be Appeal Court judges, and four had to be judges in the courts of first instance, the *Tribunali*. Since the First President and Prosecutor General of the Court of Cassation were members of the CSM *ex officio*, the result was to ensure that a majority of the CSM's judicial members would be drawn from ranks representing less than 3 per cent of the corps' members. Moreover, it was also stipulated that each member of the judiciary could vote only for candidates belonging to his or her own category (Neppi Modona 1997: 124–5).

In 1975 the electoral system was changed in such a way as to make the CSM more representative. From then on, all members of the judiciary were to be able to vote for all of the candidates – among whom the available seats were to be distributed, within a single national college, on a proportional basis. With this reform, a three-stage process leading to the emergence of the individual magistrate endowed with the autonomy enjoined by the Constitution could be said to have reached a culmination. The first stage, marked by the establishment of the Constitutional Court, saw the removal from the senior ranks of their monopoly on interpretations of constitutional legitimacy. The second stage, marked by the establishment of the CSM, saw the removal from the executive of much of its power to control the judiciary. The third stage, marked by the reform of judicial careers and the system of election of the CSM, saw the removal of much of the ability of the senior ranks to control the judicial activity of the lower ranks.

From a political point of view, the importance of this new autonomy lay in the increased potential it gave to public prosecutors to deploy their very significant power. Such power derived, first, from their *de facto* discretion in deciding what to investigate and what charges, if any, to press. Though article 112 of the Constitution obliges them to prosecute all cases that come to their attention, the volume of work makes this impossible, while the article makes it possible for them to initiate investigations, not only on request from external bodies, but also on their own initiative in relation to crimes they think *may* have been committed. Second, public prosecutors belong to the same profession as trial judges – that is, both are part of the judicial corps administered by the CSM. This, it is often suggested, allows for an imperfect separation between the roles of judge and prosecutor, with the result that trials can sometimes represent little more than the formal confirmation of prosecutors' investigations.[3]

As a consequence, from the mid-1970s the judiciary came under increasingly frequent attack from politicians, who began to complain of an illegitimate politicization of the institution. For, as a new generation of public prosecutors and judges increasingly replaced those who had been socialized under Fascism, there developed a new 'protagonism' on the part of members of the judiciary. Far from seeing their role as being to act as a passive 'bouche de la loi' (Guarnieri 1997: 158), significant numbers of judges and prosecutors adopted a far more active stance and – through penal initiatives in the areas of workplace safety, environmental pollution, tax evasion, fraud and so forth – sought to use their powers to act as problem solvers, attempting to tackle the great social issues of the day (Di Federico 1989: 33). In a number of celebrated instances, such initiatives were 'inconvenient' or embarrassing for members of the 'political class'. For example, in 1981 judicial investigations surrounding the Masonic lodge P2 and the collapse of the Banco Ambrosiano, revealed that the banker and P2 member Roberto Calvi had made illegal payments of $7 million to the Socialist Party. In July 1981 Calvi was sentenced to four years in prison for his part in the Banco Ambrosiano collapse. The violent reactions of politicians to Calvi's arrest included calls for political controls over the activities of public prosecutors.

Although the prosecution of such cases was undoubtedly facilitated by the institutional reforms described above, this is not to suggest that individual politicians were powerless in the face of judicial investigations damaging to them. On the contrary: despite the measures taken to develop and consolidate traditions of external and internal independence of the judiciary, not all hierarchical features of the judiciary's internal organization were abolished. Politicians were able to use such features to establish informal relations of connivance with individual members of the judiciary whereby they could protect themselves, and/or trade political favours (e.g. help in getting a seat in Parliament) for judicial favours (such as damaging a political opponent). For example, the work of public prosecutors' offices is directed by judges of the Court of Appeal or the Court of Cassation, whose responsibility it is, among other things, to assign cases to the individual prosecutors working under them. Directors of public prosecutors' offices have the power to remove individual prosecutors from specific cases on grounds of 'grave impediment' or 'significant reasons of service'. Likewise, when cases are ready to be brought to trial, decisions have to be taken concerning the individual judges to whom to assign them (decisions usually made by the presidents of the courts in question, the presidents themselves being appointed by the CSM). Each court, and its associated public prosecutor's office, has jurisdiction over a defined geographical area, except that the Court of Cassation can, for example, move trials from a given jurisdiction 'when security or public safety or the freedom of decision-making of the persons involved are prejudiced by serious local circumstances such as to disturb the trial and not otherwise eliminable' (article 45 of the Code of Criminal Procedure, quoted by Pizzorusso 1990: 144). Prosecutors General associated with the Appeal Court can take over cases from public prosecutors on the grounds that they have failed to act according to the terms established by law. Such procedures all created a number of points at which political pressures could be brought to bear. Emblematic of such pressures was the epithet that came to be associated with the Rome public prosecutor's office from the time of the terrorism trials associated with the 'strategy of tension' (see chapter 6). Called upon to adjudicate between the conflicting claims to jurisdiction of different public prosecutors' offices, the Court of Cassation tended to favour the Rome office, whose capacity to use all kinds of mysterious means to 'bury' politically sensitive cases and prevent them from coming to trial earned it the name of the 'foggy port'. The collusion that took place between individual politicians and members of the judiciary was well symbolized by the case of Claudio Vitalone:

According to the boss of the Roman DC Vittorio Sbardella, the career of Claudio Vitalone, ex-magistrate, senator and DC minister closely associated with Andreotti, resulted from a transaction between the two men: 'Since Vitalone had no electoral or political support of his own he got Andreotti's support by performing miracles in order to get him politically advantageous results by judicial means. What I mean is you can do something which will gain the appreciation of a politician either by judicial favours for their friends and supporters or, on the other hand, damaging political personalities who might inconvenience your friend judicially' . . . Claudio Martelli, justice minister in Andreotti's final government, stated: 'Claudio Vitalone was a man very close to Andreotti who had, at the same time, considerable influence in Roman judicial circles; not just in the Roman Public Prosecutor's office but also among judging magistrates and the Court of Cassation. You could say that Vitalone was the "long arm" of Andreotti in judicial circles.' (Della Porta 1998: 10)

Such relationships should not occasion surprise. Moving in the same social circles, sitting on the same government committees, having the same cultural outlooks,

members of Parliament and senior members of the judiciary would often be personally acquainted. That this could often give rise to the sense that, cutting across professional distinctions, there were common interests to be defended, was testified to by
the membership list of the P2 Masonic lodge. Besides those of the heads of the secret
services, various army officers, bankers, journalists, ambassadors and members of Parliament, the list also contained the names of eighteen high-ranking members of the
judiciary, including a former vice-president of the CSM.

Collusion between politicians and members of the judiciary was also encouraged by
the lack of prolonged training prior to entry into the profession and by the lack of any
separation in the careers of trial judges and prosecutors. These factors prevented the
development of 'a coherent set of values concerning . . . professional integrity and
ethos', leading instead to 'a corporatist logic according to which the judiciary . . . tried
to oppose any measure which could reduce . . . [its] "privileges" and status' (Alberti
1996: 285). These circumstances in turn made it difficult for the judiciary to remain
free of the political dynamics of the political parties whose support they sought in
opposing undesired measures. Second, the fact that twenty of the thirty-three members
of the CSM were elected by members of the judiciary as a whole, *whatever* their rank,
gave rise to a tendency for it to take decisions according to political, rather than hierarchical, criteria. Consequently, matters such as the distribution of resources, disciplinary sanctions, transfers from one judicial office to another, became highly political
issues on which individual members of the judiciary had an incentive to ally themselves with one party or the other.

Given all of this, political parties were often able to influence, through the judicial
factions closest to them ideologically, 'the assignment of magistrates to various posts
and in particular the choice of the heads of judicial offices' (Di Federico 1989: 35;
quoted by Alberti 1996: 287). The judiciary, for its part, was so highly politicized that
its members were often willing to turn a blind eye to acts of corruption in order to
maintain their privileges. Many prosecutors 'tried to break such a system but [were]
always blocked during their investigations either by indirect political pressures on high
level judges or by the non-cooperation of other colleagues. Thus . . . not all members
of the judiciary [were] inactive, but . . . it was sufficient to have the key positions
"covered" to neutralize most efforts' (Alberti 1996: 287).

By the end of 1980s, then, it could be said that judicial activities had come to express
the influence of two contradictory forces. On the one hand, the conquest of external
and internal independence allowed for judicial assertiveness in the political system. In
this, the abolition of judicial careers was especially significant; for, once advancement
had been uncoupled from the race for positions in the higher courts, positions in the
'front line' acquired a new attractiveness. It meant that judges and prosecutors with
several years' experience could remain active in positions that kept them in close
contact with social problems and ordinary people (Bruti Liberati 1997: 228). On the
other hand, judicial activities were subject to frequent, strenuous and meticulous efforts
by the political class to ensure that they were carried on under an informal system of
political tutelage that would prevent damage to the interests of the politically powerful. These contradictory forces would explode in the early 1990s, producing dramatic
changes in the scope of action of magistrates and in their relationship with the political sphere.

Table 8.1   Average duration of civil proceedings, in days, in courts of first instance and in appeal courts

Year	First instance	Appeal
1991	804	868
1992	900	1,004
1993	850	963
1994	859	1,004
1995	833	1,074
1996	864	1,031
1997	802	986
1998	815	997
1999	789	940
2000	839	950

Source: ISTAT 2001[a]: 250, table 5.3

This is not to suggest that, by the end of the 1980s, the judiciary was a popular institution. On the contrary. There has always been a lack of public confidence in the institution, which is partly a reflection of a lack of trust in the State at a general level, but at the same time reinforced by perceived shortcomings of the judicial function. These include the length of judicial procedures, perceived departures from norms of impartiality and due process, occasional miscarriages of justice, and the lack of professionalism. Both civil and criminal proceedings in Italy are usually very lengthy, and it is not uncommon for trials to carry on for three or more years before conclusions are reached (Guarnieri 2001: 76) (see table 8.1). The reason for this, at least in the case of criminal law, is essentially twofold. On the one hand, the so-called obligation to initiate criminal proceedings embodied in article 112 of the Constitution creates a volume of work for public prosecutors that is far larger than can reasonably be coped with (with the result that the obligation is often interpreted in a formalistic way, files being opened on cases that are then left pending until the statute of limitations has to be applied (Guarnieri 1997: 167)). On the other hand, the Italian legal system concedes an automatic right to appeal – on both legal grounds and grounds of fact – sentences handed down by courts of first instance. Following this, sentences can be further appealed on legal grounds to the Court of Cassation. Moreover, it is open to defendants to have recourse to the Court of Cassation to challenge, not just sentences, but any judicial measure for which there are no other mechanisms available for its reconsideration (Guarnieri 2001: 72). A number of so-called *riti alternativi* ('alternative procedures') were introduced with the reform of the Code of Criminal Procedure that was introduced in 1988. These were designed to increase the throughput of cases by making plea bargaining available to defendants willing to forgo a formal hearing and see their cases dealt with at the instruction phase. In fact, the desired effects have not been obtained, because the length of trials makes it more worthwhile for defendants to insist on the full procedure and to rely on the statute of limitations to prevent them from having to pay any kind of penalty (Guarnieri 2001: 70).

The fact that such stratagems are more widely available to those with the material resources to sustain long trials than to those of more humble means only adds to perceptions that the legal system frequently falls short of the obligation to ensure equality before the law. And if there are objective risks of bias in the legal system – such as the discretionary powers given to prosecutors by the sheer number of laws on the statute books and by the vagueness with which some criminal offences are defined (Guarnieri 1997: 167) – then the perception that such risks frequently lead to actual bias has tended to be reinforced by the numerous instances of apparent manipulation of proceedings, such as those leading to the acquittal of the P2 Masons in 1983 (Bruti Liberati 1997: 212).

Meanwhile, popular hostility towards the judiciary is occasionally aroused by high-profile instances of what appear to be miscarriages of justice. One particularly famous instance concerned the television presenter Enzo Tortora, who in 1985 was found guilty of drug trafficking and association with the Neapolitan Camorra and was sentenced to ten years in prison. The significance of this case was that much of the evidence against Tortora was based on the statements of criminals who had decided to take advantage of measures designed to facilitate proceedings against suspected terrorists and those involved in organized crime by offering incentives to those willing to turn 'state's witness'. The problem was that the measures contained insufficient protection of the rights of the accused in terms of provisions for verifying the truthfulness of statements made by such persons. In Tortora's case, the sentence handed down by the court of first instance was overturned by the Appeal Court, and his acquittal was then confirmed by the Court of Cassation. When he died of cancer a short time afterwards, it was widely believed that his legal difficulties had played a not insignificant part in the onset and development of his illness.

Finally, the judicial corps is often criticized for the supposedly poor quality of the training of its personnel. Entry to the profession is by means of a public competition, open to law graduates of at least 21 years of age, instigated periodically by the Ministry of Justice, and which consists of a series of oral and written examinations designed to establish candidates' knowledge of the law. This is then followed by a period of training, which in theory should be of at least two years, but in practice is often less (Pizzorusso 1990: 200), before the functions of prosecutor or trial judge are fully assumed. Frequently viewed negatively is the fact that the entrance examinations test no more than theoretical and juridical knowledge, and that there is a lack of opportunities for formal training after the functions of trial judge or prosecutor have been assumed. President Cossiga expressed in colourful terms a widely felt sentiment when he told the CSM: 'It is not possible to think that a boy, merely because he has undertaken a competition in Roman law is capable of conducting complex investigations against the Mafia and drug trafficking ... I would not entrust the administration of a farmhouse to such a boy' (quoted by Bruti Liberati 1997: 222). Given the dedication of large numbers of young judges to the struggle against organized crime (some paying with their lives in the process), it is likely that many who heard such remarks would have found them to be in bad taste. Yet, however lacking in respect for the commitment of those to whom they referred, expressed by the President of the Republic, they could hardly be expected to raise levels of popular respect for the judiciary as an institution.

CHANGES IN THE BUREAUCRACY AND JUDICIARY SINCE THE EARLY 1990s

The period since the early 1990s has witnessed considerable ongoing change in both the bureaucracy and the judiciary, albeit overlaid by elements of continuity with the past. Bureaucratic reform was prompted essentially by the pressures deriving from the Maastricht convergence criteria and Italy's need to qualify for membership of the European Single Currency. On the one hand, if Italy were left out of Economic and Monetary Union (EMU), there was the risk of being relegated to a marginal place in Europe, the country's industries – unable to benefit from the low interest rates and fiscal discipline that were thought to be the likely consequences of EMU – being placed in a position of competitive disadvantage. On the other hand, in order to qualify, steps had to be taken to reform the public finances – which pointed naturally in the direction of reform of the public administration, bearing in mind the close relationship between administrative arrangements and levels of public expenditure. Not surprisingly, the reforms coincided with eclipse of the traditional governing parties, and so began with the Amato and Ciampi governments in 1992 and 1993. Three sets of legislative interventions stand out as having been especially important.

The first, legislative decree no. 29 of 1993, changed the legal basis of public employees' contracts, stipulating that they would henceforth be based on private rather than public law. The effect of this was to undermine job security by abolishing the employment guarantees embodied in the previous legal framework, to insist on the principles of mobility and of pay differentials on the basis of productivity, and to impose targets on the managers of public offices. It also seemed likely that it would cap public-sector salaries, since contracts arrived at on the basis of collective bargaining and private law would remove the possibility that groups of employees had previously had to seek to protect the purchasing power of earnings through Parliament and by having recourse to the Regional Administrative Tribunals or 'TARs' (Capano 1992: 263).

The second, a series of measures taken by the Ciampi government in 1993–4, aimed at reducing the costs of administration through reform of structures and administrative procedures. Regarding the former, the Ministries of Transport and Merchant Shipping were amalgamated, and thirteen inter-ministerial committees and seventy-five collegial bodies were abolished (Della Cananea 1996: 327–8).[5] The government was given delegated powers to abolish a number of parallel administrations where these were found no longer to be performing any obviously useful functions. In the area of administrative procedures, an attempt was made to give effect to earlier reforms, which had remained unimplemented, concerning matters such as self-certification and the publication of time limits within which citizens could expect administrative activities to be completed. The remit of the *Corte dei Conti* (Financial Audit Office) was modified so that it would henceforth assess the efficiency and effectiveness of expenditure, not merely its formal legitimacy, and would assess activities rather than individual actions (Della Cananea 1996: 328). A 'Charter of Public Services' was published, laying down codes of practice for the delivery of administrative services to the public and means of seeking remedies for deficient service. Some of these reforms had a very significant impact on the legal framework governing the public administration; others were less successful, because they required action under delegated legislation, which was not taken by the government that succeeded that of Ciampi.

Table 8.2 The structure of the Berlusconi government as of 14 August 2004

Role	Current incumbent
Prime Minister	Silvio Berlusconi
Deputy Prime Minister	Gianfranco Fini
Undersecretaries of State attached to the Prime Minister's Office	Gianni Letta Paolo Bonaiuti
Ministers without Portfolio	
Regional Affairs	Enrico La Loggia (Undersecretary: Alberto Gagliardi)
Government Legislative Programme	Claudio Scajola
Civil Service	Luigi Mazzella (Undersecretary: Learco Saporito)
Innovation and Technology	Lucio Stanca
Italians Resident Abroad	Mirko Tremaglia
Equal Opportunities	Stefania Prestigiacomo
European Union Legislation	Rocco Buttiglione
Institutional Reform and Devolution	Roberto Calderoli (Undersecretary: Aldo Brancher)
Relations with Parliament	Carlo Giovanardi (Undersecretary: Cosimo Ventucci)
Ministries/Ministers	
Foreign Affairs	Franco Frattini (Undersecretaries: Roberto Antonione, Mario Baccini, Margherita Boniver, Alfredo Luigi Martica)
Interior	Giuseppe Pisanu (Undersecretaries: Maurizio Balocchi, Antonio D'Alì, Alfredo Mantovano)
Justice	Roberto Castelli (Undersecretaries: Jole Santelli, Giuseppe Valentino, Michele Vietti)
Economy and Finance	Domenico Siniscalco (Deputy Ministers: Mario Baldassarri, Gianfranco Micchè) (Undersecretaries: Maria Teresa Armosino, Manlio Contento, Daniele Molgora, Giuseppe Vegas, Gianluigi Magri)
Productive Activities	Antonio Marzano (Deputy Minister: Adolfo Urso) (Undersecretaries: Giovanni Dell'Elce, Giuseppe Galati, Mario Valducci)
Education, Universities and Scientific Research	Letizia Moratti (Deputy Minister: Guido Possa) (Undersecretaries: Valentina Aprea, Stefano Caldoro, Maria Grazia Siliquini)
Work and Social Services	Roberto Maroni (Undersecretaries: Alberto Brambilla, Maurizio Sacconi, Grazia Sestini, Pasquale Viespoli)

Table 8.2 *(continued)*

Role	Current incumbent
Defence	Antonio Martino (Undersecretaries: Filippo Berselli, Francesco Bosi, Salvatore Cicu)
Agriculture and Forests	Giovanni Alemanno (Undersecretaries: Teresio Delfino, Gianpaolo Dozzo, Paolo Scarpa Bonazza Buora)
Environment and Territorial Protection	Altero Matteoli (Undersecretaries: Antonio Martusciello, Francesco Nucara, Roberto Tortoli)
Infrastructure and Transport	Pietro Lunardi (Deputy Ministers: Ugo Martinat, Mario Tassone) (Undersecretaries: Paolo Mammola, Nino Sospiri, Guido Viceconte Paolo Uggè
Health	Girolamo Sirchia (Undersecretaries: Cesare Cursi, Antonio Guidi)
Culture	Giuliano Urbani (Undersecretaries: Nicola Bono, Mario Pescante)
Communications	Maurizio Gasparri (Undersecretaries: Massimo Baldini, Giancarlo Innocenzi)

Source: <www.governo.it/Governo/Ministeri/ministri_gov.html>

The third set of measures, law no. 59/1997 and law no. 127/1997 (known as the Bassanini laws, after their sponsor Franco Bassanini, the Minister for Local Government), were inspired at least in part by the realization that administrative complexity has indirect, as well as direct, effects on public finances (by virtue of the costs it imposes on the private sector). They were also inspired by the awareness that the traditional reliance on primary legislation as the means of regulating administrative conduct not only undermined still further the ideal of impartiality (by allowing officials to decide which of thousands of different sets of regulations to appeal to in dealing with any given case), but also made reform difficult – since it required most innovations themselves to be carried out through legislation. Thus, besides delegating to the regions and the local authorities a number of administrative functions via a process of legislative decree, the laws also contained, in their own words, 'urgent measures for the simplification of administrative practices and procedures of decision-making and control'. In this respect they were very much a continuation of the reform process begun under the Ciampi government (Rugge 1997: 720), and their 'vigorous slashing of the exasperating red tape surrounding the request for even the most basic documents such as the certificate of "civil status", or the rules governing participation in public examinations [seemed likely to] prove to be a boon for every citizen' (Gilbert 2000: 145).

With regard to the judiciary, the changes were a consequence of the explosion of the Tangentopoli scandal of the 1990s, which itself can be fruitfully interpreted as the outcome of an effort by a section of the judiciary to break free of the political constraints that had until then frequently conditioned their work. In this, a decisive role seems to have been played by magistrates' awareness – in the light of the unprecedented outcome of the 1992 election and especially of the result in Milan, where the investigations began – that the governing parties had been severely weakened. In particular, the explosive growth in support for parties such as the Northern League, whose own perceived *raison d'être* (at least rhetorically) was the struggle against the clientelism and corruption of the Rome-based *partitocrazia*, made it clear that the governing parties were very much on the defensive. It was thus evident that the magistrates would have the decisive backing of a public opinion 'excited by the idea that some of the most powerful persons in Italy, for long considered untouchable, would at last be made to account for their actions' (Ginsborg 1998: 504). The support of public opinion was crucial, for it ensured that as the investigations gathered momentum, the threat that politicians would be able to use their powers of *insabbiamento* – to manipulate proceedings using their contacts within the judiciary to avoid personally undesirable outcomes – was diminished. More generally, it reduced the likelihood that the political class as a whole would be able to respond to the onslaught by taking the kinds of legislative measures to which they had in the past been able to resort on occasion, to reduce judicial power.[6]

The judiciary's new-found freedom from the informal political ties that had in the past 'balanced' or checked its growing power must have seemed to not a few politicians a particularly threatening development. This is undoubtedly what explains the increasingly shrill reactions of politicians of the centre right whenever, in the period since Tangentopoli, the news of some new investigation, or progress in an existing investigation, has broken into the public domain. Such politicians' reactions have centred on the idea that large numbers of judicial investigators are biased in favour of the left and have been using their powers to damage politicians with whom they disagree. Prime Minister Berlusconi himself has been especially shrill in his denunciation of investigations into allegations against him as the work of Communist sympathizers who have been 'using the judicial system to eliminate political adversaries, riding rough-shod over the law, due process and reality itself, by means of contrived investigations, witnesses invented ad hoc, contradictory accusations, farcical trials and monstrous sentences' (*La Repubblica*, 5 September 1998, p. 13; quoted by Della Porta and Vannucci 1999a: 56).

The constant repetition of these sorts of claims has had a significant effect on public opinion – at the time of Tangentopoli almost unanimous in its support for the judiciary, now much more divided, and in many cases definitely hostile – thereby confirming that public support for the institution has always been fragile and highly changeable. Given the judiciary's long-term shortcomings, centre-right politicians have successfully drawn on such popular feelings to portray the institution as one that is inefficient, politically biased and in need of extensive reform. However, the government's proposals include plans to change the organization and functioning of the judiciary in such a way that its independence would be severely compromised. For example, the constitutional obligation on prosecutors to pursue all cases of suspected wrongdoing of which they are aware would be replaced with a power of Parliament to establish an order of priority of the types of cases to be pursued. Moreover, the proposals have been accompanied by a number of other proposals and items of legislation, which, by making the judiciary's work more difficult, have apparently been designed to serve the personal interests of Berlusconi and his closest allies.[7] The Prime Minister thus stands accused by many politicians and commentators of abusing his position in ways that undermine impartial application of the law as well as fundamental principles of the Constitution.

While, for Berlusconi, this simply confirms the political bias of the judiciary, there is a fundamental irony in the centre right's attempts to reform the judiciary: by exploiting popular hostility towards the institution in order to act in ways that so obviously infringe norms of due process, the political class risks perpetuating those feelings of cynicism and mistrust towards the State that have been such long-standing features of Italian political culture. And by perpetuating such feelings, in the long run the political class undermines the very security of its position that its judicial reforms are apparently designed to reinforce. But conflict between the judiciary and the executive/legislative branches of government is not the only way in which the position of the political class has been challenged in recent years: another is through conflicts between central and sub-national levels of government. It is to this issue that we turn in the next chapter.

9

CENTRAL–LOCAL RELATIONS AND SUB-NATIONAL GOVERNMENT

INTRODUCTION

In the last two chapters we looked at how power is distributed between the various structures of central government; in this chapter we look at how power is distributed geographically between central government and the various units of sub-national government. This is an especially significant issue in the Italian case, for, over a hundred years after the creation of the Italian State out of a heterogeneous group of independent kingdoms, the agitation of parties such as the Lega Nord for a form of regional autonomy that at times has been little short of a demand for independence highlights the continuing existence of a problem of national integration. Moreover, political scientists frequently argue that, partly as a consequence of globalization, governance is everywhere slipping away from national authorities to be partially relocated at sub-national and supra-national levels (Barrett 1996: 6). For this reason, policy is something that emerges from consultation and negotiation between decision-makers located in a wide range of institutional settings. This implies that a more than partial understanding of how governance and policy making are carried on in Italy requires an appreciation of the characteristics of the country's sub-national institutions and of how they interact with the institutions of central government. In considering this issue, we begin, as before, by describing the formal arrangements.

SUB-NATIONAL GOVERNMENT: FORMAL ARRANGEMENTS

In setting out the tiers of government below the national level, the Constitution establishes regions of two types: ordinary regions (fifteen) and the *regioni a statuto speciale* (Sicilia, Sardegna, Trentino-Alto Adige, Friuli-Venezia Giulia, Valle d'Aosta). The latter have statutes with the status of constitutional legislation (that is, legislation which, having been 'expressly provided for' by the Constitution, has the same legal status as the articles of the Constitution itself), whereas, prior to 1999, the statutes of the ordinary regions, once drafted, were sent to Parliament for approval. A little noticed constitutional change approved in November of that year authorized *all* the regions to decide upon new statutes for themselves, as well as their own electoral laws, while considerably reducing central government influence over their content – thus ensuring that the power of the centre to impose uniformity in these areas was correspondingly reduced (Newell 2000a: 169). Until 2001, when they were extended to all regions, exclusive competences were confined to the special regions, the ordinary regions having legislative powers that were concurrent only.

But more important than the legal distinctions is the symbolic significance of the difference between the two. The establishment of the special regions was a way of providing official acknowledgement of the claims of certain areas that they had particular needs and interests. Located on Italy's borders and on the two islands, and threatened by separatism and ethnic problems, the special regions were established early on precisely in order to defuse such threats. Thus, though Friuli-Venezia Giulia had to wait upon resolution of the Trieste dispute with Yugoslavia and was not established until 1963, the other four came into existence in 1948.

The ordinary regions, though provided for in the Constitution along with the special regions, had to wait until 1970 before the enabling legislation giving life to them could be passed. This was for straightforward reasons of party politics. The Christian Democrats in the Constituent Assembly, fearful of the consequences of centralized authority in a state open to capture by an apparently anti-system opposition, sought a strong system of regional government as a way of meeting this eventuality, while the Communists, for obvious ideological reasons implying the subordination of local particularism to the idea of national planning, opposed it. From the early 1950s onwards, the positions of the two parties began to reverse themselves. The Christian Democrats' realization that their hold on national power was likely – in the absence of any change in the basic parameters of the Cold War – to be indefinite led them to lose interest in regional devolution, as did their realization that to favour devolution would be to favour giving power to the Communists, who were electorally strong in the 'red belt' central regions. The Communists, meanwhile, came to favour subnational autonomy for exactly the same reasons: facing indefinite exclusion from power at the national level, regionalization offered the party a potential means of making an impact in the meantime, and indeed seemed to offer it a potential way out of its isolation in so far as the regional administrations could act as 'testing grounds' for the national-level alliances which it sought to build. Regionalization came when it did, then, in essence because Communist pressure conspired with a number of other political circumstances working in its favour to ensure that the Christian Democrats were unable to postpone it any longer. One of these factors was the growing belief that decentralization would increase administrative efficiency; another – and one which gained considerable motive power from the '1968 movement' – was the belief that regional government would raise levels of democracy by fostering citizen participation and responsiveness to local needs (Putnam 1993: 20).

Besides drawing the distinction between ordinary and special regions, the Constitution also establishes in outline (articles 121 and 122) the internal structures of each region, their powers and functions (while article 123 leaves it to each region's individual statute to resolve any more detailed questions concerning the powers and functions of its governing institutions). In each case there are three basic structures: the regional council, the *giunta* (executive) and the presidency. The council is the region's legislative body, and, as introduced in March 1995, the electoral law currently in force provides for regional councils to be elected once every five years by means of a mixed simple plurality/proportional representation electoral system.[1] The members of the executive are chosen by the regional president who is elected at the same time as the council.[2] The president's responsibilities are to represent the region in its external relations, to co-ordinate the policies of the executive, to promulgate regional legislation, and to supervise the execution of administrative tasks delegated by the State to the region. If a council passes a vote of no confidence in the regional president, the latter, along with the executive, is obliged to resign – but successful no-confidence votes also result in the automatic dissolution of the council as well, and the calling of fresh elections. Dissolution is also the consequence of a decision of the President to resign – a provision introduced by the above-mentioned constitutional reform of 1999 and clearly designed to improve the efficiency and effectiveness of regional policy making.

Finally, article 119 of the Constitution stipulates that the regions (along with the local communes, the metropolitan cities and the provinces) 'have financial autonomy both in terms of income and expenditure'. However, their freedom to impose their own taxes and to establish their own patterns of expenditure are in fact limited by the stipulation that such activities are to be carried on in conformity with 'the principles of co-ordination of public finance and the tax system' and by the powers which article 117 reserves to the State, to establish the fundamental principles whereby such co-ordination is itself to be achieved. Moreover, sub-national units of government are prohibited from borrowing money except to finance investment expenditure, while the State is not allowed to guarantee any loans made to them.

Below the regions are the provinces, and below them the communes – the lowest tier of government. Unlike those of the regions, the functions of these tiers are determined entirely by ordinary legislation. Organizationally, both tiers reflect the regional pattern: in each case there is a council and an executive whose members are chosen by a directly elected president (or mayor in the case of the communes), who also represents the province or commune with regard to its external relations. In practice, the communes are more important as units of local government than are the provinces. Formally speaking, the autonomy of both is less than that of the regions, for, in addition to having no constitutionally specified competences, they are obliged to carry out functions delegated to them by the regions. Analytically, the functions of both entities may be thought of as falling into one or another of three categories: (1) delegated powers to issue regulations in areas (such as local police, health, public works) which the commune or province is expected to organize, for the benefit of its inhabitants, on its own behalf; (2) administrative functions (such as the maintenance of military call-up lists) carried out on behalf of the central authorities; (3) rule-making and administrative functions delegated by the regions.

Prior to 2001, just as regional measures were supervised from above through the activities of a Government Commissioner, so the measures of the provinces and communes were similarly supervised. In this case the relevant supervision – which extended to the legitimacy and (where legislation stipulated) also to the merits of measures – was carried out by Regional Control Commissions based one in each regional capital, comprising three members elected by the regional council, one member nominated by the Government Commissioner, and a judge drawn from the TAR. In 2001, both the Government Commissioner and the Regional Control Commissions were abolished (see nn. 5 and 6 below).

Finally, though mentioned in the Constitution only with the reform of 2001, the 'metropolitan city' first made its appearance in an earlier wide-ranging piece of ordinary legislation designed to reform the system of sub-national government, law no. 142 of 1990. Processes of urbanization and industrialization over the post-war decades had led to an increasing concentration of population and economic activity in a small number of urban areas, giving rise to strategic and co-ordination needs not always adequately met by existing divisions of competence between communes and provinces. The problem was that the Constitution, through article 133, made provision only for altering the boundaries of communes and provinces, not for altering the functions attributed to them. Law no. 142 thus denoted specific large cities as 'metropolitan areas', and made it possible for the communes within the boundaries of such areas to come together to form metropolitan cities. These would acquire the functions otherwise given to the provinces, together with those of the functions of the participating communes that the latter decided to transfer to them.

SUB-NATIONAL AUTONOMY AND THE DEGREE OF CENTRAL CONTROL

The machinery of sub-national government described above gives its operators a capacity for discretionary decision making whose limits in practice have been set by two sets of factors: on the one hand, the attempts of the central authorities to impose legal, financial and policy controls; on the other hand, by the sub-national units' countervailing powers and by the way in which the controls themselves, paradoxically, empower the sub-national units.

Legal controls are intended to ensure that citizens are treated in accordance with universalistic, non-arbitrary criteria, and therefore aim to ensure that the acts of sub-national units of government are not *ultra vires* and that they are undertaken according to the correct, legally established procedures. However, the effectiveness of the control bodies mentioned above was often limited by clientelism, which is particularly well suited to the attempts of local authorities to resist legal controls. In accordance with the legalistic ethos that tends to pervade Italian public administration, control procedures are of a rather complex nature. '[T]he more complicated, frustrating and time-consuming the legal procedure, the more will some "special" intervention be necessary for getting the desired result' (Dente 1985: 144). Such 'special intervention' will usually aim to achieve objectives of a rather specific and immediate kind. Given that clientelism, by definition, involves the bending of (universalistic) rules as part of a (particularistic) exchange of favours, it will be the more successful the more specific the matter to which it is applied. In short, attempts by local authorities to resist legal controls makes clientelism more necessary and more likely to be successful.

Financial controls have two aims: to maintain a check on the total level of public expenditure pursuant on the national government's responsibilities in the macroeconomic sphere; and second, to ensure the reduction and eventual elimination of territorially based economic imbalances. These controls are achieved, first, by restricting locally based revenue-raising powers so that the income of local authorities comes essentially from nationally allocated grants (see table 9.1); second, by ensuring that the allocated funds are earmarked for specific purposes.

The exercise of these controls is, as far as regional government is concerned, in essence governed by law no. 281 of 1970. This allows regions not to impose their own taxes, but to retain the revenue yielded by certain types of taxes and to vary the rates – within nationally determined limits – of fees and charges for certain permits and regionally provided services. In 1988 these two sources together yielded no more than 3 per cent of regional income. The remaining taxes gathered by the regions all go into a common fund held by the Treasury, and are redistributed among the regions on the basis of such criteria as the regions' population, size, rate of emigration and rate of unemployment. A fourth source of regional income established by law no. 281 is a fund for the finance of regional development plans, whose monies are distributed among the regions according to annually established criteria and with particular regard to the development needs of the Mezzogiorno. Finally, regions receive income from 'special contributions' from the centre for specific purposes. These contributions rose steadily as a proportion of regional income throughout the 1980s, so that by 1990,

Table 9.1 Sources of regional income, current account, 1974–2000 (%)

Year	1974	1975	1976	1977	1978	1979	1980	1981	1982	1983	1984	1985	1986
Investment income	4.7	2.0	2.3	2.4	3.5	2.8	2.4	2.3	1.9	1.0	1.1	1.4	1.6
Taxes	8.0	4.6	4.2	3.2	3.1	2.5	1.6	1.7	1.3	0.9	0.9	0.9	1.0
Transfers	81.7	92.7	92.8	93.3	92.9	94.2	95.7	95.4	96.4	97.7	97.5	97.4	97.3
Other income	5.5	0.7	0.7	1.2	0.4	0.6	0.4	0.5	0.5	0.3	0.5	0.4	0.2
Total	99.9	100	100	100.1	99.9	100.1	100.1	99.9	100.1	99.9	100	100.1	100.1

1987	1988	1989	1990	1991	1992	1993	1994	1995	1996	1997	1998	1999	2000
1.7			0.5	0.4	0.3	0.5	0.4	0.4	0.4	0.6	0.8	0.3	0.4
0.9			1.7	1.9	9.6	14.9	4.5	8.1	8.8	11.8	32.9	34.0	38.3
97.1			97.5	97.5	89.9	84.4	94.9	91.3	90.6	87.4	66.0	65.2	60.9
0.3			0.3	0.2	0.2	0.2	0.2	0.2	0.2	0.2	0.2	0.5	0.4
100	100	100	100	100	100	100	100	100	100	100	99.9	100	100

Sources: ISTAT 1978b: 340, table 240; 1980b: 354, table 231; 1982b: 330, table 212; 1985b: 347, table 228; 1987b: 527, table 19.7; 1989b: 525, table 19.7; 1993b: 543, table 19.7; 1998b: 212, table 18.4; 2002b: 246, table 18.3

approximately 90 per cent of regional income was tied to precise instructions, laid down by the central authorities, about when, where and how it was to be spent.

At the communal level, control of income and expenditure takes place by similar means. In 1973 there was a major change in the laws regulating the income side, for in that year most communal taxes (which accounted for more than half of communal current revenues) were abolished and replaced by central government grants. From something of the order of two-fifths before the reform, central government grants rose to about two-thirds as a proportion of communal current revenues in the period following (Fraschini 1993: 82).

The reliance on central government grants does not unequivocally restrict the capacity for discretionary decision making. Nor does it matter whether government grants are tightly earmarked (as at regional level) or not (as at communal level). What counts is whether, as a general rule, ceilings are placed on local authority expenditure with the government grants only *then* being made available, or whether, on the contrary, the local authorities are given greater freedom to make their own spending decisions, which the central authorities then agree to underwrite by the provision of the necessary funds. As far as communal expenditure is concerned, the first of these situations prevailed only after 1977, when it became clear that the 1973 reform would have to be supplemented by measures to contain local expenditure. And even if ceilings *are* imposed, a presumption in favour of central government funding empowers the poorer areas, enabling them to provide services to a standard that they would be unable to achieve if they had to rely largely or wholly on their own autonomous sources of income. This is a particularly significant consideration in a country like Italy, bearing in mind the awesome north–south divide.

Controls over policy, or controls over the content of sub-national units' measures, are a consequence of the post-liberal welfare state, which assumes responsibility not just for protecting its citizens against internal disorder and external attack, but for protecting them against a whole range of problems, from ill health to unemployment to lack of education and so forth. In such circumstances, the objective of control becomes that of ensuring minimum and maximum levels of service provision regardless of where citizens happen to live. The principal instruments of control are the legal controls discussed above, and, aside from clientelism, their effectiveness has often been limited in post-war Italy by the party fragmentation existing at the heart of central government. Because of this, against such mechanisms as the power of the Government Commissioner to withhold approval of regional legislation – to take one example – the sub-national units could count on the fact that as unstable coalitions most of the time, Italian governments did not usually find it easy to take united stands on issues. Inter-party relationships at the national level have tended, in effect, to represent a network of interlocking vetoes giving rise on occasion to quasi-consociational arrangements. In such circumstances, local-level needs and initiatives are added to, and become part of, the quasi-consociational bargain whereby it is through the ties of party between national and local-level representatives that the demands of the latter gain a hearing. Given a complex process of bargaining, with a number of parties jockeying for advantage, it is not always clear that to veto the initiatives of this or that sub-national unit of government represents a particularly worthwhile proposition for a party.

It is precisely this lack of clarity which explains the failure, so far, to reform the 8,101 communes, the majority of which are too small to provide more than a limited range of services. Such communes would need to be amalgamated with others for services to be provided properly. That this has not happened so far is probably to be explained in terms of the sheer difficulty of knowing which parties would win and which would lose power as a result of such a general reshuffling of the cards (Dente 1985: 104). In the absence of a general reform, the main approach of government has been to encourage a series of *ad hoc* measures. In reality, the problem is twofold. On the one hand, there are diseconomies of scale arising from municipalities that are too small; on the other hand, there is an issue of remoteness in the case of communes that are too large (in 1971, forty-seven communes had more than 100,000 inhabitants). These problems have been addressed by the creation of organizations that complicate the basic three-tier structure: the creation of a series of inter-communal consortia in order to meet the first problem and the creation of sub-communal *circoscrizioni* in order to meet the second. The latter come in two forms: those that are elected (these also tend to have some decision-making power) and those that are appointed (these tend to have only a consultative status). In 1990, as part of the above-mentioned law no. 142, it was decided to provide financial incentives to encourage the amalgamation of the smaller *comuni* and to place a bar on the subdivision of *comuni* where this would result in the creation of entities with fewer than 10,000 inhabitants.

In short, power relationships between centre and localities in Italy are of a highly complex nature, and it is possible that the Italian system may be both centralized and fragmented at the same time. For strict controls on the *mode* of local authority action need not coexist with strict controls over the *content* of what they do. Moreover, the sheer heterogeneity of Italian local authorities in terms of such things as population, economic infrastructure and the wealth of their inhabitants, bring with it a corresponding heterogeneity in the autonomy enjoyed by each. Since policy is the outcome of a fragmented process of bargaining, local diversity means that the authorities are able to wield varying degrees of influence at the bargaining table. Italian sub-national authorities are therefore neither federal bodies nor mere agents of central government, but something in-between. This partly reflects the 'ineradicable ambiguity' (Sharpe 1981) at the heart of local governments everywhere: namely, that they are ultimately subordinate to national government (state or provincial government in federal systems), while also expected to respond to locally expressed political preferences.

ASSESSING SUB-NATIONAL GOVERNMENT PERFORMANCE

An obvious criterion by which to assess such responsiveness is the degree of efficiency with which demands are responded to. For governments which meet the demands of their citizens efficiently perform 'better' than less efficient governments in the sense that they are, by definition, able to meet the same demands for a lower volume of resources. Sub-national government performance, thus understood, varies considerably from one part of the country to another.

In attempting to explain this difference, Putnam (1993) has argued that what is important is variation in the degree to which the authorities' surroundings approximate the ideal of a 'civic community'. A 'civic community' is one in which citizens participate in public affairs, while allowing self-interest to be tempered by a recognition and pursuit of the public interest. They conceive of each other as political equals, are trustful of each other, and tolerant of political opponents. In turn, variation in the presence of civic attitudes and behaviours is, Putnam argues, appropriately understood in terms of the presence/absence of social patterns stretching back over a long time, possibly several centuries. Thus, in the north, relatively well-developed norms of social co-operation and trust – norms largely absent in the south – are a function of the considerably more participatory character of political life in the independent northern communes. What makes these historical traditions so powerful is that they are largely self-perpetuating through virtuous and vicious circles, whereby trust or its opposite leads individuals to act in such a way as to validate their trust or the lack of it, which in turn reinforces the grounds for trust or mistrust in the first place.

If this thesis about the importance of historical continuities bears any weight, then it is not surprising that the establishment of regional government in 1970 largely failed to meet the expectations of its supporters that it would succeed in cleaning up public administration and in modernizing the Italian state. The most powerful parties in the system had every incentive to ensure that the reform would leave traditional political practices intact. Consequently, elections at five-year intervals beginning in 1970 meant that the regions were simply taken over by established political élites. Clientelism and *lottizzazione* were simply reproduced at the level of the regions, the latter in effect becoming components of an overall power apparatus to be bargained over. For example, in the aftermath of the regional elections of 1980, the PSDI sought to enhance its prospects of re-entering the national-level coalition of which it was not then a member, by offering to exclude the PCI from power in three regions – Liguria, Lazio and Marche – where negotiations were proving difficult (Graziano, Girotti and Bonet 1984: 437). This is not to suggest that peripheral negotiations were always rigidly controlled from the centre. On the contrary, since the main aim in post-election negotiations was to manipulate as many contractual resources as possible, to be subsequently employed in the arenas of greatest strategic interest including central government,

[c]entral direction then had to be clever enough not to disclose a more global design. Indeed, in the context of very articulate negotiations in which parties tend to use as a resource the very opposition of their own local groups to the party line and the vetoes of other political forces, it would be counter productive to show too great a capacity for control of local tensions and conflicts. (Graziano, Girotti and Bonet 1984: 435)

But what is clear is that the impact of the 1970 reform was entirely dependent on the vicissitudes of the national-level party system with a consequent failure of anything like a genuinely distinct sub-national, or regional-level, political system to emerge. Meanwhile the almost total absence of administrative reform involved in, or accompanying, the transfer of competences to the regions (Leonardi, Nanetti and Putnam 1987: 101) meant that the inefficiency of the state machine would both survive the establishment of the regions and affect their operation.

The problems involved in trying to use the new regional structures to develop innovative forms of governance are best illustrated by reference to the case where such forms were most to be expected: Emilia-Romagna. Here, where the city of Bologna had long been held up as an example of efficient and innovative Communist government,[3] the PCI was widely associated with the so-called Emilian model of sub-national government. The principal components of the model were the attempt to turn into progressive public policy – and thus to base PCI rule upon – a social alliance between the working class, agricultural labourers and the rural and urban middle class in a social context that was predominantly rural but that also had an industrial presence based on small firms and 'sufficiently developed to sustain a significant working class movement' (Gundle 1986: 75). In such circumstances, the role of Communist local government was to help sustain the alliance by meeting and defending material interests and reducing the tensions arising out of economic development. For example, from the mid-1950s, Communist local government in Emilia sought to give expression to the anti-monopoly alliance formula by negotiating industrialization in such a way 'as broadly to favour the small industrial and commercial middle class and block the penetration of monopoly capital' (Gundle 1986: 77). By means of directed public spending, co-ordinated urban development, infrastructural provision and so forth, Communist local government was able to steer the process of industrial development in such a way as to avoid the sudden disruption of established life-styles. Through the development of neighbourhood councils, attempts were made to provide fora that could act as yet further instruments for the mediation and thus containment of conflict.

But such attempts at squaring the circle of conflicting interests encountered significant difficulties. In 1977 the demonstrations in Bologna of students and the far left, who accused the PCI of trying to smother dissent, made it clear that the attempt to impose consensus, with the party acting as sole mediator, was bound to antagonize those groups and forces which for one reason or another could not be brought under the consensual umbrella. Relatively minor in themselves (though one person was killed), the Bologna disturbances inevitably tarnished the party and indicated that its alliance strategy would have to be rethought (Edwards 2004). Later, more serious incidents (such as the Bologna railway station bombing in 1980 and the Italicus train bombing in 1984) seemed to add confirmation to the view that it was illusory to believe that the PCI's alliance strategy really could make of Emilia-Romagna 'a happy island in the troubled waters of mainstream Italy' (Gundle 1986: 90). Though a wider range of more efficiently delivered services was to be found in Emilia-Romagna than elsewhere, the region and its Communist-dominated administration could not escape the impact of the economic recession of the early 1980s.[4]

As long as economic growth was steady and continuous, the attempts of local authorities to mediate between different social groups would not be difficult; but when economic recession brought the groups' interests into direct conflict, converting a positive-sum into a zero-sum game, mediation was bound to be far more problematic. For example, a specific problem in the 1980s was the spread of algae along the Emilia-Romagna coast. This posed a significant threat to the regional economy because of the importance of the tourist industry. However, it was clear from the beginning that if anything was to be done about the problem, the region would have to enlist the active support and co-operation of the national government and of the other regions bordering the River Po, since it was the pollution of the river's waters by industrial activity and dumping in the interior that was responsible for the algae in the first place. Yet it was not until ecological disaster hit the Adriatic in 1989, leading to the wholesale cancellation of block bookings by foreign tour companies, that a national government, itself acting under economic constraints to cut levels of public expenditure, could be persuaded to allocate the funds necessary to tackle the problem.

If the achievement of co-operation was not without its difficulties in Emilia-Romagna – the one region where it was perceived to be at its most successful – the problems encountered elsewhere are not hard to imagine. Unlike in Emilia ('the buckle of the red belt'), the PCI had nothing like the same degree of 'social embeddedness' on which to rely to engineer consensus. On the contrary, outside the central red belt regions, and especially in the large cities, the party was forced to come to terms with a whole series of new social problems consequent upon rapid industrialization and large-scale internal migration. As a consequence, it had to deal with new political forces and groups, which could not simply be incorporated into an already established sub-cultural network of flanking organizations of the kind to be found in the red belt areas. The most striking examples of the problems of governance come from the large cities. In Naples, for instance, the PCI found itself in an impossible position: efforts to eliminate corruption meant that a number of social problems that had in effect been dealt with by illegal means could no longer be ignored by the authorities. However, in tackling these problems, the PCI needed the co-operation of people in key administrative posts controlled by its opponents, the DC, whose domination of the city over the previous thirty years gave it a vested interest in the maintenance of much of the situation that the PCI was trying to tackle in the first place.

By the mid-1980s, then, the experience of Communist influence in local and regional government was judged by most observers to have been a disappointment, and, not surprisingly, the party's showing in local and regional elections tended to reflect its declining fortunes at national level. Overall, one had to conclude that the regional reform had failed to alter the basic patterns of Italian politics to any appreciable degree, and that it had failed to live up to the expectations invested in it. Yet, in spite of this disappointment, public opinion in subsequent years continued to support the principle of regional reform. Furthermore, notwithstanding discontent with the performance of regional government, even greater dissatisfaction with the performance of the *national*-level authorities was eventually channelled – through the Northern League – into strong popular support for radical decentralization. The League's role in helping to bring about the electoral downfall, and eventually the disintegration, of the traditional governing parties enabled it to create an opening large enough to oblige the central authorities to concede reforms which, from the early 1990s onwards, were sufficiently thoroughgoing to usher in fundamental change. Just like the reform of 1970, therefore, reforms since the early 1990s have been a product of the vicissitudes of the national-level party system. If the 1970 reform was disappointing partly because of the concern of the dominant parties at the time that any reform should not disturb prevailing practices, then the disintegration of those parties, and thus of the system of power relationships they sustained, opened the door to a series of reforms that can fairly be said to have led to a renaissance of sub-national government in Italy.

REFORMS SINCE THE EARLY 1990s

The growth of the north–south economic divide in the 1970s and 1980s (see table 9.2), and in particular the emergence of the so-called Third Italy based on efficient small enterprises in the central and north-eastern regions, meant the emergence of a large

Table 9.2 Family expenditure in northern and southern Italy as percentages of the national average for family expenditure

Geographical area	1973	1978	1982		1987		1996
North-west	108	106	108	**North**	108	**North and**	111
North-east	111	112	114			**Centre**	
Centre	105	108	107		107		
South	83	82	85		84		77

Source: ISTAT 1975a: 409, table 354; 1980a: 323, table 305; 1983a: 322, table 314; 1988a: 629, table 20.1; 1998a: 288, table 11.10

constituency whose economic interests in the provision of efficient public services and low taxes conflicted with the reliance of the governing parties on clientele politics. Not only did the latter bring wasteful public expenditure and public-sector inefficiencies, but it was most widely practised in the less developed south. This created an opportunity for the Northern League – taking advantage of long-standing latent hostility towards southerners and the waning strength of anti-communism as an electoral mobilizer following the collapse of the Berlin Wall – to garner electoral support by arguing that a corrupt, party-dominated bureaucracy in far-away Rome sought to appropriate the resources of the north in order to maintain its own power in the underdeveloped south. Therefore, it argued that a set of federalist arrangements were needed, as these – by limiting the functions of the state to external defence, internal security, the administration of justice, and the provision of only the most indispensable of public goods – would remove from the central authorities those functions which allowed them to tax the north while giving very little in return. In other words, apparently wasteful public expenditure on the southern regions, combined with the fact that most of the total tax revenue needed to finance it necessarily came from the richer north, allowed the League to argue that the tax and spending activities of the traditional governing parties were regionally biased against the north. In this way, the League managed to use the taxation and resources issue to focus popular discontent with the traditional parties on the supposed need for regional autonomy.

The League's success in draining away support from the traditional parties, and thus its role (alongside the Tangentopoli corruption investigations and the other events of the early 1990s) in bringing about their demise, has meant that the parties that succeeded them have all felt obliged, with the sole exception of Communist Refoundation, to declare themselves in favour of a federal reform of the State (even though differing on what this means in practice). This can be seen in the substance of the decentralization proposals put forward by the coalitions of the centre left and of the centre right in recent years.

The first significant item of legislation was law no. 81 of 1993. It principally provided for the direct election of mayors, but also sought to increase the efficiency and effectiveness of local and provincial governments through concentrating power in the hands of their chief executives. From now on, directly elected mayors and provincial presidents with absolute majorities to back them were able to appoint and dismiss members of their executives without reference to their legislatures, were free to appoint such members from among non-elected experts, and could try to force the adoption of policies by threatening resignation (since this would lead automatically to the dissolution of the council). Since these changes took place in tandem with a decimation of the old political class by the Tangentopoli investigations, the outcome was, as Dente (1997: 184) points out, 'spectacular':

Between 1992 and 1993, the class of municipal politicians was completely renewed through the election of mayors who were either new to politics (e.g. Castellani in Turin, Sansa in Genoa, Illy in Trieste and Di Cagno in Bari) or different to the usual politicians (e.g. Cacciari in Venice, Rutelli in Rome, Orlando in Palermo and Bianco in Catania). Furthermore, the composition of the executives ('personally selected' by the mayors), combined with the transfer of power away from local authority legislatures, completely transformed local policymaking by substantially depoliticising it.

The momentum created by this success then stimulated further reform legislation. The year 1994 saw the definitive introduction of the *imposta comunale sugli immobili* (local property tax, ICI), giving local councils the power to tax property and hence a considerably enhanced level of financial autonomy; in March and May 1997, Parliament sought to remove the threat to local government autonomy and effectiveness posed by centrally imposed bureaucratic controls and procedures through the passage of two major pieces of legislation (law nos. 59/1997 and 127/1997) known after their sponsor, the Minister for Regional Affairs and Public Administration, as Bassanini 1 and Bassanini 2.[5]

Since the party system upheavals of the early 1990s, sub-national politicians have had considerably more freedom from their traditional subordination to the demands of national-level intra-party and inter-party power brokering. In the PCI, the definitive extinction of democratic centralism that was part and parcel of its transformation meant a considerable relaxation of national control over coalition formation at sub-national level. The larger number of small parties in the party system freed the hands of local politicians in so far as the lack of organizational and power resources in smaller parties made central control more difficult than it is in larger parties. Regional-level politicians and the mayors of large cities were not slow to take advantage of their new freedom, attempting, wherever possible, to build power bases independent of the national-level structures of the parties to which they belong. A clear example of this was the so-called 'Mayors' Party' – a loosely organized cross-party structure surrounding the charismatic mayor of Venice, Massimo Cacciari – which, in the aftermath of the 1996 general election, attempted to cut the ground from under the Northern League by campaigning for decentralizing reforms on an explicitly cross-party basis.

In seeking to respond to the electoral challenge posed by the new 'federalism' issue, the centre left was aware that it had to advance proposals that would offer a convincing increase in regional autonomy, but without depriving the centre of the instruments necessary to ensure equality in public-service delivery between rich and poor areas of the country. It therefore seemed possible, following the failure of the parliamentary Commission for Constitutional Reform in 1998, that the centre left government would not go beyond the Bassanini laws. However, the centre left government was also aware of the apparent strength of feeling in the north. November 1999 had seen the passage of a constitutional amendment which had changed the way in which regional presidents were elected, thereby increasing their political standing, and many of them exploited their new status to maintain pressure for a federalist reform. Moreover, the government presumably felt, in the light of the forthcoming May 2001 general elections, that it needed 'to make it difficult for the centre-right to introduce a radical version of federalism in case they formed a government' (Cento Bull 2002: 190).

The government therefore secured modification of Title V of Part II of the Constitution, which sought to reconcile the competing demands of regional autonomy and the maintenance of equality. On the one hand, the concurrent legislative powers conferred on the regions by article 117 were replaced by the stipulation that the State has exclusive legislative powers in matters which are listed in detail; the State and regions have concurrent legislative powers in other matters, which are also fully listed; and the regions have exclusive legislative powers in all remaining matters (which are not listed).[6] On the other hand, the exclusive legislative powers conferred on the State include 'the equalization of financial resources' and 'determination of the essential levels of service concerning the civil and social rights which must be guaranteed throughout the national territory'.

Whether the centre left government can be said to have succeeded in reconciling autonomy and equality in this way may be doubted. For instance, the clause that attributes to the State the power to ensure that minimum standards of service are guaranteed across the peninsula is susceptible to being interpreted in many different ways (Cammelli 2003: 88): it could be used by the State to minimize the legislative powers granted to the regions, or it could be branded as justification for reducing to a bare minimum the transfer of resources from the richer to the poorer regions (Cento Bull 2002), and observers have also pointed to a number of other shortcomings of the reform. First, there was no attempt to transform the Senate into a Chamber of the Regions (which would be necessary in order for anything that informed observers would agree to call 'genuine federalism' to be achieved). Second, the clause conferring concurrent legislative powers fails to draw a clear-cut division among tasks and responsibilities – with the consequence that the disputes between different layers of government that were the norm prior to the reform (Hine 1993a: 258) seem set to continue. Third, there are a large number of functions listed as falling within the purview of the State (either because subject to concurrent powers or because subject to the exclusive legislative powers of the State) – which has left many observers wondering about the extent of the additional competences that the regions have actually acquired (Cento Bull 2002: 190–1; Capotorto 2002: 16–19).

For its part, the centre right criticized the reform on just this ground (among others). Northern League leader, Bossi, declared after the Cabinet had approved the centre right's preferred reform on 13 December 2001 that, thanks to the government's decision, 'Today everything has changed . . . we no longer have the minifederalism of the left with the small-scale competences that the regions more or less had already' (quoted by Luciani 2002: 141). In fact, a number of observers (Cento Bull 2002; Luciani 2002; Parker and McDonnell 2003) have expressed doubts about how much the centre right's proposals really add to the degree of sub-national autonomy that the centre left's reform had granted already.

It is true that in the immediate aftermath of the 2001 election it looked as though the new government just might pursue something quite radical. At the beginning of July 2001, the new Minister for Institutional Reform, Umberto Bossi himself, presented proposals providing for a revision of article 117 giving regions the power to invoke, or to 'activate', on their own authority, exclusive legislative powers in four areas, including health, schools and local policing.[7] Moreover, the regions were to be given a new role in electing members of the Constitutional Court,[8] a proposal thought to be motivated by a perceived anti-regional bias on the part of the Court and by a desire to give the Court a right-wing majority, since most of the regions are currently run by coalitions of the centre right. In addition, the constitutional provision giving parliamentarians immunity from prosecution for opinions expressed during the course of their duties was to be extended to regional councillors (a proposal thought to be motivated by a long-standing animosity of the League towards the judiciary arising from periodic prosecutions of its representatives for defamation, vilification and so forth). However, under pressure from his allies, Bossi was subsequently forced to moderate his position, and the latter two provisions were dropped from the proposal, which was then presented to Parliament.[9]

The most significant likely effects of the bill are twofold. First, it is up to each region to decide whether to take the powers granted to it by the proposed constitutional change or to continue to rely on the State as in other areas. On the one hand, this represents a radical new departure in central/sub-national relations, one reminiscent of Spain – where sub-national tiers of government enjoy varying degrees of autonomy, according to their size, wealth and preparedness for self-government. On the other hand, the centre left's reform already makes possible such a system in so far as article 116 of the Constitution stipulates that 'Additional specific forms and conditions of autonomy . . . can be given to [the] Regions by State law on the initiative of the Region concerned'. What is different about the centre right's proposal is that it allows the regions to take powers unilaterally, even *without* the agreement of the central authorities. Second, the areas in which the bill allows the regions to take exclusive powers – health, education and policing – are big spending areas, highly significant in citizens' everyday lives. Therefore, differentiation and competition between regions could become a salient feature of public life in Italy. The implications of this are potentially significant. Giving the regions powers to legislate in different ways and to organize functions differently means that they can compete with each other in terms of the quality and efficiency of the services they provide. For, even if we assume that all regions have access to the same level of funding, they will spend it in different ways. While this is welcomed by the centre right, because seen as conducive to an overall, if non-uniform, improvement in standards, it is opposed by the left as subversive of the principle of equality of service provision across the national territory.

Finally, it is noteworthy that the bill contains no reference to the 'Chamber of Autonomies', to replace the existing Senate, which had initially appeared to be one of Bossi's priorities. If, as has been claimed, the omission is to be explained by a desire deliberately to exclude the creation of a body in which each region would have the same power regardless of wealth (Manzella 2001; quoted by Cento Bull 2002: 195), then it may be symptomatic of lingering separatist designs in so far as it implicitly prioritizes the interests of the north over the project of a reform of the Italian State as a whole.

CONCLUSION

As Cento Bull (2002: 199) and others have suggested, the current situation with regard to devolution 'can only be described as transitional', in at least two senses. First, it is often pointed out that the concrete effects of the recent constitutional reform will become clear only as the new provisions are applied and argued over before the Constitutional Court and in other fora. Second, and in a broader and deeper sense, the issue of the relationship between centre and sub-national levels has become a matter of relatively clear-cut differentiation between government and opposition,[10] and one of the effects of this has been – arguably – to weaken the Constitution as a whole. By setting the precedent of securing significant constitutional change unilaterally, the centre left government has – it may be suggested – increased the likelihood that the Constitution 'ceases to be the fixed and enduring point of reference for all players and becomes terrain at the disposal of temporary majorities and of inevitably partial and precarious measures supported by such majorities' (Cammelli 2003: 91). And to the extent that constitutional change does become piecemeal in this way, so the overall coherence of the founding document is undermined, thus weakening it still further.

Whatever the outcome of the current process of transition in Italy, it is clear that the institutional arrangements governing central–local relations that finally bed down will both reflect and have very significant implications for the distribution of power between the political forces at the national level. Politicians of the right such as Giulio Tremonti (Minister of Finance in the second Berlusconi government) have responded to the League's demands by seeking to tie the dissatisfactions spearheaded by them more closely to their own concerns to reduce taxation and levels of public expenditure wherever they may be undertaken or incurred: north, south, east or west (Tremonti and Vitaletti 1994). Politicians of Tremonti's persuasion emphasize what they see as a basic flaw in existing arrangements governing financial relations between centre and periphery: namely, the fact that by far the largest proportion of the expenditure of sub-national units of government is financed by means of transfers from the centre. As far as they are concerned, this gives rise to the problem that it breaks what they think ought to be the links between electoral, taxation and spending decisions. Local legislators have no incentive to restrain public expenditure, since they are not responsible for the electorally hazardous taxation decisions that have to be made if the expenditure is to be financed. This in turn means that electors are less readily able to appreciate the taxation implications of the expenditure they vote for locally, and since national-level politicians will not want to risk electors' wrath through unpopular tax increases, they are likely to have recourse instead to the bond market. There is, therefore, an in-built tendency for both the level of public expenditure and the level of public indebtedness to rise. What Tremonti and others propose is *federalismo fiscale* (fiscal federalism), by which they mean legislation which would give sub-national units of government their own tax-raising powers while making them responsible for raising the sums required to finance the services for which they are responsible entirely from among their own citizens. In this way, it is argued, voters would be able to see clearly the precise costs attached to the spending proposals they are offered in parties' programmes, and so democratic control over expenditure would be restored.

In advancing such proposals, politicians of the right echo the concerns of those of their forebears in the Constituent Assembly who sought to use regionalism as 'a device to shift power out of the hands of the centralized state before the workers could get their hands on it' (Keating 1988: 187). With the passing of the traditional governing parties and of the *conventio ad excludendum* that once permanently shut the left out of real power, new ways had to be found to neutralize it. One of the ways of doing so is to alter the institutional framework so that, if the left can no longer be prevented from entering the *stanza dei bottoni* ('control room'), one can at least make certain – through a timely removal of the relevant powers to the regions – that a number of the levers in the 'control room' are not actually attached to anything. And if this observation thus highlights the significance of the current debate over institutional reform at the sub-national level, it also serves to re-emphasize the point that institutions matter, because it is by and through them, in Italy as everywhere, that the basic terms and resources of the political contest are established.

GOVERNING THE ECONOMY I: BIG INDUSTRY AND THE PUBLIC–PRIVATE DIVIDE

INTRODUCTION

Broadly speaking, one can view an economy from either a structural or a territorial perspective. From a *structural* perspective, O'Connor (1973) divides industrial activity into three sectors: competitive (largely small firms in traditional industrial sectors and commerce), monopoly (big private industry) and the State (publicly owned or part-publicly owned). Each country will contain a distinctive mix of sectors, and different sizes of firms within each sector. Italy's industrial structure embodies three dualisms: first, a dualism between a few large industries and a myriad of extremely small firms, with hardly any medium-sized enterprises in between; second, a dualism in large industry between a substantial state-controlled sector (the largest of any Western democracy) with a distinct model of intervention and a relatively small private sector; third, a division between traditional sectors and very modern or advanced sectors.

From a *territorial* perspective, each country will be unique in its spatial diffusion of economic sectors. There is, in Italy, a rough territorial division of industrial activity which coincides with the structural division, creating 'three Italies': the monopoly sector being dominant in the industrial triangle of the north-west; the state sector operating largely (but not only) in the underdeveloped (and until the 1960s, agrarian) south; and the competitive sector operating largely in the centre and north-east (see figure 4.2). The notion of the 'three Italies' emphasizes two distinct territorial features: first, dualism between an advanced north and a largely underdeveloped south; and second, the distinctiveness of the area of small firms and industrial districts, located in the centre and north-east, whose geographic concentration has been an important determinant of the development of a particular socio-economic model known as the 'Third Italy' (Bagnasco 1977).

It follows that, in the Italian case, the structural and territorial approaches can, to a large extent, be integrated (big industry in the north-west, the underdeveloped south, small firms in the centre and north-east), although there is inevitably a degree of overlap between the categories (e.g. the role of big industry in the south). This and the following chapter, therefore, are organized around the notion of the 'three Italies', with some adjustment to accommodate structural peculiarities that do not fit neatly into the territorial categories.[1] Whereas chapter 11 analyses the problems of the south and the distinctiveness of the centre/north-east, this chapter explores big industry from the perspective of the dualism between the public and private sectors, incorporating an analysis of the state sector, which has been particularly significant in the south. The first two sections analyse the model of state and private capitalism that developed in the period until the early 1990s. The third section analyses the changes that have occurred since the beginning of the 1990s, before concluding with an assessment of whether they amount to a transformation in the Italian post-war model of large-firm capitalism. The common theme across both chapters is the distinctive role of the State in its regulation of the economy.

BIG INDUSTRY IN THE STATE SECTOR: THE STATE HOLDINGS FORMULA

The State sector of the economy in post-war Italy was, until recently, the largest of any non-Communist state. The origins of its size lay in several factors. Italy needed to industrialize rapidly in the post-war period (over 40 per cent of the labour force was employed in the agricultural sector), yet the backwardness of the private sector and a restricted capital market made this difficult to achieve. At the same time, there was an inheritance from Fascism of state-controlled companies (in steel, shipbuilding, sea transport, the mechanical and electromechanical industry, and parts of the electricity industry). The liberalization measures taken by Einaudi in the early part of the post-war period were accompanied by the view that a special form of state leadership was needed to build up industries in what were defined as 'strategic' areas. Private industry was too weak, and ordinary administration was viewed as too inflexible and associated with the former Fascist regime (Barca and Trento 1997). This special form of state leadership was developed through what became known as the 'state holdings' formula, which became a distinctive model, differing from the two types of public intervention ('general government' and 'public enterprises') common in post-war Western democracies (Padoa Schioppa Kostoris 1993: 27).

In the state holdings formula, the State set up large holding companies which (in 1956) were placed under the general jurisdiction of the newly created Ministry of State Holdings (*Ministero per le partecipazioni statali*). The holding companies either controlled companies or had a stake in them, while allowing them to be run like private companies with boards of directors and shareholders. It was felt that these companies would have more autonomy and incentives than their counterparts in public enterprises to pursue commercial objectives. At the same time, they could be used to further certain industrial and social goals (Padoa Schioppa Kostoris 1993: 23).[2] Three main state holding companies were set up:[3]

1   *IRI*   The most important holding company was the Institute for Industrial Reconstruction (*Istituto per la ricostruzione industriale*, IRI), which provided a model for the others. It was originally set up in 1933 under Fascism (to help industry after the Depression) and was kept intact after the war to assist in building up Italy's steel and engineering sectors. IRI developed into Europe's largest single company

(excluding oil companies), owning, by the late 1980s (before privatization) over 600 subsidiaries through several sectoral holding companies. These included Ilva (originally Finsider, the bulk of Italy's steel industry); Finmeccanica (engineering); Finmare (maritime insurance); STET (telecommunications, with control over SIP – telephones – and Italtel – telecommunications equipment); Alitalia (state airline); RAI (state broadcasting corporation, with three television and three radio channels); SME (food group); SACI (television advertising agency); ERI (RAI's publishing arm); CIT (state tourism holding); *Autostrade* (motorways); three major national banks, and CARIPLO, the world's largest savings bank.

2 *ENI* The *Ente Nazionale Idrocarburi* (ENI, National Hydrocarbons Corporation), was set up in 1953 and was responsible for coal and oil, manufacturing, chemicals, the nuclear industry, engineering and services. It controlled over a dozen important companies and some 300 agencies, and in the late 1980s was among the largest twenty-five European companies in terms of sales. The companies included AGIP (petrol and other related activities); SNAM (transport of hydrocarbons); ANIC (chemicals and refining); AGIP*Nuclear* (nuclear industry); SAIPEM (industrial plants); TESCON (textiles) SEMI (tourism and catering); *Snamprogetti* (engineering).

3 *EFIM* The function of the *Ente Partecipazioni e Finanziamenti Industria Manifatturiera* (EFIM, Agency for Financing of State's Manufacturing Industry) was to assist industrial development through control over a number of firms and holding companies. These included the *Ernesto Breda Holding Company* (mechanics); the *Breda Railway Company* (transport); SOPAL (food); and INSUD (development in the south).

The impact of the state holding companies on industrial output was considerable because of their overall size, which expanded considerably during the post-war period. By the 1990s, there were very few sectors of the Italian economy in which the State did not have a major influence or which it did not largely control, and the influence extended well beyond what were originally intended to be only 'strategic sectors'. The industries included steel, metals, shipbuilding, motorways, telecommunications, broadcasting, hydrocarbons, electricity and other forms of energy, chemicals, aerospace, arms, glass, mining, clothing and fashion, agricultural agencies, food and restaurants, shipping, insurance, film and publishing. By the 1990s, the three main holding companies (IRI, ENI and EFIM) were together responsible for almost 30 per cent of sales and 50 per cent of fixed investment in Italy. IRI employed over half a million people, and by the late 1980s had a turnover of nearly 50 trillion lire. In addition, banking and finance were also largely controlled by the State. Besides the banks owned by holding companies, the State directly owned six other national banks, all thirty-one lending banks, *Italcasse* (a group of eighty-five regional savings banks) and various big credit organizations, notably the *Istituto mobiliare italiano* (IMI), which was responsible for funding most of Italy's public works projects. It is not surprising, therefore, that post-war Italy has been portrayed as being close to a Communist state in terms of its structure of public ownership. For this reason, and because of the distinctiveness of the state holdings formula, the Italian economy has stood out from those of other Western democracies (Leon 1993: 125). The performance of the model, however, turned out to be less impressive.

If the basic idea was to use the State (in an innovative manner) to fill the entrepreneurial gap left by the private sector and promote new industry, then the first two decades witnessed a degree of success (Coltorti 1993; Leon 1993). For example, IRI rationalized and modernized the steel sector, turning it into one of the most profitable sectors of the economy. Annual net profits rose from approximately 2 billion lire in 1954–5 to 16 billion lire in 1962–3 (of publicly quoted companies, only FIAT and Edison made higher profits in the latter two years). In the energy sector, ENI was set up on the back of the discovery of natural gas reserves in the Po Valley, and oversaw a rapid rise in gas production and a proliferation of pipelines necessary to distribute the gas. A successful programme was also developed for the production of synthetic rubber and nitrous fertilizer based on natural gas. In telecommunications, a programme of modernization and expansion was begun, particularly after the telephone service companies merged to form SIP in 1964. Based on these early successes, state intervention was stepped up in the 1960s, and public administration (traditionally weak and unreformed) was increasingly bypassed by existing and newly founded bodies in the state holdings system (Barca 1997a). The nationalization of the electricity industry was the most significant undertaking, but state-controlled companies were also directed towards assisting the industrialization of the south (see chapter 11) and fulfilling the objectives of the 1966–70 plan (see chapter 2). At the same time, they were required to preserve their 'entrepreneurial function' by operating 'in keeping with strict criteria as regards cost effectiveness' (Coltorti 1993: 74).

However, when the economic climate became more difficult, so the tensions inherent in the state holdings formula came to the fore, and the formula entered into crisis. During the 1970s the companies were subject to more political control, of an anti-entrepreneurial character. The cost-effectiveness constraint was abandoned, and state-controlled companies were increasingly used to acquire troubled firms in the private sector. This led to repeated requests for increases in their endowment funds, to cover growing financial demands. Paradoxically, at precisely the time when a restructuring of industry was needed (which was made more difficult anyway in state-controlled firms because of the difficulties of decentralizing production and restrictions imposed by the labour market and trade unions), the state holdings formula imposed increasing rigidity on the system. Innovation and efficiency were sacrificed to the socio-political goal of assistance, thus altering the delicate balance between social objectives and commercial needs (Padoa Schioppa Kostoris 1993: 28).

Acquisitions were made in wide-ranging sectors that often went beyond the primary concerns of the different holding companies and also went beyond large industry. ENI, for example, purchased a number of clothing and textile companies; SME (under the control of IRI) bought Alemagna, Cirio and Star food companies; and EFIM bought the Montedison aluminium business. Moreover, new agencies were set up with the explicit purpose of expanding state control into troubled areas. The two most notorious instruments of this practice were the *Ente Autonomo di Gestione per le Aziende Minerarie Metallurgiche* (EGAM) and the *Società di Gestione e Partecipazioni Industriali* (GEPI). EGAM was created in 1958, but started its operations in 1971 to assist troubled firms in the iron and steel industry. It acquired failing companies at a rapid rate (forty in three years), with losses by the mid-1970s of 144 billion lire, and was dissolved in 1977. GEPI was set up in 1971 (under the auspices of IMI, IRI, ENI and EFIM) as a temporary means of using public funds to protect or expand employment where it was threatened by what were termed the 'short-term difficulties' of industrial firms in the private sector. If a firm was taken over, the expectation was that it would be resold fairly quickly. Through GEPI, therefore, the scope of public intervention was extended beyond state-controlled firms, and the agency quickly became a political instrument for bailing out small and medium-sized firms. By the mid-1970s more than a hundred firms employing 40,000 workers had been assisted to the tune of a total of 330 billion lire, and accumulated losses were 86 billion lire, higher than the initial capital outlay, thus requiring further financing (Coltorti 1993: 76–80). Endowment funds, originally used for investment, became simply a way of covering losses, and they were granted largely without conditions. Furthermore, it was found difficult to transfer firms back into the private sector once they had been taken over. In short, competitiveness was largely overlooked in favour of saving jobs, expanding employment in underdeveloped areas and protecting wages and working conditions (Gros-Pietro 1993: 144).

The losses of the State-controlled companies continued to rise throughout the 1970s, reaching a peak in the years 1981–3, when the combined losses of IRI (excluding banks), ENEL, ENI and EFIM amounted to 20.51 trillion lire. While the 1980s saw some reversal of this trend and improved performance (especially through IRI coming back in to profit by 1986 under the leadership of Romano Prodi), it was nevertheless clear that the state holdings formula had become an anachronistic burden on economic performance. Three factors can be identified to explain the failure of the formula:[4]

1 *Multiple objectives* To work well, the companies needed clear and compatible objectives. This was the case in the immediate post-war period when the companies were given the task of building up heavy industry in strategic sectors. Yet, through accretion of tasks over time, the state holdings formula ended up with so many goals that it lost its *raison d'être* (Bianchi et al. 1988: 93). In this context, it became easy to use the companies as a vehicle for offsetting the effects of market failure, a tendency that was reinforced by the political context.

2 *Political (mis)use* The sector became the main vehicle for the patronage exercised by the political parties. The state holdings and the agencies and companies they controlled became subject to a meticulous system of distribution between the different factions of the DC and those of other parties (and notably, from the 1960s onwards, the PSI). This led to the creation of a 'state bourgeoisie': large numbers of public managers who were appointed for their political affiliations to one of the ruling parties and factions. This created not only institutional deficiencies, but also economic distortions, because the parties' influence extended also to commercial policy and investment decisions. These were often based on the need to provide jobs for party supporters (especially in the south), votes for the parties (e.g. through 'welfarist' policies to protect employment and wages), and money for parties and individuals (through obtaining bribes for awarding public works contracts). This mix of clientelism and corruption not only had damaging consequences for the performance of the state sector of the economy, but also helped to corrode relations with the private sector (see below).[5]

3 *Incoherent industrial policy* The success of the formula also depended on the existence of a coherent industrial policy. Yet, until the late 1970s there was no single

source of authority for industrial policy; rather, it consisted of different initiatives from various committees and ministries. Actions taken to regulate industry were excessively interventionist and dogmatic, at the same time as being characterized by improvization, an absence of strategic (structural) objectives, and a gap between the decisions that were taken and the measures that were actually implemented (Prodi and De Giovanni 1993: 31–2). The institutional division between the public and private sectors – which was established with the creation of the Ministry of State Holdings alongside the Ministry of Industry – hindered the development of a strategy for the whole of industry. The Ministry of Industry's jurisdiction was limited to the private sector, while the control of much of the activity of the state holding companies proved, in practice, to be beyond the Ministry of State Holdings. The ministers always came from different parties (or competing factions within the same party), which generated competition rather than co-operation between the two ministries and a dualism in the regulation of industry (Prodi and De Giovanni 1993: 46).

The above factors also help to explain why attempts to reform the State sector of the economy failed. Several inquiries into and reports on the performance of state-owned enterprises were commissioned in the 1970s and 1980s, but the proposed reforms were either inadequate or were blocked by those in political power (Woods 1998: 34–6). Attempts to rationalize industrial policy by centralizing its management under the Committee for the Co-ordination of Industrial Policy (CIPI) were unsuccessful. CIPI experienced planning deficiencies, operational sluggishness and a tendency (mirroring the state holdings experience) to develop projects of a social assistance nature, particularly wage maintenance for redundant workers (Ferrera 1989: 121–2; Adams 1990: esp. 222–3; and Furlong 1994: ch. 9).

Nor did the ideology of privatization that swept across Europe in the 1980s have much impact in Italy, despite the fact that the conditions might have been regarded as ideal: a large number of state-controlled companies whose performance was such that profitability could subsequently be increased fairly easily, and a State badly in need of reducing the rising public debt (meaning attractive flotation prices). While other countries (notably Britain) embarked on ambitious privatization programmes in the 1980s, it took a further decade for anything similar to develop in Italy. The privatization measures in the 1980s were limited in nature, and constituted part of Romano Prodi's attempt (as head of IRI) to rationalize state-controlled enterprises through a strategy of partial privatization (by reducing the shares held by holding companies in certain firms, and by the direct sale of some enterprises to firms in the private sector). Yet, the only significant achievements were IRI's sale of Alfa Romeo (cars) to FIAT and ENI's sale of Lanerossi (textiles) to Marzotto. Others foundered or were blocked (for example, Bettino Craxi blocked the sale of the food group SME to De Benedetti). The process of privatization did not form part of government policy, and the transfers were not subject to the formal approval of the government and Parliament. They were decided upon by the holding companies themselves (and approved by CIPI), which also defined the procedures and received the funds produced by the sales, rather than them going into the Treasury (Cassese 1994b: 125–7). A common element in these reform failures was the role of the Ministry of State Holdings itself. It had a vested interest in opposing measures which threatened to reduce its power, and it thereby 'became increasingly adept at placing obstacles in the path of the much needed rationalisation of industry' (Prodi and de Giovanni 1993: 33).

LARGE FIRMS IN THE PRIVATE SECTOR:
THE DOMINANCE OF 'FAMILY' CAPITALISM

The post-war Italian economy failed to develop a thriving and diverse private sector of large firms. As a percentage of the total number of firms, employees and sales turnover, the large private firm sector (in both the manufacturing and the service industry) has constituted one of the smallest of post-Communist states, and is considerably below the EU average in terms of production and employment (see tables 10.1, 10.2 and 10.3). Even if one were to include the state holding companies, Italy has rarely had more than ten companies listed in *Fortune*'s annual list of the top 500 non-American companies. Britain has about seven times as many companies cited, and France and Germany five times. Italy's figure is lower even than those of such countries as Finland and South Korea.

Despite post-war economic development and restructuring, large firms in the private sector remain in the hands of a small number of powerful groupings (or coalitions), which are often family-based, exercising control over various sectors, and whose leaders have become influential and powerful figures in Italian public life. By the early 1990s, 35 per cent of listed firms were subject to either family or coalition control (with 50 per cent of the rest being under state control), and 96 per cent of the top 500 non-financial firms had an absolute-majority shareholder (compared with 55 per cent in France and 5 per cent in Britain) (McCann 2000b: 58).

The most vivid example of this economic structure is the late Gianni Agnelli's FIAT, which at its peak accounted for approximately 4 per cent of Italian GDP and 60 per cent of the domestic automobile market (the largest in Western Europe). The family's influence (exerted through its finance holding, *Istituto finanziario italiano*, IFI) has extended beyond cars to include finance, the media, department stores and cultural events. The Agnelli empire's power and influence are legendary and controversial (Friedman 1988). Yet, Agnelli has not been alone. Other notable commercial empires include those of Silvio Berlusconi, who, through Fininvest, built up a multi-media empire and also extended into football (owning A. C. Milan) and politics (becoming leader of his own party, Forza Italia, and Prime Minister in 1994 and 2001) (Travaglio and Veltri 2001); Carlo De Benedetti (Olivetti), who built an empire in computers, finance, fashion and food (Turani 1988); the late Raoul Gardini, who rapidly built up the Ferruzzi agro-industrial empire and extended also into the media; and Luciano Benetton (textiles), who is now the world's largest purchaser of wool. The Pirelli, Falk, Mondadori, Rizzoli, Marzotto and Beretta families also exercise considerable influence in different sectors.[6] The dominance of a small number of family-based empires has been facilitated by five factors.

First, the Italian capital market has remained considerably underdeveloped, thus restricting the growth in the number of firms. The number quoted on the Milan Stock Exchange over the years (approximately 200) has grown only slowly (one estimate

Table 10.1   Distribution of economic activity in industrial manufacturing sector by firm size (number of employees), 2000

No. of employees	Firms (% of total)	Employees (% of total)	Sales turnover (% of total)
1–9	83.5	25.1	11.0
10–19	9.6	15.1	9.9
20–99	5.9	15.8	23.7
100–249	0.6	11.0	13.7
250+	0.3	23.0	41.6
Total	100.0	100.0	100.0

Source: Adapted from Onida 2004: 50

Table 10.2   Distribution of economic activity in service sector by firm size (number of employees), 2000

No. of employees	Firms (% of total)	Employees (% of total)	Sales turnover (% of total)
1–9	97.4	60.0	43.8
10–19	1.7	7.9	11.3
20–99	0.8	10.9	17.0
100–249	0.1	4.8	7.4
250+	0.0	16.5	20.5
Total	100.0	100.0	100.0

Source: Adapted from Onida 2004: 50

Table 10.3   Distribution of production and employment in industrial manufacturing by number of employees: Italy (1996) compared with EU average, 1997 (%)

		Micro 1–9	Small 10–49	Medium 50–249	Large 250+	Total
Production	Italy	10.0	24.3	22.7	42.6	100
	EU avge (15)	6.9	13.3	18.3	63.7	100
Employment	Italy	23.9	30.9	19.0	26.3	100
	EU avge (15)	14.6	19.9	19.4	46.1	100

Source: Adapted from Onida 2004: 44–5

suggesting that in 1999 only 10 per cent of eligible companies were listed on the Italian market), and the level of market capitalization remained very low until the late 1990s (Della Sala 2001: 207–8). The capital market has not, therefore, been a major source of finance or corporate restructuring (McCann 2000b: 58).

Second, the main industrial empires have exercised their financial muscle through control of Mediobanca, Italy's only merchant bank, which was set up after the war and chaired for most of the post-war period by Enrico Cuccia. The original idea behind Mediobanca was that it would acquire shares in companies and make long-term loans to them, thus promoting new industry. Cuccia, however, used it rather to build up and protect the positions of the key dynasties in the private sector and to make inroads into the increasingly party-politicized public sector. Mediobanca, moreover, established for itself an almost unique position as a 'special credit institution' through long-term lending and equity stakes in many firms. This was due to the fact that until 1993 banks (almost all of which were state-owned) with short-term liabilities were not allowed to acquire significant shareholdings in non-financial companies, and were therefore restricted to short-term lending (as a result of a supervisory policy that enforced separation between banking and industry). The banking sector therefore failed to provide the sort of medium- and long-term financial resources available to big private firms in other countries, and Mediobanca has been the only credit institution to play a central role in Italian corporate governance (Bianchi et al. 2001: 163–4).

Third, Mediobanca and the large industrial empires reinforced their control, and helped to restrict competitive growth, through two practices: pyramiding and elaborate alliances (McCann 2000a: 51–2). The structure of the Italian corporate world is pyramidal in shape, where large numbers of companies constitute complex chains of ownership, with the family-dominated holding companies exercising control from the top. In 1992 over half of all industrial firms and virtually all large firms (i.e. those with 1,000 employees or more) belonged to a pyramidal group. The pyramidal structure enables small groups of individuals to control a wide range of assets and activities by spreading the voting rights of minority shareholders over a large number of firms, while they concentrate their own shareholdings in the company at the apex of the pyramid (Bianchi et al. 2001: 169). These pyramidal structures are reinforced by a complex web of interlocking alliances and shareholdings, which have created a system of mutual dependence or trust, with Mediobanca at the system's heart.

Fourth, these practices have been facilitated by legal provisions and practices concerning shareholding and the Stock Exchange, which privilege 'insiders' and reduce the influence of minority shareholders. Pyramidal groups have been accepted by the Stock Exchange. They have also been favoured by the State through a neutral tax policy (where dividends are taxed only once, no matter how long the chain) and the absence of legal provisions regarding conflicts of interest between controlling groups and minority shareholders (meaning that the latter have no redress if they feel that their interests in a smaller company are being sacrificed to those of the larger group). This lack of regulation is perhaps unsurprising in view of the fact that the State itself has indulged in pyramiding activities (Bianchi et al. 2001: 161). Meanwhile, company management boards have traditionally been appointed by dominant shareholding families and are usually concerned wholly with such families' interests, there being no obligation to appoint to boards minority shareholders, who can be denied even the most basic information about the company's performance. Furthermore, sales of companies have traditionally been carried out through a 'friendly' private agreement between the bidder, management and the main shareholding group, a disproportionate share of the price being paid to the controlling shareholders. There has been no tradition of 'hostile' bids, and the right of controlling shareholders to purchase the shares of minority shareholders in the event of such bids have made them even less likely (McCann 2000b: 59–60).

Fifth, at a more general level, state regulation of the private sector has proved wanting. The absence of a coherent industrial policy for the whole of industry has already been noted, and that which exists has tended to favour state-controlled companies. This has been complemented by an excessive degree of (indirect) state regulation of the private sector, consisting of a myriad of rules, regulations, conditions, prohibitions, etc., which has been onerous and poorly administered and has undermined competition (Padoa Schioppa Kostoris 1993: 30–1). At the same time, other forms of regulation, of a 'facilitative' nature – such as antitrust policies, manpower policies, industrial relations – have been weakly developed and institutionalized, if not distorted, in their functioning. For example, the independent regulatory body set up in 1974 to regulate companies and the Stock Exchange (the Consob) was heavily conditioned by the affiliations of its members, who favoured economic groups close to influential party members, refrained from acting when wider public interests were at stake, and were happy to take bribes and benefits from 'regulated' firms (La Spina 2003b: 172–3). Large firms, unlike their smaller counterparts (see chapter 11), have often been unable to adapt or develop other forms of regulation to overcome the weaknesses of the public regulatory system (Prodi and De Giovanni 1993: 39–40; Padoa Schioppa Kostoris 1996: 277–84; Regini 1995).

To summarize, the Italian model of large private capitalism which developed in the post-war period proved to be distinctive from both the Atlantic 'outsider/shareholder' model (typical of the US and the UK) and the Rhenish 'insider/stakeholder' model (typical of Germany) (Albert 1993), although it has much stronger affinities with the latter.[7] The Atlantic model is characterized by diffused ownership, a separation (or anonymous relationship) between shareholders and managers, the prioritization of shareholders' interests and short-term financial profits, with few restrictions on predatory behaviour (through mergers and acquisitions). The Rhenish model is characterized by a concentration of share ownership, a large role for banks in corporate finance, cross-ownership of firms and/or banks, a close relationship between owners and managers, and a prioritization of consensus and long-term results, with little predatory behaviour in the form of 'hostile' takeovers.

The regulation and corporate culture typical of Italian capitalism have not favoured the development of the sort of mechanisms and culture that sustain either the Atlantic model or the close relations between banks and companies typical of the German one. The Italian large-firm sector has been dominated by a combination of families, pyramidal coalitions, Mediobanca and, more generally, the State, which have, between them, concentrated share ownership and provided finance to support growth. With an absence of 'anonymous' capital and of monitoring through banks or takeovers, there has been a dependence on informal and implicit practices, emanating from the common interests and values of families, coalitions and owners. It has been a robust, 'clannish', family-based model in which the separation between ownership and control has been limited (Bianchi et al. 2001: 184).

The 'clannish' nature of the large-firm private sector, moreover, has owed much to the politicized nature of the state sector. The more that public ownership was used to protect uncompetitive industries (and, in the process, expand the state bourgeoisie and party clienteles), the more the private sector was constrained in terms of its potential for development, so leaving the few family-based industrial empires dominant. The relationship between the public and private sectors was both competitive and collusive (Coltorti 1993: 77–8; Gros Pietro 1993: 148). FIAT, for example, is known to have benefited (in exchange for its political support) from DC government policies that protected the domestic car market, kept petrol prices low, and constructed motorways while leaving public transport undeveloped. The collusive side of the relationship between the two sectors led to more direct forms of corruption. McCarthy (1995: 100) argues that there was a 'tacit agreement, which each tried to change to its advantage. The state did not create a free market by extensive antitrust legislation, did not protect the small shareholder, and watched while publicly owned banks made dangerous loans. In return the companies paid bribes/taxes on public contracts and did not foster opposition to DC–PSI rule.' This is not to say that the large-firm private sector was sluggish or performed poorly. On the contrary, its dynamism has often been noted; but its small numbers, onerous and inefficient regulation, and the corrosive public–private relationship meant that the most internationally competitive part of Italian industry was associated with small enterprise (see chapter 11).

RESHAPING OF THE PUBLIC AND PRIVATE SECTORS SINCE THE EARLY 1990s

In the period since the early 1990s, several important changes have occurred in the essential characteristics of large-firm Italian capitalism, which suggest that the old model is, if not redundant, at least under challenge and in decline. The most visible causes of these changes were the corruption scandals, involving many top economic actors and exposing to the public glare the collusive relationship between the public and private sectors.[8] These scandals made the need for reform pressing if large industry were to perform more efficiently. However, there have also been broader factors at work, including globalization (notably the international integration of capital markets) and Europeanization (notably the single market and currency) (see chapter 12), which have brought into sharp relief the distinctive (or anomalous) nature of Italian capitalism. These processes have placed common pressures on European political economies to move in the direction of the Anglo-Saxon capitalist model (Rhodes and Apeldoorn 1998: 413–21). Two areas of change are especially relevant to the Italian case: the public–private divide and regulatory reform/corporate governance.

Privatization: remapping the public–private divide

After failing to make inroads into the political debate in any substantial manner in the 1980s, privatization, in the early 1990s, became the main policy response of the Italian political class to the changed national and international climate. Widespread public intervention in the economy was no longer seen as an effective instrument of industrial policy, and the market was seen as a solution to economic inefficiency and politicization. The parties perceived a decisive swing in the public mood, symbolized in the abolition of the Ministry of State Holdings in 1993 via a referendum which, with seven others, was aimed at cutting away the ruling parties' system of patronage and power

Table 10.4 Principal privatizations of the 1990s

Year	Company (Group)	Method of sale	Percentage Sold	Gross yield (billions of lire)
1993	Italgel (IRI)	Private deal	62.12	431.1
	Cirio–Bertolli–De Rica (IRI)	Private deal	62.12	310.7
	Credito Italiano	Public issue	58.09	1801.1
	SIV (EFIM)	Auction	100.00	210.0
Total for year				**2752.9**
1994	IMI 1st tranche	Public issue	32.89	1794.0
	COMIT (IRI)	Public issue	54.35	2891.2
	Nuovo Pignone (ENI)	Auction	69.33	699.0
	INA 1st tranche	Public issue	47.25	4530.0
	Acciai Speciali Terni (IRI)	Private deal	100.0	624.0
	SME 1st tranche	Private deal	32.0	723.0
	Other cos. (ENI)			1087.0
Total for year				**12348.2**
1995	Italtel (IRI)	Auction	40.0	1000.0
	Ilva Laminati Piani (IRI)	Private deal	100.0	2514.0
	Enichem Augusta	Auction	70.0	300.0
	IMI 2nd tranche	Private deal	19.03	913.0
	SME 2nd tranche	Accepted takeover bid	14.91	341.4
	INA 2nd tranche	Private deal	18.37	1687.0
	ENI 1st tranche	Public issue	15.00	6299.0
	ISE (IRI)	Auction	73.96	370.0
	Other cos. (ENI)			336.0
Total for year				**13760.4**
1996	Dalmine (IRI)	Auction	84.08	301.5
	Italimpianti (IRI)	Auction	100.0	41.6
	Nuova Tirrena	Auction	91.14	548.0
	SME 3rd tranche (IRI)	Public offer of acquisition	15.21	120.9
	INA 3rd tranche	Conventional bond issue	31.08	4200.0
	MAC (IRI)	Auction	50.0	223.0
	IMI 3rd tranche	Public issue	6.94	501.2
	Montefibre (ENI)	Public issue	65.0	183.0
	ENI 2nd tranche	Public issue	15.82	8872.0
Total for year				**14991.2**
1997	ENI 3rd tranche	Public issue	17.6	13231.0
	Aeroporti di Roma (IRI)	Public issue	45.0	594.0

Table 10.4 *(continued)*

Year	Company (Group)	Method of sale	Percentage Sold	Gross yield (billions of lire)
	Telecom Italia	Core investors + public issue	39.54	22883.0
	SEAT editoria	Core investors + public issue	61.27	1653.0
	Banco di Roma (IRI)	Public issue + liabilities	36.5	1898.0
	Istituto Bancario San Paolo di Torino	Public issue	3.36	286.0
Total for year				**40545.0**
1998	SAIPEM (ENI)	Public issue	18.75	1140.0
	ENI 4th tranche	Public issue	14.83	12995.0
	BNL	Public issue	67.85	6707.0
Total for year				**20842.0**
1999	Enel	Public issue	31.7	32045.0
	Autostrade (IRI)	Auction + public issue	82.4	13016.0
	Mediocredito Centrale	Auction	100.0	3944.0
	UNIM	Public offer of acquisition	1.90	41.0
	Aeroporti di Roma	Auction	3.00	100.0
Total for year				**49146.0**
2000	Aeroporti di Roma	Direct negotiation	51.2	2569.0
	Finmeccanica	Public issue	43.7	10660.0
	Credito Industriale Sardo	Direct negotiation	53.3	41.0
	Mediobanca	Direct negotiation	7.3	82.0
	Mediolombardo	Direct negotiation	3.4	79.0
	COFIRI	Direct negotiation	100.0	975.0
	Banco di Napoli	Public offer of acquistion	16.2	955.0
Total for year				**15361.0**
Grand total				**169746.7**

Source: Adapted from Tabella 1.4. Principali privatizzazioni in Italia negli anni '90, *Review dell'OCSE della riforma della regolazione in Italia* © OECD, 2001 (OECD 2001a: 36–8)

(Newell and Bull 1993). A consensus quickly developed amongst virtually all the parties (except Communist Refoundation) that privatization was desirable (Marrelli and Stroffolini 1998: 150; Reviglio 1994: 129).

The privatization programme that was launched in the early 1990s was consequently of an entirely different nature from the more limited attempts of the 1980s. In 1992 Giuliano Amato's government presented a report on the state holdings system, in which the main causes of its crisis were identified as lying in excessive political interference and the setting of multiple, and at times contradictory, objectives. In contrast with previous inquiries, reforming the system was not advocated, but rather its wholesale privatization (Woods 1998: 23). The key objectives of this programme were to increase economic efficiency (especially where the newly privatized firms were concerned with public utilities), to make the industrial structure more competitive by increasing the number of big private groups in the economy from about half a dozen to closer to a dozen, to promote a degree of 'people's capitalism' by making the ownership of corporate stock more widespread, to encourage foreign investment in the Italian Stock Exchange, and to reduce the public debt (Marrelli and Stroffolini 1998: 158–9; Cassese 1996: 326; Graziani 1994).

As compared to those of many other privatization programmes in Europe, these objectives were highly ambitious. They reveal how important privatization was perceived to be in Italy, the aims driving it being to reform the public *and* private sectors and the corrosive relationship between them. On the one hand, a reduction in the size of the public sector would reduce the level of state and political interference in the regulation of the economy, and thus the political protection afforded to poor managers and entrepreneurs. On the other hand, significant privatization had the potential to achieve structural reform in the large-firm private sector through the challenges it might pose to the existing system of family-dominated corporate governance. The introduction of new large private and financial actors offered a potential challenge to the existing groups. The offer of large numbers of shares in new private companies had the potential to render share ownership more widespread. A larger and more liquid market would encourage the development of hostile takeover bidding, if new firms were committed to 'releasing shareholder value' and were transparent in their operations and open to outsiders. Finally, privatization of the banking system threatened directly the financial foundations of the so-called Northern Galaxy system, based as it was on Mediobanca's special relationship with two state-owned banks (Comit and Credit) and on the absence of alternatives for those seeking finance (McCann 2000a: 52–3).

In view of the size of some of the state-owned organizations, and of the public sector generally, the procedures and timetable were quite complex (Cassese 1996). In 1992 IRI, ENEL, ENI and INA were transformed into public limited companies, allowing them to be listed on the Stock Exchange and to be subject to the provisions of civil law. In June of the follow year, a Permanent Committee for Privatization was set up by the Prime Minister to oversee the privatization programme as a whole, which was scheduled to involve state holdings, public enterprises, railways, postal services, public banks, corporations owned by local governments and public real estate. The privatizations that followed were of an unprecedented scale (see table 10.4). Between 1992 and 1995, eleven IRI companies (including Comit and Credit, the fourth and sixth largest banks in Italy), eight ENI enterprises, IMI (a special credit bank) and INA (the second largest insurance company in Italy) were sold, while EFIM was dissolved. The sales covered a wide range of sectors: steel, manufacturing, cement, coal, gas, engineering, mining, chemicals, glass, food and catering, medical equipment, banking and insurance (Scobie et al. 1996: 92–8; Marrelli and Stroffolini 1998: 162). Since the end of 1995, sales have included regional public banks and Telecom Italia (communications, formerly STET), which was the largest privatization in Europe. IRI, meanwhile, had its last annual general meeting in July 2000 to approve its dissolution, its remaining cash pile (14,000 billion lire) and stakes in about half a dozen firms being transferred to the Treasury in anticipation of privatization.[9]

Regulatory reform and changes in corporate governance

The privatization programme has been accompanied by regulatory reform and changes in corporate governance. Regarding the former, since in Italy 'market failure' was traditionally tackled through state control of industry, it was perhaps inevitable that privatization would be accompanied by a growth in independent regulatory bodies (IRBs), and this was spurred on by a power vacuum created by the collapse of the parties in the early part of the decade and the influence of several technocratically minded minsters. Consequently, beginning in 1990 with the strengthening of the Consob and the creation of a new antitrust body, the *Autorità garante della concorrenza e del mercato*, Italy has followed other European countries, such as Britain and France, in setting up IRBs across a diverse range of sectors: strikes in public services, information systems for public administration, banking sector supervision, transport, industrial relations, advertising contracts of public broadcasting companies, energy and telecommunications (Amato 1996; La Spina 2000; OECD 2001a; La Spina 2003b).

With respect to corporate governance, a comprehensive banking law (heavily conditioned by EU directives) was passed in 1993, which liberalized and expanded the financial activities permissible for banks (including acquiring stakes in non-financial firms), and increased the accessibility of foreign financial institutions. This reform, it was hoped, would strengthen and make more co-operative the relationship between banks and firms along German lines (Deeg and Perez 2000: 135). In 1998, privatization of the Italian Stock Exchange was accompanied by a reform of market regulations. Together these measures were aimed at discouraging Italian firms from listing on markets overseas (a growing trend), and increasing the number of firms listed nationally, thus making the Italian financial markets more competitive. A law of the same year addressed deficiencies in previous laws on financial markets, at the same time as responding to demands from the EU. The rights of minority shareholders were strengthened, not only in relation to voting rights but also in takeovers. A more robust mandatory bid rule for takeovers now requires any shareholder or group of shareholders who gain over 30 per cent of the voting stock to make an offer to purchase the remaining shares within thirty days (at a price which reflects any consequent rise in value of the stock). This is aimed at preventing control being passed from one group of shareholders to another without benefit to minority shareholders. A later ruling by the Stock Market regulator, Consob, also prevents bidders from gaining control of a pyramid simply by buying the company at the top of the control chain. Bidders are now required to make an offer for all the shares that the company controls, thus ensuring that control of a company does not change hands without benefit to minority shareholders (Vaciago 2000: 196–9; McCann 2000b: 60–2).

These has also been a reform of the company tax structure (in 1998), which makes the Italian tax system more compatible with those of other countries and provides the potential for a higher level of integration into the global financial system (Vaciago 2000: 198–9).

LARGE PUBLIC AND PRIVATE INDUSTRY TODAY: TRANSFORMATION OR ADAPTATION?

How significant are the reforms carried out since the early 1990s? To what extent are they transforming the regulation of large public and private industry? That they have had an impact on both sectors is undeniable. The privatization programme has considerably reduced the size of the public sector. The first wave of privatization divested the State of shares worth over 25,000 billion lire, while by 2000 the value of assets disposed of by IRI alone amounted to more than 100,000 billion lire. Many of the privatizations were accompanied by management shake-ups, reductions in stock holdings and redundancies, all of which had significant effects on economic performance. The debts of the major state-owned and state-controlled enterprises quickly became a thing of the past: 1993's losses of over 10,000 billion lire (with a consolidated debt of 72,000 billion lire) were reversed within a year to a 1,288 billion lire profit (Marrelli and Stroffolini 1998: 163). Privatization has also reduced the weight of the State in the ownership of listed companies (which by 1998 had dropped to less than 10 per cent from 30 per cent only two years previously), and the degree of concentration of share ownership in large shareholders generally (see table 10.5). Assisted by a reformed Stock Exchange, there has been an increase in both the level of market capitalization (from 12.1 per cent in 1985 to 71.1 per cent in 2000) and the number of listed firms (from 161 in 1985 to 238 in 2000) (Della Sala 2001: 207–8).

In relation to the large-firm private sector, the changes to corporate governance have increased competition; globalization has increased shareholder power and placed pressure on executives to perform; and the launch of the single currency has removed the government's devaluation option and removed the currency risk for investors (so facilitating investment and takeovers). Several of the groups operating in the more competitive sectors (e.g. Olivetti, Pirelli) have been experiencing considerable financial difficulties, while Agnelli's FIAT entered into crisis in 2002. Too long dependent on the domestic market, the company is suffering acutely from foreign competition, which is making considerable inroads into its domestic share of the market. The result of these developments is a trend towards simplification of pyramidal groups, as some groups seek to protect their 'core' businesses by divesting themselves of companies lower down the chain (which has been the Agnelli group's approach since 1996). This is diluting ownership and causing instability in ownership and control structures, through substantial reductions in voting-block concentrations since 1996 (notably for large companies) and reductions in controlling stakes to keep below the new 30 per cent threshold (Bianchi et al. 2001: 183). Companies are also more likely now than before to forge alliances with foreign partners to address their financial difficulties. The

Table 10.5 Changing concentration of share ownership, 2000–2002*

	2000	2001	2002
Largest shareholders	44.0	42.2	40.7
Other major shareholders	9.4	9.2	8.0
Market	46.6	48.6	51.2
Total	100.0	100.0	100.0

* Year-end data, as a percentage of the total market value of the
ordinary share capital of the companies listed on the Stock Exchange.
Source: Adapted from Table 26. Concentration of share ownership.
Year-end data, *OECD Economic Surveys: Italy – Volume 2003 Issue 13* ©
OECD, 2003 (OECD 2003: 128)

securing of a cross-shareholding alliance by FIAT in 2000 with an American partner (General Motors) was an unusual event in Italy's traditionally provincial capitalist structure.

In this new context, banks and financial institutions are beginning to play a more significant role, with a visible waning of the position of Mediobanca, which is finding it increasingly difficult to hold together its Byzantine network of cross-shareholdings, especially since the death of its founding chairman, Enrico Cuccia, in June 2000. The past few years have witnessed unprecedented mergers and alliances, which have consolidated the banking world into fewer, much larger, financial institutions. This has been designed both to reduce the risk of takeovers by foreign groups and to challenge Mediobanca's dominance. All of this appears to be spawning a new corporate culture in which hostile takeover bids, once unthinkable, are now a possibility, something from which even Mediobanca is not regarded as safe. Olivetti's audacious, hostile takeover of Telecom Italia (a firm seven times its size) in 1999 was unprecedented (indeed, it was post-war Europe's largest hostile takeover) and suggests that individual shareholder power and managerial accountability now count (Woods 2000: 164). Finally, the rapid expansion of IRBs has effected a redistribution of power through creation of a new administrative 'branch' of government, which has undercut some of the functions previously exercised by the political parties.

Nevertheless, while change is undoubtedly occurring, its transformative potential should not be overestimated; nor should it be assumed that the process is consistent, unopposed and producing an inevitable convergence with the Anglo-Saxon model. Despite the change in the political class that has occurred since the early 1990s, the lobby of politicians, bureaucrats, state holdings managers, financial institutions and trade unionists against the adoption of wholesale privatization and neo-liberalism remains strong. The changes in corporate governance in 1998, for example, were a consequence of the existence of a fortuitous combination of reformers in key positions (Prodi as Prime Minister, D'Alema as leader of the largest party of government, and Ciampi at the Treasury) who were committed to liberalizing Italian capitalism (McCann 2000b: 66–9). The privatization programme has proceeded at a very slow pace, especially after the successful first phase of sell-offs in the mid-1990s. The Olive-tree

Alliance (Ulivo), despite being brought to power in 1996 with a commitment to accelerate the process, did not achieve much beyond the privatization of Telecom Italia. The second Berlusconi government (elected in May 2001) has done very little in its first three years to meet its manifesto commitment to further privatization and liberalization (the state of the world economy and share prices not making things easy). The State still has control of over twenty holdings, some of which it inherited from IRI, others of which (such as ENEL) were earmarked for privatization back in 1992. Significantly, holdings such as ENEL, ENI (which sold off eight companies in the first tranche of privatizations, and whose fortunes were subsequently turned around by Franco Bernabé) and Finmeccanica (scheduled to have been broken up and sold off in 1997) remain active in new ventures, buying up privatized firms in a manner that resembles the old IRI strategy.[10]

Furthermore, while the pace has been slow, the privatizations that have been achieved (even if radical compared with those of the 1980s) have, in fact, been less 'liberalizing' than at first appears – as criticism from the EU's competition commissioner has confirmed. Besides ambiguities and inconsistencies in privatization procedures, the emphasis on increasing budget revenues has overshadowed the link between privatization and competition policy. This has resulted in the granting of exclusive concessions, the absence of competitive bidding, and the continuing dominance of previous incumbents (OECD 2002: 6). Often 'the control structure of privatised companies is an intricate puzzle: even when the privatisation has been fully realised, a mix of regulatory measures (such as the "golden share") and bye-law provisions (such as voting caps) reduces the role of the market for corporate control' (Bianchi et al. 2001: 183). Some companies have been only partially privatized. Many banks, for example, are still controlled by 'foundations' created by a 1990 law to facilitate privatization (Bianchi et al. 2001: 164), and they have been able, under the 1993 banking law, to buy shares in privatized firms, thus paradoxically *reversing* the state disinvestment process (Goldstein 1998: 182). A law passed in 1999 (known as the Ciampi law) appeared to resolve this situation, fixing a deadline of mid-2003 or, at the latest, mid-2006 for an end to the control exercised by the foundations. However, the Berlusconi government of 2001 undermined the Ciampi legislation through further legislative measures that postponed almost indefinitely the divesting of control at the same time as increasing the political tutelage over the foundations (Costi 2003). The impact of the privatization of the two large banks, Comit and Credit, was effectively nullified by Mediobanca, which, in the weeks following their sale, used its networks to mould coalitions and purchase sufficient numbers of shares to secure control of both (McCann 2000a: 54–5).

This situation is complemented by the persistence of some of the old corporate practices. There remains a scarcity of big firms (meaning that certain sectors rely heavily on the performance of a few large-sized companies), and a high concentration of public equity ownership, with control still exercised chiefly through pyramidal groups, cross-holdings and alliances. Indeed, Mediobanca has attempted to raise its game in the past few years, to shore up its waning position in the face of challenges from others using the same techniques. Consequently, what appear to be mould-breaking events in the corporate world also display features of continuity with the past. FIAT's alliance with General Motors amounted to a management, not a shareholder, decision, Agnelli making it clear that the remaining shares would never be sold and that FIAT would remain Italian. Olivetti's takeover of Telecom Italia, while unprecedented, could also be interpreted as the result of a failed privatization. Without any major restructuring before privatization (which granted a 3.4 per cent 'golden share' to government and 9 per cent to a core group of shareholders), there followed nearly two years of management turmoil and a low stock price, which made the company ripe for a takeover. The bid was supported by Mediobanca, and, once successful, Roberto Colaninno (who masterminded the bid) set about protecting his new assets using the traditional Mediobanca-style techniques (Woods 2000). In a comparative study, Deeg and Perez (2000: 139) argue that 'the most notable feature of the evolution of corporate governance . . . is the *reinforcement* of various "insider" models of corporate governance in the face of liberalization'. Italy is a case in point: in comparative indexes of 'economic freedom' and 'competitiveness', the country, despite having made some progress, still languishes behind her Western counterparts.[11]

Finally, the involvement and intervention of government and politicians in these affairs confirms how deeply ingrained remain the State's interventionist instincts. For example, despite claims of neutrality, the government became actively involved in the Olivetti/Telecom saga, as it did in the case of FIAT's crisis in 2002–3, when some members of the government openly supported the idea of rescuing FIAT through one of the state holdings. There has also been no attempt to 'depoliticize' appointments to the state sector of the economy (or, indeed, elsewhere). On the contrary, the new Berlusconi government quickly reinforced the potential for making political appointments through the Frattini law (passed in August 2002). This strengthened certain aspects of a law passed by the Ulivo government that had formalized and regulated the so-called spoils system. Finally, IRBs, in the period since 1994, have increasingly been viewed by the parties as a means to multiply patronage opportunities through securing 'friendly' placemen, with the danger that some areas of this independent and supposedly neutral structure will become emasculated over time (La Spina 2003b: 181–2).

Conclusion

Under both national and international pressures, the old model of 'state capitalism' and 'clannish private capitalism' is undergoing change in Italy. The weight of the public sector has been considerably modified, and this is part of a more general phenomenon of a 'hollowing out' of the State through a displacement of its authority in key areas (Della Sala 1997). Changes in corporate governance, the globalization of industry and financial markets, and the launch of the single currency have exposed the relatively weak structure of the large groups, accustomed as they have been to state support and collusive, protective practices. The full force of competition and the end of public funding at favourable rates has placed several large groups in difficulties, and has begun to call into question the long-term viability of Italian large industry (Gallino 2003; De Cecco 2004). Perhaps the most potent symbols of these changes have been the deaths of the chairman of Mediobanca, Enrico Cuccia (in June 2000), and the head of FIAT, Giovanni Agnelli (in January 2003). The Mediobanca–FIAT relationship, and the political influence in Rome which each wielded, constituted the main axis on which post-war large-group capitalism rested. By the time of their deaths, their unquestioned corporate power was under challenge. Mediobanca has lost its unchallenged supremacy at the heart of the Italian financial world, while the future of the Agnelli dynasty is in doubt due to FIAT's financial crisis. Yet there remain various sources of resistance to these changes, notably the State, some of whose representatives still seem to be wedded to the idea that certain large firms must be protected as national champions, because they are strategic to the country's interests.

In short, while the old model is evidently passing, it remains unclear what will be the main characteristics of the emerging new system. In the short term, despite international pressures, a straightforward convergence along Anglo-American lines is unlikely. As Albert (2001: 389) has noted, 'Italian capitalism is in complete transformation, but principally on a national basis.' The new model is therefore more likely to constitute a mix of greater liberalization and some practices derived from the more state-driven, clannish past.

GOVERNING THE ECONOMY II:
THE SOUTH AND THE 'THIRD ITALY'

INTRODUCTION

Chapter 10 analysed big industry from the particular perspective of the dualism between the public and private sectors (and the role these have played in the north-west and the south). This chapter, by analysing the distinctive economies of the south, on the one hand, and the centre/north-east, on the other, completes the analysis of the territorial and structural dualisms of the Italian economy as outlined at the beginning of the previous chapter.

THE PROBLEM OF THE SOUTH

The south (Mezzogiorno) is an area south of Rome that is larger than some European countries, comprising eight regions, 36 per cent of Italy's population and 25 per cent of its Gross National Product. Its long-term economic and political underdevelopment relative to the north, and the dualism this has created, has constituted the 'southern problem' (*la questione meridionale*). Economically, in 1951 southern income was less than half that of the north, there was widespread illiteracy (one in four), high unemployment (up to 50 per cent in rural areas), widespread underemployment and no industry. Geographically, the south was viewed as having unfavourable natural conditions and a remoteness from the markets of the central European countries during the industrialization period (while the northern regions received a direct stimulus). The politics of the south were viewed as distinctly different from those of the north, based on traditional patron–client relations, a weak bourgeoisie and an alliance, formed during the 1880s, between southern landowners and northern industrialists (Gramsci's 'historic bloc') which hindered modernization. These traits were reinforced at the social level by Mafia practices and organized crime in large areas of the south. Finally, southern culture was viewed as different, being characterized by 'amoral familism' (see chapter 1) and the absence of 'civic traditions'.

The above constitute what might be described as orthodox perspectives on the south. In fact, the origins and dimensions of the problem (geographic, cultural, social, economic and political) have been the subject of intense debate and a huge literature spanning various disciplines, in which all of the conventional wisdoms have been challenged. Indeed, historical revisionist research in the past decade takes issue even with the very existence of a southern problem or something distinct called the 'south' (beyond historical stereotyping).[1] Nevertheless, what is important from our perspective is that policy-makers and the political class have been considerably influenced by their perception of the existence of the problem, especially in their attempts to tackle its economic aspect.[2]

Indeed, so glaring was the southern problem in the immediate post-war period that a radical change occurred in the State's approach, through the launch of the first modern policy for the south. In the period after Unification, the classical economic doctrine of market balance (fostered by bourgeois economists from the north) prevailed in government thinking. This view, rejected by Marx, was predicated on the assumption that the elimination of all obstacles to free competition would assist the more backward areas. As a consequence, little was done to help the south, and fiscal and economic policies tended to favour the north. The break with this approach occurred in 1950, with the establishment of the *Cassa per il Mezzogiorno* (Fund for the South), an administrative unit working under the auspices of the Ministry for the South.[3]

The legislation (which was subsequently modified several times) called for the targeting of considerable public funding and a ten-year plan. The south was identified as an area that required public intervention of an 'extraordinary' nature over the long term. Although the agency was, formally speaking, part of the general government sector, the rationale behind its establishment was the same as for the state holding companies (see chapter 10). The Cassa was given special powers: it could act in sectors traditionally reserved to other ministries; its actions would supplement, and not replace, the activities of other ministries; it received independent funding and a large degree of autonomy over its funds; and it was responsible for implementing its decisions. The launch of this policy and its ambitious objective (solving the southern problem once and for all) raised considerable expectations. Yet, the policy of extraordinary intervention, which lasted just over forty years, ultimately failed to meet that objective, and the policy itself helped to shape the State's problematic relationship with the south in the post-war period.

A HISTORY OF FAILURE: FORTY YEARS OF SPECIAL INTERVENTION IN THE SOUTH (1950–1992)

The post-war policy of intervention in the south through the Cassa has been described as a 'festival of re-thinking' (Sarcina 2002), its changing nature being a reflection of its ongoing failure to secure its objectives. In the period until 1950, the Cassa's policies were concentrated on developing agriculture (the largest economic sector) through infrastructural investment. The idea – which was in keeping with liberal theories of industrialization in the 1950s and 1960s (e.g. Lutz 1975) – was that the provision of infrastructure (roads, railways, housing, sanitation, etc.), coupled with a rise in agri-

Table 11.1   Financial investments by the *Cassa per il Mezzogiorno*, 1951–1975, by sector (%)

	1951–5	1956–60	1961–5	1966–70	1971–5
Infrastructure	82.5	46.2	23.3	22.7	30.6
Industry	9.0	35.3	58.8	63.3	59.2
Other sectors	8.5	18.5	17.9	14.0	10.2
Total	100.0	100.0	100.0	100.0	100.0

Source: Reproduced from Balcet, *L'économie italienne* © Editions La Découverte, Paris 1995 (Balcet 1997: 99)

cultural incomes, would provide a natural stimulus to industrial development. This would occur not only directly, but also through the so-called multiplier effect: attracting private investment and thus expanding southern markets, which were regarded as prerequisites for industrialization. However, by the mid-1950s it was evident that improvement in infrastructure was insufficient to attract industry, which needed to be *compensated* for the disadvantages of setting up in the south. Indeed, rather than seeing southern markets expanding, the south strengthened northern industry through 'leakage', because much of the Cassa's expenditure went on purchasing goods produced in the north.

This led to a shift, in 1957, towards a policy of planned industrialization through direct intervention. The Cassa's funds were increased by 50 per cent, and the proportion going to agriculture was reduced in favour of industry, with an increasing volume of resources being directed towards industry in the period until the mid-1970s (see table 11.1). Potential 'growth areas' were targeted, with the Cassa funding the creation of local consortia responsible for promoting and attracting industry. A series of incentives was developed for private industry and state holding companies, and firms under their control were compelled to locate 40 per cent of their overall investments and 60 per cent of new investments (in industrial enterprises) in the south (until then the investment figures were much lower, respectively 19 per cent and 30 per cent). The priorities, therefore, as refined in the mid-1960s, were industry (over agriculture), large private firms (over small ones) and public companies (over private industry).

By the mid-1970s, this policy was having noticeable distorting effects. There was a massive agricultural exodus, which, while raising per capita incomes in the south, also led to growing social problems in northern cities, whose facilities could not meet the demands of the new population. Industrialization caused growing imbalances within the south itself, some of the poorest regions not having been allocated any industrial growth areas. The shift towards big (and largely public) industry did not generate the expected outcomes, because the big firms tended to be capital-rather than labour-intensive (thus failing to improve unemployment). They were often not genuine southern companies, but rather branches of enterprises based in the north (from where they tended to import their goods), and big firms consequently failed to generate a network of small and medium-sized firms around them. They became *cattedrali nel deserto* ('cathedrals in the desert'), large, capital-intensive, state-backed projects located in backward regions, which remained backward – a process defined as 'industrialization without development' (Hytten and Marchioni 1970). This was also the period in which the state holding companies were becoming increasingly costly burdens on the State.

In this context, the 1970s witnessed the beginning of a gradual retreat from special intervention in the south. A new law in 1971 (reinforced in 1976) devolved several of the Cassa's responsibilities to the newly created regional governments, and gave overall responsibility for the policy to a *Comitato Interministeriale per la Pianificazione Economica* (Interministerial Committee for Economic Planning, CIPE). Additional industrial incentives were offered through state subsidization of national insurance contributions, to which firms would otherwise be liable. There was an increase in required investments for state holding firms (to 60 per cent of their total investments and 80 per cent of new investments). At the same time, there was a shift away from the idea of a 'growth area' policy based on the big firm towards the creation of networks of small industries and the goal of assisting the most backward areas. The main focus of the Cassa's activities became inter-sectoral and inter-regional 'special projects'. However, the economic crisis of the 1970s had a devastating impact on both the southern economy and government aid. Besides causing major failures in big industry (e.g. chemicals and steel), national economic policy was oriented towards protecting production and employment in the north rather than developing the south. This trend was confirmed in 1977, when a new law was passed whose aim was to incorporate industrial policy for the south into national industrial policy, as a means of harmonizing policies for the south with national policies generally.

The 1980s saw an increasing emphasis on the private sector, at the same time as a continuation of the gradual phasing out of special intervention. In 1984, Parliament voted to abolish the Cassa, which, in 1986, was replaced with an 'Agency for the Development of the Mezzogiorno', although in practice the new body carried out largely similar functions to the old (Barca 2001: 171). In the same year, a new law provided funding for the next decade to attract new business from the north and overseas, based on planning contracts between state and industry, programmatic agreements between the State and public agencies, and funding packages for small and medium-sized enterprises. The government's main objective was to encourage investment in research and development and in high-technology sectors (such as pharmaceuticals and electronics) which would have an effect on jobs, training and regional development. This policy had some success, but its limits were also revealed in bureaucratic slowness and complexities (which in particular discouraged small and medium-sized firms), difficulties in co-ordination and the influence of clientelism and corruption. The aid packages, moreover, were subsequently contested by the European Commission.

In the 1990s, the sweeping changes in Italian politics (notably the rapid electoral growth of the Northern League), combined with other factors (see below), undermined the long-term consensus on the need to provide aid to the south. In 1992 the basis of the financing was changed, undermining its special nature. The following year the policy of special aid to the south was ended (La Spina 2003a: 255). This effective abandonment of the south by the State was reinforced two years later with the abolition (at the insistence of the European Commission) of State subsidization of firms' national insurance contributions, signifying the end of labour cost advantages.

THE PARADOX OF STATE INTERVENTION IN THE SOUTH OVER FOUR DECADES

What was the impact of forty years of special intervention in the south, and why did it fail? On the one hand, it could be argued that the redistributive policies increased incomes in the south and improved living conditions generally. For example, between 1951 and 1992, GDP grew by over 550 per cent, compared with 473 per cent for the centre–north (Bevilacqua 1996: 89).[4] Moreover, considerable investments in the south were made by Italian private and state-owned companies (e.g. IRI, FIAT, Olivetti, Barilla, Merloni) as well as foreign-run companies (e.g. Texas Instruments, Bridgestone-Firestone, Siemens). By the mid-1990s, for example, FIAT had more than forty southern plants, employing about a sixth of its total workforce, including factories in Lazio, Molise and Basilicata that were considered the most advanced in the world.

On the other hand, the main objective of special intervention, the reduction of the north–south gap, was not achieved. The gap narrowed only during the period of most intense industrialization (1960–75). It widened again during the 1980s (Padoa Schioppa Kostoris 1993: 106; D'Antonio 1993: 189; Boccella 1994: 429–31). As special intervention ended, economists emphasized the continuing problems of the south compared with the rest of Italy (e.g. D'Antonio 1993; Trigilia 1992; Padoa Schioppa Kostoris 1993: chs 7–8; Balcet 1997: ch. 6). Per capita income in the south remained not much more than half that of the north; its 36 per cent of the population was producing only a quarter of Italy's GDP; unemployment was almost three times that of the north, and economic growth consistently below the national average.

The difference between evaluations based on absolute criteria (improvement in living conditions) and those based on relative criteria (size of the north–south gap) illuminate the difficulty of reaching any definitive conclusion on the success or failure of the policy. As Bevilacqua (1996: 88) has commented, forty years of extraordinary intervention cannot be condemned as a failure without critics asking themselves, 'even in hypothetical terms, what the Mezzogiorno would be like today if there had been no extraordinary intervention. How big would the divide between the two large parts of Italy now be if the spontaneous mechanisms of the market had been left to themselves?' Yet, what is unquestionable is that the policy failed to generate a *self-perpetuating* – or *autonomous* – process of development (Trigilia 1992: 171), and this qualitative (rather than quantitative) aspect was probably the policy's most glaring shortcoming. Moreover, there is a paradox in this shortcoming, in so far as it was the very intervention in the south that inhibited this process of development, turning the south into 'a publicly subsidized economy' (Graziani 1979: 63). Two interrelated factors lie at the heart of this failure: first, the political nature of extraordinary intervention; and second, the effects of the broader context of governmental intervention at the local level (Graziani 1979; Trigilia 1992; Padoa Schioppa Kostoris 1993).

First, the Cassa and the extension of the public sector into the south constituted one of the main pillars of Christian Democracy's system of clientelism and patronage (see chapters 2 and 10). Decisions were often determined less by economic rationality than by the need to win support in the south. Many companies were fragile, because 'they were not born of real economic necessity, and remained alienated from local traditions, culture and *savoir faire* . . . and they did not "fertilize" the entrepreneurial soil in which they were set' (Bevilacqua 1996: 90). Indeed, the Cassa constituted a vested interest against industrialization of the south because of the implications it carried for the social base of the governing parties (Allum 1981).

Second, even though special intervention in the south was probably unprecedented in post-war Europe, it constituted only a small part of government activity overall. Paradoxically, the constantly improving per capita income in the south was achieved in a context where per capita state expenditure, seen as a whole, was not distributed in a way that clearly favoured the south (it was marginally lower for the south than for the centre and north). The redistribution, therefore, came about less through expenditure to promote development than through a discrepancy in productive return (or 'value added') – where the south's was one-third of that of the centre and north – and (inseparable from the first) through welfare and other benefits payments. In short, public intervention in the south was too oriented towards supporting demand than investing in supply and development.

These factors were significant in view of the political context of the south. The introduction of a growing number of resources – through the extension of the welfare state and special intervention – increased the power of the local political class. This class had low levels of legitimacy, forced as it was 'continually [to attempt] to construct what [was] an unstable and precarious consensus because of the weakness of shared values, in a context characterised by strong particularistic demands' (Trigilia 1992: 174). The outcome was a growth in clientelistic policies, a failure of the investment in public services and collective goods, and little stimulus to economic development. This also helped to foster corruption and organized crime, in terms of the abuse of procurement contracts (the instrument for implementing public investment) to launder money, which further discouraged outside investment and internal initiatives. In general, the increased power given to the local political class was used 'for distributing public expenditure in such a way that preserve[d] the political *status quo*' (Graziani 1979: 65). There were, in short, perverse effects of public intervention to promote industrialization: 'the efforts of the public sector . . . not only failed almost completely to instil an entrepreneurial spirit where it was lacking but in certain instances . . . accentuated the tendency to wait passively for solutions from on high (and from the centre of the country) rather than from within the economy of the Mezzogiorno itself' (Padoa Schioppa Kostoris 1993: 105).

A TURNING POINT? THE MEZZOGIORNO SINCE THE EARLY 1990s

What is evident from the above analysis is that, however good the original intentions behind post-war policies for the south, their failure was bound up with their location within a particular political-economic model. Perhaps inevitably, therefore, the crisis of that model caused a watershed moment in southern policy too.

The organizational and electoral collapse of the governing parties, the rapid rise of the Northern League, and the outcome of the 1993 referendum all had the effect of discrediting the policy for the south. The decision to abolish the Cassa and end special intervention was reinforced by the fiscal crisis of the State and the exit of the lira from the ERM in 1992. The policies of monetary rigour and financial discipline that followed between 1992 and 1998 (in order to qualify for EMU) further reduced the room for redistributive policies. Moreover, the privatization policies pursued by successive governments in this period cut investment in the south, because they resulted in the privatization of many of the state-controlled companies and state holdings which had been required to invest in the south in the post-war period.[5] In addition, the banking system in the south effectively collapsed, with most of the principal banks in the area being acquired by northern institutions (Viesti 2001: 701). External pressures increased the significance of these domestic factors. The EMU convergence criteria acted, of course, as a rigid constraint on Italian policy-makers. More generally, the EU's hostility to state intervention, and the new competitive free-market philosophy of the global economy constituted a competitive challenge to all states. This made extraordinary intervention in the south appear to be an anachronism, at odds with the need 'to introduce individual initiative and agency in a competitive society, especially in the south' (Della Sala 2000: 186).

The immediate economic impact of these changes on the south, as a long-term 'subsidized economy', was considerable, and the gap between the north and the south in terms of economic growth widened further (see table 11.2). After 1992, GDP in the southern regions remained static, and unemployment rose from 17.1 per cent in 1993 to 21.9 per cent in 1998, both being the worst results in the whole of Europe. Furthermore, this fall in employment was most marked in the blue-collar sector, indicating that the elusive post-war goal of industrialization of the south was becoming more distant than ever. Fixed investments as a percentage of GDP fell from 21.2 per cent in 1993 to 16.6 per cent in 1997. New building works came to a halt, commerce suffered from a decline in internal demand, and the function of public employment to reduce social tension began to dry up. The early 1990s witnessed the end of the 'great redistributive agreement', the rapid withdrawal of the State, and therefore the removal of the main element which had secured any growth in the south in the post-war period, but without any alternative being implemented (Viesti 2001: 701; De Vivo 2002: 714–15).

However, despite these economic reversals in the first half of the 1990s, the second half of the decade witnessed an equally dramatic turn-around, with the south outperforming the north and the centre in terms of economic growth (see table 11.2). GDP has continued to grow faster in the south than in the centre–north into the millennium: 2.2 per cent versus 1.8 per cent in 2001, 1.1 per cent versus 0.1 per cent in 2002, and 0.3 per cent versus 0.2 per cent in 2003 (Svimez 2002, 2003, 2004). The withdrawal of the State in the 1990s, combined with the policies of financial and monetary rigour, had a rationalizing effect on Italian industry and enterprise in the south. At the same time, the lira's exit from the ERM in 1992 meant that those companies that did survive were, alongside new businesses, in a position to benefit from the devaluation of the currency. In the period between 1992 and 1996, the value of exports rose from 20 to 35 billion lire, while the number of exporters increased from 12,000 to 18,000, and these trends continued even after the lira began to stabilize in 1996. Finally, the south avoided the immediate impact of the downturn in the international economy because of its lower levels of integration internationally, compared with the centre and north.

Table 11.2 Turn-around in economic growth in the south in the 1990s: regional deviations from national growth across two periods

Regions or Areas	1990–5*	1995–8*	Improvement/regression
Italy	0	0	0
North-west	−24	−6	18
North-east	92	16	−76
Centre	−4	−27	−23
South,	**−46**	**15**	**60**
comprising:			
Sicilia	**−59**	**52**	**111**
Campania	**−107**	**−8**	**99**
Basilicata	**86**	**170**	**85**
Sardegna	**−23**	**32**	**55**
Molise	**0**	**40**	**40**
Puglia	**−26**	**−7**	**19**
Abruzzo	**5**	**−15**	**−20**
Calabria	**26**	**−17**	**−44**

* % deviation

Source: Adapted from Table 3. Annual deviation from national growth 1990–95 and 1995–98, *OECD Territorial Reviews Italy* © OECD, 2001 (OECD 2001b: 169)

Levels of growth over the past decade have not been uniform, with the more backward regions (e.g. Sicily, Sardinia) generally achieving greater improvement than those (such as Abruzzo) which are closer to northern levels of development. Yet, the most notable characteristic of the economic turn-around in the south is its innovatory aspect: the development of small enterprises involved in specialized production, which have, along the lines of the north-east (see below in this chapter), developed industrial districts to exploit the benefits of territorial proximity. For example, there has been a mushrooming of dozens of smaller firms in the so-called *triangolo del salotto* (between Altamura, Santeramo in Colle and Matera) and related areas, producing furniture, shoes, leather goods, paper and so on. Industrial districts have developed in Grumo Nevano (shoes and clothing), Solofra (leather production), Arzano and Casavatore (paper goods) and Castellammare di Stabia (cut flowers) (Burroni and Trigilia 2001: 69–75). A weak lira also gave a boost to international tourism, with the number of overseas visitors to the south increasing from 10 million in 1993 to 18 million in 1999. Changes in employment nationally have confirmed these trends, with levels of employment in both agriculture and large-scale industrial manufacturing continuing a long-term decline, while the tertiary sector continues to grow (see figure 11.1).

The spontaneity of this economic turn-around was assisted by the formulation and launch of a new policy framework for the south in the late 1990s. This emphasized 'a different role for the state, a more enhanced role for parts of civil society and new relationships between centre and periphery' (Della Sala 2000: 189). It embodied a shift from an 'inward investment' to an 'endogenous development' approach to regional

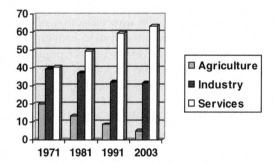

Figure 11.1   Changing distribution of national employment by sector, 1991–2003 (%). For data, see table 5.1.
Source: ISTAT, 2004a

policy: instead of simply attempting to attract capital from outside the region, in order to strengthen exports and employment, the new approach aims to reduce regional disparities by increasing the endogenous potential of the south, and this by building institutional capacity (Bull and Baudner 2004). New instruments, such as 'planning agreements', 'planning programmes', 'territorial pacts' and 'area contracts' were launched, all of which were based on the principle of co-ordination between different bodies (local authorities, firms, financial institutions, interest groups and associations), with the State providing a role of facilitation and support, especially in the context of securing EU structural funds to assist development.

At the same time, the government decided to merge the various agencies concerned with promoting development in the south, which in the aftermath of the ending of special intervention were dissipated and fragmented. In January 1999 a single agency, *Sviluppo Italia*, was created, into which were merged seven existing development agencies. The new holding agency, which operates under the auspices of the Treasury, has the function of attracting domestic and foreign capital and investment, assisting in the securing of EU structural funds, promoting economic activities which will stimulate new business and employment, and several other support functions. In 1999 it identified nine sectors as motors of development, in which it has been working since: biotechnology, agrofood, information technology, tourism, fashion, the environment, aerospace, female entrepreneurship and microsystem technologies (Della Sala 2000: 197–8). A new development programme for the period 2000–6 was launched, after negotiations between central government, regions, communes and interest groups, which is based on developing industrial districts, improving transport and instilling more competitiveness in the labour market and the goods and services sector. The programme confirms a more limited role for the State than in the past, as a facilitator of *local* resources on the basis of which development is expected to take place.

Two other factors also contributed to the economic turn-around and the new policy response. First, there was a concerted attempt by central government to reassert a level of legality in the south after the assassinations of anti-Mafia prosecutors Giovanni Falcone and Paolo Borsellino in 1992 (see chapter 6), and between 1991 and 1996 approximately ninety communal municipalities in the south were dissolved on the grounds of Mafia infiltration. Second, the direct election of local mayors was introduced, and the first elections under the new system brought to the fore a new local political class (see chapter 9). These mayors had direct popular legitimacy, and many of them were committed to reversing the decline of their cities, and consequently injected a new vitality and confidence into the civil, political and economic management of their municipalities.

To summarize, there can be little doubt that the 1990s have witnessed a sea change in both the approach of the State to the problem of the south and the economic development of the region itself. This is not to suggest that the south is necessarily better off now than it was in the early 1990s. On the contrary, it is, on several indicators, poorer. However, that can be viewed as a consequence of the drastic economic transition required by the changes of the early 1990s. Moreover, the quality of the new development is of a different order than before, and contains the potential for more stable and prolonged growth. This is because the growth is more spontaneous than in the past, and based on the sort of model (flexible specialization and industrial districts) which has proved to be successful in the centre and north-east of Italy (see below). Painfully freed from the suffocating embrace of forty years of the *stato assistenziale*, the Mezzogiorno is revealing the potential of some of its own economic and political resources, and through this the extent of difference within the south itself (Cipoletta 1999). After the failure of industrialization, the south may now be undergoing a transformation from an agricultural to a post-industrial society without the industrialized stage in between.

These developments suggest to many that the entire premiss of the southern problem may have become outdated. Both the growth of small firms in the north-east – which makes that area distinguishable from other parts of the north – and the growing diversity of development within the south are undermining the notion that Italy's economy can be seen as constituting a straightforward dualism between north and south. The south has become subject to 'diffuse industrialization', with some regions experiencing levels of development higher than the south's average.[6] 'Revisionist' historians have taken this argument further by maintaining that the southern problem is, to a large extent, artificial. Its origins can be traced to the politics of the late nineteenth century rather than economic reality, and its continued existence has been maintained largely by comparing the south to a level and type of development 'normally' expected in advanced European democracies.[7]

Nevertheless, the significance of the turn-around should not be overstated. It is neither robust nor widespread enough to justify predictions of long-term change in the economic and social nature of some regions of the south. The striking differences that continue to distinguish the south and the centre–north in terms of GDP, productivity and rates of employment/unemployment should not be underestimated (see table 11.3). For example, at the end of the 1990s, the unemployment rate in the south was not only significantly higher than the national average, but also above the average of the EU's Objective 1 regions (identified as the poorest regions in the EU) (OECD 2003: 111–12). Calculations of the overall contribution of the south, compared with the centre and north, to the national economy are also revealing (see figure 11.2).

Table 11.3 Regional difference (north–centre v. south) in macro-economic performance in 1995 and 2001

	Italy		North–Centre		South	
	1995	2001	1995	2001	1995	2001
GDP at mkt prices (share)	100.0	100.0	75.8	75.6	24.2	24.4
GDP per capita	100.0	100.0	119.2	118.0	66.4	67.8
Productivity	100.0	100.0	105.3	104.9	86.3	87.2
Employment rate*	57.4	61.0	60.9	65.3	51.1	53.2
Unemployment rate+	11.6	9.1	7.6	4.8	20.4	18.6

* As % of working population (2001 data refer to Jan. 2003).
+ As % of labour force (2001 data refer to Jan. 2003).
Source: Adapted from Table 3. Regional differential in macroeconomic performance 1995 and 2001, *OECD Economic Surveys: Italy – Volume 2003 Issue 13* © OECD, 2003 (OECD 2003: 42)

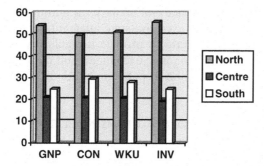

Figure 11.2 Contribution to the economy by territorial area (north, centre, south), 2002 (%). GNP = Gross National Product; CON = consumption; WKU = work units (calculated through conversion of all working positions held by each person employed during the year into 'full-time units'); INV = investments.
Source: ISTAT 2004a

It could be argued that diversity of development within the south (which to some extent has created a 'south of the south') is evidence of continuing dualism in the Italian economy, because otherwise one would expect a tendency towards balanced growth within the region as a whole. This would apply not just to territory, but to the size of industry. If small and medium-sized enterprises (SMEs) are a new phenomenon in the south, they are appearing at a time when the big Italian groups (such as FIAT and Pirelli) have completed their expansion into the area (and there are signs of the beginnings of a retreat).[8] Furthermore, amongst small and medium-sized enterprises, there are fewer signs of the innovative approach to resisting the farming out of phases of production to Central and Eastern Europe (where labour costs can be up to ten times less) which has been a characteristic of their counterparts in the centre and north-east. Finally, the new policy for the south has experienced difficulties in implementation, and has also been subject to a change in direction (if not a return to earlier thinking) as a consequence of the alternation in government in 2001.[9]

These factors point to the importance of a key variable: the nature of state intervention. The ending of special intervention in the early 1990s constituted a turning point in policy regarding the south. It was a consequence not just of the exhaustion of a particular policy (forced industrialization) but of the passing of a national and political model of development. This model of development had been exploited by the political class – and especially the two main governing parties (the DC and the PSI) whose voting support had become increasingly concentrated in the south – for its own interests. When the State was 'brought back in' by the centre left governments in the period after 1996, there was a marked shift towards attempting to construct a role which would facilitate development 'from below' rather than force it 'from above'. The changes were effectively responding to spontaneous new forms of growth, and the new role of state intervention was more embryonic and gradual than comprehensive and complete. If it is to attract private and public investment, the south will have to confront the considerable problems of lack of infrastructure, the need for greater flexibility and deregulation, the need for greater security in terms of public order and justice, and the poverty or incapacity of some local administrations and élites. The main problem today is no longer excessive state intervention and its 'perverse' effects, but rather the inability of the State to provide a regulatory framework sufficiently strong to provide certainty to 'economic exchanges' and reinforce respect for citizens' rights and responsibilities in relation to public institutions (De Vivo 2001: 719).

THE 'THIRD ITALY': THE RISE OF SMALL FIRMS IN THE CENTRE AND NORTH-EAST

The 'Third Italy' was first identified as a distinct area in the 1970s, and the notion was refined and developed during the 1980s.[10] This is not to suggest that the presence of small firms was an entirely new phenomenon. On the contrary, one of the dualisms in the Italian economy has always been the coexistence of a small number of large industries and a myriad of small firms, with very little in between (see chapter 10). Yet, there is a notable difference between the first real expansion (measured in terms of employment) of this sector in the 1950s (during the economic miracle) and that experienced from the 1970s onwards. In fact, the sector's share of the economy as a whole actually declined in the 1960s, the period when large private and public firms increased their share notably, even though it remained higher than the European average. Moreover, economists' interpretation of the role and function of small firms in the economy was traditionally a negative one, emanating from a broader interpretation of dualistic development. Small firms were viewed as traditional parts of the underdeveloped economy, which were low in technology and productivity, high in labour intensity, and dependent largely on domestic markets.[11] But, from the 1970s onwards, there were changes – of both a quantitative and a qualitative nature – which transformed the Italian economy and the manner in which it was studied.

From a quantitative perspective, small and medium-sized firms, as a proportion of total employment, productivity and number of firms in Italy, grew markedly between

Table 11.4 Employment distribution in manufacturing industry by
firm size (number of employees), 1951–2000

	1951	1961	1971	1981	1991	2000
1–9	32.1	30.0	22.3	23.9	26.2	25.1
10–99	22.1	26.9	28.3	34.9	41.7	40.9
100–499	20.4	21.6	18.6	18.3	19.2	34.0
500+	25.4	21.5	30.8	22.9	12.9	34.0
Total	100	100	100	100	100	100

Source: Adapted from Balcet 1997: 112 and Onida 2004: 49–50

the early 1970s and early 1990s, giving the Italian economy a 'size' distinctiveness which marks it out from the European average today (see table 11.4 and tables 10.1, 10.2 and 10.3).

These developments were accompanied by qualitative changes, relating to the specific nature of the sector (traditional), its economic performance (increasingly strong), its diversity (different types of small firms), its distinctive practices (flexible), its territorial location (primarily in the centre and north-east), its internal relationships (both competitive and co-operative) and its external relationship to big firms ('decentralization') and local government (highly supportive). Together, these changes amounted to the emergence not just of a distinctive sector of the Italian economy, but an alternative socio-economic model of development, which has seen its peak in the development of 'industrial districts' within which the above features have become institutionalized. There are three key characteristics of this socio-economic model of development.

Flexibility

The firms are based on the principle of 'flexibility' (*flessibilità*). By remaining small, they are able to escape most of the bureaucratic regulation imposed on firms by the State relating to employment, insurance, taxation and other matters. Firms below a certain size in terms of personnel and annual turnover are not required to make their statements of accounts available to the tax authorities, beyond a declaration that their income is below the threshold amount. Nor need they be unionized, or pay minimum wages and other social benefits. This means that they can, without problems, employ categories of workers often shunned by larger firms (youth, women, pensioners, immigrants), pay lower wages, operate flexible work patterns, and evade fiscal and insurance burdens, all this reducing costs and boosting profits.

The importance of these differences is evidenced in the fact that more than 90 per cent of Italian firms declare themselves to be in this category. This explains the growing attention paid to Italy's so-called informal economy in the 1980s. Until the 1980s, what was known as the 'black' (or 'underground') economy was denounced both for its evasive practices and its exploitation of workers and their rights. In the 1980s, however, there was a gradual shift in attitude towards it (Saba 1978). It was recognized that 'black work' (*lavoro nero*) was often as much a *preference* of workers as a necessity, and that the informal economy was part of a more general economic trend towards diffusion, which was producing a real benefit to the economy overall. It was estimated that the informal economy employed as many as 4 million people and raised GDP by 20–30 per cent above the official figures. Its significance was such that, in the 1980s, the decision was taken to adjust national economic statistics to take account of it, on the grounds that it hid Italy's true position in the international economic league (Pugliese 1994).[12] Certainly, the performance of this sector was impressive, particularly in view of the fact that most firms were operating in traditional sectors (clothing, shoes, textiles and so on). Indeed, it became apparent that the maintenance of Italy's competitiveness abroad was becoming increasingly dependent on small and medium-sized firms, which – contrary to the conventional wisdom – were proving able to compete with Third World countries where labour costs were much lower.

Flexible specialization

Flexibility relates not just to work practices but to a firm's relationship to larger firms and different markets, a phenomenon known as 'flexible specialization' (*specializzazione flessibile*), and which constitutes the core of larger processes known as 'industrial decentralization' and 'industrial diffusion' (Brusco 1982). On the one hand, small firms have taken advantage of the restructuring of large firms, which, since the 1970s, have had to reduce employment and make themselves more responsive to economic cycles. This has led them towards 'decentralizing' the production and supply of certain goods and services to small firms, which, being more flexible, can adapt to the changes in demand and labour supply more easily than their larger counterparts. On the other hand, there has been a process of industrial diffusion, with the multiplication of highly volatile and fluctuating markets requiring rapid adaptation and penetration on the part of firms in order to be successful. Small firms have proved to be the ideal formula for this activity. A good example is the rapid penetration of the Chinese market for machine tools that opened up in the late 1980s. In 1985, Italian exports to China in this sector were equal to 3.7 per cent of all exports. By 1993, the figure had risen to 10.5 per cent, and China had become the second largest importer of Italian machine tools (Saba 1995: 49).

Diversity of firms, then, is a hallmark of the sector, although, broadly speaking, four principal types can be identified (Balcet 1997: 114): first, marginal firms working in sectors protected by natural monopolies and public subsidies; second, firms that are satellites of big firms, operating within a network that provides them with a constant set of outlets; third, niche firms in technological and other sectors, which maintain their presence through their ability to adapt quickly; and finally, specialized suppliers, which are independent of big firms, very competitive and usually located in 'industrial districts'. The type of goods that these firms produce is also rich in diversity, but, generally speaking, of a traditional nature: clothing, shoes, glass, household goods, jewellery, machine tools, leather products, agricultural machinery, toys and so on. In short, there is a range of traditional-style products produced in a small-scale, technologically advanced setting (Regini 1988).

Territorial concentration

The bulk of the more productive firms are territorially concentrated in the centre and north-eastern parts of the country, particularly in the regions of Emilia-Romagna, Tuscany, Friuli-Venezia Giulia, the Veneto and the Marche. This territorial concentration, however, is more than simply a geographic expression that might distinguish the area from the traditional industrial triangle of the north-west. Rather, the firms have actively sought to exploit their territorial proximity to each other and their local environment in order to develop mutual support systems. The areas where these mutual support systems have been most highly developed have been described as 'industrial districts'.[13] An industrial district is characterized by the presence of a number of small-scale firms in a specific (either traditional or specialized) area of production, with specialized labour forces. The firms have a relationship of competition and co-operation with each other, and are also deeply rooted in their local socio-political environments, from which they draw support. By 1991 there were 238 industrial districts employing 1.7 million workers, compared with 149 employing 360,000 in 1951 (Brusco and Paba 1997).[14] Examples include Prato and Empoli (textiles and clothes), Murano (glass), Sassuolo (ceramics), Reggio Emilia (agricultural machinery and cheese), Parma and San Daniele (ham), Vigevano and Macerata (shoes), Valenza and Arezzo (gold jewelry), Poggibonsi and Bassano (furniture), Santa Croce sull'Arno (leather).

The competition between firms maintains quality, while co-operation occurs in areas such as administrative and financial services, purchase of raw materials, subcontracting, relocating labour and so on. In addition, the firms draw on support from local and regional government in terms of services, infrastructure, professional training, market information, etc. Moreover, the districts act as a point of reference for entrepreneurs, employees, local trade unions and local politicians and officials, in negotiations on work practices as well as in lobbying the central government. In short, industrial districts have developed into genuine socio-economic systems that are highly flexible, relying on carefully developed external economies and based on a strong sense of solidarity and community.

EXPLAINING THE RISE AND SUCCESS OF THE THIRD ITALY

The emergence of the Third Italy can be seen as a structural ('spontaneous') development in the Italian economy, and one that is part of a more general trend in economic development towards industrial decentralization and flexible work practices, witnessed in other countries (notably Japan). The rise of the small-firm sector should therefore be viewed in the context of the crisis of the big firms in the 1970s and the changes imposed on their nature and strategies by the demands of the economy. From this perspective, the essential features of flexibility and the importance of the local environment are not limited to small firms, but constitute part of a general model of economic development 'from below', of which the Third Italy is a particularly noteworthy example (Trigilia 1992: 24–7).

Important as this general context may be, it does not adequately explain why the phenomenon should be so territorially concentrated in the centre and north-east (despite the emergence of industrial districts elsewhere in the country), and why it has become so deep-rooted in Italy (compared with other countries). The answer to the first question (why the north-east?) lies in the distinctive socio-political environment that is found in these areas. The strong sense of community and solidarity arises in those regions where the subcultures (both 'red' and 'white') have been deeply rooted; research, therefore, has posited a relationship between political and economic patterns of territorial development (Bagnasco and Trigilia 1984, 1985; Trigilia 1986; Cento Bull and Gilbert 2001). In other words, the emergence of a model of development 'from below' is predicated to a large extent on non-economic factors. These regions, more-over, are precisely those which Putnam (1993: 161) found to have a strong history of civic traditions and thus 'high performance regional government'.

The answer to the second question (why Italy?) lies in the particular nature of post-war state regulation and industrial policy, the broad pattern of which was outlined in chapter 10. Two points should be made about this type of regulation (Bianchi and Gualtieri 1990). First, it has been extensive, restrictive and onerous, but at the same time poorly administered and implemented. Its restrictive nature reached its height in the early 1970s, when various laws (partly stemming from the Workers' Statute) were passed. This created a strong incentive for entrepreneurs to devise ways and means of avoiding regulation by the State, such incentive in turn acting as a catalyst towards more general processes at work. Second, forms of regulation which are designed to be 'facilitative' rather than restrictive (e.g. in manpower policies and industrial relations) have been weakly developed and institutionalized. The nature of – and distortions in – industrial policies towards large firms were addressed in chapter 10. Policies towards small and medium-sized firms have not proved to be more innovative, as the difficul-ties in facilitating and regulating new growth in the south have shown. Industrial poli-cies have been subject to fierce criticism by the European Union, which 'blames Italy outright for the exclusive centralising intervention as a support to structural imbal-ances rather than a means of creating an environment to overcome them' (Bianchi 1993: 161).

Consequently, two forms of regulation emerged in the 1980s and coexisted: 'weak institutional regulation' alongside 'ad hoc voluntaristic regulation', the latter develop-ing spontaneously as a means of overcoming the former (Regini 1995). It is mainly small firms that have been able to develop these forms of regulation, because of their flexibility and the importance of the local socio-political structures. In short, the very nature of state regulation in Italy has been a prime determinant in the emergence and success of an alternative model of politico-economic development, one that is predicated on a rejection of the idea of centralized state intervention in the economy. Small firms have thrived because of – not despite – the absence of the State. They are 'sheltered by their very nature from public intervention, which no longer acts in the interest of industrial policy, but, rather, as an unwelcome inter-ference in the daily lives of firms impeding their every decision' (Prodi and De Giovanni 1993: 53).

The characteristics of the 'Third Italy' have provided firms with significant competitive advantages. Economic studies have confirmed that firms located in industrial districts have higher rates of income generation, labour productivity and capacity to export goods. Indeed, the major Italian exporters that have been the bedrock of the 'made in Italy' success story are small and medium-sized enterprises located in industrial districts. Italians have consequently become world leaders in the export of specialized goods such as spectacles, furniture, ceramics, machine tools, shoes, textiles, clothing and other consumer goods. By 1995 the industrial districts were producing approximately 22 per cent of all Italian exports, with even higher percentages in certain sectors: 66 per cent in textiles, 37 per cent in clothing and 34 per cent in furniture (Berger and Locke 2001: 384). Despite this success, however, the 1990s have witnessed the emergence of the strongest challenge the sector has known since its emergence, and its fortunes appear to be rapidly changing.

THE GLOBALIZED 'NEW ECONOMY' AND THE CHINESE CHALLENGE

Globalization and the rise of the 'new economy' in the early 1990s posed considerable challenges to a sector of the national economy that is fragmented and small and has relatively low levels of capital accumulation. The Third Italy appeared to respond well to the new demands, at least in the first part of the 1990s. In particular, the challenge of cheap labour markets in Central and Eastern Europe was met while retaining the bulk of production locally. Industrial districts exploited the existence of cheaper labour markets abroad to expand, rather than substitute, their local productive capacity, through adapting certain aspects of their organization and manufacturing processes (Berger and Locke 2001: 396–8).

However, the second half of the 1990s saw the emergence of a far more significant challenge, the so-called Chinese threat. Between 1996 and 2002, the Chinese share of world exports rose from 2.8 per cent to 6.5 per cent, placing it third in the league table of world exporters in 2002. This has affected the export shares of most of the advanced Western democracies, but especially of Italy, which dropped to eighth position in 2002, and whose reduction in share of world trade fell by 20 per cent between 1995 and 2002 (see tables 2.7 and 2.8). This is because Chinese competition is focused precisely on those products in which Italy (through its small firms) has become a world leader in the past thirty years: clothing, shoes, jewels, lighting, furniture, taps, spectacles, engineering components and industrial machines. Almost all of the sectors associated with the Third Italy's production have seen their share of exports decline in this period. A comparative study of imports by the fifteen countries of the EU of fifteen types of goods typical of the Third Italy's production base reveals that between 1990 and 2002 Italy's share rose by half as much again, while China's increased tenfold. Since the late 1990s, the European and other markets have been flooded with Chinese products in sectors that are traditional Italian strongholds. Moreover, the production and distribution of many of the goods are based on unfair or illegal practices. The counterfeiting of Italian brand names has become so widespread that it has forced the European Commission to take action, passing a new regulation against counterfeiting, and Italy is taking measures to protect its intellectual copyrights.

Table 11.5   Italian exporters by size of firm (number of employees), 2001

Category (employee size)	Number of exporting firms	% of total firms in that category	% of all exporters	% of all firms	Value (millions of euros)	% of total value
1–4	73,858	1.9	41.8	88.5	18,599	7.1
5–9	35,133	12.0	19.9	6.81	9,455	3.6
10–19	32,351	25.7	18.3	2.93	18,562	7.1
20–49	22,233	42.6	12.6	0.21	34,163	13.0
50–99	7,130	53.4	4.0	0.31	29,525	11.3
100–249	3,987	58.4	2.3	0.16	41,725	15.9
250–499	1,143	58.6	0.6	0.05	28,250	10.8
500+	839	62.4	0.5	0.03	81,894	31.2
Total	176,674	4.1	100	100	262,172	100

Source: Onida 2004: 86

Inevitably, Italy itself has increased its share of Chinese imports, but it has been unable to offset this increase through its own exports to China, which in 2002 amounted to less than half the value of Italian imports of Chinese goods (Fortis and Curzio 2003). This has prompted the formulation of the 'Marco Polo' project, which co-ordinates the action not just of industrial districts in the north-east and elsewhere, but also of large firms. The aim is to make a co-ordinated assault on the Chinese market, shifting production processes abroad where necessary, with large firms being assisted by their smaller counterparts (Morelli 2003: 5).

The Chinese threat has prompted a wide-ranging debate amongst politicians, entre-preneurs and economists, and many speak of the sector as being in crisis. Paradoxi-cally, the very characteristics that have been at the root of its success may now hinder an adequate response to this latest challenge. Industrial districts encourage smallness and avoid what are perceived to be onerous forms of central regulation. As long as the broader financial and regulatory framework acts as a constraint rather than a facil-itating condition for the innovatory capacity and growth of small firms, this situation is difficult to change (see chapter 2). Indeed, while the total share of employment of small and medium-sized firms has not risen in the past decade, the actual number of firms grew (by 784,000) between 1991 and 2001, fuelled partly by the break-up of some of the larger enterprises and groups. The average number of employees per firm has fallen consistently since 1971, from 5 to 4.4 (1991), 3.9 (1996) and 3.8 (2001). Italy's exporting capacity is heavily skewed towards these firms, making it highly dependent on too few sectors (see table 11.5).

In short, what began as a source of strength (small firms in industrial districts) has expanded on a general basis to become a potential Achilles' heel: there is a tendency in virtually all sectors for smallness and specialization to dominate, with SMEs either reluctant or unable to grow, and the question is whether an advanced economy of the West can withstand competition in a globalized economy with this sort of struc-ture (Trento 2003; Onida 2004). Since the early 1990s, these firms have struggled to exploit the technological innovations of the 'new economy' at the same time as having to adapt to a single currency whose existence removes the possibility of devaluation to aid exports. Yet, the unsatisfactory financial and regulatory conditions in Italy tend to hinder innovation and act as a disincentive to growth in firm size (see chapter 2).

CONCLUSION

The focus of the last two chapters has been on the part that state regulation and politics has played in shaping the nature and development of the economy. It could be argued that the State has – wittingly or unwittingly – played a key role in producing what Saba (1995: 110) has described as Italy's 'two innovative formulae' in industrial development. The first is the State holding formula (see chapter 10). This proved at first to be a success, and a model admired abroad, but then – for both economic and political reasons – entered into a crisis from which it has never fully recovered. Moreover, use of the formula to try to address the problem of the south had only a brief period of success (in terms of reducing the north–south gap), for largely similar reasons. The second innovative formula is the small-firm industrial district model of development. This emerged in the 1970s and 1980s, partly as a reaction to the inhibiting nature of state regulation, and developed its own forms of voluntary regulation to increase its productivity and performance. It has proved to be very successful, and the growth of industrial districts in the south is evidence of how it may now be replacing the first formula as a means of resolving Italy's oldest economic problem (the underdevelopment of an area larger than some European countries).

The focus on state regulation also highlights the changing nature of the Italian economy today. Italy is witnessing the gradual passing of a distinct political-economic 'model' which has characterized the post-war period. That model has been primarily based on a large state sector that has dominated the economy as a whole, a large underdeveloped south, and a thriving small-firm sector. This model of development cannot be separated from the 'party regime' within which all three features were shaped. For this reason, the gradual passing of the model cannot be divorced from the broader context of the collapse of the old regime and the economic watershed that occurred during the 1990s. The programme of privatization has reshaped the public–private divide, making clientelistic and corrupt practices more difficult, and it can be seen partly as a natural consequence of the ending of the old DC regime. The abolition of special intervention in the south, bringing to an end decades of political mismanagement and clientelism, can also be seen as a natural consequence of the collapse of the old order. Finally, the difficulties being encountered by the Third Italy have exposed the extent to which the Italian economy has become dependent on this sector and the degree to which, due to the inefficiencies of state regulation, the economy's industrial structure has now developed a general 'dimensional' problem. For if, as appears to be the case, the Third Italy is entering into a manufacturing crisis under the weight of Chinese competition, it is not clear whether the changes to the other two Italies will be sufficiently rapid or incisive to offset the damage such a crisis could cause.

Italy and the European Union

Introduction

In the immediate post-war period, European integration was largely perceived as a single aspect of a nation's foreign policy. Today, it is as much a domestic as an overseas issue, due to the impact it is having on national political systems (a concept known as Europeanization). The importance of the European Union (EU) to Italy can hardly be understated. Telò (1996: 131–2 and 145–6) argues that the EU has been much more important to Italy than to any other member state, since it has been at the heart of an extraordinary process of socio-economic modernization as well as an anchoring point for a fledgling democracy.

It is perhaps unsurprising, therefore, that the most notable aspect of the Italy–Europe relationship has been the country's unequivocal and constant support for the process of European integration throughout the post-war period. This combination (of modernization and pro-Europeanism) would appear to suggest that the Italy–Europe relationship has been nothing but successful. The reality, however, is more complex, as this chapter will argue. Having first explained Italy's Europeanism, the chapter then evaluates the Italy–European relationship along two dimensions (the 'upstream' phase and the 'downstream' phase) and across two phases, with the early 1990s marking an important juncture. It will emphasize the importance of the EU in the passing of the First Republic's political-economic model and the changes that have occurred in Italy's Europeanism in the past decade.

Explaining Italy's Europeanism

The Italian position on European integration stands out over time for its consistency and maximalist nature. Pistone (1991: 179–82) argues that the European policies of successive Italian governments have been shaped by four tendencies, which display more federalist traits than the European policies of any other member government during the post-war period: the preference for a 'global' form of integration, incorporating political, military and economic aspects; the insistence on a strict link between 'positive' and 'negative' economic integration; support for the democratization of the institutions of the EU, especially through strengthening the role of the European Parliament; and a belief in the limits of intergovernmentalism as a means to achieve reform. There are five closely interrelated factors that explain this position, their importance relative to each other having changed over time.

International benefits: reintegration, status and influence

The two pillars of Italy's post-war foreign policy were NATO and the EEC. The conventional wisdom that the latter was a secondary consideration for Italy has been overturned by recent research, which has showed that De Gasperi's priority was to achieve recognition of Italy as an important and autonomous actor in Europe and the Mediterranean, thus recovering her international status. This was viewed as best achieved through a European Community of nations, and Italy resisted joining the Atlantic Alliance until it became clear that the European choice could not prevail, and that isolation would follow. The Atlantic Alliance therefore became a surrogate for De Gasperi's preferred alternative, a shield within which the European ideal could develop (Varsori 1995; Galante 1992; Ellwood 1995). Italy's international position, moreover, influenced this Europeanism in a supra-national, rather than intergovernmental, direction. Vanquished countries, humiliated by military defeat and economic destruction, are more likely to cede sovereignty in exchange for legitimation: paradoxically, in order to recover national sovereignty, it may be necessary to give some up to supra-national institutions (Telò 1996: 142–3). More generally, countries with low status in the international community stand to gain more from supra-nationalism than countries with high status, since it provides an introduction (albeit indirectly) to the 'big league of international politics' (Cotta 1992: 208). Italy was viewed as more significant than the small powers of northern and southern Europe, but not as a power ranking alongside Germany, Britain and France. European integration has therefore provided a significant incentive and instrument for Italy to attempt to enter the 'big league'.

Political benefits: stabilization of a fragile democracy

As a nascent democracy emerging from a fascist dictatorship, Italy was confronted with a long period of consolidation. The threat of democratic breakdown was real, both because of the Cold War and because of the presence of anti-system extremes in the party system (see chapters 1 and 3). A united Europe was seen as a means whereby Italy could be integrated into a framework of nations, thus making the Communist threat less tenable. In his memoirs, Guido Carli (1993: 164–5) argues that fear of communism (rather than economic benefits) was the decisive factor behind membership of the EEC.

Economic benefits: modernization

From the early 1960s onwards, the economic benefits of EC membership came increasingly to influence Italy's position. Italy's 'economic miracle', because it was primarily export-driven (see chapter 2), was given a significant boost by the EEC's creation of a free-trade zone, and the percentage of Italian goods exported to member states rose considerably. From there on, scepticism on the part of small industry and agriculture abated, and membership was regarded by most economic elites as essential to economic growth and modernization.

Policy-making benefits: discipline and the 'vincolo esterno'

Romano (1991) and Coralluzzo (1994) argue that a nation-state's European policy can be either 'behavioural' or 'institutionalist' in style. In the former, a member state exhibits behaviour that makes possible the creation of common European institutions and policies. In the latter, a member state sets up institutions as a means of *constraining its own representatives* to behave in ways which make common European policies possible. Supra-nationalism, therefore, constitutes an 'external constraint' (*vincolo esterno*). Italy's European policy has always been shaped by an institutionalist approach, which, Romano (1991: 666) argues, derives from a deep-rooted pessimism about the capacity of the country to rectify its deficiencies through its own political will. From this perspective, renovation of the political system can be achieved only through the pressure and support of an external force. Consequently, the EU is used by those seeking reform to legitimize what might be harsh and unpopular measures (Cotta 1992: 211; Hine 1992: 57–8; Bindi 1996: 101), and to overcome vested interests preventing reform. Europe has always been seen as a great panacea or a mythical saviour: a means of resolving problems in the Italian political system that the political class itself is unable or unwilling to resolve by itself (Coralluzzo 1994: 116; Dyson and Featherstone 1996).

The pressures from Italian society

Surveys by Eurobarometer and Doxa since the 1970s show that Italy has consistently been one of the countries that has been most supportive of European integration (Wertman 1983; Panebianco 1994; Martinotti and Stefanizzi 1995).[1] Even today, when (as will be argued below) there are stronger elements of scepticism about the EU in some quarters, Italy is consistently above the (pre-2004 expansion) EU average in terms of support on key issues (see tables 12.1 and 12.2).

   In the period since the former PCI began to shift its position on Europe, the consensus has been a broad one: from the general public to the media, interest groups, parliamentarians and political parties (Walker 1976; Galante 1988; Maggiorani 1998). Italy is unusual in the EU in so far as parties and governments feel under constant pressure to be more committed to European integration (Hine 1992: 53).[2] The Italian public's high levels of support for Europe are closely correlated with their dissatisfaction with Italian democracy, and Italy is consistently bottom of the table in approving the functioning of its own democracy and among those at the top in support of membership of the EU (see tables 12.3 and 12.4). In creating a typology of different types of national and supra-national orientation Martinotti and Stefanizzi (1995: 176–7) found that the vast majority of Italians are 'innovators' or 'escapists': 'they hope either

Table 12.1 Italy and support for Europe on key issues, compared with other EU member states, Spring 2004

Country	Membership: good thing	Benefit from membership	Trust in European Community	Support for ... Single currency	Common FP	Common DSP*	Enlargement	EU Constitution
Italy	**54**	**49**	**63**	**69**	**77**	**83**	**55**	**78**
Belgium	57	58	63	83	71	77	38	72
Denmark	54	64	47	50	50	61	59	37
Germany	45	39	39	58	74	80	28	68
Greece	71	82	63	64	78	80	66	66
Spain	64	69	53	74	69	74	59	70
France	43	46	52	68	66	75	37	62
Ireland	71	80	61	83	66	60	60	59
Luxembourg	75	69	66	88	77	83	37	75
Netherlands	64	55	54	58	69	77	44	70
Austria	30	38	37	68	62	57	34	60
Portugal	55	66	56	67	62	68	52	57
Finland	46	46	59	73	55	57	48	52
Sweden	37	27	48	45	49	55	54	53
UK	29	30	26	26	39	52	31	42
EU15(av.)	48	47	47	60	65	72	42	63

* DSP = Defence and Security Policy

Source: Eurobarometer 61 (<www.europa.eu.int>)

Table 12.2 Italy and changing support for the single currency, compared with other EU participating countries, 1995–2004 (%)

Country	Autumn 1995	Spring 2001	Autumn 2004
Italy	68	83	69
Luxembourg	59	81	88
Belgium	51	75	83
Greece	52	72	64
Ireland	60	72	83
Spain	58	68	74
France	58	67	68
Netherlands	64	66	58
Austria	23	59	68
Portugal	46	59	67
Germany	34	53	58
Finland	33	49	73

Source: Eurispes 2002: 264–5 and Eurobarometer 61 (<www.europa.eu.int>)

Table 12.3 Italians and trust in national institutions and in the EU, 2002–3 (%)

	Trust: 2002	No trust: 2002	Trust: 2003	No trust: 2003
National Political Parties	15	75	11	78
National Government	34	53	27	62
National Parliament	41	45	33	53
European Union	59	24	57	25

Source: Eurobarometer 61 (<www.europa.eu.int>)

Table 12.4 Italians and evaluation of functioning of democracy in Italy and in the EU, 2002–3 (%)

		Very satisfied	Reasonably satisfied	Not very satisfied	Not at all satisfied	Don't know
Autumn	Italy	3	30	44	22	1
2002	EU	3	42	29	9	17
Autumn	Italy	2	31	46	19	2
2003	EU	3	42	30	8	18

Source: Eurobarometer 61 (<www.europa.eu.int>)

that European integration will provide leverage for innovation or reform in their national system or they regard it as an escape hatch through which the deficiencies of the national system can be circumvented.'

If these five factors explain the rationale and strength of Italy's Europeanism, several qualifications need to be made. First, the reintegration of Italy into the Western community of nations has never led to its acceptance as a first-rank power. Second, whatever support European integration has offered to the consolidation of Italian democracy, for the majority of Italians the latter has remained a poorly functioning one. Third, despite the economic modernization of the country, considerable structural disparities in its development have remained. Fourth, there is an evident paradox in a country 'benefiting' from the rigour of an external constraint because it is unable to carry through of its own accord the policies required. This raises the question as to whether Europe can be seen, from Italy's perspective, as an arena in which the country has genuinely exercised any real choices.[3] Finally, the consensus behind the European ideal seems to have a primarily negative foundation, with Italians supporting Europe largely as a means of escaping the inadequacies of their own democracy, and possibly, therefore, doing so in ignorance of the problems or implications that membership involves.

These qualifications point to a more complex picture, which can be explored across two temporal periods, with the early 1990s as a watershed, and within these periods from two perspectives: the *fase ascendente* ('upstream phase'), referring to Italy's input into the European integration process, and the *fase discendente* ('downstream phase'), referring to Italy's response and adjustment to the demands of Europe, as well as to the more general impact of the EU on its domestic structures.

'FLAWED EUROPEANISM': THE ITALY–EUROPE RELATIONSHIP UNTIL THE EARLY 1990S

'Upstream' phase

Despite some notable achievements over the years, Italy has never had a consistent overall European policy. In fact, it has often been little more than the sum of foreign sectoral policies (Coralluzzo 1994: 109 and 117–19). This has caused significant shortcomings, in so far as foreign policy itself has long been noted for its general weakness and low profile, if not, at times, non-existence. This originated in Italy's 'choice of camp' (NATO) in a Cold War context and the presence of the largest Communist party in the West. The framework within which foreign policy had to be conducted was one of American hegemony, and in the effective absence of independent objectives, foreign policy lacked any dynamism and became dependent on the only two tangible symbols of reintegration into the post-war order: NATO and the EEC (Rimanelli 1989). It was feared that excessive activism would aggravate internal disorder (Telò 1996: 171). Consequently, 'foreign policy was removed from the arena of debate, and domestic politics became virtually all-inclusive. Foreign policy stances and actions were evaluated almost exclusively in terms of domestic political considerations' (Aliboni 1985: 3). This situation was exacerbated by the absence of coherence normally provided to foreign policy through strong party government. The DC maintained a monopoly of influence over the Ministry of Foreign Affairs, but it was also aware that a low-profile foreign policy was more conducive to its hold on power. The party maintained, therefore, a 'polycentric presence' (Pilati 1982: 82–3), its input and influence varying according to the individuals occupying the key ministries, many of whom regarded themselves as effectively independent of the party (Santoro 1988: 72–3). European policy, in this respect, was simply an offshoot of foreign policy, and this has hindered the development of a strong Italian presence at the European level to match that of countries such as France and Germany.[4] It has been characterized by five shortcomings.

First, there has been little interest in developing a coherent European policy amongst the main political forces, or in providing any significant leadership. Except for the period under De Gasperi, the DC showed little interest in European integration and did little or nothing in the way of developing new ideas in the area of Community policy (Pridham 1980: 81). Its Europeanism was of a bland, unsophisticated kind which, rather than leading others, tended to follow initiatives taken by individuals in government (Bull 1996b). This characteristic, moreover, was not unique to the DC, but common to all of the parties (Tizzano 1979: 80–2).[5] Debate about the nature of Italy's European policy and how well Italian interests were being represented seldom occurred. There was, in short, a long-term failure on the part of parties and Parliament to try to exercise any control over European policy, this reflecting a lack of *collective* leadership, an essential feature of a strong national presence at the European level. Countries such as France and Germany typify such presence, but it is also visible in countries such as Britain (despite its more conflictual relationship with the EU) and Spain. It has been largely absent in the Italian case (Attinà 1996: 43–7). This also reflects Italy's disregard for the quality of its staff in Brussels, which 'has been considered as a sort of exile by the infinitely preferable Roman ministries' (Ginsborg 1996b: 89). The European Parliament has been regarded as a form of retirement or substitute for politicians ousted from Rome, and Italian MEPs have not been known for their regular attendance (Bindi 1996: 115). Furthermore, at the national level, the minister without portfolio responsible for co-ordinating EU policies has rarely been a political heavyweight and often not closely associated with the Prime Minister (Hine 2000: 38).

Second, there has been a failure of co-ordination between different ministries over European policy below the level of the Prime Minister or Ministry of Foreign Affairs. For a long time a co-ordinating ministry never existed, and when one was created in the 1980s, it was provided with insufficient powers to prevent the taking up of contradictory positions in Brussels by different Italian ministries. Italian delegates in Brussels have had a degree of autonomy in negotiating their country's position not enjoyed by delegates from countries such as France and Britain, which exercise close control at each stage of the negotiating process in Brussels. There has always been, therefore, the risk of an 'uncoupling' of the negotiating action taking place in the EU arena, particularly as a consequence of rivalry or a conflict of interests, between the Prime Minister's office and the Ministry of Foreign Affairs. Official governmental and parliamentary studies carried out in the early 1990s found that, in most sectors, the national interest was being defined by individual departments, resulting in a fragmented sectoral perspective (which is hardly surprising given strong traditions of ministerial autonomy), and that the country was relatively absent in the day-to-day work of shaping EU law. Italian participation was found to be largely reactive, with Italian influence failing to be registered until well on in the negotiating process (Bindi 1996: 111–12; Hine 2000: 30).

Third, there is a tendency for particular initiatives to be identified with particular prime ministers or ministers of foreign affairs – so that the initiatives are left to stagnate when there is a change of personnel. The high turnover of ministers undermines Italy's credibility, since foreign counterparts are never sure whether or not a commitment will later be respected (Bindi 1996: 114). Moreover, many of the initiatives are influenced by the demands of internal politics (to increase the prestige of an individual or the profile of a party), and are therefore poorly formulated and quickly left to lapse (Coralluzzo 1994: 110–11). The consequence is discontinuity in both the nature and the implementation of the Italian line over time.

Fourth, there is a lack of preparation of Italian negotiators arriving in Brussels. As Ferrera (1991: 82–3) has noted, if a country is to protect its interests in the EU, it requires informed and assiduous negotiators as well as careful preparation of a set of objectives and preferences before arriving in Brussels, two conditions which are rarely met in the Italian case. This undermines the compactness and efficiency of the Italian delegation, resulting in a tendency to let others take the initiative and to retreat from its original preferences. Pietro Quaroni's comments (1967: 817) about Italian foreign policy generally have a precise echo in the European arena: a consistent failure to make a critical and realistic assessment of the situation, of the possibilities for effective Italian action, and of the means that are really at the country's disposal to achieve its goals.

Fifth, almost to make up for (or mask) its shortcomings as a European partner, Italy's approach has tended to focus on enthusiasm, unrealistic 'maximalism' and 'presence'. Sometimes, this has meant the pursuit of overly ambitious objectives without sufficient awareness of the diplomatic and negotiating skills necessary for their successful achievement. At other times, Italy has been concerned more with a presence at the European table for the prestige it has brought than for the realization of concrete objectives (Rimanelli 1989: 32–3). In Quaroni's words (1967: 811), 'we want to be present, but in a certain sense it should be added that we are content to be no more than present.'

These shortcomings have at times resulted in agreements against Italy's interests, but which are justified in terms of the 'European interest'. For example, the outcome of negotiations in the 1960s over the Common Agricultural Policy (CAP) had a negative long-term impact on Italian agriculture, specifically in the south, helping to maintain the disparities between the north and the south and between Italy and the other member states of the Community (Roccas 1980: esp. 109–11).[6]

This situation was not, of course, unchanging. Having, in the 1970s, been dubbed the 'sick man of Europe', Italy's image abroad improved considerably in the subsequent decade, and there was greater European activity in the context of a more dynamic foreign policy (Aliboni 1985; LaPalombara 1989; Rimanelli 1989). Italy's assumption of the EU presidency in 1985 and 1990 resulted in uncharacteristic levels of activism, with both presidencies launching intergovernmental conferences (IGCs) of considerable importance to the integration process (Daniels, Hine and Gualdesi 1991).[7] Yet, whether or not all this resulted in a more coherent European policy and a more assiduous defence of Italian interests is open to question. It could be argued that, even if foreign policy became more dynamic and linked to the new forms of domestic political competition, it was precisely the European component that remained stagnant, and that the displays of activism were consistent with the tendency to pursue 'maximalist' objectives.[8] Certainly, the reactions of others did not suggest that much had changed in their perceptions of Italy's Europeanism.[9]

'Downstream' phase

The 'downstream' phase involves two aspects: first, the implementation of EU law through translating EU directives into national law and through compliance with the decisions of the European Court of Justice; second, the adjustment of economic and budgetary policies to the needs of the EU, and the implementation of EU funding decisions accordingly, such that convergence of the economies of the member states can continue to occur.

With regard to both aspects, the Italian record in the period until the early 1990s was lamentable. First, by late 1990 Italy had the lowest figures of any member state for implementation of the internal market programme and the highest number of infringement proceedings against it for failure to comply with EU law (Hine 1992: 54–5). Second, by the early 1990s, despite being (with France) the country most enthusiastic about monetary union, Italy was confronted with the likelihood of not making the single currency. This was due to the glaring divergences between the Italian political economy and those of most other member states, as was revealed in the formulation of the Maastricht criteria in 1990–1. The origin of the difficulties went back nearly twenty years, yet successive governments failed to take any measures, with no visible sign of a likely change in the early 1990s (see chapter 2).[10] Despite Europe being an essential foreign policy option, Italy traditionally seemed unwilling to draw the consequences in terms of domestic action, seeking instead EU solidarity with, and compensation for, less affluent countries (Giolitti 1984: 51).

Yet, even when securing aid and structural funds, Italy's performance was poor. In the early 1990s, Italy was last in implementing projects co-financed by the EU. At the end of 1993, only 47 per cent of resources available under the Community Support Frameworks for 1989–93 had been spent by Italy, compared with almost 90 per cent by Portugal and Spain, and, by the end of 1994, 95 per cent by Greece (Apicella 1996: 124–5). The utilization of structural funds by southern regions was alarming: in 1991, for example, only 1.7 per cent of the funding allocated to Campania was used. Finally, in using the funds, Italy had a reputation for the highest number of frauds (Bindi 1996: 110).

Many of the problems in the 'downstream' phase stem from the same factor as in the 'upstream' phase: the dominance of the Ministry of Foreign Affairs, which has made the domestic management of European policy notable for its fragmentation and lack of co-ordination. The Ministry is divided into six Directorates-General, each with its own EU desk, although most of the EU work is done by the Directorate-General for Economic Affairs (which deals with all of the EU's internal economic business) and, to a lesser extent, the Directorate-General for Political Affairs (which deals with European Political Co-operation, the Council of Europe and the Western Political Union). All information on EU issues is sent from Brussels to the Directorate-General for Economic Affairs, which then disseminates the information to various bodies: other directorates-general in the Ministry, other ministries, the EU committees established in the Chamber of Deputies and the Senate, the two chambers themselves, the regions and other relevant groups (Bindi 1996: 108). In addition, the two chambers of Parliament have committees dedicated to the EU (the 'Executive for Community Affairs' established by the Senate in 1968 and the 'Special Commission for Community Affairs' established by the Chamber of Deputies in 1990), but they have only consultative powers. There is also a biannual conference of the State and the Regions (established in 1989) to provide the regions with an opportunity to discuss EU regional policy and its implementation. In Brussels, there is a Permanent Delegation, which is made up of the ambassador to the EU and his or her deputy, a legal councillor and representatives from the most important Italian ministries.

The inadequacy of a system dominated by the Ministry of Foreign Affairs became apparent as the EU began increasingly to impinge on complex domestic issues, especially with the development of the single market programme and technical harmonization in industrial standards. As Hine (1992: 61–2) has pointed out, 'The *Farnesina* is at its best in identifying the Italian interest on large but relatively non-technical issues', but is unable to deal easily with issues in complex areas such as health, product standards, and public procurement law. Yet, reform was hampered by a form of jurisdictional struggle between the Ministry of Foreign Affairs (anxious to preserve its control over European policy) and the Prime Minister's office. In 1980–1 a minister without portfolio attached to the Prime Minister's office was created and given responsibility for co-ordinating EU policies. The incumbent became head of a new Department of European Policy Co-ordination. The purpose of this department was to make Italy's participation in the integration process more efficient and incisive, through better co-ordination of the activities of different parts of the administration in both the 'downstream' and the 'upstream' phases. However, the new department had several weaknesses (Hine 1992: 62–3) and was later dubbed the Cinderella of Italian ministries (Bindi 1996: 108), little more than an 'intermediary' body rather than one of genuine co-ordination.

Furthermore, the responsibilities of the department in the 'upstream' phase were later removed from it, marking the successful retention of such responsibilities by the Ministry of Foreign Affairs. In 1987 there were further reforms, but these also failed to reinforce the authority of the department (Hine 2000: 33–4). More significantly, in 1989 Parliament passed a reform designed to improve Italy's implementation of EU legislation. The Pergola law (which subsequently became known as the *legge comunitaria*) established a fixed parliamentary session for the annual approval of all EU legislation that needed to be translated into national law. Each year, the government was required to submit a set of proposals containing a schedule for completion and authorizing it to complete the process through decree or other forms of administrative delegation. However, while this law increased the control of the executive over the domestic management of EU legislation (Fabbrini and Donà 2003), its effects were, in the short term, disappointing (Italy saw little improvement in its relative position until the late 1990s).

To summarize, Italy's post-war Europeanism until the early 1990s was flawed, in so far as its consistent and enthusiastic pro-European stance was contradicted and undermined by its failure to play a productive role at the European level and to bring its legal, political and economic structures up to the European average. There was, of course, a connection between the poor performance in both 'phases', in so far as part of the explanation for Italy's lack of credibility in the European arena was its dismal performance in the 'downstream' phase (Olivi 1977: 205; Hine 1992: 55–6). All of this has made its enthusiasm for deeper integration ring hollow. Responsibility for this failure has been rooted at the level of policy making, institutions and the political and administrative class. To a large extent, therefore, the failings were rooted in the very nature of the political system that developed in the post-war period and which was a consequence of the DC's fifty-year hold on power. Italy's failure in Europe, then, was a product of the blocked nature of its political system in general. Consequently, only changes in the political system – starting with the removal of the 'regime party' from office – could help the country overcome its flawed Europeanism (Bull 1994). This is what was to occur in the 1990s. However, if the changed Italy–Europe relationship was a consequence of more general changes in the political system, the paradox was that these more general changes were partly prompted by a deepening of the European integration process in the first place.

EUROPEANIZATION OF ITALY SINCE THE EARLY 1990s

The considerable change in Italy's relationship with the EU since the early 1990s has been due primarily to the deepening of the process of European integration (symbolized most forcefully in European Monetary Union) and its impact on the political economies of all member states. The 'downstream' phase is increasingly characterized by two closely interwoven aspects: first, the adjustments formally required by member states in legal and political-economic terms; and second, the knock-on effect of those adjustments (or needed adjustments) on other areas of the system, as well as the more general impact of European integration on the domestic politics of member states. This process has been called 'Europeanization', and it can be defined as a process of convergence by which national features give way to a common supra-national character across different domains: institutions, political dynamics, cultures and policies.[11]

The Europeanization process has had particular resonance in the Italian case, for two reasons. The first is the distance separating the Italian polity from the European 'average' in various areas. Risse, Cowles and Caporaso (2001), for example, theorize a degree of change in member states which is determined by the 'goodness of fit' between Europeanization (i.e. convergence), on the one hand, and national institutional settings, rules and practices, on the other. The less good the fit, the stronger the pressures to adapt, and the greater the degree to which institutions and structures have to change. The second reason is that Italian politics in the early 1990s underwent a dramatic crisis and entered a long period of change that is still ongoing (see chapter 1). This period of change coincided more or less precisely with a deepening of the process of European integration, and this timing has focused attention on Europeanization as a cause of the changes. Indeed, for some observers, European integration has been the main driving force of the changes in the Italian polity since the early 1990s.[12] The impact of the EU and the changing nature of the Italy–EU relationship in both the 'upstream' and the 'downstream' phases since the early 1990s can be summarized under four headings.

Europe as a factor in the destabilization of Italian politics in the early 1990s

The EU's decision to move to EMU prompted the formulation of tough convergence criteria in 1990–1. At the time, Italy met only one of the five criteria, the most significant of which was the stipulation that budget deficits should be no more than 3 per cent of GDP. Italy's was nearer 10 per cent, and was compounded by a level of debt that, by 1991, was higher than that of any country in the world except Japan and the United States (see chapter 2). The signing of the Maastricht Treaty therefore fully exposed the flawed Europeanism at the heart of Italy's position.

This was seen most clearly, between April 1991 and June 1992, in the European strategy pursued by what was the last government to be led by the DC (the party collapsed and split into different fragments in 1994). Prime Minister Andreotti, broadly in keeping with the traditional Italian approach, supported a deepening of integration, which would give Italy more influence in (an increasingly federal) Europe, at the same time as anchoring the country to northern Europe specifically through the influence of the Franco–German axis in the EU. Andreotti therefore viewed any faltering in the integration process which raised the prospect of a looser structure for a united Europe as a threat (hence the government's disappointment with the outcome of the Danish referendum rejecting the Maastricht Treaty in 1992). Yet, this strategy was also predicated on an assumption that anchoring Italy securely within a federated Europe would result in the country complying painlessly with the requirements of closer integration, and that Italy was essential to the achievement of political and economic union. The debate in the late 1980s and early 1990s on the prospects of a 'two-speed' Europe, and the currency crisis of September 1992 resulting in the lira's exit from the ERM, shattered these assumptions.

The economic demands of EMU therefore had distinct political implications. It was evident that, at a minimum, significant tax increases and cuts in public expenditure would be needed in order to meet the Maastricht requirements. The former would be politically difficult to carry through, and the latter threatened the clientelistic base of the DC and the other ruling parties. Yet, failure to meet Maastricht would have potentially devastating consequences in a country so enthusiastic about the EU. The demands of EMU coincided with the emergence of several domestic factors, and together they produced a devastating electoral result for the governing parties in 1992.

Meeting Maastricht and the emergence of a 'culture of stability'

In the period between 1992 and 1998, Italy, through several governments (three of them strictly 'transitional' in nature), was able to bring about a drastic change in the state of its public finances (see chapter 2). This resulted in it unexpectedly meeting the Maastricht requirement on public deficits and qualifying with the first wave of entrants for EMU (Sbragia 2001; Vassallo 2000; Radaelli 2001).[13] This achievement was attributable to a successful synergy of budgetary policy, incomes policy and a restrictive monetary policy (Radaelli 2001: 229). How was this successful synergy achieved? A short answer would be that the old political class was swept away, and a new class bent on reform took its place. While there is an element of truth in this, the reality was, in fact, more complex.

The negotiations over the Maastricht Treaty (before the transformation of the parties took place) witnessed the first visible development in the internal debate over Europe in Italy. There was a differentiated set of Italian motives at work in the negotiations that took place (Dyson and Featherstone 1996). On the one hand, there were the key (party-based) ministers (and notably the Prime Minister, Giulio Andreotti, and the Foreign Minister, Gianni De Michelis), whose approach was consistent with the broad thrust of Italian European policy in the post-war period. They were mainly concerned with Italy remaining at the forefront of the integration process, with the creation of a European Monetary System as part of a broader package of integration measures. On the other hand, there was a small group of technocrats around the Treasury Minister, Guido Carli (himself a former Governor of the Bank of Italy), who saw EMU as a necessary *vincolo esterno* ('external constraint'). EMU would, in their view, impose economic and monetary discipline and reform on a political class which had neither the political capability nor the will to carry through reform by itself. Whether or not the political leaders were aware of the implications and consequences of EMU is not clear, but the broadness of their own objectives, and the indifference with which they regarded detailed policy content, gave the technocrats a good deal of latitude in conducting the negotiations. This also resulted in the Italians agreeing to rather tough convergence criteria, since to the technocrats 'the domestic gains from almost any EMU bargain outweighed the costs to Italian bargaining positions (and would translate into long-term international gains)' (Dyson and Featherstone 1996: 276).

The technocrats negotiating the Maastricht Treaty formed part of a larger consensus of opinion amongst economists, other experts and politicians, based on the importance of sound public finance. Once the Treaty was signed, this consensus was crucial to underpinning the action of successive governments to meet the demands of Maastricht (Radaelli 1998). This is not to say that this consensus was unopposed. On the contrary, the signing of the Maastricht Treaty marked the end of the old unanimity on the European issue, since there was opposition to the sound finance position from a more traditional approach. This placed less emphasis on the health of the public finances, and was hostile to the schedule and timing of the requirements of the Maastricht Treaty. It also raised questions about the costs involved in meeting Maastricht, and questioned the effectiveness of the *vincolo esterno*, especially since it would involve sharing the economic and monetary choices of Germany. Parts of the commercial world, which were used to the assistance of the Italian State, were also hesitant about Maastricht's provisions for a move towards open and fair economic competition. The final parliamentary motion that ratified the Maastricht Treaty was not uncritical of it. On the contrary, it committed the government to seeking the improvement of certain operational aspects of the EU. Moreover, in accepting the motion, several contributors to the parliamentary debate made evident their view that the convergence criteria ought to be made subject to a degree of discretion or flexibility (Gualdesi 1994: 42–7).[14] This attitude was adopted by the most significant of the new political forces to emerge in the 1990s, Forza Italia. Antonio Martino, Minister of Foreign Affairs in the first Berlusconi government (1994), argued that the convergence criteria were arbitrary, and neither a necessary nor sufficient condition for arriving at a single currency (Dastoli 1996: 172–3).

The debate continued as long as there remained a question mark over Italy's participation in the single currency and over the possibility that the timetable might be postponed.[15] However, once this had been firmly ruled out (by French and German insistence in late 1995), a strong elite-level consensus prevailed on the fiscal adjustment needed. It was reinforced by a striking continuity (in the context of political party

Table 12.5 Degree of convergence of Italy with EU economies on key economic indicators, 2003

	Deficit GDP*	Debt GDP*	Inflation rate	Employment rate
Italy	**−2.4**	**106.2**	**2.8**	**55.5**
Austria	−1.1	64.9	1.3	69.3
Belgium	0.2	100.5	1.5	59.9
Finland	2.3	45.3	1.3	68.1
France	−4.1	63.3	2.2	63.0
Germany	−3.9	64.2	1.0	65.3
Greece	−3.2	103.0	3.4	56.7
Ireland	0.2	32.4	4.0	65.3
Luxembourg	−0.1	4.9	2.5	63.7
Netherlands	−3.2	54.8	2.2	74.4
Portugal	−2.8	59.9	3.3	68.2
Spain	0.3	50.8	3.1	58.4
Denmark	1.5	45.0	2.0	75.9
UK	−3.2	39.9	1.4	71.1
Switzerland	0.7	51.9	2.3	73.6
New members (av.)	−5.7	42.9	–	55.9

* As percentages of GDP. Minus signs represent actual deficit; absence of minus signs a surplus.
Source: ISTAT (2004a)

and government upheaval) in influential networks of expertise committed to sound finance (Radaelli 1998: 9–10), and (for the most part) the holding of the premiership by politicians or technocrats influenced by those networks (Amato, Ciampi, Dini, Prodi).[16] In the course of the decade, therefore, the general culture of economic policy shifted towards the philosophy of sound public finance: sound monetary policy, central bank independence and control of inflation, as priorities over full employment or other economic criteria (Radaelli 1998: 6–7). This has been reflected in figures for the public sector deficit and inflation rate which are more in keeping with the European average (the public debt and unemployment have proved harder to tackle) (see table 12.5). The Italian European Commissioner, Mario Monti, has referred to the consolidation of a 'culture of stability' in Italy thanks to Maastricht, not just through the single currency but also through a constitution and body of rules (quoted in Di Palma 2000: 43).

This achievement has been echoed in an improvement in the other aspect of the 'downstream' phase. Between 1992 and 1998, Italy remained amongst the last three member states in terms of its implementation of EU legislation. However, since the mid-1990s there has been a gradual improvement in the Italian record. With specific regard to the Single Market directives, whereas in 1998 Italy still had the poorest record among the fifteen member states, by the following year it had escaped the group of the five worst countries. However, the number of infringement proceedings against Italy remains high (Giuliani 2000: 61–4; 2003: 155).

Policy reform

The new 'culture of stability' has had an impact beyond budgetary and monetary policy. The Maastricht criteria were met primarily thanks to fiscal (rather than structural) adjustment, and fiscal adjustment was secured mainly through an increase in tax pressure (and notably Prodi's special 'tax for Europe'). Yet, there were structural implications, not only in the expenditure cuts that were needed, but also in the fact that the pressure from Europe did not abate once participation in the single currency had been secured. Consequently, the past decade has witnessed the carrying through of reforms (mostly partial and continuing) in a substantial number of policy areas, including pensions, health and welfare, labour relations, privatization, competition policy and regulatory reform, budgetary procedures, the south, decentralization and administrative reform.[17] These reforms have been concerned with reducing expenditure and strengthening the role of the core executive and the Treasury, both in policy domains traditionally subject to high spending, and in the budgetary process and macro-economic policy as a whole (Radaelli 2001: 228–9).[18]

Institutional management of European policy

The domestic political crisis of the first half of the 1990s did little for the credibility of Italy and Italian negotiators abroad (Ammendola and Isernia 2000: 375–6). There was a (continued) stagnation in European policy, and Italy proved to be one of the countries least able to influence policy at the European level in this period (Giuliani 1997a). The 1996 Italian presidency of the EU, for example, received mixed reactions. Bonvicini (1996) regarded it as a general failure, rooted in the long-term institutional and organizational weaknesses in Italy's management of EU affairs.[19] However, the domestic convulsion, combined with significant demands emanating from the European level, also led to several efforts to improve the EU co-ordinating mechanisms in the context of a strengthening of the Prime Minister's power. These culminated in the passing of two decrees in 1999, each of which has significantly reduced the control of the Ministry of Foreign Affairs over EU matters by limiting its jurisdiction to 'second pillar' issues (the Common Foreign and Security Policy), the EU's external relations and EU treaty revision mechanisms. While the ministry still retains general responsibility for co-ordinating European policy, this is also limited by the specific allocation to the Prime Minister of the task of promoting and co-ordinating action to ensure Italy's maximum participation in the EU. In short, primary responsibility for co-ordination, coherence and strategic guidance in European policy now rests, formally at least, with the Prime Minister (Hine 2000: 42).

This has occurred at a time when foreign policy itself has had to become more dynamic and independent of the old Cold War divisions. New challenges have arisen since the early 1990s, especially in the form of international crises: the Gulf War, the intervention in Somalia, the Bosnian crisis, and the wars in Afghanistan and Iraq. Unusually in Italian foreign policy, there have been specific national interests at stake, and governments have been unable to 'insulate' foreign policy from domestic political competition. Coalitions of interests have had to be built behind decisions, since the old Cold War divisions can no longer be relied upon (Ammendola and Isernia 2000). In the Iraq War, for example, the government was forced to choose between the symbol of the Atlantic Alliance (America) and the EU's central axis (France and Germany).

These factors, combined with a decline in the level of political instability since the mid-1990s, have produced a more active European policy, and one can see a more consistent identification of, and action upon, Italian national interests in Europe. This has been evidenced in the more sceptical and intransigent approach towards Europe that has been characteristic of the second Berlusconi government. The government has come into conflict with its European partners over several issues, and is not hesitant about sticking to a position even if it means isolation abroad, a relatively new phenomenon in foreign and European policy management. Renato Ruggiero, the Minister of Foreign Affairs in Berlusconi's second government, resigned in January 2002 over the implied Euro-scepticism in the government's lukewarm reaction to the launch of the euro. This was followed by indications by more than one minister (including the Prime Minister himself) that the euro had much to answer for with regard to Italy's recent economic difficulties, something also reflected in a decline in public enthusiasm for the new coinage since its launch (see table 12.2). Forza Italia generally does not adhere to the perception of the European Union as a necessary 'external constraint' to promote modernization. Rather, the party has a tendency to view European rules as obstacles to the free development of domestic policy. While this 'Euro-scepticism' should not be equated to the hostility towards Europe encountered in, say, the British variant, it nevertheless signals a clear decline in traditional Italian Europeanism,

However, it is not clear to what extent Italy's credibility in Brussels has risen as a consequence of this more independent stance, largely because of the degree to which, in Brussels and in the rest of Europe, Berlusconi is viewed as a controversial figure. The 2003 Italian presidency of the EU, for example, was commonly regarded as a failure, characterized by Berlusconi's gaffes, the approval of a 'soft' stability pact to assist the Germans and French, and the failure to ratify the new European Constitution. In fact, a more robust analysis of the presidency (based on its specific goals and subsequent achievements) suggests that, like other presidencies, it achieved some of its goals while failing to realize others (Di Quirico 2003a and 2003b). However, there is little doubt that Berlusconi's conflict of interests and his ongoing court cases do little to improve Italy's standing in Brussels, something not helped by the fact that the President of the European Commission was, until November 2004, his arch political rival, Romano Prodi.

CONCLUSION: A 'GOOD EUROPEAN' NOW?

Italy is often described as having been 'rescued by Europe'; and certainly it seems highly improbable that the achievements of the 1990s could have been secured without the tightening of the European 'external constraint' that occurred. Yet, the key question is how permanent this shift will turn out to have been, or to what extent, paradoxically, the 'external constraint' might have now served its purpose in so far as its core philosophy has been internalized. Some observers emphasize the extraordinary nature of the crisis of the 1990s, which, combined with the tough demands arising from Maastricht, created a unique situation. This was exploited by a part of the political-technocratic élite to drive through the necessary fiscal adjustment. In other words, there were largely conjunctural factors at work, and with the Maastricht deadline met and the crisis over, there is the possibility that the performance, and therefore continued convergence, cannot be sustained (Vassallo 2000: 321–3). This view is reinforced by the argument that, if Europeanization has occurred in Italy, it has been at the level of actors, practices and policies, rather than structures and institutions (Giuliani 2000: 66–8). The Italian turn-around was achieved without any formal changes in the institutional and constitutional framework beyond a strengthening of the core executive over financial matters; there is no institutional or structural guarantee, therefore, that the improved performance can be sustained.

Other observers, however, point to the continued external pressure deriving from an independent European Central Bank in charge of monetary policy, the EU's Growth and Stability Pact, and the role of EMU in providing stability to member states (e.g. Radaelli 1998: 8; 2001: 234–5). Moreover, the informal changes caused by Europeanization may, in fact, be more important than constitutional reform, in so far as they may gradually alter the manner in which national institutions function without modifying their formal architecture (Giuliani 2000: 67), if not, as we concluded in chapter 1, eventually forcing constitutional change itself.

NOTES

Except where evident, translations from Italian are by the authors.

Introduction

1 For example, Hine (1993a) and Furlong (1994), although these texts are not free of a different problem. The criticism made by Paci (Paci and Romanelli 1994: 106) of the three main contemporary histories of Italy published at the beginning of the 1990s (Ginsborg 1990, Lanaro 1992, Scoppola 1991), that their limits are evident in their failure to anticipate, in their analyses, the dramatic changes of the 1990s, could equally be applied to the political science texts published in the same period (although this of course also applies to many of the other works produced on the cusp of the changes).

2 This is not to suggest that this cannot be a useful exercise in chronological form – e.g. Bufacchi and Burgess (2001), Tranfaglia (2003) and, to a lesser extent, Gilbert (1995) – but straightforward political histories (as opposed to thematic analyses) do not have to confront the time frame issue as elaborated here.

3 This is essentially the approach adopted by Pasquino (2002b) and Fabbrini (2000), although the latter (beyond the theory) is not so different from Bufacchi and Burgess (2001) in its chronological approach.

4 The distinction originated with Mortati (1940). For a more recent discussion, see Ferrajoli (1996).

5 This is especially the case for the sector which has experienced the most change, the party system (see Newell 2000b).

6 Of note is that the 'spread' adopted in Pasquino (2002b) is much narrower than the one in this book, so making a chronological approach to the organization of the time frame more manageable.

Chapter 1   Understanding Political Change in Post-War Italy

1 Allum (1973a: ch. 1), Cazzola (1981: chs 1–2), Hine (1993: ch. 1) and Sassoon (1997: Introduction) are typical examples.

2 The Action Party was a radical party on the left of the political spectrum, originally founded by Mazzini in 1853, but which did not survive the period of the post-war settlement.

3 Quoted in Vercellone 1972: 124.

4   For a fuller discussion of the leftist aspirations behind these clauses see Sassoon 1997: 208–11.

5   For a fuller discussion see Vercellone 1972: 124–6.

6   For overviews of the liberal order see Mack Smith (1997) and Di Scala (2004).

7   For an account of the continuities in Italian history across the three regimes, which emphasizes the failure to achieve alternation in government, see Salvadori (1994).

8   In the national elections of the same year the governing coalition narrowly failed to secure the necessary number of votes to obtain the premium, and the law was repealed the following year.

9   Tarrow (1990: 309) defines 'soft hegemony' as 'a pattern of political relationships based on a flexible centrist governing formula, an interclass social base, friendship to business but solicitousness to marginal groups, and a governing style . . . based heavily on distributive policy'. With hindsight, however, it is clear that he underestimated the role of clientelism and corruption, suggesting that scholars who emphasize these elements 'often miss the point that corruption and clientelism are only the extreme expressions of a system of governance based on political exchange'.

10   Hence our description of the system as characterized by 'stable instability' (Bull and Newell 1993).

11   On the relationship between institutions and government, on the one hand, and cultural outlooks and social capital, on the other, see Sabetti (2000) and Putnam (1993).

12   We say 'effectively' because it was still exploited thereafter by Berlusconi, and a party of communism continued to exist (Communist Refoundation), but the nature of the 'Communist question' and its long-term influence on the party and political system became a thing of the past with the transformation of the PCI.

13   Whether a different reaction or handling of events would have saved the DC and the PSI from extinction obviously remains an open question, and is dependent on the emphasis one chooses to give to agency versus structure in the collapse of the system. Gilbert (1997: 224) believes it would have done so. We would emphasize the difficulty of the parties responding in any other way than they did, because of the logic of the system they had developed, within which their autonomy, let alone their ability to break that logic, had become increasingly circumscribed. For our own separate contributions to this debate see Bull (1996c) and Newell (2000b: ch. 1).

14   Hine and Vassallo (2000) capture this nicely in the subtitle of their book: *Italian Politics: The Return of Politics*.

15   In 2002, this represents a rise from 41.7 per cent in 1997. The figures for the state-run RAI channels are 46.4 per cent in 2002 and 48.1 per cent in 1997 (ISTAT 2003).

Chapter 2   The Post-War Economy and Macro-Economic Policy Making

1   The European Commission's first formal assessment, in April 1997, of the likely entrants in the first wave, had concluded that Italy was still adrift.

2   Berlusconi I's record was more mixed. His period in government was characterized, amongst other things, by much looser budgetary policies, a halting of the privatization programme, clashes with the Bank of Italy, and a decline in Italy's international credit rating. It would be premature to judge Berlusconi II, but, in terms of international credibility, Italy's position is compromised by the controversies surrounding Berlusconi himself (his conflict of interests and trials – see chapter 1).

Chapter 3   Political Parties and the Party System

1   Catholic Action was founded in 1867 as the Society of Italian Catholic Youth, with the purpose of involving laypersons actively in the life of the Church through proselytizing activities and charitable works (<www.azionecattolica.it/aci/Chi_siamo/Storia/#>

2   According to one estimate, party membership went down from 3,804,000 in 1991 to 1,330,000 in 1993 when Tangentopoli was at its height (Follini 1997: 250).

3   Namely, PDS–*Sinistra Europea* (PDS–European Left); *Partito Sardo d'Azione* (Sardinian Action Party); *Verdi* (Greens); Pop. SVP-PRI-UD-Prodi; *Lista Dini–Rinnovamento Italiano* (Dini List–Italian Renewal).

4   That is, non-institutionalized formations: e.g. parliamentary elites without stable territorial organizations ('parties on the ground'), or social movements with politico-electoral ambitions which have not achieved, or sustained, significant parliamentary representation (Donovan 2002: 122).

5   The fourteen parties and quasi-parties were PDS; *Comunisti Unitari* (United Communists); *Cristiani Sociali* (Social Christians); *Laburisti* (Labour); *La Rete* (the Network); *Partito Sardo d'Azione*; *Verdi*; PPI; *Unione Democratica* (Democratic Union); PRI; *Lista Dini*; *Patto Segni* (Segni Pact); *Socialisti Italiani* (Italian Socialists, SI) and the *Movimento Italiano Democratico* (Italian Democratic Movement).

6   That is, the *Democratici di Sinistra* (Left Democrats, DS); the *Girasole* (or Sunflower); the *Partito dei Comunisti Italiani* (Party of Italian Communists, PdCI) and the *Margherita* (or Daisy).

7   That is, the PdCI, the DS (as the PDS called itself from Feb. 1998 when it in effect absorbed four minor groupings), the *Socialisti Democratici Italiani* (Italian Democratic Socialists, SDI), the Greens, the Democrats, the PPI, *Rinnovamento Italiano* (Italian Renewal, RI) and the *Unione dei Democratici per l'Europa* (Union of Democrats for Europe, UDEUR).

8   See n. 6.

9   In March 2002 the parties merged with the Democrats, turning the 2001 *Margherita* list into a party of the same name.

10 At that election the Ulivo concluded a stand-down agreement with RC whereby, in exchange for a 'free run' in a number of single-member constituencies where no Ulivo candidates were fielded against RC candidates (who ran under the 'Progressive Alliance' symbol used in 1994), RC agreed not to field candidates in the remaining constituencies and to invite its supporters living there to vote for the Ulivo candidates (Pasquino 2000b: 220).

11 Formed at the end of 1999, most UDEUR parliamentarians had originally been elected as part of Berlusconi's coalition.

12 Following his victory in the 1994 elections, Berlusconi formed a government which, however, fell in December the same year after League leader, Umberto Bossi, withdrew his support, fearful of the consequences for his party's identity and organizational integrity of the similarities between his own battle cries and those of FI. This event put the centre right in Opposition for the next six-and-a-half years. For the Berlusconi government was replaced by a government of technocrats before fresh elections were held in April 1996 – elections won by the centre left, in no small measure because of the inability of Berlusconi and Bossi to repair their broken alliance. Yet in the longer term these elections brought the two back together. For, having failed in 1996 to capture the balance of power in Parliament and now rapidly losing support, in February 2000, Bossi once more embraced Berlusconi, the centre right coalition now taking the name, *Casa delle libertà* (House – or 'Home' – of Freedoms) (Newell 2002a: 4).

13 In October 1998, the Ulivo government, dependent for an overall majority in the Chamber of Deputies on the votes of RC, was brought down when a majority of RC deputies refused to support it on a confidence motion. This episode led the UDR to lend the Ulivo its voting support, thus making possible the formation of a new centre-left government under DS leader Massimo D'Alema.

14 For detailed discussions of the 2001 outcome see Newell and Bull (2001), (2002), Newell (2002b).

Chapter 4   Political Culture, Elections and Voting Behaviour

1   Originally appearing in the weekly magazine *Candido*, the stories were witten by cartoonist Giovannino Guareschi (1908–68), who was editor of the magazine. The central characters are a Catholic priest (Don Camillo) and Communist mayor (Peppone) of a small village in the Po River Valley in the years just following the Second World War. 'Don Camillo, the big cleric with fists of steel and heart of gold, converses frequently (and colorfully) with the Lord, Who continually challenges him to take the higher path in his dealings with his Marxist adversary, Peppone. The feisty priest, alas, isn't quite able to confine his methods to the purely spiritual . . . but neither is Peppone always able to toe *his* Party's line, so that the two find themselves seeing disconcertingly eye-to-eye at times' (<http://mywebpages.comcast.net/doncamillo/genintro.htm>).

2   The essence of the 'historic compromise' strategy was the attempt to build a wide-ranging set of social alliances to include a political alliance with the Christian Democrats. During the second half of the 1970s, the PCI supported a strong line against left-wing terrorism; 1981 saw the famous *strappo* (break) with the Soviet Union; the eighteenth party congress in March 1989 saw the party's official acceptance of the 'irreversibility' of capital accumulation and of the market economy (Bull 1991a, 1991b). Yet the party's support at successive elections continued to decline.

3   This is measured as half the absolute sum of the differences in the percentage of the vote received by each individual party between successive pairs of elections (Pedersen 1979: 1–26).

4   For a more detailed explanation of how the electoral system works see Hine (1993b).

5   For analyses of the principal features of this new style of campaigning, see the contributions in Newell (2002b).

Chapter 5   The Representation of Interests

1   We use the terms 'interest group' and 'pressure group' interchangeably in this chapter.

2   'By 1958, the association claimed 13,556 local sections . . . representing a total of 7,768,100 persons' (LaPalombara 1964: 237).

3   'Peasant farmers in each district are told what combination of preference-vote numbers to cast. While this method does not completely destroy secrecy of the ballot, it does give the leadership an opportunity to gauge how closely each district adheres to the line established by the leaders. Where deviation is too pronounced, retaliatory measures can be taken' (LaPalombara 1964: 242).

4   <http://www.coldiretti.it/organismi/coldiretti.asp>

5   <http://www.vatican.va/holy_father/john_xxiii/encyclicals/documents/hf_j-xxiii_enc_11041963_pacem_en.html>

6   As in the case of the Amato, Ciampi and Dini governments of 1992, 1993 and 1995 respectively.

7   As in the case of the Prodi government.

8   In addition to the 1992 and 1993 agreements mentioned in chapter 2, these included the 1995 reform of the pensions system, the 1996 'Labour Agreement' providing for a number of labour market reforms, and the 1998 'Social Pact' which aimed to reduce labour costs by 3 per cent over five years (for details see Contarino 2000).

9   The most significant of the attempted reforms was modification of the employment protection provisions contained in article 18 of the so-called Workers' Statute passed by Parliament in 1970 in the wake of the 'hot autumn'. For details see Accornero and Como (2003).

10   The support of Catholic social teaching for capitalism and private enterprise has always been distinctly qualified, while traditional, nineteenth-century forms of that teaching explicitly rejected industrialization as a key element in the country's future (Bedani 1995: 69).

Chapter 6   Informal Institutions

1   A member of the DC later referred to the existence of a tacit compromise between leaders De Gasperi and Togliatti whereby the PCI was not to be outlawed in return for renouncing revolutionary action (Leonardi 1991: 82).

2   Quoted in Ferraresi (1992: 29). As he points out (1992: 39), either the establishment of Gladio should have been subject to approval by Parliament (if it were not attached to NATO) or (if it were), its existence and activities should have been reported to the secret services executive committee (CESIS) and parliamentary committee, both of which were established in 1977 with the reform of the Secret Services.

3   The most notable exclusion was six times Prime Minister Amintore Fanfani, because the secret services feared that he was the type of person who would want to know more (Ferraresi 1992: 39–40).

4   The reformist centre left government (which, some would argue, was the most radical government of the First Republic) gave way to one having a more conservative orientation.

5   The PSU was the result of a merger in 1966 of the PSI and the Italian Social Democratic Party (PSDI), a significant venture in view of the fact that the latter had been heavily funded from the outset by American money, and was in some respects therefore a disguised vehicle for right-wing politicians. The PSU obtained only 14.5 per cent of the vote, and split up into its original two components shortly after.

6   It also included people who would later become politically significant, such as Berlusconi.

7   In fact, Mario Moretti, who became leader of the Red Brigades after Renato Curcio's arrest, was long suspected as an infiltrator, although no proof has yet been found of this.

8   The literature on the Moro kidnapping is huge. For succinct summaries of the main issues see Galli 1991: 213–22; Silj 1994: ch. 9.

9   One of the most notorious concerned Ciro Cirillo, a DC regional councillor from Naples, who had been responsible for awarding many of the contracts financed by the State after the 1981 Basilicata earthquake. Much of the money disappeared as a consequence of corruption and the Mafia. The DC not only paid a ransom for his release, but used the Camorra as a mediator (Behan 1996: ch. 5).

10   This was partly because, according to senior KGB sources, the Soviet Union was not keen on changing the Yalta settlement (Fasanella et al. 2000: 86).

11   This is Pellegrino's essential thesis (Fasanella et al. 2000: 84–96).

12   Mafia is a generic term in and beyond Sicily. *Cosa Nostra* is a term restricted specifically to groups of individuals who operate (in Sicily and elsewhere) in specific 'families' or 'clans'. The Camorra and 'ndrangheta are the two other main Mafia groups, operating respectively in Naples and Calabria.

13   Engaging in political relationships was not novel. Before Fascism, with the extension of suffrage, the Mafia had found itself in an ideal position to deliver safe majorities to northern politicians.

14   There is, of course, considerable debate over how much exactly has changed, and this depends on one's interpretation of the nature and functions of the Mafia over time. See, e.g., Gambetta (1996) and, for a critical summary of different interpretations, Catanzaro (1993).

15   Although there are strong differences of opinion on exactly 'how formally organized is organized crime' (Catanzaro 1993: 334–5).

16   Data presented by Arlacchi (1996: 92) show that, in western Sicily, between half and three-quarters of DC deputies and about 40 per cent of all deputies elected to the Chamber of Deputies were supported by *Cosa Nostra* families.

17   The 1962 parliamentary commission, e.g., did not submit its report until 1976.

18   The Court of Cassation confirmed the maxi-trial verdicts on 30 Jan. 1992, and several important Mafia bosses remained in prison.

19   This led to formal charges being made against Andreotti for association with the Mafia, and complicity in murder, charges on which he was eventually (ten years later) acquitted. This and other trials produced sufficient evidence of the 'dangerous' relationships established between the political class and organized crime to raise questions about the political responsibility of the former, irrespective of legal outcomes (Sciarrone 2001).

20   Francesco Saverio Borelli, in an interview conducted by Barbacetto et al. (2002: 700).

Chapter 7   The Government, Parliament and the President

1   The precise number required varied over time and between the two chambers.

2   The exceptions concern the budget, the ratification of international treaties, laws on constitutional and electoral matters, and the delegation of law-making powers to the government (Di Palma 1977: 194).

3   At the same time, *consociativismo* was widely condemned as a practice which, by undermining the ordinary political division of labour between government and opposition (Giuliani 1997b: 67), also undermined the accountability function of elections, because it made it difficult for voters to locate responsibility for given policies.

4   That is, they are composed of coalitions formed prior to elections and directly endorsed by election outcomes themselves rather than being composed of coalitions formed only *after* the election results are known.

5   For details of the 1988 law and its consequences, see Barrera (1990); Hine (1993a: ch. 7); Hine and Finocchi (1991).

6   In fact, Berlusconi's analysis was mistaken on both counts. First, he had not received a Westminster-style mandate (see above). Second, even had he done so, this would not have added to his case, since, notwithstanding its presumption that election outcomes determine the composition of governments directly and thus give them mandates, there is nothing in the so-called Westminster model to which he appealed that enjoins dissolution as the automatic consequence of a government's resignation.

7   The proposed legislation sought to circumvent anti-trust legislation and a series of decisions of the Constitutional Court, the effects of which were to place a legal obligation on Berlusconi either to sell one of his terrestrial television stations, *Retequattro*, or to turn it into a satellite station, by the end of December 2003.

8   The 'Cirami law', so-called after its sponsor, the Forza Italia Deputy Melchiore Cirami, allows a defendent to ask the Court of Cassation to transfer proceedings against them to another court on grounds of 'legitimate suspicion' concerning the impartiality of the judges involved in trying the case. It was widely suspected that the legislation was being pursued in order to allow Berlusconi's lawyers to delay proceedings against him in the Sme–Ariosto corruption trial, whose judges were expected to give a verdict that autumn.

9   If the parties and government are weak, the President may play his accordion to the full. In the opposite case, there is little room for the President to play his accordion, and he may just choose to keep, or be content with keeping, it closed.

Chapter 8   The Bureaucracy and the Judiciary

1   The Constitutional Court is, in effect, an appeal court, since proceedings are normally initiated only when a case is passed up from another court, only a limited number of applicants having the right to initiate 'direct review' independent of any other proceedings: notably the State and the regions (Certoma 1985: 157).

2   Its predecessor, the *Associazione generale fra i magistrati d'Italia*, was suppressed in 1926 (Bruti Liberati 1997: 152).

3 For details see Newell (2000b: 57).

4 TARs are administrative courts of first instance, called such simply because their territorial competence is defined on a regional basis (Certoma 1985: 159).

5 The structure of the current government is shown in table 8.2.

6 A good example of this is the 1987 referendum on the civil liability of members of the judiciary, which the Socialists, in populist fashion, sponsored and won by an overwhelming majority in the wake of the public outcry over the Tortora affair.

7 These proposals include a considerable tightening of the conditions that must be met for evidence gathered abroad to be admissible in Italian criminal proceedings; the so-called Cirami law allowing defendants to ask the Court of Cassation to transfer proceedings against them to another court on grounds of 'legitimate suspicion' concerning the impartiality of the judges involved in trying the case; proposals that would, among other things, oblige investigating magistrates to inform a suspect that they are under investigation as soon as a file is opened on them – a provision which, prominent members of the judiciary have argued, would allow suspects to destroy evidence because it removes the secrecy from investigations.

Chapter 9   Central–Local Relations and Sub-National Government

1 For details of how the system works, see Neppi Modona (1995: 410–12) and Newell (2000a: 170).

2 See above, n. 1. Presidents are elected according to the simple plurality system: the presidential candidate who wins the most votes in the region is elected.

3 'And when they ask us what we would do, what path we would take if we dominated the whole of Italy, we modestly give the example of what our party has managed to do here' (P. Togliatti, from a speech given during the eighth Provincial Congress of the PCI in Bologna, 1956, quoted by Bellini (1990: 109)).

4 In 1982, Emilia-Romagna lost 30,000 jobs, and in 1983 the region's GDP increased by a mere 0.1 per cent in real terms (Leonardi 1990: 30).

5 Bassanini 1 empowered the government to pass legislative decrees conferring upon the regions and local authorities administrative responsibilities in all areas 'related to the protection of the interests and the promotion of the development of their respective communities', excluding such areas as foreign affairs, defence, the judiciary, the police and internal security. Among a wide range of provisions, Bassanini 2 placed limits on the powers of the Regional Control Commissions. For details see Newell (1998). In 2001, the Commissions were abolished altogether by the centre left government's reform of Title V, Part II of the Constitution.

6 In addition, the reform abolishes the post of Government Commissioner (which had been provided for by article 124 of the 1948 Constitution) along with the various 'ex-ante' controls on regional laws that had been associated with the post (and provided for by article 127), leaving the central authorities only with the 'ex-post' power of referring regional laws to the Constitutional Court. Among other things, this means that the central authorities can object to regional laws only on grounds of constitutional legitimacy, no longer on grounds of merit (which old article 127 allowed them to do by placing questions of merit before the two chambers of Parliament).

7 More specifically, the four areas were (a) health care and organization; (b) school organization, management of schools and training institutions; (c) definition of educational and training syllabuses of specific interest to the region; (d) local policing.

8 As things stand at the moment, article 135 of the Constitution provides that one-third of the judges of the Constitutional Court are appointed by the President of the Republic, one-third by Parliament, and one-third by the members of the ordinary and administrative supreme courts for a period of nine years.

9   *Disegno di Legge* 1187 was presented in the Senate on 26 Feb. 2002 and approved on 5
    Dec. 2002. It was then approved by the Chamber of Deputies on 14 April 2003. It would
    appear, however, that neither the two provisions nor the proposal to establish a 'Senate of
    the Regions' have been abandoned entirely. On 11 April 2003 the Cabinet agreed to a more
    wide-ranging constitutional reform that apparently incorporates Bossi's more limited pro-
    posal within it and allows for a Constitutional Court whose members would be appointed
    by a new Senate of the Regions.

10 The one stressing competition and diversification, the other stressing equality and col-
    laboration (Cento Bull 2002: 199).

Chapter 10 Governing the Economy I: Big Industry and the Public–Private Divide

1   Allum (1995: Part I) shows the uses of combining O'Connor's (1973) (structural) analysis and
    Bagnasco's (1977) (territorial) insights to analyse the development of the economies of
    Western Europe. These analytical distinctions are not free from problems. Indeed, the notion
    of the 'three Italies' has been criticized for being too simplistic, because of the existence of
    structural characteristics outside the territorial identifications: e.g. the development of small
    industry and industrial districts in the south and the north-west. For contrasting approaches,
    see Garofoli (1983) and, more radically, Locke (1995). For the purposes of this text, we find
    the model of the 'three Italies' (adjusted as indicated in the text) most useful; its continued
    validity, moreover, has recently been confirmed in work by Burroni and Trigilia (2001: 55).

2   The classic treatments in English of the state holdings model are Posner and Woolf (1967)
    and Holland (1972). In Italian, see Saraceno (1975); Maggia and Fornengo (1976); and
    Serrani (1978).

3   For useful inventories see Ward (1993: 236–8); Mignone (1995: 109–11); and Travaglia
    (1994). Other holding companies/agencies included the *Istituto Nazionale delle Assicu-
    razioni* (National Insurance Institute, INA) and the *Ente Gestione per le Aziende Cine-
    matografiche* (Agency for Film Studios). Some of the literature includes the National
    Electricity Authority, ENEL, as a holding company/agency because of the way it developed,
    although formally speaking it should be defined as a 'public enterprise'.

4   A fourth is that the 'middle way' (public companies operating in a private setting) is bound,
    economically, to fail, because the public aspect will always end up dominating. Certainly,
    this occurred in the Italian case. It is for this reason (i.e. the economic behaviour of state-
    controlled companies in practice) that Padoa Schioppa Kostoris (1993: ch. 1) argues
    that both traditional public enterprises and state-controlled companies should be viewed
    together as 'public corporations'.

5   The literature on the politicization of the state sector of the economy and its consequences is
    enormous. For early polemical treatments see Scalfari and Turani (1974) and Galli and
    Nannei (1976). For general academic analyses see Orfei (1976), Cazzola (1979) and
    Tamburrano (1974). For a more recent treatment which incorporates the more recent find-
    ings of corruption into the analysis, see McCarthy (1995: chs 4–5). Some literature concen-
    trates on specific individuals, for whom the state holdings formula became a real power base.
    Enrico Mattei, e.g. built up a significant network of industrial and political power through
    his control of ENI, eventually founding a faction inside the DC (Frankel 1966; Votaw 1964).

6   For an analysis of the structures of finance and power of the main groups in the period
    until the 1990s, see Brioschi, Buzzachi and Colombo (1990).

7   In fact, Rhodes and van Apeldoorn (1998: 408–11), defining the Rhenish model as
    'Network-oriented' (in contrast to the Anglo-Saxon 'Market-oriented' model), subdivide it
    into 'Germanic' and 'Latin' (the latter incorporating Italy). Amyot (2004: 80) also sees Italy
    as a particular variant of the Rhenish model.

8 People placed under investigation included Enrico Cuccia, Cesare Romiti (Agnelli's chief man at FIAT), Raoul Gardini (who committed suicide) and Silvio Berlusconi.

9 Although IRI has continued to exist because of ongoing legal disputes concerning its subsidiaries.

10 Berlusconi, e.g. has said that 'No reasonable, common-sense person would think of privatising ENI' (quoted in Rizzo 2002: 2). However, this stance is perhaps not surprising in view of the fact that he is himself an important head of one of the most important large corporate financial groups (Fininvest).

11 In the *Centro Einaudi* 2002 'Index of Economic Freedom', Italy was placed 14th, second from last of EU countries (ahead only of Greece), and behind the Czech Republic (<www.centroeinaudi.it>). In the World Economic Forum's 2002 'Index of Competitiveness', Italy dropped to 39th (behind countries such as Greece, Trinidad and Tobago, Lithuania and Mauritius) from 26th in 2001 (*Corriere della Sera*, 30 Nov. 2002).

Chapter 11   Governing the Economy II: The South and the 'Third Italy'

1 See Villari (1974) for a useful anthology of writings on the south. On the new revisionist history, see below (n. 7).

2 The economic aspect, moreover, is 'the kernel of Italy's dualism, and the aspect of it which is least open to discussion' (Lupo 1996: 249).

3 The other major change in this period in relation to the south was the introduction of agricultural reform, with the break-up of the old landed estates and a much wider distribution of land.

4 See Trigilia (1992: ch. 1) for a comprehensive evaluation.

5 As a consequence, more than 80,000 jobs were privatized by the end of the decade (Viesti 2001: 701).

6 This diversification is not new – Barbagallo (1994b) having earlier earlier described it as 'imbalanced modernization' – but it is becoming greater. Cersosimo and Donzelli (1997), have argued that if one excludes from the analysis the four regions where organized crime operates extensively (Campania, Puglia, Calabria and Sicilia) – and which constitute, it should be said, a large part of the south – the other regions show levels of growth similar to their central and northern counterparts. Viesti (2001: 706–7) identifies 'four Mezzogiorns': of the cities, the 'districts', the 'internal areas' and the 'most weak areas'. Only the last resembles the old idea of the Mezzogiorno.

7 Consequently, it is argued, all research into the south has been distorted, because it has started from these premises, and the revisionists' objective is to analyse the 'south without meridionalization' (from the title of Giarizzo 1992). For a flavour of this revisionism, see Schneider (1998) and Lumley and Morris (1997); and for evaluations of its merits, Davis (1996) and Riall (2000).

8 There was a view in the early 1990s that for big companies the south represented a 'virgin' territory of opportunities, without the industrial conflicts and environmental problems characteristic of other regions. The head of FIAT until the early 1990s, Giovanni Agnelli, e.g., stated that 'We must act with the awareness that the Mezzogiorno is the new frontier of Italy's economic and social development' (quoted in 'Survey of Italy', *Financial Times*, 6 June 1991). It is not clear that this view is any longer prevalent amongst the big companies. Certainly, the crisis of FIAT in 2002 has dealt a blow to future investment in the south by big companies.

9 The Berlusconi government has made a partial return to a 'cement [i.e. infrastructure] and incentives' approach, managed by a small central government committee. This was the product of a compromise reached within the governing majority in 2002 following exten-

sive disagreement over the future shape of policy for the south. At one stage the Minister for Productive Activities threatened to resign, commenting that 'we seem to be back in the time of the *Cassa per il Mezzogiorno*' (quoted in Sarcina 2002).

10   The classic work is Bagnasco (1977). See also Bagnasco (1988).

11   See, e.g., Graziani (1969) and Fuà (1976).

12   This was what led to the controversial economic *sorpasso* ('overtaking') of Britain by Italy in the late 1980s. The impact of the adjustment, however, should not be exaggerated (Pugliese 1994: 405).

13   On industrial districts see Bianchi and Gualtieri (1990); Goodman and Bamford (1991); Pyke, Beccatini and Sengenberger (1990); Saba (1995).

14   Evidently, what counts as an 'industrial district' will depend on which criteria are adopted. Saba (1995: 159–60), e.g., identifies only sixty-five industrial districts across the whole of Italy, but encompassing nearly 52,000 firms.

Chapter 12   Italy and the European Union

1   For example, on the eve of the launch of the European single currency, the proportion of citizens in favour of its introduction was higher in Italy than in any other EU country (Radaelli 2001: 226).

2   In his survey of elite and mass attitudes to European integration in member states, Wessels (1995: 152–5) found that the greatest similarities between the average position of parties and the average position of party supporters are to be found in Italy, France, Luxembourg and Ireland.

3   Romano (1993: 115), e.g., describes it as 'impotent Europeanism'. We prefer the expression 'flawed Europeanism' to capture the broader complexity of the Italy–Europe relationship (see Bull 1994 and 1996b).

4   This is evidenced in general analyses of the development of the EU, which, as Sbragia (1992: 79) has noted, have tended to overlook the role played by Italy in contrast with Britain, France and Germany.

5   Although it was not necessarily characteristic of all individuals. Altiero Spinelli was a significant exception, but even mainstream politicians, such as Andreotti and Fanfani, were at times active on the European front.

6   Podbielski (1981: 348) has noted that 'Italian negotiators were known in Community circles to have frequently put up a weak defence of the Italian point of view, to have adopted decisions too readily and uncritically and to have made concessions too quickly'.

7   In particular, Italy was the only country to support without reservation the European Parliament's project for reform of the treaties and an increase in its powers, which helped to relaunch the integration process in the early 1980s. It also used its 1985 presidency, in the face of strong opposition from Britain, Denmark and France, to force a vote on the issue of an IGC to consider amendments to the Treaty of Rome, whence came the Single European Act (SEA).

8   It is notable, e.g., that the origins of the Italian insistence on the 1985 vote on the IGC lay in domestic political competition over the European credentials of the Christian Democratic and Socialist parties (Keating and Murphy 1992: 232–3).

9   This lack of respect was perhaps exemplified in the *Economist*'s now (in)famous description of the Italian presidency in 1990 as a 'ride on a bus driven by the Marx brothers' (20 Oct. 1990). Alternatively, in fact, the outcome of the presidency could be viewed in quite positive terms (Coralluzzo 1994: 23).

10   See Daniels (1993: 202–6) on the implications of the Maastricht Treaty and the inadequacies of the government response at the time.

11   On Europeanization see Hix and Goetz (2000); Featherstone and Kazamias (2000); and, specifically in relation to Italy, Giuliani (2000).

12   See, e.g., Perissich (1996: 55); Romano (1996: 15); Monti (1998:13); and the chapters in Di Palma, Fabbrini and Freddi (2000). As Di Palma (2000) points out in his introduction, almost all of the contributions to the volume emphasize the impact of the EU.

13   Italy achieved a deficit of 2.7 per cent (of GDP) in 1997, and entered the euro zone with ten other states the following year.

14   This did not, however, prevent RC, the MSI, the Greens and the *Rete* (Network) from voting against the Treaty.

15   See Dastoli (1996) for an account of Prime Minister Dini's vain efforts to secure agreement for a postponement of the timetable if Italy was not ready. Dini, while committed to sound finance, was doubtful that the adjustment could be made in time, and the Italian government's position heightened the scepticism and criticism of Maastricht by others.

16   The significance of Ciampi should be emphasized here, since he was the first non-party Prime Minister to be appointed since the Badoglio government in the immediate post-war period.

17   See other chapters in this book, as well as Di Palma, Fabbrini and Freddi (2000); Fabbrini (2003); Ferrera and Gualmini (2004); Amato (1996); La Spina and Majone (2000: ch. 6); La Spina (2003a: ch. IV); Bull and Baudner (2004).

18   This is part of a general trend towards a 'hardening' of the state as a consequence of European integration and convergence (Della Sala 1997).

19   For a more positive assessment, see Attinà (1996), who none the less viewed it as less noticeable than the previous presidencies in terms of high-profile political achievements.

REFERENCES

Accornero, Aris and Eliana Como (2003), 'La mancata riforma dell'articolo 18', in Blondel and Segatti (2003).

Adams, Pamela (1990), 'La politica industriale', in Dente (1990).

Albert, Michel (1993), *Capitalism Against Capitalism* (London: Whurr Publishers).

Albert, Michel (2001), 'Capitalismo contro capitalismo: Dieci anni dopo', *Il Mulino*, 3 (395).

Alberti, A. (1996), 'Political corruption and the role of public prosecutors in Italy', *Crime, Law and Social Change*, 24.

Aliboni, Roberto (1985), 'Italy and the new international context: an emerging foreign policy profile', *International Spectator*, 20 (1) (Jan.–Mar.).

Allum, Felia and James Newell (eds) (2003), 'Introduction' (to 'Aspects of the transition'), *Journal of Modern Italian Studies*, 8 (2) (Summer).

Allum, Percy A. (1973a), *Italy – Republic without Government?* (New York: Norton & Company).

Allum, Percy A. (1973b), *Politics and Society in Post-War Naples* (Cambridge: Cambridge University Press).

Allum, Percy A. (1981), 'Thirty years of southern policy in Italy', *Political Quarterly*, repr. in Donovan (1998).

Allum, Percy A. (1993), 'Chronicle of a death foretold: the first Italian Republic', *University of Reading Department of Politics*, Occasional Paper no. 12, Jan. (Reading: Department of Politics, University of Reading).

Allum, Percy A. (1995), *State and Society in Western Europe* (Cambridge: Polity).

Allum, Percy A. (1997), '"From two into one": the faces of the Italian Christian Democratic Party', *Party Politics*, 3 (1).

Almond, Gabriel A. and G. Bingham Powell, Jr., et al. (1992), *Comparative Politics Today: A World View* (New York: Harper Collins).

Amato, Giuliano (1996), 'The impact of Europe on national policies: Italian anti-trust policy', in Yves Mény and Jean-Louis Quermanne (eds), *Adjusting to Europe: The Impact of the European Union on National Institutions and Policies* (London: Routledge).

Ammendola, Teresa and Pierangelo Isernia (2000), 'Continuità e mutamento nella politica estera italiana', in Di Palma, Fabbrini and Freddi (2000).

Amyot, Grant (2004), *Business, the State and Economic Policy: The Case of Italy* (London: Routledge).

Apicella, Vincenzo (1996), 'Southern Italy and the underdeveloped regions of Europe', *Review of Economic Conditions in Italy*, no. 1 (Jan.–June).

Arlacchi, Pino (1988), *Mafia Business: The Mafia Ethic and the Spirit of Capitalism* (Oxford: Oxford University Press).

Arlacchi, Pino (1995), 'The Mafia, Cosa Nostra, and Italian institutions today', in Sechi (1995).

Arlacchi, Pino (1996), 'Mafia: the Sicilian Cosa Nostra', *South European Society and Politics*, 1 (1) (Summer).

Attinà, Fulvio (1996), 'La prima repubblica in Europa', *Europa Europe*, 1.

Bagnasco, Arnaldo (1977), *Tre Italie: la problematica territoriale dello sviluppo italiano* (Bologna: Mulino).

Bagnasco, Arnaldo (1988), *La costruzione sociale del mercato: Studi sullo sviluppo di piccola impresa in Italia* (Bologna: Mulino).

Bagnasco, Arnaldo and Carlo Trigilia (eds) (1984), *Società e politica nelle aree di piccola impresa: il caso di Bassano* (Venice: Marsilio).

Bagnasco, Arnaldo and Carlo Trigilia (eds) (1985), *Società e politica nelle aree di piccola impresa: il caso di Valdelsa* (Milan: Franco Angeli).

Balcet, Giovanni (1997), *L'economia italiana: Evoluzione, problemi e paradossi* (Milan: Feltrinelli).

Baldassarri, Mario (ed.) (1993), *Industrial Policy in Italy, 1945–90* (London: Macmillan).

Baldassarri, Mario and Franco Modigliani (eds) (1995), *The Italian Economy: What Next?* (London: Macmillan).

Banfield, Edward (1958), *The Moral Basis of a Backward Society* (New York: Free Press).

Barbacetto, Gianni, Peter Gomez and Marco Travaglio (2002), *Mani Pulite: La vera storia: Da Mario Chiesa a Sivlio Berlusconi* (Rome: Editori Riuniti).

Barbagallo, Francesco (1994a), 'La formazione dell'Italia democratica', in Barbagallo (1994c).

Barbagallo, Francesco (1994b), *La modernità squilibrata del Mezzogiorno d'Italia* (Turin: Einaudi).

Barbagallo, Francesco (coordinator) (1994c), *Storia dell'Italia repubblicana*, Vol. 1: *La costruzione della democrazia: dalla caduta del fascismo agli anni cinquanta* (Turin: Einaudi).

Barbagallo, Francesco (coordinator) (1997), *Storia dell'Italia repubblicana*, Vol. 3: *L'Italia nella crisi mondiale: L'Ultimo ventennio. Istituzioni, politiche, culture* (Turin: Einaudi).

Barca, Fabrizio (1997a), 'Introduzione', in Barca (1997b).

Barca, Fabrizio (1997b), *Storia del capitalismo italiano* (Rome: Donzelli).

Barca, Fabrizio (2001), 'Nuove tendenze del Mezzogiorno d'Italia e la svolta nella politica di sviluppo', in Padoa-Schioppa and Graubard (2001).

Barca, Fabrizio and Sandro Trento (1997), 'State ownership and the evolution of Italian corporate governance', *Industrial and Corporate Change*, 6 (3).

Bardi, Luciano and Martin Rhodes (eds) (1998), *Italian Politics: Mapping the Future* (Boulder, CO: Westview Press).

Barnes, Samuel H. (1994), 'L'elettorato italiano e la teoria della democratizzazione', in Caciagli et al. (1994).

Barrera, Pietro (1990), 'The first institutional reform: new discipline in government activity', in: Nanetti and Catanzaro (1990).

Barrett, Chris (1996), 'Globalization: implications for democracy', Case Studies for Politics, no. 34 (Department of Politics, University of York).

Bartolini, Stefano and Roberto D'Alimonte (1994), 'La competizione maggioritaria: Le origini elettorali del parlamento diviso', *Rivista Italiana di Scienza Politica*, 24 (3) (Dec.).

Battente, Saverio (2001), 'Nation and state building in Italy: recent historiographical interpretations (1989–1997), II: from fascism to the Republic', *Journal of Modern Italian Studies*, 6 (1).

Battista, Pierluigi (2002), 'Se la storia si fa con i "forse"', *Panorama*, 8 Aug.: 131.

Bedani, Gino (1995), *Politics and Ideology in the Italian Workers' Movement: Union Development and the Changing Role of the Catholic and Communist Subcultures in Postwar Italy*, (Oxford: Berg).

Bedeschi, Giuseppe (2002), 'La teoria del doppio Stato: Complottomania', *Liberal*, 13 (Aug.–Sept.).

Behan, Tom (1996), *The Camorra* (London: Routledge).

Bellini, Nicola (1990), 'The management of the economy in Emilia-Romagna: the PCI and the regional experience', in Leonardi and Nanetti (1990).

Bellu, Giovanni Maria (1993), 'Cento i deputati di Tangentopoli per questo resta l'immunità', *La Repubblica*, 19 June, p. 15.

Bellucci, Paolo and Martin Bull (eds) (2002), *Italian Politics: The Return of Berlusconi* (Oxford and New York: Berghahn).

Berger, Suzanne and Richard M. Locke (2001), 'Il "caso italiano" e la globalizzazione', in Padoa-Schioppa and Graubard (2001).

Bevilacqua, Piero (1996), 'New and old in the southern question', *Modern Italy*, 1 (2).

Bianchi, Marcello, Magda Bianco and Luca Enriques (2001), 'Pyramidal groups and the separation between ownership and control in Italy', in Fabrizio Barca and Marco Brecht (eds), *The Control of Corporate Europe* (Oxford: Oxford University Press).

Bianchi, Patrizio (1993), 'Industrial policies for small and medium firms and the new direction of European Community policies', in Baldassarri (1993).

Bianchi, Patrizio and Giuseppina Gualtieri (1990), 'Emilia-Romagna and its industrial districts: the evolution of a model', in Leonardi and Nanetti (1990).

Bianchi, Patrizio, Sabino Cassese and Vincent della Sala (1988), 'Privatisation in Italy: aims and constraints', *West European Politics* (Oct.).

Bindi, Federiga Maria (1996), 'Italy: in need of more EU democracy', in Svein S. Andersen and Kjell A. Eliassen (eds), *The European Union: How Democratic is it?* (London: Sage).

Blondel, Jean and Paolo Segatti (eds) (2003), *Politica in Italia: I fatti dell'anno e le interpretazioni* (Bologna: Mulino).

Bobbio, Norberto (1980), 'La democrazia e il potere invisibile', *Rivista Italiana di Scienza Politica*, 10 (2) (Aug.).

Boccella, Nicola (1994), 'Mezzogiorno più lontano dal Nord', in Ginsborg (1994).

Bonvicini, Gianni (1996), 'Riflessioni sulla Presidenza Italiana dell'Unione Europea', *Politica Internazionale*, nos 3–4 (May–Aug.).

Brioschi, Francesco, Luigi Buzzacchi and Massimo G. Colombo (1990), *Gruppi di imprese e mercato finanziario: La struttura di potere nell'industria italiana* (Rome: La Nuova Italia Scientifica).

Brusco, Sebastiano (1982), 'The Emilian model: productive decentralisation and social integration', *Cambridge Journal of Economics*, 6.

Brusco, Sebastiano and Sergio Paba (1997), 'Per una storia dei distretti industriali italiani dal secondo dopoguerra agli anni novanta', in Barca (1997b).

Bruti Liberati, Edmondo (1997), 'La magistratura dall'attuazione della Costituzione agli anni novanta', in Barbagallo (1997).

Bruzzone, Emanuele (1994), 'I contadini: estinzione o ridefinizione?', in Paul Ginsborg (ed.), *Stato dell'Italia* (Milan: Mondadori).

Bufacchi, Vittorio and Simon Burgess (2001), *Italy since 1989: Events and Interpretations* (London: Palgrave).

Bull, Martin J. (1988), 'From pluralism to pluralism: Italy and the corporatist debate', in Andrew W. Cox and Noel O'Sullivan (eds), *The Corporate State: Corporatism and the State Tradition in Western Europe* (London: Edward Elgar).

Bull, Martin J. (1991a), 'The unremarkable death of the Italian Communist Party', in Sabetti and Catanzaro (1991).

Bull, Martin J. (1991b), 'Whatever happened to Italian communism? Explaining the dissolution of the largest Communist party in the West', *West European Politics*, 14 (4).

Bull, Martin J. (1992), 'Villains of the peace: terrorism and the Secret Services in Italy', *Intelligence and National Security*, 7 (4).

Bull, Martin J. (1994), 'The European Community and "Regime Parties": a case study of Italian Christian Democracy', *EUI Working Paper*, SPS no. 94/4.

Bull, Martin J. (1996a), *Contemporary Italy: A Research Guide* (Westport, Conn.: Greenwood Press).

Bull, Martin J. (1996b), 'Italian Christian Democracy', in John Gaffney (ed.), *Political Parties and the European Community* (London: Routledge).

Bull, Martin J. (1996c), 'The roots of the Italian crisis', *Southern European Society and Politics*, 1 (1) (Spring).

Bull, Martin J. and Joerg Baudner (2004), 'Europeanisation and Italian policy for the *Mezzogiorno*', *Journal of European Public Policy*, 11 (6) (Dec.).

Bull, Martin J. and James L. Newell (1993), 'Italian politics and the 1992 elections: from "stable instability" to instability and change', *Parliamentary Affairs*, 46 (2).

Bull, Martin, and Martin Rhodes (1997a), 'Between crisis and transition: Italian politics in the 1990s', in Bull and Rhodes (1997b).

Bull, Martin and Martin Rhodes (eds) (1997b), *Crisis and Transition in Italian Politics* (London: Frank Cass). Originally a special issue of *West European Politics*, 20 (1) (Jan.).

Burroni, Luigi and Carlo Trigilia (2001), 'Italy: economic development through local economies', in Colin Crouch, Patrick Le Galès, Carlo Trigilia and Helmut Voelzkow (eds), *Local Production Systems in Europe: Rise or Demise?* (Oxford: Oxford University Press).

Caciagli, Mario (1982), 'The mass clientelism party and conservative politics: Christian Democracy in southern Italy', in Zig Layton-Henry (ed.), *Conservative Politics in Western Europe* (New York: St Martin's Press).

Caciagli, Mario and David Kertzer (eds) (1996), *Italian Politics: The Stalled Transition* (Boulder, Colo.: Westview Press).

Caciagli, Mario and Alan S. Zuckerman (eds) (2001), *Italian Politics: Emerging Themes and Institutional Responses* (Oxford and New York: Berghahn).

Caciagli, Mario, F. Cazzola, L. Morlino and S. Passigli (eds) (1994), *L'Italia fra crisi e transizione* (Bari and Rome: Laterza).

Calandra, Piero (1986), *Il governo della Repubblica* (Bologna: Mulino).

Calise, Mauro (1993), 'Remaking the Italian party system: how Lijphart got it wrong by saying it right', *West European Politics*, 16 (4) (Oct.).

Calise, Mauro (1994), 'Il governo tra istituzione e politica', in Caciagli et al. (1994).

Cammelli, Marco (2003), 'Un grande caos chiamato *devolution*', *Il Mulino*, (1) 52 (405).

Campus, Donatella (2002), 'La formazione del governo Berlusconi', in Pasquino (2002b).

Capano, Giliberto (1992), 'Verso l'ennesima riforma del pubblico impiego?', *Il Mulino*, 340 (Mar.–Apr.).

Capano, Giliberto and Marco Giuliani (2003), 'The Italian parliament: in search of a new role?', *Journal of Legislative Studies*, 9 (2).

Capo, Enrico (1985), 'Quarant'anni di Coldiretti: passato e avvenire', *Protezione Sociale*, 6.

Capotorto, Sebastiano (2002), 'Relazione introduttiva', paper presented to the seminar, il nuovo titolo quinto della Costituzione: Roma capitale', Campidoglio, Rome, 8 Feb. 2002.

Carli, Guido (1993), *Cinquant'anni di vita italiana* (Bari: Laterza).

Cartocci, Roberto (1994), 'Il deficit di integrazione in Italia: una lettura culturale della crisi di oggi', in Caciagli et al. (1994).

Cassese, Sabino (1983), *Il sistema amministrativo italiano* (Bologna: Mulino).

Cassese, Sabino (1994a), 'Il sistema amministrativo italiano, ovvero l'arte di arrangiarsi', in: Sabino Cassese and Claudio Franchini (eds), *L'amministrazione publica italiana: Un profilo* (Bologna: Mulino).

Cassese, Sabino (1994b), 'Italy: privatizations announced, semi-privatizations and pseudo-privatizations', in Vincent Wright (ed.), *Privatization in Western Europe: Pressures, Problems and Paradoxes* (London: Pinter).

Cassese, Sabino (1996), 'Le privatizzazioni in Italia', *Stato e mercato*, no. 47 (Aug.).

Catanzaro, Raimondo (1985), 'Enforcers, entrepreneurs and survivors: how the *mafia* has adapted to change', *British Journal of Sociology*, 36 (1); repr. in Donovan (1998).

Catanzaro, Raimondo (1988), *Men of Respect: A Social History of the Mafia* (New York: Free Press).

Catanzaro, Raimondo (1993), 'Recenti studi sulla Mafia', *Polis*, 7 (2).

Cazzola, Franco (ed.) (1979), *Anatomia del potere DC: enti pubblici e 'centralità democristiana'* (Bari: De Donato).

Cazzola, Franco (1981), *Il sistema politico dell'Italia contemporanea* (Turin: Loescher).

Cento Bull, Anna (2002), 'Towards a federal state? Competing proposals for constitutional revision', in Bellucci and Bull (2002).

Cento Bull, Anna and Mark Gilbert (2001), *The Lega Nord and the Northern Question in Italian Politics* (London: Palgrave).

Cersosimo, Domenico and Carmine Donzelli (1997), 'Mezzo giorno e mezzo no', *Meridiana* (Spring).

Certoma, G. Leroy (1985), *The Italian Legal System* (London: Butterworths).

Chubb, Judith (1982), *Patronage, Power and Poverty in Southern Italy: A Tale of Two Cities* (Cambridge: Cambridge University Press).

Cipoletta, Innocenza (1995), 'Italy: an ever-lagging economy?', in Baldassarri and Modigliani (1995).

Cipoletta, Innocenzo (1999), 'Un Mezzogiorno debole ma migliore', in A. D'Amato and G. Rosa (eds), *Nel Sud per competere* (Rome and Bari: Laterza).

Colarizi, Simona (1998), *Storia dei partiti nell'Italia repubblicana*, 3rd edn (Rome and Bari: Laterza).

Coltorti, Fulvio (1993), 'Phases of industrial development and the relationship between the public and private sectors', in Baldassarri (1993).

Contarino, Michael (2000), 'Italy's December 1998 "Social Pact for Development and Employment": towards a new political economy for a "normal country"?', in Gilbert and Pasquino (2000).

Coralluzzo, Walter (1994), 'La politica europea dell'Italia: antichi vizi e opinabili virtù', *Teoria Politica*, 10 (2).

Corbetta, Piergiorgio and Arturo M. L. Parisi (1997), 'Introduzione', in: Piergiorgio Corbetta and Arturo M. L. Parisi (eds), *A domanda risponde: Il cambiamento del voto degli italiani nelle elezioni del 1994 e del 1996* (Bologna: Mulino).

Costi, Renzo (2003), 'Le fondazioni bancarie: un assalto respinto?', in Blondel and Segatti (2003).

Cotta, Maurizio (1992), 'European integration and the Italian political system', in Francesco Francioni (ed.), *Italy and EC Membership Evaluated* (London: Pinter).

Cotta, Maurizio (1994), 'The rise and fall of the "centrality" of the Italian Parliament: transformations of the executive-legislative subsystem after the Second World War', in Gary W. Copeland and Samuel C. Patterson (eds), *Parliaments in the Modern World: Changing Institutions* (Ann Arbor: University of Michigan Press).

Cotta, Maurizio (1996), 'La crisi del governo di partito all'italiana', in Cotta and Isernia (1996).

Cotta, Maurizio and P. Isernia (eds) (1996), *Il gigante dai piedi d'argilla: La crisi del regime partitocratico in Italia* (Bologna: Mulino).

Cowles, Maria Green, James Caporaso and Thomas Risse (eds) (2001), *Transforming Europe: Europeanization and Domestic Change* (Ithaca, NY: Cornell University Press).

Criscitiello, Annarita (1993), 'Majority summits: decision-making inside the Cabinet and out: Italy 1970–1990', *West Euopean Politics*, 16 (4) (Oct.).

Cucchiarelli, Paolo and Aldo Giannuli (1997), *Lo stato parallelo: L'Italia 'oscura' nei documenti e nelle relazioni della Commissione Stragi* (Rome: Gamberetti).

D'Alimonte, Roberto and Stefano Bartolini (1997), ' "Electoral transition" and party system change in Italy', in Bull and Rhodes (1997b).

D'Antonio, Mariano (1993), 'The tortuous road of industry through the Mezzogiorno', in Baldassarri (1993).

Dahrendorf, Ralf (1988), *The Modern Social Conflict: An Essay on the Politics of Liberty* (London: Weidenfeld & Nicolson).

Daniels, Philip (1988), 'The end of the Craxi era? The Italian parliamentary elections of June 1987', *Parliamentary Affairs*, 41.

Daniels, Philip (1993), 'L'Italia e il trattato di Maastricht', in Hellman and Pasquino (1993).

Daniels, Philip, David Hine and Marinella Neri Gualdesi (1991), 'Italy, the European Community and the 1990 presidency: policy trends and policy performance', *Centre for Mediterranean Studies Occasional Paper*, No. 3 (University of Bristol, June).

Dastoli, Pier Virgilio (1996), 'The stone guest: Italy on the threshold of European Monetary Union', in Caciagli and Kertzer (1996).

Davis, John A. (1996), 'Changing perspectives on Italy's "southern problem" ', in Levy (1996).

De Bernardi, Alberto (1994), 'Clientelismo', in Ginsborg (1994).

De Cecco, Marcello (2004), 'Il declino della grande impresa', in Toniolo and Visco (2004).

De Felice, Franco (1989), 'Doppia lealtà e doppio stato', *Studi Storici*, 30 (3) (July–Sept.).

De Grand, Alexander (1989), *The Italian Left in the Twentieth Century: A History of the Socialist and Communist Parties* (Bloomington and Indianapolis: Indiana University Press).

De Lutiis, Giuseppe (1996), *Il lato oscuro del potere: Associazioni politiche e strutture paramilitari segrete dal 1946 a oggi* (Rome: Editori Riuniti).

De Vivo, Paola (2001), 'I molti volti del Sud: Fra imprenditorialità diffusa, azione pubblica e società', *Il Mulino*, 4 (396) (July–Aug.).

Deeg, Richard and Sofia Perez (2000), 'International capital mobility and domestic institutions: corporate finance and governance in four European cases', *Governance*, 13 (2).

Della Cananea, Giacinto (1996), 'Reforming the state: the policy of administrative reform in Italy under the Ciampi government', *West European Politics*, 19 (2) (Apr.).

Della Cananea, Giacinto (1997), 'The reform of finance and administration in Italy: contrasting achievements', in Bull and Rhodes (1997b).

Della Porta, Donatella (1993), 'La capitale immorale: le tangenti di Milano', in Hellman and Pasquino (1993).

Della Porta, Donatella (1996), 'Actors in corruption: business politicians in Italy', *International Social Science Journal*, 149 (Sept.).

Della Porta, Donatella (1998), 'A judges' revolution? Political corruption and the judiciary in Italy', paper presented to the workshop on 'Italy: Changes, Constraints and Choices', ECPR Joint Sessions of Workshops, University of Warwick, 23–8 Mar. 1998.

Della Porta, Donatella and Alberto Vannucci (1999a), *Corrupt Exchanges: Actors, Resources, and Mechanisms of Political Corruption* (New York: De Gruyter).

Della Porta, Donatella and Alberto Vannucci (1999b), *Un paese anormale: Come la classe politica ha perso l'occasione di Mani Pulite* (Rome and Bari: Laterza).

Della Sala, Vincent (1997), 'Hollowing out and hardening the State: European integration and the Italian economy', in Bull and Rhodes (1997b).

Della Sala, Vincent (2000), 'The new south in the new Europe: the case of Sviluppo Italia', in Gilbert and Pasquino (2000).

Della Sala, Vincent (2001), 'A new *Confindustria* for a new model of Italian capitalism', in Caciagli and Zuckerman (2001).

Della Sala, Vincent and Sergio Fabbrini (eds) (2004), *Politica in Italia: I fatti dell'anno e le interpretazioni* (Bologna: Mulino).

Dente, Bruno (1985), 'Centre–local relations in Italy: the impact of the legal and political structures', in Yves Mény and Vincent Wright (eds), *Centre–Periphery Relations in Western Europe* (London: George Allen & Unwin).

Dente, Bruno (ed.) (1990), *Le politiche pubbliche in Italia* (Bologna: Mulino).

Dente, Bruno (1997), 'Sub-national governments in the long Italian transition', in Bull and Rhodes (1997b).

Di Federico, Giuseppe (1989), 'The crisis of the justice system and the referendum on the judiciary', in Leonardi and Corbetta (1989).

Di Palma, Giuseppe (1977), *Surviving without Governing: The Italian Parties in Parliament* (Berkeley: University of California Press).

Di Palma, Giuseppe (2000), 'Introduzione: Istituzioni e politiche nell'Italia che cambia', in Di Palma, Fabbrini and Freddi (2000).

Di Palma, Giuseppe, Sergio Fabbrini and Giorgio Freddi (eds) (2000), *Condannata al successo? L'Italia nell'Europa integrata* (Bologna: Mulino).

Di Quirico, Roberto (2003a), 'Italy, Europe and the European presidency of 2003', Groupement D'Études et de Recherches, Notre Europe, *Research and European Issues*, no. 27 (July).

Di Quirico, Roberto (2003b), 'Italy in the European Union', presentation at workshop 'Italy in the European Union and in the Atlantic Community', Robert Schuman Centre for Advanced Studies, European University Institute, 8 Dec.

Di Scala, Spencer M. (2004), *Italy: From Revolution to Republic, 1700 to the Present* (Boulder, Colo.: Westview Press).

Donovan, Mark (ed.) (1998), *Italy* (Aldershot: Ashgate).

Donovan, Mark (2002), 'The processes of alliance formation', in Newell (2002b).

Donovan, Mark (2003a), 'Berlusconi, strong government and the Italian state', *Journal of Modern Italian Studies*, 8 (2) (Summer).

Donovan, Mark (2003b), 'The Italian state: no longer Catholic, no longer Christian', *West European Politics*, 26 (1) (Jan.).

Dossi, Rosella (2001), 'Italy's invisible government', *Contemporary Europe Research Centre (CERC) Working Papers Series*, no. 1.

Duggan, Christopher (1995), 'Italy in the Cold War years and the legacy of fascism', in Christopher Duggan and Christopher Wagstaff (eds), *Italy in the Cold War: Politics, Culture and Society, 1945–58* (Oxford: Berg).

Dyson, Kenneth and Kevin Featherstone (1996), 'Italy and EMU as a *"vincolo esterno"*: empowering the technocrats, transforming the State', *Southern European Society and Politics*, 1 (2) (Autumn).

Edwards, Philip (2004), 'Struggling to protest: the Italian Communist Party and the protest cycle, 1972–1977', (unpub. Ph.D. thesis, University of Salford).

Ellwood, David (1995), 'Italy, Europe and the Cold War: the politics and economics of limited sovereignty', in Christopher Duggan and Christopher Wagstaff (eds), *Italy in the Cold War: Politics, Culture and Society, 1948–58* (Oxford: Berg).

Esping-Andersen, Gøsta (1985), *Politics against Markets: The Social Democratic Road to Power* (Princeton, Princeton University Press).

Eurispes (2002), *Rapporto Italia 2002* (Rome: Eurispes).

Eurispes (2004), *Rapporto Italia 2004* (Rome: Eurispes).

Fabbrini, Sergio (2000), *Tra pressioni e veti: Il cambiamento politico in Italia* (Rome and Bari: Laterza).

Fabbrini, Sergio (ed.) (2003), *L'europeizzazione dell'Italia: L'impatto dell'Unione Europea sulle istituzioni e le politiche italiane* (Rome and Bari: Laterza).

Fabbrini, Sergio and Alessia Donà (2003), 'Europeanisation as strengthening of domestic executive power? The Italian experience and the case of the *"Legge Comunitaria"'*, *Journal of European Integration*, 25 (1) (Mar.).

Fasanella, Giovanni and Claudio Sestieri, with Giovanni Pellegrino (2000), *Segreto di Stato: La verità da Gladio al caso Moro* (Turin: Einaudi).

Featherstone, Kevin and George Kazamias (2000), 'Introduction: southern Europe and the process of "Europeanization"', *West European Politics*, 23 (4) (Oct.).

Ferrajoli, Luigi (1996), 'Democracy and the Constitution in Italy', *Political Studies*, 44.

Ferraresi, Franco (1992), 'A secret structure codenamed Gladio', in Stephen Hellman and Gianfranco Pasquino (eds), *Italian Politics: A Review*, Vol. 8 (London: Pinter).

Ferrera, Maurizio (1989), 'Politics, institutional features, and the government of industry', in Lange and Regini (1989).

Ferrera, Maurizio (1991), 'Italia: aspirazioni e vincoli del "quarto grande"', in Maurizio Ferrera (ed.), *Le dodici Europe* (Bologna: Mulino).

Ferrera, Maurizio and Elisabetta Gualmini (2004), *Rescued by Europe? Social and Labour Market Reforms in Italy from Maastricht to Berlusconi* (Amsterdam: Amsterdam University Press).

Follini, Marco (1997), 'Il ritorno dei partiti', *Il Mulino*, 370 (Mar.–Apr.).

Fortis, Marco and Alberto Quadrio Curzio (2003), 'Alle prese con la concorrenza asiatica', *Il Mulino*, 410 (6) (Nov.–Dec.).

Frankel, P. (1966), *Mattei: Oil and Power Politics* (London: Faber & Faber).

Fraschini, Angela (1993), 'Financing communal government in Italy', in: John Gibson and Richard Batley (eds), *Financing European Local Governments* (London: Frank Cass).

Friedman, Alan (1988), *Agnelli and the Network of Italian Power* (London: Harrap).

Fuà, G. (1976), *Occupazione e capacità produttiva: la realtà italiana* (Bologna: Mulino).

Furlong, Paul (1990), 'Parliament in Italian politics', *West European Politics*, 13 (3).

Furlong, Paul (1994), *Modern Italy: Representation and Reform* (London: Routledge).

Fusaro, Carlo (1998), 'The politics of constitutional reform in Italy: a framework for analysis', *South European Society and Politics*, 3 (2) (Autumn).

Galante, Sergio (1988), *Il Partito comunista italiano e l'integrazione europea* (Padua: Liviana Editrice).

Galante, Sergio (1992), 'In search of lost power: the international policies of the Italian Christian Democrat and Communist parties in the fifties', in Ennio di Nolfo (ed.), *Power in Europe? II Great Britain, France, Germany and Italy and the Origins of the EEC, 1952–1957* (Berlin: De Gruyter).

Galli, Giorgio (1991), *Affari di Stato: L'Italia sotterranea 1943–1990: storia politica, partiti, corruzione, misteri, scandali* (Milan: Kaos).

Galli, Giorgio and Alessandra Nannei (1976), *Il capitalismo assistenziale: Ascesa e declino del sistema economico italiano 1960–1975* (Milan: SugarCo).

Galli, Giorgio and Alfonso Prandi (1970), *Patterns of Political Participation in Italy* (New Haven: Yale University Press).

Gallino, Luciano (2003), *La scomparsa dell'Italia industiale* (Turin: Einaudi).

Gambetta, Diego (1996), *The Sicilian Mafia: The Business of Private Protection* (Cambridge, Mass.: Harvard University Press).

Garofoli, G. (1983), 'Modalità dello sviluppo territoriale: l'emergere dei sistemi territoriali ad economia diffusa', in IRER, *Industrializzazione diffusa in Lombardia* (Milan: Franco Angeli).

Giarizzo, Giuseppe (1992), *Mezzogiorno senza meridionalismo: La Sicilia, lo sviluppo, il potere* (Venice: Marsilio).

Giavazzi, Francesco and Luigi Spaventa (eds) (1988), *High Public Debt: The Italian Experience* (Cambridge: Cambridge University Press).

Gilbert, Mark (1995), *The Italian Revolution: The End of Politics, Italian Style?* (Boulder, Colo.: Westview Press).

Gilbert, Mark (1997), 'Italy's third fall', *Journal of Modern Italian Studies*, 2 (2).

Gilbert, Mark (2000), 'The Bassanini laws: a half-way house in local government reform', in Hine and Vassallo (2000).

Gilbert, Mark, and Gianfranco Pasquino (eds) (2000), *Italian Politics: The Faltering Transition* (Oxford: Berghahn).

Ginsborg, Paul (1990), *A History of Contemporary Italy: Society and Politics 1943–1988* (London: Penguin).

Ginsborg, Paul (ed.) (1994), *Stato dell'Italia* (Milan: Mondadori).

Ginsborg, Paul (1996a), 'Explaining Italy's crisis', in Gundle and Parker (1996).

Ginsborg, Paul (1996b), 'L'Italia e l'Unione europea', *Passato e presente*, 14 (37).

Ginsborg, Paul (1998), *L'Italia del tempo presente: Famiglia, società civile, Stato* (Turin: Einaudi).

Ginsborg, Paul (2003), *Berlusconi: Ambizioni patrimoniali in una democrazia mediatica* (Turin: Einaudi).

Giolitti, Antonio (1984), 'Italy and the Community after thirty years of experience', *International Spectator*, 19 (2) (April/June).

Giuliani, Marco (1997a), 'L'Italia fra politica interna e politica europea', *Italian Politics and Society*, no. 47 (Spring).

Giuliani, Marco (1997b), 'Measures of consensual law-making: Italian "Consociativismo"', *South European Society and Politics*, 2 (1).

Giuliani, Marco (2000), 'Europeanization and Italy: a bottom-up process?', *South European Society and Politics*, 5 (2) (Autumn).

Giuliani, Marco (2003), 'Italy and Europe: policy domains and policy dynamics', in Leonardi and Fedele (2003).

Goldstein, Andrea (1998), 'Recent works on Italian capitalism: a review essay', *Journal of Modern Italian Studies*, 3 (2).

Goodman, Edward and Julia Bamford (1991), *Small Firms and Industrial Districts in Italy* (London: Routledge).

Graziani, Augusto (1969), *Lo sviluppo di una economia aperta* (Naples: Esi).

Graziani, Augusto (1972), *L'economia italiana: 1945–1970* (Bologna: Mulino).

Graziani, Augusto (1979), *L'economia italiana dal 1945 ad oggi* (Bologna: Mulino).

Graziani, Augusto (1991), 'Export-led growth: the Italian experience', in Carluccio Bianchi and Carlo Casarosa (eds), *The Recent Performance of the Italian Economy: Market Outcomes and State Policy* (Milan: Franco Angeli).

Graziani, Augusto (1994), 'Le privatizzazioni', in Ginsborg (1994).

Graziano, Luigi (1980), *Clientelismo e Sistema Politico: Il Caso dell'Italia* (Milan: Franco Angeli).

Graziano, Luigi, Fiorenzo Girotti and Luciano Bonet (1984), 'Coalition politics at the regional level and centre–periphery relationships', *International Political Science Review*, 5 (4).

Gribaudi, G. (1991), *Mediatori: Antropologia del potere democristiano nel Mezzogiorno* (Turin: Rosenberg and Sellier).

Gros-Pietro, Gian Maria (1993), 'The restructuring of large-sized industrial groups', in Baldassarri (1993).

Gualdesi, Marinella Neri (1994), 'L'Italia e l'integrazione europea', in Istituto Affari Internazionale, *L'Italia nella Politica Internazionale, Anno Ventunesimo, Edizione 1994* (Rome: Editore SIPI).

Guarnieri, Carlo (1997), 'The judiciary in the Italian political crisis', in Bull and Rhodes (1997b).

Guarnieri, Carlo (2001), *La giustizia in Italia* (Bologna: il Mulino).

Gundle, Stephen (1986), 'Urban dreams and metropolitan nightmares: models and crises of Communist local government in Italy', in Bogdan Szajkowski (ed.), *Marxist Local Governments in Western Europe and Japan* (London: Pinter).

Gundle, Stephen and Simon Parker (eds) (1996), *The New Italian Republic: From the Fall of the Berlin Wall to Berlusconi* (London: Routledge).

Guzzini, Stefano (1995), 'The "long night of the First Republic": years of clientelistic implosion in Italy', *Review of International Political Economy*, 2 (1) (Winter).

Hellman, Stephen and Gianfranco Pasquino (eds) (1993), *Politica in Italia: I fatti dell'anno e le interpretazioni* (Bologna: Mulino).

Hine, David (1979), 'The Italian Socialist Party under Craxi: surviving but not reviving', in Lange and Tarrow (1979).

Hine, David (1990), 'The consolidation of democracy in post-war Italy', in Geoffrey Pridham (ed.), *Securing Democracy: Political Parties and Democratic Consolidation in Southern Europe* (London: Routledge).

Hine, David (1992), 'Italy and Europe: the Italian presidency and the domestic management of the European Community', in Leonardi and Anderlini (1992).

Hine, David (1993a), *Governing Italy: The Politics of Bargained Pluralism* (Oxford: Clarendon Press).

Hine, David (1993b), 'The new Italian electoral system', *ASMI Newsletter*, no. 24 (Autumn).

Hine, David (2000), 'European policy making and the machinery of Italian government', *South European Society and Politics*, 15 (2) (Autumn).

Hine, David (2002), 'Silvio Berlusconi, the media and the conflict of interest issue', in Bellucci and Bull (2002).

Hine, David and Renato Finocchi (1991), 'The Italian Prime Minister', *West European Politics*, 14 (2).

Hine, David and Salvatore Vassallo (eds) (2000), *Italian Politics: The Return of Politics* (London: Berghahn).

Hix, Simon and Klaus H. Goetz (2000), 'Introduction: European integration and national political systems', *West European Politics*, 23 (4) (Oct.).

Hobsbawm, E. J. (1971), *Primitive Rebels: Studies in Archaic Forms of Social Movement in the Nineteenth and Twentieth Centuries* (Manchester: Manchester University Press).

Holland, Stuart (1972), *The State as Entrepreneur: New Dimensions for Public Enterprise: The IRI State Share-Holding Formula* (London: Weidenfeld & Nicolson).

Hopkin, J. and Paolucci, C. (1999), 'The business firm model of party organisation: cases from Spain and Italy', *European Journal of Political Research*, 35.

Hytten, Eyvind and Marco Marchioni (1970), *Industrializzazione senza sviluppo: Gela: una storia meridionale* (Milan: Franco Angeli).

Ignazi, Piero (2003), 'La storia infinita della questione istituzionale', *Il Mulino*, 1 (405).

ISTAT [Istituto Nazionale di Statistica] (various years a), *Annuario Statistico Italiano* (Rome: Poligrafico dello Stato) and <www.istat.it>

ISTAT [Istituto Nazionale di Statistica] (various years b), *Compendio Statistico Italiano* (Rome: Poligrafico dello Stato).

ISTAT [Istituto Nazionale di Statistica] (various years c), *Rapporto sull'Italia Edzione . . .* (Rome: Poligrafico dello Stato), and <www.istat.it>

ITANES [Italian National Election Study] (2001), *Perché ha vinto il centro-destra* (Bologna: Mulino).

Jamieson, Alison (2000), *The Antimafia: Italy's Fight against Organized Crime* (London: Macmillan).

Jensen, Carsten Strøby (2004), 'Trade unionism: differences and similarities – a comparative view on Europe, USA and Asia', paper presented at the International Industrial Relations Association Congress, Seoul, 23–6 June.

Keating, Michael (1988), 'Does regional government work? The experience of Italy, France and Spain', *Governance*, 1 (2) (Apr.).

Keating, Robert Patrick and Anna Murphy (1992), 'The European Council's ad hoc Committee of Institutional Affairs (1984–85)', in Roy Pryce (ed.), *The Dynamics of European Union* (London: Croom Helm).

Koff, Sandra Z. and Stephen P. Koff (2000), *Italy: From the First to the Second Republic* (London: Routledge).

La Spina, Antonio (2000), 'L'esperienza italiana', in La Spina and Majone (2000).

La Spina, Antonio (2003a), *La politica per il Mezzogiorno* (Bologna: Mulino).

La Spina, Antonio (2003b), 'The role of independent regulatory bodies in Italy today', in Leonardi and Fedele (2003).

La Spina, Antonio and Giandomenico Majone (2000), *Lo Stato regolatore* (Bologna: Mulino).

Lanaro, Silvio (1992), *Storia dell'Italia Repubblicana: dalla fine della guerra agli anni novanta* (Venice: Marsilio).

Lane, David (2004), *Berlusconi's Shadow: Crime, Justice and the Pursuit of Power* (London: Allen Lane).

Lange, Peter (1986), 'The end of an era: the wage indexation referendum of 1985', in Nanetti and Leonardi (1986).

Lange, Peter and Marino Regini (eds) (1989), *State, Market and Social Regulation: New Perspectives on Italy* (Cambridge: Cambridge University Press).

Lange, Peter and Sidney Tarrow (eds) (1979), *Italy in Transition: Conflict and Consensus* (London: Frank Cass).

Lange, Peter, G. Ross and M. Vannicelli (1982), *Unions, Change and Crisis: French and Italian Union Strategy and the Political Economy, 1948–80* (London: George Allen & Unwin).

Lanza, Orazio (1991), 'L'agricoltura, la Coldiretti e la DC', in: Morlino (1991a).

LaPalombara, Joseph (1964), *Interest Groups in Italian Politics* (Princeton: Princeton University Press).

LaPalombara, Joseph (1989), 'Politica estera italiana: Immobilismo al tramonto', *Relazione Internazionali* (Sept.).

Lauth, Hans-Joachim (2000), 'Informal institutions and democracy', *Democratization*, 7 (4).

Lelli, Susy Monica (2004), 'Appendice documentaria', in Della Sala and Fabbrini (2004).

Leon, Paolo (1993), 'Public enterprises and industrial policies', in Baldassarri (1993).

Leonardi, Robert (1990), 'Political developments and institutional change in Emilia-Romagna 1970–1990', in Leonardi and Nanetti (1990).

Leonardi, Robert (1991), 'The international context of democratic transition in postwar Italy: a case of penetration', in Geoffrey Pridham (ed.), *Encouraging Democracy: The Transitional Context of Regime Transition within Europe* (Leicester: Leicester University Press).

Leonardi, Robert and Douglas A. Wertman (1989), *Italian Christian Democracy* (London: Macmillan).

Leonardi, Robert and Fausto Anderlini (eds) (1992), *Italian Politics: A Review*, vol. 6 (London: Pinter).

Leonardi, Robert and Marcello Fedele (eds) (2003), *Italy: Politics and Policy*, vol. 2 (Aldershot: Dartmouth).

Leonardi, Robert and Piergiorgio Corbetta (eds) (1989), *Italian Politics: A Review*, vol. 3 (London: Pinter).

Leonardi, Robert and Raffaella Y. Nanetti (eds) (1990), *The Regions and European Integration: The Case of Emilia-Romagna* (London: Pinter).

Leonardi, Robert, Raffaella Y. Nanetti and Robert D. Putnam (1987), 'Italy – territorial politics in the post-war years: the case of regional reform', *West European Politics*, 10 (4).

Levy, Carl (ed.) (1996), *Regionalism, History, Identity and Politics* (Oxford: Berg).

Lewis, Norman (1984), *The Honoured Society: The Sicilian Mafia Observed* (London: Eland).

Locke, Richard (1995), *Remaking the Italian Economy* (Ithaca, NY: Cornell University Press).

Luciani, Massimo (2002), 'Federalismo', in Francesco Tuccari (ed.), *Il governo Berlusconi: le parole, i fatti, i rischi* (Rome, Bari: Laterza).

Lumley, Robert and Jonathan Morris (eds) (1997), *The New History of the Italian South: The Mezzogiorno Revisited* (Exeter: Exeter University Press).

Lupo, Salvatore (1996), 'The changing Mezzogiorno: between representations and reality', in Gundle and Parker (1996).

Lutz, Vera (1975), *Italy: A Study in Economic Development* (Westport, Conn.: Greenwood Press; originally published in 1962 by Oxford University Press).

Mack Smith, Dennis (1997), *Modern Italy: A Political History* (New Haven: Yale University Press).

Maggia, G. and G. Fornengo (1976), *Appunti sul sistema delle partecipazioni statali* (Turin: Einaudi).

Maggiorani, Mauro (1998), (Istituto Gramsci Emilia-Romagna), *Comunisti italiani e integrazione europea (1957–1969)* (Rome: Carocci Editore).

Magister, Sandro (1979), *La politica vaticana e l'Italia 1943–1978* (Rome: Editori Riuniti).

Mannheimer, Renato and Giacomo Sani (1987), *Il mercato elettorale: Identikit dell' elettore italiano* (Bologna: Mulino).

Mannheimer Renato and Giacomo Sani (2000), 'Reassembling the centre and the electoral spectrum', in Hine and Vassallo (2000).

Manzella, A. (2001), 'Le regioni divise nell'Italia di Bossi', *La Repubblica*, 31 July.

March, J. G. and J. P. Olsen (1989), *Rediscovering Institutions: The Organizational Basis of Politics* (New York: Free Press).

Marrelli, Massimo and Francesca Stroffolini (1998), 'Privatisation in Italy: a tale of "capture"', in David Parker (ed.), *Privatisation in the European Union: Theory and Policy Perspectives* (London: Routledge).

Martinotti, Guido and Sonia Stefanizzi (1995), 'Europeans and the nation state', in Oskar Niedermayer and Richard Sinnot (eds), *Public Opinion and Internationalized Governance* (Oxford: Oxford University Press).

Massari, Oreste and Simon Parker (2000), 'The two Lefts: between rupture and recomposition', in Hine and Vassallo (2000).

Mastropaolo, Alfio (1994), 'Perché è entrata in crisi la democrazia italiana? Un'ipotesi sugli anni Ottanta', in Caciagli et al. (1994).

Mattina, Liborio (1991), 'La Confindustria oltre la simbiosi', in Morlino (1991a).

McCann, Dermot (2000a), 'The "Anglo-American" model, privatization and the transformation of private capitalism in Italy', *Modern Italy*, 5 (1).

McCann, Dermot (2000b), 'Economic internationalization, domestic political crisis and corporate governance reform in Italy', *South European Society and Politics*, 5 (1) (Summer).

McCarthy, Patrick (1995), *The Crisis of the Italian State: From the Origins of the Cold War to the Fall of Berlusconi and Beyond* (New York: St Martin's Press).

McCarthy, Patrick (2000), 'The Church in post-war Italy', in Patrick McCarthy (ed.), *Italy since 1945* (Oxford: Oxford University Press).

Melis, Guido (1996), *Storia dell'Amministrazione Italiana 1861–1993* (Bologna: Mulino).

Mershon, Carol and Gianfranco Pasquino (eds) (1994), *Politica in Italia: i fatti dell'anno e le interpretazioni. Edizione 1994* (Bologna: Mulino).

Mignone, Mario B. (1995), *Italy Today: A Country in Transition* (New York: Peter Lang).

Monti, Mario (1998), *Intervista sull'Italia in Europa* (Rome: Laterza).

Morelli, Roberto (2003), 'Se non puoi fermarli attaccarli', *CorrierEconomia, Corriere della Sera*, 15 Dec.

Morlino, Leonardo (ed.) (1991a), *Costruire la democrazia. Gruppi e partiti in Italia* (Bologna: Mulino).

Morlino, Leonardo (1991b), 'Introduzione', in Morlino (1991a).

Morlino, Leonardo (1991c), 'La relazione fra gruppi e partiti', in Morlino (1991a).

Morlino, Leonardo and Marco Tarchi (1996), 'The dissatisfied society: the roots of political change in Italy', *European Journal of Political Research*, 30 (July).

Mortati, C. (1940), *La costituzione in senso materiale* (Milan: Giuffré).

Nanetti, Raffaella Y. and Raimondo Catanzaro (eds) (1990), *Italian Politics: A Review*, vol. 4 (London: Pinter).

Nanetti, Raffaella Y. and Robert Leonardi (eds) (1986), *Italian Politics: A Review*, vol. 1 (London: Pinter).

Neppi Modona, Guido (1995), *Stato della Costituzione: Principi, regole, equilibri* (Milano: il Saggiatore).

Neppi Modona, Guido (1997), 'La magistratura dalla Liberazione agli anni cinquanta', in Barbagallo (1997).

Nevola, Gaspare (2003), 'From the "Republic of Parties" to a "Fatherland for Italians": the Italian political system in search of a new principle of legitimation', *Journal of Modern Italian Studies*, 8 (2) (Summer).

Newell, James L. (1998), 'At the start of a journey: steps on the road to decentralization', in Bardi and Rhodes (1998).

Newell, James L. (2000a), 'Actors at a dress rehearsal: the Italian regional elections of April 2000', *Regional and Federal Studies*, 10 (3) (Autumn).

Newell, James L. (2000b), *Parties and Democracy in Italy* (Aldershot: Ashgate).

Newell, James L. (2000c), 'Turning over a new leaf? Cohesion and discipline in the Italian parliament', *Journal of Legislative Studies*, 4 (4) (Winter).

Newell, James L. (2002a), 'Introduction' in Newell (2002b).

Newell, James L. (2002b) (ed.), *The Italian General Election of 2001: Berlusconi's Victory* (Manchester: Manchester University Press).

Newell, James L. and Martin J. Bull (1993), 'The Italian referenda of April 1993: real change at last?', *West European Politics*, 16 (4) (Oct.).

Newell, James L. and Martin J. Bull (1997), 'Party organisations and alliances in the 1990s: a revolution of sorts', in Bull and Rhodes (1997b).

Newell, James L. and Martin J. Bull (2001), 'The Italian General Election of May 2001', Keele European Parties Research Unit (KEPRU), Working Paper no. 4 (University of Keele).

Newell, James L. and Martin J. Bull (2002), 'Italian politics after the 2001 General Election: *Plus ça change plus c'est la même chose?*', *Parliamentary Affairs*, 55, (4) (Oct.).

Newell, James L. and Martin J. Bull (2003), 'Political corruption in Italy', in Martin J. Bull and James L. Newell (eds), *Corruption in Contemporary Politics* (London: Palgrave Macmillan).

O'Connor, James (1973), *The Fiscal Crisis of the State* (New York: St Martin's Press).

OECD (2001a), *Review dell'OCSE della riforma della regolazione in Italia* (OECD <www.oecd.org>).

OECD (2001b), *Territorial Reviews. Italy* (OECD, <www.oecd.org>).

OECD (2002), *Economic Survey of Italy, 2001* (OECD, <www.oecd.org>).

OECD (2003), *Economic Surveys 2002–2003: Italy* (OECD, <www.oecd.org>).

Olivi, Bino (1977), 'L'Italia nella Cee degli anni '70 – problemi e prospettivi', in Natalino Ronzitti (ed.), *Istituto Affari Internazionali, La politica estera italiana. Autonomia, interdependenza, integrazione e sicurezza* (Varese: Edizioni di Comunità – Istituto Affari Internazionali).

Onida, Fabrizio (2004), *Se il piccolo non cresce: Piccole e medie imprese italiane in affanno* (Bologna: Mulino).

Orfei, Ruggero (1976), *L'Occupazione del potere: I democristiani 1945–1975* (Milan: Longanesi).

Paci, Massimo and Raffaele Romanelli (1994), 'Recenti volumi di storia dell'Italia repubblicana', *Stato e Mercato*, no. 40 (Apr.).

Padoa-Schioppa, Tommaso and Stephen R. Graubard (eds) (2001), *Il caso italiano 2. Dove sta andando il nostro paese?* (Milan: Garzanti).

Padoa Schioppa Kostoris, Fiorella (1993), *Italy: The Sheltered Economy: Structural Problems in the Italian Economy* (Oxford: Clarendon Press).

Padoa Schioppa Kostoris, Fiorella (1996), 'Excesses and limits of the public sector in the Italian economy', in Gundle and Parker (1996).

Panebianco, S. (1994), 'I cittadini e lo sviluppo politico dell'Unione', in Fulvio Attinà, F. Longo and S. Panebianco (eds), *Identità, partiti ed elezioni nell'Unione europea* (Bari: Cacucci).

Paoli, Letizia (2001), 'La mafia è sconfitta?', *Il Mulino*, 3 (395).

Pappalardo, Adriano (2002), 'Il sistema partitico italiano fra bipolarismo e destrutturazione', in Pasquino (2002a).

Parisi, Arturo and Gianfranco Pasquino (eds) (1977), *Continuità e mutamento elettorale in Italia* (Bologna: Mulino).

Parker, Simon and Duncan McDonnell (2003), 'Devolution or neo-centralism? Centre-left cities in centre-right regions: the cases of Genoa and Venice', paper presented to the panel, 'Italian politics I: Party politics at the national and sub-national levels' at the 53rd Annual Conference of the UK Political Studies Association, University of Leicester, 15–17 Apr.

Partridge, Hilary (1998), *Italian Politics Today* (Manchester: Manchester University Press).

Pasquino, Gianfranco (1994), 'Le coalizioni di pentapartito (1980–91): quale governo dei partiti?', in Caciagli et al. (1994).

Pasquino, Gianfranco (1998), 'Reforming the Italian Constitution', *Journal of Modern Italian Studies*, 3 (1).

Pasquino, Gianfranco (1999), *La classe politica* (Bologna: Mulino).

Pasquino, Gianfranco (2000a), 'A postmortem of the bicamerale', in Hine and Vassallo (2000).

Pasquino, Gianfranco (2000b), *La transizione a parole* (Bologna: Mulino).

Pasquino, Gianfranco (2001a), *Critica della Sinistra Italiana* (Rome and Bari: Laterza).

Pasquino, Gianfranco (2001b), 'Teorie della transizione e analisi del sistema politico: il caso italiano', *Rivista Italiana di Scienza Politica*, no. 2 (Aug.).

Pasquino, Gianfranco (ed.) (2002a), *Dall'Ulivo al governo Berlusconi: Le elezioni del 13 maggio 2001 e il sistema politico italiano* (Bologna: Mulino).

Pasquino, Gianfranco (2002b), *Il sistema politico italiano: Autorità, istituzioni, società* (Bologna: Bononia University Press).

Pasquino, Gianfranco (2003), 'The Government, the Opposition and the President of the Republic under Berlusconi', paper presented to the panel, 'Italian Politics II: The Second Berlusconi Government' at the 53rd Annual Conference of the UK Political Studies Association, University of Leicester, 15–17 Apr.

Pasquino, Gianfranco (2004), "The Italian party system: from polarised pluralism to imperfect bipolar competition', paper prepared for presentation to the panel, 'Political parties and party-system change in Italy: current states and future prospects II' at the 54th Annual Conference of the UK Political Studies Association, University of Lincoln, 6–8 Apr.

Pasquino, Gianfranco and Salvatore Vassallo (1994), 'Il governo di Carlo Azeglio Ciampi', in Mershon and Pasquino (1994).

Pedersen, Mogens N. (1979), 'The dynamics of European party systems: changing patterns of electoral volatility', *European Journal of Political Research*, 7 (1).

Perrisich, Riccardo (1996), 'The costs and benefits of international liberalisation and deregulation: an Italian view', *International Spectator*, 31 (2) (Apr.–June).

Perulli, Angela, 'Com'è cambiata l'occupazione', in Ginsborg (1994).

Petrarca, Carmina (2004), 'I valori del neoconservatorismo in Gran Bretagna e in Italia: un'analisi dell'elettorato' (unpublished Ph.D. thesis, University of Siena).

Pilati, Antonio (1982), 'Obiettivi e vincoli dei partiti sulla scena internazionale', *Politica Internazionale*, no. 2 (Feb.).

Pistone, Sergio (1991), 'Italia e l'integrazione europea', *L'Italia e Europa*, nos 28–9.

Pizzorrusso, Alessandro (1990), *L'organizzazione della giustizia in Italia: La magistratura nel sistema politico e istituzionale* (Turin: Einaudi).

Pizzuti, Felice Roberto (1994), 'Introduzione', in Felice Roberto Pizzuti (ed.), *L'economia italiana dagli anni '70 agli anni '90: Pragmatismo, disciplina e saggezza convenzionale* (Milan: McGraw-Hill).

Podbielski, Gisele (1981), 'The Common Agricultural Policy and the Mezzogiorno', *Journal of Common Market Studies*, 19 (4) (June).

Posner, M. V. and Stuart J. Woolf (1967), *Italian Public Enterprise* (London: Duckworth).

Pridham, Geoffrey (1980), 'Concepts of Italy's approach to the European Community', *Journal of Common Market Studies*, 19 (1) (Sept.).

Prodi, Romano and Daniele De Giovanni (1993), 'Forty-five years of industrial policy in Italy: protagonists, objectives and instruments', in Baldassari (1993).

Pugliese, Enrico (1994), 'Economia informale', in Ginsborg (1994).

Putnam, Robert D. (1993) *Making Democracy Work: Civic Traditions in Modern Italy* (Princeton: Princeton University Press).

Pyke, Frank, Giacomo Becattini and Werner Sengenberger (1990), *Industrial Districts and Inter-Firm Cooperation in Italy* (Geneva: Institute for Labour Studies).

Quaroni, P. (1967), 'Chi è che fa la politica estera in Italia', in M. Bonanni (ed.), *La politica estera della Repubblica italiana* (Milan: Comunità).

Radaelli, Claudio (1998), 'Networks of expertise and policy change in Italy', *South European Society and Politics*, 3 (2) (Autumn).

Radaelli, Claudio (2001), 'The Italian State and the euro: institutions, discourse, and policy regimes', in Kenneth Dyson (ed.), *European States and the Euro: Europeanization, Variation, and Convergence* (Oxford: Oxford University Press).

Regalia, Ida and Marino Regini (1998), 'Italy: the dual character of industrial relations', in Anthony Ferner and Richard Hyman (eds), *Changing Industrial Relations in Europe* (Oxford: Blackwell).

Regini, Marino (ed.) (1988), *La sfida della flessibilità* (Milan: Franco Angeli).

Regini, Marino (1995), 'La varietà italiana di capitalismo: Istituzioni sociali e struttura produttiva negli anni ottanta', *Stato e Mercato*, no. 43 (Apr.).

Regini, Marino and Ida Regalia (1997), 'Employers, unions and the State: the resurgence of concertation in Italy', in Bull and Rhodes (1997b).

Reviglio, Franco (1994), *Meno Stato più mercato: Come ridurre lo Stato per risanare il Paese* (Milan: Mondadori).

Rhodes, Martin (1997), 'Financing party politics in Italy: a case of systemic corruption', in Bull and Rhodes (1997b).

Rhodes, Martin, and Bastiaan van Apeldoorn (1998), 'Capital unbound? The transformation of European corporate governance', *Journal of European Public Policy*, 5 (3) (Sept.).

Riall, Lucy (2000), 'Which road to the south? Revisionists revisit the Mezzogiorno', *Journal of Modern Italian Studies*, 5 (1).

Rimanelli, Marco (1989), 'From ashes to renewal: post-war Italian foreign policy', *Italian Journal*, 3 (4).

Risse, Thomas, Maria Green Cowles and James Caporaso (2001), 'Europeanization and domestic change: introduction', in Cowles, Caporaso and Risse (2001).

Rizzo, Sergio (2002), 'Avanza la carica dei neocorporativi', *CorrierEconomia, Corriere della Sera*, 25 Nov.

Roccas, Massimo (1980), 'Italy', in Dudley Seers and Constantine Vaitsos (eds), *Integration and Unequal Development: The Experience of the EEC* (London: Macmillan).

Romano, Sergio (1991), 'La cambiale europea dell'Italia', *Il Mulino*, 40 (336) (July–Aug.).

Romano, Sergio (1993), *L'Italia scappata di mano* (Milan: Longanesi).

Romano, Sergio (1996), 'Italy's constitutional crisis', *International Spectator*, 31 (2) (Apr.–June).

Rugge, Fabio (1997), 'Le leggi "Bassanini": continuità e innovazioni del reformismo amminis-trativo', *il Mulino*, 372 (July–Aug.).

Ruzza, Carlo and Oliver Schmidtke (1996), 'Towards a modern right: Alleanza Nazionale and the "Italian Revolution"', in Gundle and Parker (1996).

Saba, Andrea (1978), *L'Industria sommersa: nuovo modello di sviluppo* (Venice: Marsilio).

Saba, Andrea (1995), *Il Modello italiano: La "specializzazione flessibile" e i distretti industriali* (Milan: Franco Angeli).

Sabbatucci, Giovanni (1999), 'I misteri del caso Moro', in Giovanni Belardelli, Luciano Cafagna, Giovanni Sabbatucci and Ernesto Galli della Loggia, *Miti e Storia dell'Italia unità* (Bologna: Mulino).

Sabetti, Filippo (1990), 'The Mafia and antimafia: moments in the struggle for justice and self-governance in Sicily', in Nanetti and Catanzaro (1990).

Sabetti, Filippo (2000), *The Search for Good Government: Understanding the Paradox of Italian Democracy* (Montral: McGill–Queen's University Press).

Sabetti, Filippo and Raimondo Catanzaro (eds) (1991), *Italian Politics: A Review*, vol. 5 (London: Pinter).

Salvadori, Massimo (1994), *Storia d'Italia e crisi di regime: Alle radici della politica italiana* (Bologna: Mulino).

Salvati, Michele (1972), 'The impasse of Italian capitalism', *New Left Review*, no. 76 (Nov.–Dec.).

Salvati, Michele (1979), 'Muddling through: economics and politics in Italy 1969–1979', in Lange and Tarrow (1979).

Salvati, Michele (1984), *Economia e politica in Italia dal dopoguerra a oggi* (Milan: Garzanti).

Salvati, Michele (2000), *Occasioni mancate: Economia e politica in Italia dagli anni '60 a oggi* (Rome and Bari: Laterza).

Santomassimo, Gianpasquale (ed.) (2003), *La notte della democrazia italiana: Dal regime fascista al governo Berlusconi* (Milan: il Saggiatore).

Santoro, Carlo M. (1988), *L'Italia e il Mediterraneo: Questioni di politica estera* (Milan: Franco Angeli).

Saraceno, P. (1975), *Il sistema delle impresa partecipazione statale* (Milan: Giuffré).

Sarcina, Giuseppe (2002), 'Sud-story, festival dei ripensamenti', *Corriere della Sera*, 4 Oct.

Sartori, Giovanni (1959), 'Gruppi di pressione o gruppi di interesse?', *Il Mulino*, 8.

Sartori, Giovanni (1966), 'European political parties: the case of polarized pluralism' in J. LaPalombara and M. Weiner (eds), *Political Parties and Political Development* (Princeton: Princeton University Press).

Sartori, Giovanni (1976), *Parties and Party Systems: A Framework for Analysis* (Cambridge: Cambridge University Press).

Sartori, Giovanni (2002), 'Il problema è la minoranza', *Corriere della Sera*, 5 Feb.

Sassoon, Donald (1997), *Contemporary Italy: Politics, Economy and Society since 1945* (London: Longman).

Sbragia, Alberta (1992), 'Italia/CEE: Un partner sottovalutato', *Relazioni Internazionali* (June).

Sbragia, Alberta (2001), 'Italy pays for Europe: political leadership, political choice and insti-tutional adaptation', in Cowles, Caporaso and Risse (2001).

Scalfari, Eugenio and Giuseppe Turani (1974), *Razza padrona: Storia della borghesia di stato* (Milan: Feltrinelli).

Schneider, Jane (ed.) (1998), *Italy's 'Southern Question': Orientalism in One Country* (Oxford and New York: Berg).

Sciarrone, Rocco (2001), 'Il processo Andreotti and la lotta alla mafia', *Il Mulino*, no. 395.

Scobie, H. M., S. Mortali, S. Persaud and P. Docile (1996), *The Italian Economy in the 1990s* (London: Routledge).

Scoppola, Pietro (1991), *La Repubblica dei partiti: profilo storico della democrazia in Italia, 1945–1990* (Bologna: Mulino).

Sechi, Salvatore (ed.) (1995), *Deconstructing Italy: Italy in the Nineties* (Berkeley: University of California Press).

Serrani, Donatello (1978), *Il potere per enti: enti pubblici e sistema politico in Italia* (Bologna: Mulino).

Sharpe, Lawrence J. (1981), 'Is there a fiscal crisis in European local government?', in Lawrence J. Sharpe (ed.), *The Local Fiscal Crisis in Western Europe* (London: Sage).

Signorini, Luigi Federico (2001), 'L'economia italiana: un'introduzione', in Padoa-Schioppa and Graubard (2001).

Silj, Alessandro (1994), *Malpaese: Criminalità, corruzione e politica nell'Italia della prima Repubblica 1943–1994* (Rome: Donzelli).

Spotts, Frederic and Theodor Wieser (1986), *Italy: A Difficult Democracy* (Cambridge: Cambridge University Press).

Stern, R. M. (1967), *Foreign Trade and Economic Growth in Italy* (New York: Praeger).

Stille, Alexander (1996), *Excellent Cadavers: The Mafia and the Death of the First Italian Republic* (London: Vintage).

Svimez (various years), *Rapporto . . . sull'economia del Mezzogiorno* (Rome: Svimez), <www.svimez.it>

Sylos Labini, Paolo (1974), *Saggio sulle classi sociali* (Bari: Laterza).

Tamburrano, Giuseppe (1974), *L'iceberg democristiano* (Milan: SugarCo).

Tarchi, Marco and Emanuela Poli (2000), 'The parties of the *Polo*: united to what end?', in Hine and Vassallo (2000).

Tarrow, Sidney (1990), 'Maintaining hegemony in Italy: "The softer they rise the slower they fall!"', in T. J. Pempel (ed.), *Uncommon Democracies: The One-Party Dominant Regimes* (Ithaca, NY: Cornell University Press).

Telò, Mario (1996), 'L'Italia nel processo di costruzione europea', in *Storia dell'Italia repubblicana, vol. 3: L'Italia nella crisi mondiale: L'ultimo ventennio. I. Economia e società* (Turin: Einaudi).

Tizzano, Antonio (1979), 'Forze politiche italiane e collegamenti europei nella prospettiva della elezione del parlamento Europeo', in Centro Nazionale di Prevenzione e Difesa Sociale, *Parlamento Europeo, Forze politiche e diritti dei cittadini* (Milan: Franco Angeli).

Toniolo, Gianni and Vincenzo Visco (eds) (2004), *Il declino economico dell'Italia: Cause e rimedi* (Milan: Mondadori).

Tranfaglia, Nicola (1994), *L'Italia democratica: Profilo del primo cinquantennio* (Milan: Mondadori).

Tranfaglia, Nicola (1997), 'Un capitolo del "doppio stato": La stagione delle stragi e dei terrorismi, 1969–84', in Barbagallo (1997).

Tranfaglia, Nicola (2003), *La transizione italiana: Storia di un decennio* (Milan: Garzanti).

Travaglia, Sergio (1994), *Come funziona l'Italia: Le istituzioni pubbliche e private, gli organigrammi di enti e associazioni, le sigle misteriose* (Milan: Sperling and Kupfer).

Travaglio, Marco and E. Veltri (2001), *L'Odore dei soldi* (Rome: Editori Riuniti).

Tremonti, Giulio and Giuseppe Vitaletti (1994), *Il federalismo fiscale: Autonomia municipale e solidarietà sociale* (Rome and Bari: Laterza).

Trento, Sandro (2003), 'Stagnazione e frammentazione produttiva', *Il Mulino*, 6 (410).

Trigilia, Carlo (1986), *Grandi partiti e piccole imprese: Comunisti e democristiani nelle regioni a economia diffusa* (Bologna: Mulino).

Trigilia, Carlo (1992), *Sviluppo senza autonomia* (Bologna: Mulino).

Trigilia, Carlo (1994), 'I paradossi di un capitalismo leggero', in Ginsborg (1994).

Trigilia, Carlo (1996), 'Italy at the crossroads: economy and society in the 1990s', presentation made at the European University Institute, Florence, 12 Dec.

Turani, G. (1988), *L'Ingegnere* (Milan: Sperling and Kupfer).

Vaciago, Giacomo (2000), 'Finance between market and politics', in Hine and Vassallo (2000).

Valli, Vittorio (1982), *L'Economia e la politica economica italiana dal 1945 ad oggi* (Milan: Etas).

Varsori, Antonio (1995), 'Italy's policy towards European integration (1947–58)', in Christopher Duggan and Christopher Wagstaff (eds), *Italy in the Cold War: Politics, Culture and Society, 1948–58* (Oxford: Berg).

Vassallo, Salvatore (1994), *Il governo di partito in Italia (1943–93)* (Bologna: Mulino).

Vassallo, Salvatore (2000), 'La politica di bilancio: le condizioni e gli effetti istituzionali della convergenza', in Di Palma, Fabbrini and Freddi (2000).

Vercellone, P. (1972), 'The Italian Constitution of 1947–48', in Woolf (1972a).

Verzichelli, Luca and Maurizio Cotta (2002), 'Still a central institution? New patterns of parliamentary democracy in Italy, 1992–2002', paper presented at the workshop, 'A Renewal of Parliaments in Europe? MPs, behaviours and action constraints', ECPR Joint Sessions of Workshops, Turin, 22–27 March.

Viesti, Gianfranco (2001), 'Un Mezzogiorno diverso', *Il Mulino*, 4 (396) (July–Aug.).

Villari, Rosario (1974), *Il sud nella storia d'Italia: antologia della questione meridionale* (Bari: Laterza).

Visco, Vincenzo (2004), 'Alle origine del declino', in Toniolo and Visco (2004).

Votaw, Dow (1964), *The Six-Legged Dog: Mattei and ENI – A Study in Power* (Berkeley: University of California Press).

Walker, Richard (1976), *Dal confronto al consenso: I partiti politici italiani e l'integrazione europea* (Rome: Istituto Affari Internazionali).

Ward, William (1993), *Getting it Right in Italy: A Manual for the 1990s* (London: Bloomsbury).

Watts, Ronald L. (1991), 'Federalism', in Vernon Bogdanor (ed.), *The Blackwell Encyclopaedia of Political Science* (Oxford: Blackwell).

Wertman, Douglas (1983), 'Italian attitudes on foreign policy issues: are there generational differences?', in Stephen S. Szabo (ed.), *The Successor Generation: International Perspectives of Postwar Europeans* (London: Butterworths).

Wessels, Bernhard (1995), 'Support for integration: elite or mass-driven?', in Oskar Niedemayer and Richard Sinnot (eds), *Public Opinion and Internationalized Governance* (Oxford: Oxford University Press).

Willan, Philip (1991), *Puppet Masters: The Political Use of Terrorism in Italy* (London: Constable).

Woods, Dwayne (1998), 'The crisis (collapse) of Italy's public enterprise system: a revised property rights perspective', *Journal of Modern Italian Studies*, 3 (1).

Woods, Dwayne (2000), 'Transformations in Italian capitalism: an analysis of Olivetti's takeover of Telecom Italia', in Gilbert and Pasquino (2000).

Woolf, Stuart J. (ed.), (1972a), *The Rebirth of Italy 1943–50* (London: Longman).

Woolf, Stuart J. (1972b), 'The rebirth of Italy 1943–50', in Woolf (1972a).

INDEX